# THE ART AND SCIENCE
# OF PERSONALITY DEVELOPMENT

# The Art
# and Science of
# Personality
# Development

Dan P. McAdams

THE GUILFORD PRESS
New York    London

© 2015 The Guilford Press
A Division of Guilford Publications, Inc.
370 Seventh Avenue, Suite 1200, New York, NY 10001
www.guilford.com

Paperback edition 2018

Printed in the United States of America

This book is printed on acid-free paper.

Last digit is print number: 9 8 7 6 5 4

**Library of Congress Cataloging-in-Publication Data**

McAdams, Dan P.
  The art and science of personality development / Dan P. McAdams.
     pages cm
  Includes bibliographical references and index.
  ISBN 978-1-4625-1995-8 (hardback); ISBN 978-1-4625-2932-2 (paperback)
  1. Personality.   2. Social psychology.   I. Title.
  BF698.M347 2015
  155.2′5—dc23
                                                        2014039361

*For my students—past, present, and future*

# About the Author

Dan P. McAdams, PhD, is the Henry Wade Rogers Professor of Psychology and Human Development at Northwestern University. He is a Fellow of the Society for Personality and Social Psychology (SPSP, Division 8 of the American Psychological Association) and the American Psychological Society, has served on the Executive Committee of SPSP, and is a founding member of the Association for Research in Personality. Dr. McAdams works in the areas of personality and lifespan developmental psychology. His research focuses on concepts of self and identity in contemporary American society and on themes of power, intimacy, redemption, and generativity across the adult life course. He has published over 200 scientific articles and chapters and numerous books.

# Acknowledgments

In graduate school at Harvard in the late 1970s, I received my training in a program specializing in "personality *and* developmental psychology." I learned about personality psychology from Professors David McClelland, Brendan Maher, John Kihlstrom, Bonnie Spring, and Ross Rizley. I learned about developmental psychology from Professors Jerome Kagan, Dante Cicchetti, Sheldon White, and Carol Gilligan. I was a teaching assistant for George Goethals's legendary class "The Psychology of the Human Life Cycle," which blended themes from both personality and developmental psychology. Goethals and McClelland—both now deceased—had the greatest influence on me, and many years ago I dedicated a book to their memory. With this new book—on *personality development*—I feel that I have finally brought together the two different strands of my training, now more than three decades after I began graduate school. It seems apt, therefore, to thank again those stellar teachers I had back then, as well as the professors who were so instrumental in my intellectual development before I went off to graduate school—especially Arlin Meyer, Bill Olmsted, and Warren Rubel at Christ College, an honors program in the humanities and social sciences at Valparaiso University. None of these three master teachers is a psychologist, but they all stimulated my interest in the art and science of personality development.

Since then, I have taught and conducted research in personality and developmental psychology at two different universities: Loyola University of Chicago (1980–1989) and Northwestern University (since 1989). The colleagues, students, and friends who have helped to shape my understanding of personality development during my time at Loyola and Northwestern are too numerous to name now. But let me give a shout-out to a small number of people who have informed my thinking about personality development and human lives in positive ways over the last few years, as I have been writing this book: Jon Adler, Jim Anderson, Keith Cox, Colin De Young, Jeremy Frimer, Phil Hammack, Kathryn Hanek, Brady Jones, Christian Kandler, Jiffy Lansing, Jennifer Pals Lilgendahl, Jennifer Lodi-Smith, Gina Logan, Erika Manczak, Sarah Mangelsdorf, Kate McLean, Robin Nusslock, Andrew Ortony, Monisha Pasupathi, Mike Pratt, Bill Revelle, Mark Schwehn, Josh Wilt, and Claudia Zapata-Gietl.

Thanks also to Hank Neuberger for helping me out with Jay-Z. I owe a huge debt of gratitude to Will Dunlop and to my wife, Rebecca Pallmeyer, who both read early versions of all the chapters in this book and provided me with both constructive criticism and encouragement. In a similar vein, I am delighted to extend gratitude to Jefferson Singer, Emily Durbin, Rebecca Shiner, Ken Sheldon, and Paul Griffin, who all served so conscientiously as reviewers of early drafts of the chapters. Their critiques had a big influence on the rewriting I have done over the past few months in order to give the book a more consistent tone and clearer message. Thanks also to Seymour Weingarten of The Guilford Press for originally proposing my writing a book on personality development. Finally, let me gratefully acknowledge the Foley Family Foundation of Milwaukee, Wisconsin, which has provided financial support for my research and writing on personality development over the past 15 years, while funding Northwestern University's Foley Center for the Study of Lives.

# Contents

# THE ART AND SCIENCE
# OF PERSONALITY DEVELOPMENT

# Prologue

There is a sense in which every human life is a work of art. The product of the artist's labor is a unique form, a patterning of events, characters, and characteristics that has never happened before, and can never be exactly reproduced again, even if there existed in the universe an ultimate three-dimensional printer. My life can never be exactly like yours, even if you happen to be my identical twin, sharing all my genes, for my experiences and my consciousness are not yours. Every person fashions a once-in-eternity, never-to-be-repeated life or helps to fashion it, for every human life is profoundly shaped by forces beyond the artist's creative purview, from forces of history to genetics, from gender to race to social class to the vagaries of chance. We each do what we can with the resources at hand. We each try to make a life out of the materials we are given, with its own self-identifying colors, shadings, and shapes.

Yet all lives resemble one another in at least a few ways. Humans are born into social groups and, if health and fortune permit them to thrive, they grow up to live among their peers, confronting a series of challenges that humans have perennially faced. These include, of course, learning how to live successfully in human groups or communities, cooperating and competing with others group members, forming alliances, finding mates, reproducing and raising children, caring for others (especially members of the next generation), obtaining the goods that are necessary to flourish within the group, or at least garnering those resources that are needed to survive.

The shapes and textures of human lives are constrained by the adaptive challenges that all humans face. Therefore, the individual artistry of any human life must ultimately come down to a variation on the theme

1

of human nature. The possible variations are many, but they are not infinite. Moreover, certain variations seem to resemble other variations. The *Mona Lisa* is more like Raphael's *Madonna of the Meadow* than it is like Picasso's *Guernica*. Everyday observations suggest to us that there are certain *kinds* of people out there, certain kinds of lives. Science seems to confirm those observations.

If every human life is a unique work of *art*, then *science* enters the picture when we begin to sense regularities amid all the diversity. Science enters when we see rough or approximate similarities amid the cornucopia of differences. As artists, we each fashion a singular, self-affirming life. As scientists, we notice how the life we have fashioned resembles certain other lives; we detect similarities, regularities, and trends. In recognizing the broad contours of our own psychological individuality, we see how we are similar to and different from others. As a result, we say things like this: *I am kind of like my mother because we both worry a lot; my sister is more hardworking than I am, but I am much more sociable and caring; my best friend has overcome huge obstacles in his life, and in that way my life is very much like his; and I am nothing like my first roommate in college, who was so selfish and disagreeable that I had to move out in the middle of my freshman year.*

Observations about psychological similarities and differences in the kinds of people we are, and in the kinds of lives we live, lead naturally to observations about change: *I used to be really shy, but I have opened up as I have gotten older; third grade was a turning point in my life; I never thought I would find a soul mate, and then she came along; I became much wiser in my 40s, after our children were launched and I finally found time to pursue what I have always wanted and valued in life; I have never been the same since my brother died.* From the standpoint of life's artistry, each life unfolds in its own unique way. Yet resemblances may be observed here, too. We may note similarities in life trajectories, overall maturational trends, predictable seasons, phases, passages, or epochs in human lives. My journey through life may be unique to me, yet it may resemble your journey in certain ways.

From the systematizing perspective of psychological science, therefore, similarities and differences may be noted in (1) the kinds of persons we are and (2) the paths we follow as we move through time. Put differently, we all take careful note of similarities and differences in (1) *personality* (what kind of person I am) and (2) *development* (how I have changed over time).

My goal in this book is to tell a compelling story about *personality development* as it plays out in individual human lives across the human life course. It is a story that recognizes the artistry of individual lives while examining what contemporary science has to tell us about how human lives are psychologically patterned and how these patterns develop over time. The scientific study of personality development has made tremendous strides in the last decade or two. We know a great deal more about trends and regularities in personality development than we did just a few years ago, and this scientific knowledge augments and enhances our understanding of individual human lives, in all their artistry and uniqueness. Therefore, this book has much to say about people in general, but it also holds individual insights for you, the reader, whose life is exactly like no other for sure yet may resemble other lives in some, if not many, ways.

I read scientific articles on personality development nearly every day in my role as a college professor. I conduct scientific research on personality development. I teach the topic. I read novels and short stories that describe the artistry of a person's development over time. I have been doing this sort of thing for about 40 years, ever since college, and I still have not read a single, full, coherent, evidence-based account of the development of personality across the human life course—this despite the significant advances that have occurred in the scientific study of personality development in recent years. This surprising gap in the literature inspired me to write this book. It represents my attempt to bring together scientific findings and theory to tell a coherent and accessible story about personality development. Why was such a book not written before? There are at least two reasons.

First, many of the most important scientific findings about personality development are scattered across two very different fields of study, and psychological scientists who work in either one of these two fields rarely talk to those who work in the other. Researchers in *personality psychology* study individual differences in basic traits, motives, and other personality variables as they are expressed in the lives of adults. Personality psychologists are especially eager to detect *continuity* in psychological functioning over time. Focusing mainly on children instead, researchers in *developmental psychology* rarely even use the term "personality" but instead examine what they call "temperament" and "socioemotional development." They are especially keen to detect *change*. Although a few efforts have been made among scientists themselves to link personality psychology and the study of human development (e.g., Mroczek & Little, 2006), the two fields are still worlds apart.

The second reason a coherent story of personality development has not been told to date is that nobody has yet provided the kind of integrative *theory* or conceptual framework that would make such a story possible. Scientific findings about temperament, socioemotional development, and adult personality can pile up forever, but until somebody comes along to make conceptual sense of it all, our understanding remains dim. In this book, therefore, I aim to describe and explain the development of personality across the human life course in terms of a new and broadly integrative *theory of personality development.* The outlines of the theory have appeared in professional sources, such as McAdams and Cox (2010) and McAdams and Olson (2010), but this book marks the first attempt to spell out the details and put it all together for a broader audience of students, professionals, researchers, and curious people who are looking for evidence-based insights into their own personality development. The theory itself draws upon ideas in both personality and developmental psychology, as well as the fields of evolutionary biology, affective and cognitive neuroscience, behavior genetics, social psychology, life-course sociology, and the interdisciplinary study of life narratives.

The framework within which I have organized this book's argument is disarmingly simple. It begins with human nature, designed as it has been by millions of years of human *evolution*. As I conceive of it, personality is a person's *characteristic variation on the evolved design for human nature.* Each variation on evolution's general design is unique, an artful configuration of psychological individuality, developing over time and within culture. Your personality is a unique, never-to-be-repeated variation on the general pattern for human nature, situated in history and society. The developing configuration that comprises your personality consists of *three layers*. To follow personality development over the human life course, then, is to track three different layers or lines of personal growth, as depicted in Figure P.1. Each of the three layers corresponds to a particular standpoint or perspective from which the whole person may be understood—personality from the standpoints of the *actor*, the *agent*, and the *author*.

We begin life as *social actors.* Shakespeare was profoundly right when he wrote that all the world's a stage and each of us a player upon it. Human beings evolved to live in complex social groups, striving to get along and get ahead in social life. Playacting, therefore, has always been for keeps, for if we perform badly as an actor with our peers—if we consistently botch the script or fail to deliver the lines in effective ways—we will find ourselves severely compromised in the great Darwinian challenge of earthly life, diminished in our ability to pass copies of our genes down to subsequent generations. For our hunting-and-gathering forebears and for

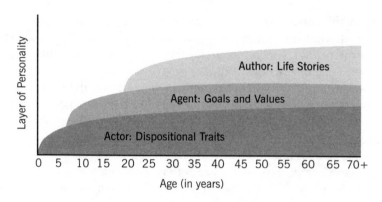

**FIGURE P.1.** Three layers of personality.

modern people today, there is nothing superficial about playing a social role. Indeed, we human beings never leave the stage to go home and live our real lives in some more authentic and comfortable place because real and authentic human life *is*, and always has been, *social* life. Therefore, not only is each of us born with a propensity to develop remarkable facility as a social actor, but each of us also comes to the stage equipped with the makings of a unique presentational *style*.

Developmental psychologists call that style *temperament*. Over developmental time and across a lifetime of performances, temperament gradually morphs into the basic dispositional traits of human personality—fundamental dimensions of psychological individuality such as extraversion, neuroticism, and conscientiousness. From the standpoint of the social actor, then, your personality comprises the broad dispositional traits that give your performances their recognizable social and emotional brand. We know each other first (and in most cases, foremost) as social actors, endowed with those signature traits that begin to reveal themselves in all their artistry in the first few months of life, and continue to capture and convey the kind of person we are even at the very end.

As inveterate actors, we never leave the theater of everyday social life. But by the time we reach middle childhood, a second layer of psychological individuality has begun to emerge, layered over dispositional traits. The second layer consists of a dynamic arrangement of evolving goals, motives, strivings, values, plans, programs, and projects that speak to what a person aims to accomplish or realize in life. This developing motivational agenda for human life, as it begins to emerge around second or third grade, reveals personality from the standpoint of the *motivated agent.* In the fullest sense, to be an *agent* is to articulate and pursue goals in life that instantiate what you want and what you value. To be an agent is to make decisions about where you want your life to go *in the future.* The dispositional traits that give shape to your performances today—your exuberant extraversion, say, or your overall tendency to feel emotions in a very intense way—do not necessarily express what you want and what you value as you imagine your life moving forward into tomorrow and beyond. In other words, traits are not motives; how we *act now* may say little about what we *want* for the *future.*

Developmental research shows that even babies act to achieve momentary goals. But it is not until the grade-school years that children begin to organize their daily lives and their future dreams in terms of self-chosen goals, values, plans, and projects. At this developmental juncture, personality "thickens" as it accommodates a second layer of psychological individuality. The 9-year-old child, equipped with traits and goals, is more complex than the 1-year-old infant, who has only traits to display. For a full understanding of personality, we must consider the older child from the standpoints of both the social actor and the motivated agent. By contrast, the infant is a simpler case, though perhaps no less interesting.

The plot thickens again in our late-teenage years. Going back to the classic writings of Erik Erikson (1963), developmental psychologists have typically argued that adolescents and young adults must confront and resolve the challenge of *identity.* They must figure out who they are and how they are to live, love, and work in adult society. They must find a way to draw upon their talents, traits, and past experiences to articulate and embody a meaningful adult life, a life that situates them within a satisfying and productive niche in society and provides them with a deep sense of psychological continuity, fidelity, and meaning.

The challenge of identity is especially acute in modern industrial and postindustrial societies, which provide their young-adult citizens with a bewildering array of choices and possibilities for the construction of a meaningful life, even as each person faces unique perils and constraints (Giddens, 1991). Identity construction is hard work, and it requires lots of developmental time—so much time, that social scientists have now demarcated a special "stage" in the human life course that is typically given over to concerted identity work. This is the stage of *emerging adulthood,* that period from the late teens through the 20s, wherein many people in modern societies obtain the training they often need to establish themselves in the workplace, while experimenting with different lifestyles, ideologies, and relationships before they eventually "settle down" to become bona fide "adults" (Arnett, 2000). In the modern world, the struggle for identity is both exciting and scary. There are so many ways to construct a life of strong purpose and deep meaning. And there are so many ways to fall short.

What does the construction of identity mean for personality development? In some ways, identity entails the extension of the person as a social actor and a motivated agent. In emerging adulthood, people learn to adopt new social roles wherein they continue to refine and express their basic performance traits. Research in personality psychology shows, for example, that dispositions toward conscientiousness and agreeableness may continue to develop and strengthen during the emerging adulthood years, and after (Roberts, Walton, & Viechtbauer, 2006). The adoption of adult social roles—spouse, parent, citizen—may enhance our tendencies to behave in responsible, industrious, and caring ways within the many different arenas of adult social life, even as we each continue to perform our roles in individually unique ways.

Moreover, identity centrally involves goals, plans, projects, and values—implicating the person as a motivated agent. Research in developmental psychology demonstrates that a key feature of identity construction in the emerging adulthood years is the exploration of various ideological and occupational options and the subsequent commitment to long-term life values and goals (Kroger & Marcia, 2011). Ideally, then, the construction of a positive identity in the modern world brings with it important changes in dispositional personality traits, signaling growing maturity, and the clear articulation of personal values and goals. In other words, identity marks further development of the person as a social actor and a motivated agent.

But there is more to identity than that. Beyond today's successful social performance and the striving to achieve tomorrow's goals, identity involves the formulation of a meaningful *story* for your life (McAdams & McLean, 2013). Over half a century ago, Erik Erikson (1958) hinted, perhaps unwittingly, at this deep psychological truth:

> To be [an] adult means among other things to see one's own life in continuous perspective, both *in retrospect and prospect*. By accepting some definition as to who he is, usually on the basis of a function in an economy, a place in the sequence of generations, and a status in the structure of society, the adult is able *to selectively reconstruct his past in such a way that, step for step, it seems to have planned him, or better, he seems to have planned it*. In this sense, psychologically we do choose our parents, our family history, and the history of our kings, heroes, and gods. By making them our own, we maneuver

ourselves into the inner position of proprietors, of creators. (pp. 111–112, emphasis added)

In the emerging adulthood years, a third layer of personality begins to form. In our efforts to find a meaningful identity for life, we begin "to selectively reconstruct" the past, as Erikson wrote, and imagine the future to create a *life story*, or what psychological scientists today often call a *narrative identity*. As such, we become *autobiographical authors* in emerging adulthood, a way of being that is layered over the self as a motivated agent, which in turn is layered over the self as a social actor. In order to provide our lives with the sense of temporal continuity and deep meaning that Erikson believed identity should confer, we must author a personalized life story that integrates our understanding of who we once were, who we are today, and who we may become in the future. The story explains, for the author and the author's world, why the social actor does what it does and why the motivated agent wants what it wants, and how the person as a whole has developed over time, from the past's reconstructed beginning to the future's imagined ending. We draw deeply upon our own past experiences to create a life story that is unique to each of us, but we also borrow widely from the images, metaphors, ideologies, and narratives that our culture provides. We are the authors of our own unique stories, for sure, but we get plenty of editorial assistance, as well as resistance, from the social, ideological, and cultural world around us.

In its full form, *personality is a developing configuration of psychological individuality that expresses a person's recognizable uniqueness, wherein life stories are layered over salient goals and values, which are layered over dispositional traits.* In its psychologically broadest, deepest, and thickest sense, personality presents the mature man or woman as an ever-developing social actor, motivated agent, and autobiographical author—a whole person expressed in a trinity of guises, moving across situations, over developmental time, and through culture. To become fully human is to express the full panoply of mature personality as actor, agent, and author. It is (1) to play out fully and effectively your signature *traits* on the many social stages where you perform; (2) to pursue your most cherished *goals* and *values* to the full extent you can pursue them; and (3) to narrate and live a *story* about your life that gives your life a full sense of meaning and purpose. To know yourself in full, then, is to know (and to know how to live with) your traits, your goals and values, and your stories.

In *The Art and Science of Personality Development*, I draw upon many of the most illuminating studies and intriguing ideas in psychological science today to describe and explain the development of human personality over the life course. Reflecting the three central metaphors in my theory of personality development, the book is divided into three parts: Becoming the Social Actor, Becoming the Motivated Agent, and Becoming the Autobiographical Author (see Table P.1). In the three sections, I move back and forth across the lifespan to sketch out a full psychological portrait of human personality and trace its development from birth through old age.

General trends in personality development are interesting in their own right, especially for psychological geeks like me. But these trends, derived from scientific research, take on deeper meaning and relevance when we observe how they play out (or sometimes don't) in the particular lives of individual human beings. The *science* of personality development reveals underlying principles, trends, and tendencies. The *art* of personality development expresses how these underlying trends are uniquely manifest in the lives of particular human beings, even if those

**TABLE P.1. Three Layers of Personality, Developing over the Human Life Course**

| Perspective | Content | Emergence | Focus | Questions |
| --- | --- | --- | --- | --- |
| Social actor | Temperament, dispositional traits | Infancy | Present | How do I act? What do I feel? |
| Motivated agent | Personal goals, plans, projects, values | Middle childhood | Present and future | What do I want? What do I value? |
| Autobiographical author | Narrative identity | Emerging adulthood | Past, present, and future | What does my life mean? Who am I? Who have I been? Who am I becoming? |

*Note.* Personality development begins with infant temperament, which gradually morphs into such basic dispositional traits as extraversion and neuroticism. Dispositional traits define personality from the perspective of the social actor. Around age 7 or 8, a second layer of personal goals and values begins to emerge, as personality "thickens" to accommodate features of the motivated agent. A third layer begins to form in late adolescence and young adulthood, as the person aims to construct an integrative life story, or narrative identity, to provide life with a sense of overall unity, meaning, and purpose. Over the course of adulthood, all three layers of personality continue to develop, and the person continues to change and adapt to changing environments from the perspectives of a social actor, motivated agent, and autobiographical author.

real, flesh-and-blood lives can never be fully reduced to the abstractions that science proposes.

The trends and processes that science discovers help us to understand the individual life, and the artistry of any given individual life may in turn reveal the concrete manifestations of general, scientific principles, regularities, trends, and tendencies. There is nonetheless a tension between the two perspectives, for the full artistry of any individual life cannot be completely conveyed through the abstractions of science. Gordon Allport, the founding father of personality psychology itself, expressed this basic conundrum back in 1937, when he distinguished between what he called the *nomothetic* and the *idiographic* approaches to personality. In the nomothetic approach, the scientist aims to produce general laws applicable to all persons; in the idiographic approach, the focus is on the particular dynamics of the individual case. Allport envisioned a constructive interplay between the two perspectives, though he realized that such a thing might be difficult to achieve. For me, it is indisputably self-evident that an individual person is not a scientific generality. There are unique people (idiographic), and there are the generalities of science (nomothetic)—two different things, to be sure. That said, I sincerely believe, like Allport, that personality development can be best appreciated and understood through a dialogue between the two contrasting perspectives of (1) the unique individual life, in all its idiographic artistry, and (2) the generalizing discourse of science.

With the competing demands of both art and science in mind, therefore, I make generous use of biographies and case studies of real (and typically well-known) people throughout this book. Through these case studies, I aim to illustrate theoretical points and to give vivid, flesh-and-blood meaning to quantitative empirical findings. I do not see these forays into the art of individual personality development to be digressions from the main story line. They are, instead, integral pieces of the book's argument, woven into the exposition of the theory. Among the stars of my presentation are Charles Darwin, U.S. Presidents Barack Obama and George W. Bush, Hillary Clinton, Mother Teresa, Mahatma Gandhi, Steve Jobs, Jane Fonda, American memoirist Mary Karr, and rapper Jay-Z.

This book's case illustrations bring personality development to life, providing compelling cameos about how real lives unfold. I also draw occasionally from my own personal experiences. If the science of personality development were disconnected from the artistry of my own unique life, I would probably never have decided to write a book on personality development in the first place. For me, then, this book is deeply personal because I want, as do many people, to understand my own personality development, and because the *idea* of personality development has been such an obsessive preoccupation in my own intellectual life. To this book's lineup of notable actors, agents, and authors, finally, I hope to add *you*, dear reader. At the end of the day, personality development is about *your* own journey to become fully human, and your unique effort to understand how you came to be and what you may become. To the extent the ideas herein connect meaningfully to your own life, then, this book will have achieved the measure of success I value most.

# Becoming an Actor

All the world's a stage,
And all the men and women merely players;
They have their exits and their entrances;
And one man in his time plays many parts,
His acts being seven ages. At first the infant . . .
—WILLIAM SHAKESPEARE, *As You Like It*

## chapter 1

# In the Beginning . . .

Your personality is a unique *variation* on the general design of human nature. Human nature itself—what we human beings have in common with each other by virtue of the fact that we are all human beings—is a product of our species' evolution. Whereas personality develops across the individual life course, from birth through old age, human nature has "developed" over millions of years of evolutionary history. And it continues to develop, of course, for evolution never goes away. For each of us, our own personality development marks an artful experiment in variation, a unique twist on the evolved pattern, as if nature were asking the cosmos: What do you think will happen if we try *this one* out? Each never-to-be-repeated experiment becomes manifest in the birth of a particular infant. But every human beginning looks back to the beginning of the human species, for every variation on the evolved design for human nature reaffirms the design itself. To appreciate the variation, then, we must understand the evolved (and evolving) design. And to understand the design, we must imagine how the design itself came to be, going back to *the beginning*.

*In the beginning, natural selection created human beings to be brainy, bipedal creatures who live together in social groups.*

The scientific understanding of human nature's beginning bears little resemblance to the ancient creation stories that you probably know, those mythic accounts of beginnings enshrined in the world's great religions, such as Judaism, Christianity, and Islam. But there is one remarkable parallel. In all of these accounts, *Homo sapiens* is portrayed as relentlessly *social* and really, really *smart*.

Recall the ancient story, as told in the book of Genesis. After God creates the first man, Adam experiences profound social isolation. He

15

is lonely; he needs a helpmate—and not just for casual sex (that comes later), but for companionship and security. And once Eve enters the scene, what gets the couple into eternal trouble? Intellectual curiosity is what. Being smart—way smarter than the birds, fish, cattle, reptiles, and wild beasts of the earth (except for the serpent, but he doesn't count). The humans cannot help but ask smart questions about how things work in the world—for example, "What happens if we eat the fruit from that enticing tree over there?" (After all, the book of Genesis describes it as a tree about *knowledge*!) Or, "what will transpire if we disobey the Powers that be?" When they are finally banished from the Garden, the original duo sets out on a difficult Darwinian journey of survival and reproduction. Their greatest assets are what got them into trouble in the first place—their need for each other, and their big brains.

## THE EVOLUTION OF BIG BRAINS AND HUMAN SOCIALITY

When scientists describe the features of human nature that cleanly differentiate us from other species, they tend to emphasize two different things. The first is obvious to everybody: Human beings are endowed with tremendous cognitive power. We are way smarter than the other animals. Of course, other animals can do amazing things that are well beyond our abilities, adapted as they are to their own evolutionary challenges and ecological niches. Your dog's sense of smell leaves yours in the dust, and you should not try to compete with birds or great whales when it comes to doing what they do best. On the intelligence front, moreover, it is surely true that scientists have taught chimpanzees to use rudimentary sign language. Some nonhuman primates use natural implements as simple tools. But the cognitive accomplishments of our smartest fellow species fall far short of what we expect from a 4-year-old human child. By virtue of our prodigious powers of mind, human beings have developed awe-inspiring technologies and promulgated cultural achievements that have transformed the globe, for better and for worse. When evolutionary scientists underscore this side of human nature, therefore, they invoke the human powers of language, reason, creativity, innovation, imagination, tool use, and the advances of science and technology.

The second broad distinguishing feature pertains to our social nature. Human beings evolved to live in groups. Nearly everything we do finds its essential contexts and meanings within a social nexus. We cooperate with other group members to meet all of life's major challenges, from obtaining food to defending ourselves against threat, from securing mates to caring for the next generation. We also compete with each other to garner resources within the group, forming social hierarchies and shifting coalitions that confer upon human social life a remarkable level of complexity. Of course, there are other social species out there. Ants and bees, for example, are so tightly bound to their respective colonies/hives that we conceive of their integrated collectivities themselves as *superorganisms* (Wilson, 2012). For ants, the colony is literally the individual, for each nearly interchangeable member of the colony (each ant) exists mainly to ensure the colony's survival.

Human beings are not so tightly bound, nor are they interchangeable. Nonetheless, the manner in which we naturally group together is unique on planet Earth for its complexity and flexibility. When evolutionary scientists, therefore, underscore this second distinguishing feature of human nature, they invoke human inclinations toward pair-bonding, family formation, group identification, cooperation and altruism, competition and warfare, religion, government, and culture. And *personality*, I will argue. At its root, personality is expressed in those consistent and artful variations in behavior, thought, and feeling that occur in social contexts, and all that goes with that. Without doubt, the powers of mind and cognition are intricately involved in personality. Individual differences in intelligence itself affect personality development, and there are features of personality expressed in creativity, innovation, and other cognitive domains. But it is mainly in the social arena, I would argue—in the spaces between people and within human groups—that personality most clearly and powerfully reveals itself (McAdams & Olson, 2010; Sullivan, 1953).

In any case, human intelligence and sociality turn out to be two sides of the same evolutionary coin, for it would appear that big brains and intense social relationships go together. As the primal couple in the biblical story would eventually learn, pair-bonding is an especially intense kind of social relationship, wherein one lover must consistently monitor and adapt to the behavior and intentions of the other. Among birds and mammals, the species with the biggest brains relative to body size tend to be those that routinely form monogamous pair-bonds (Dunbar, 2010). A moment's reflection reveals that this is no surprise. Think of all the time you have spent obsessing over the vicissitudes of pair-bonding. There is all the wooing, of course, or the playing hard-to-get, and all the planning, scheming, bluffing, weeping, and cajoling that go into securing a mate. But monogamous pair-bonding also involves holding on to what you have secured, staving off rivals, calibrating your behavior to the ever-changing whims of your mate, and coordinating the evolving relationship as it expands, over the long haul, to encompass offspring. There is so much to worry about! Moving successfully through life in a long-term partnership requires significant brainpower.

Primates have very big brains. Accounting for a great deal of the brain mass in apes, chimps, monkeys, and humans is the neocortex, which is mainly responsible for governing conscious thought, planning, and decision making. A strong line of theorizing in evolutionary biology suggests that the expanded neocortex evolved to cope with the complexity of primate *social* life (Byrne & Bates, 2007; Dunbar & Sutcliffe, 2012). Individuals have to keep track of who is who in the group, so that they can predict the behavior of other group members and coordinate their own behavior accordingly. They must be able to engage in rudimentary forms of empathy and perspective taking, wherein they sort out the inferred intentions of others and imagine how they may act in the future. The larger the group, the more there is to remember and to predict. With greater group size, then, comes greater social complexity, posing greater challenges for the social intelligence that a large neocortex confers. Research has shown that, among primates, there is a strong correlation between the relative size of the neocortex and the size of the group within which individuals typically live (Dunbar, 2010). Human beings weigh in with the greatest neocortical mass by far, making up about 80% of their exceedingly large brain volume. And their groups are, by far, the largest and the most complex.

How did it come to pass that humans should be so brainy and so social? After all, had you and I visited Earth 2 million years ago and encountered the australopithecines of Africa, we might have noted that these ancient forerunners of modern-day humans had brains that were no larger than those of the great apes who lived around them. Okay, we might *not* have noted that exactly, without the modern means to measure their brain size. But we would have surely seen that our less-than-glorious ancestors distinguished themselves from the other ape-like species mainly by their ability to walk on their hind legs. Beyond that, they were pretty unimpressive, surviving in small and simple groups scattered about the savannah. From then to now, an awful lot must have happened. But what?

Scientists of many different persuasions have tried to sketch out scenarios for how human beings evolved to live in increasingly complex social groups, based on the best paleontological and genetic evidence. Like ants, termites, bees, and a small number of other animal species, human beings exhibit what renowned evolutionary biologist E. O. Wilson (2012) calls *eusociality*. Members of eusocial species live in intricately coordinated, multigenerational groups. Through division of labor and complex social integration, individuals carry out specific tasks that contribute to the overall adaptive facility of the group. In eusocial species, individuals typically engage in altruistic acts and other prosocial behaviors that in one way or another benefit the group, even when such acts may disadvantage the individual. Of course, human groups are dramatically different from ant colonies and beehives: Human groups are less tightly organized and more fluid, and they afford individual group members a great deal of autonomy. Nonetheless, whether you are talking about social insects or human beings, eusocial species owe their success to the extraordinary sense in which their social groupings are greater than the respective sums of the individual parts. Over the past 2 million years, the line of human descent may be characterized as an evolutionary sprint to eusociality.

Appropriately enough, the sprint may have begun with *bipedalism.* The various australopithecine species that inhabited Africa between 4 and 2 million years ago had evolved to the point that they could walk on their two hind legs, freeing their hands to reach for and carry fruits, vegetables, and nuts, and to handle objects with ease and skill. A likely offshoot of the australopithecine line was *Homo habilis,* which evolved around 2.3 million years ago. With a less protruding face than their ancestors and a significantly enhanced cranial capacity (although still only about half that of modern humans), members of *Homo habilis* used their hands (and brains) to fashion primitive stone *tools* for scavenging and scraping meat off dead animals. Eventually, tools were developed for hunting, which increased the availability of *meat* sources. It turns out that meat yields much higher energy per gram eaten than do fruits and vegetables. Over evolutionary time, therefore, meat became a more prominent feature of the hominid diet. The harvesting of meat—at first through scavenging but eventually through hunting, too—became one among a suite of social tasks that required increasingly greater levels of coordination and cooperation, leading to the formation of highly organized groups.

What may be considered the next leap forward was recognized by the ancient Greeks. In Greek mythology, Prometheus stole *fire* from the gods and gave it to humankind, a theft for which he suffered eternal punishment. The ancient Greeks knew that fire was a tremendous gift, responsible for the development of human civilization. What they could hardly suspect, however, was that members of the species *Homo erectus* probably learned to control fire for domestic use around a million years ago. More graceful in appearance and endowed with substantially larger brains than other hominids, *Homo erectus* developed a litany of characteristics that ultimately made their way into human eusociality. Their breakout idea regarding fire was as Promethean as any discovery in prehistory, for it ultimately transformed the nature of hominid social relations. Fire could be used to cook meat, making it more tender and delicious. Cooking eventually became a universal human trait, and the sharing of cooked meals became a bedrock social activity, functioning not only to appease the hungry appetite but also to enhance social bonding.

Cooking led naturally to the formation of *campsites* (Wilson, 2012). Members of the group would use the campsite as a base from which to venture out into the savannah during the day, returning to the same site night after night. With the establishment of fireside campsites came greater division of labor and more complex social organizations. Group members could be organized into subgroups dedicated to specific tasks. A few young men might journey off to hunt game; another group might be authorized to gather edible vegetation or materials for a fire; still other members, most likely females, might stay behind at the campsite to care for the young and defenseless. Contingencies might be developed for the defense of the site against other groups or animals, as if the site itself were the central point in an extended tribal territory. In these ways and others, the campsite became the protohuman *nest*. All eusocial species, without exception, build nests that they defend from enemies. They raise young in the nest and forage away from it for food, returning regularly to the nest with a bounty to share with others in the group. As the primordial nest, ancient campsites may constitute the archetypal origin of the human idea of *home*.

Contemporary scientists can do no better than make educated guesses about how the human mind evolved over the course of hundreds of thousands of years to support complex social activities and the diversification of social tasks that so characterize the human brand of eusociality. Somewhere along the way, our distant ancestors developed the mental ability to understand, or at least imagine, what might be transpiring in the minds of their fellow group members—an ability that would seem to accelerate social cooperation. Michael Tomasello (2000) has argued that a key catalyst for development of complex social undertakings among humans is *shared intentionality*. If I want to work together with you in order to accomplish a task, I am greatly advantaged, as are you, by *my* ability to anticipate and comprehend *your* intentions. To the extent that we can share with each other what we each are planning to do, we will be able to work together more efficiently to accomplish a joint task.

Even before the evolution of human language, Tomasello (2000) suggests, our ancestors learned how to share their intentions with each other. Early on, shared intentionality may have applied mainly to very small groups—two or three people together, perhaps. Eventually, our increasingly brainy forebears learned how to share intentions with larger collectives, even to the point where they could manage in their minds the imagined multiple intentions of multiple constituencies: I know that these 30 people aim to accomplish A, whereas those 40 people aim to accomplish B; in that I intend to accomplish both A and B, I will need to split my alignments with both constituencies. In his celebrated book *The Righteous Mind*, Jonathan Haidt (2012) analogizes the emergence of shared intentionality to a crossing of the Rubicon in human evolution. As our ancestors became more and more adept at reading the minds of their compatriots and sharing their intentions with each other, they developed the capacity to establish the kinds of broad agreements that undergird a shared morality for the group. From there, it is a fairly short journey, Haidt argues, to the establishment of ethical codes, religious sensibilities, and human government.

Presumably endowed with the cognitive powers to engage in shared intentionality, anatomically modern *Homo sapiens* began to appear in Africa around 200,000 years ago. Their brains were larger than those of *Homo erectus* and *Homo habilis*, with disproportionate expansion in the prefrontal cortex and the temporal lobes. The prefrontal cortex was (and is) strongly linked to complex decision-making and social behavior, while the temporal lobes were to become instrumental in the emergence of human language. As hunters and gatherers, *Homo sapiens* lived in migratory social groups, employing campsites and related arrangements as home bases for social activity. Eventually, *Homo sapiens* would explode out of Africa to dominate every continent on Earth, save Antarctica. Somewhere along the way, humans developed language, most likely in a gradual manner. Like the introduction of controlled fires and cooking, language surely catalyzed the move toward greater and more sophisticated eusociality. Now members of the group could express their feelings, thoughts, and intentions in precise detail. Collectively, language enabled human groups to develop elaborate plans and scenarios to enhance survival and reproduction—everything from developing long-term projects to improve hunting and food storage to regulating social relations through precise norms, laws, and group sanctions.

Language was doubtlessly one of many factors, and perhaps the strongest factor, that led to the astounding proliferation of human creativity that seems to have begun around 50,000 years ago. The archaeological record shows that around this time *Homo sapiens* began to bury its dead, use animal hides to make clothing, develop specialized tools and strategies for more effective hunting and fishing, create jewelry and other decorative ornaments, construct musical instruments such as bone flutes, designate certain members of the tribe as shamans and seers, and portray cultural achievements in remarkable cave paintings. It appears that the average size of human groups may have increased during this time, and that different groups may have increased their contact with each other, leading to and producing more complex social organizations (Mesoudi & Jensen, 2012).

The dramatic changes in the kinds of lives that *Homo sapiens* experienced over the past 50,000 years reflect the rapid advancement and articulation of human *culture*, advances passed down from one generation to the next through social practices, social learning, and social institutions in increasingly large human groups (Cochran & Harpending, 2009). Moreover, genetic evolution itself appears to have sped up for human beings in this period of time. Findings from the Human Genome Project now suggest that the rate at which genes changed in response to selection pressures began rising around 40,000 years ago (Hawks, Wang, Cochran, Harpending, & Moyriz, 2007). With greater cultural variation and innovation, human beings experienced a wider range of selection pressures, which likely increased the rate at which genetic combinations were selected in (because they promoted adaptation) and selected out (because they didn't). Genes began to co-evolve, as it were, with cultural innovations. One of the greatest cultural innovations ever proposed and perfected by *Homo sapiens* emerged around 10,000 years ago, when humans invented agriculture. With the cultivation of crops and the domestication of animals, group size continued to increase for humans. Agriculture and the attendant advancement of trade and commerce led eventually to the establishment of small towns and, after that, cities. See Table 1.1 for a summary of the advancements made by *Homo sapiens.*

## IT'S ALL ABOUT THE GROUP

In the great city of New York, on January 3, 2007, 50-year-old Wesley Autrey, a Harlem construction worker, did something that none of the members of *Homo sapiens* who saw it will likely ever forget. A young man standing near Autrey on the 137th Street subway platform suffered a severe seizure and fell onto the tracks. With a speeding train

## TABLE 1.1.  Six Leaps Forward in the Evolution of Human Eusociality

### 1. Bipedalism

Following the divergence of chimpanzee and human lines of evolution (6 million years ago), australopithecines evolved to walk on their hind legs, freeing their hands for other uses, such as carrying food and manipulating objects. Endowed with brains no larger than those of chimps, they lived in small, simple groups that roamed over the African savannah.

### 2. Tools

Living 2.3 to 1.4 million years ago, *Homo habilis* evolved out of the australopithecine line with larger brains and more complex social arrangements. They invented simple stone tools, used most likely for scavenging and scraping meat off of dead animals.

### 3. Meat

Tool use made it easier to obtain meat, first from dead animals and later through hunting. The harvesting of meat required greater social cooperation and the development of more specialized and complex social functions.

### 4. Fire

Early hominids may have first realized that fire can tenderize meat after finding animals who had been burned to death in natural fires. Around 1 million years ago, *Homo erectus* learned to control fire, leading to the development of cooking, which enriched the diet and helped to establish social practices centered on the eating of common meals.

### 5. Campsites

As hunters and gatherers, *Homo erectus* and early *Homo sapiens* began to establish sites where cooking and other domestic activities could be located. Group members would return to the campsite after gathering food or hunting prey, sharing their bounty with other members of the group in common meals. Campsites made for greater division and coordination of labor, which themselves were enhanced by increased cognitive powers of shared intentionality. All eusocial species have nests that they defend against enemies. For early human beings, the campsite was their nest.

### 6. Culture

Beginning around 50,000 years ago, *Homo sapiens* achieved remarkable advances in the arts and technology, a creative explosion that continues to this day. A major catalyst for this development, and a key feature in the sprint to full human sociality, was probably the emergence of language. Humans invented agriculture about 10,000 years ago, and the rest is, literally, history.

*Note.* Eusocial species live in highly coordinated, interdependent, multigenerational groups. Members of the group perform functions that, in one way or another, are designed to promote the well-being of the group, including various forms of altruism and prosocial behavior.

approaching, Autrey jumped off the platform in an effort to save the young man's life. He first tried to drag the young man back up to the platform, but his weight was too much and he was still writhing from the seizure. As the lights of the incoming train appeared in the tunnel, Autrey pulled him away from the live third rail and pushed him down into a grimy drainage trough just below the tracks. Then he laid his own body on top and pressed down as hard as he could to keep the young man still, as the speeding train passed over them, with 2 inches of clearance to spare. Autrey later showed reporters grease stains on his wool hat that had come from the speeding train's undercarriage.

Subway passengers who witnessed Autrey's feat were overwhelmed with emotion. And so were the millions of newspaper and Internet readers and the television viewers who learned how the subway hero saved the young man's life. Notes of thanks, money, and television interviews came to Autrey from around the world. On the *Late Show with David Letterman* and network news interviews, Autrey repeatedly downplayed his efforts. "I just tried to do the right thing," he said. "It ain't about being a hero, it was just being there and helping the next person. That's all I did." But most everybody else saw it differently. Remarked one New Yorker: "Here and all over the world people are struck by this unselfish, heroic act. With so much evil in the world, it gives everybody hope" (Hampson, 2007, p. 1).

We might consider Wesley Autrey's altruistic act as an extraordinary example of human eusociality. Ever since Darwin proposed that human beings, like all other living things, are the products of evolution, the issue of *altruism* has intrigued scientists who aim to understand human nature. In the popular imagination, evolution plays out as a ruthless calculus in which the strongest organisms are most likely to survive and reproduce, passing copies of their genes down to the next generation. Evolution would seem to have little appetite for the milk of human kindness, except perhaps as expressed by human mothers to their helpless babies, and only then so that those genetically related infants may grow up to survive and reproduce. For nearly half a century, developmental psychologists have construed mother–infant *attachment* as a bond of love that forms in the first year of the infant's life in order to serve the evolutionary demand of protecting the helpless infant from predators and other dangers in the environment (Bowlby, 1969). It is easy to see why natural selection would promote the development of just such a bond, to ensure mother–infant proximity and motivate the mother to do nearly everything in her power, even to the point of sacrificing her own well-being, to protect her baby. Babies attach to fathers, too, and to certain other caregivers, who themselves may be primed by evolved mechanisms to exhibit care and nurturance.

The dynamics behind the mother's care for her offspring may indeed be extended to other genetically related individuals, as captured in the principle of *kin selection*—the idea that individuals may show altruism toward those with whom they share a significant allotment of genes. Siblings may exhibit kind and caring behavior to each other, again to the point of compromising their own selfish goals; cousins, even, and others related by blood may do so as well. The evolutionary logic for this behavior and sentiment is based on the fact that family members share copies of the same genes. Thus, doing something to benefit your siblings and cousins, even while incurring risk to yourself, advantages the Darwinian calculus for *them*, which may increase the chances that they will pass down copies of their own genes to the next generation, genes that they share with *you* (Hamilton, 1964). But heroic feats of altruism aimed at nonkin, and especially extreme examples such as Autrey's, would seem at first blush to be idiotic aberrations, at least as far as Autrey's own survival and reproductive prospects are concerned. And what about the survival and reproductive prospects of *his* kin? I forgot to mention that Autrey left his two daughters, ages 4 and 6, behind on the platform when he jumped down on to the tracks.

I do not know whether I would have done what Autrey did. In a crowded subway station, he was the only person who risked his life to save the stricken young man. But examples of selfless heroism appear regularly in the world's news sources. As I write these sentences today, the *New York Times* is reporting that President Obama awarded a Medal of Honor to Marine Corporal William Kyle Carpenter (Schneider, 2014). During a firefight in Afghanistan a few years back, Carpenter threw his body in the path between a fellow Marine and a live grenade. The blast blew away half of Carpenter's face and shattered his right arm. He almost died on the spot, but fellow soldiers quickly applied pressure dressings and tourniquets to his arms and frantically yelled at him to rally against death, keeping him alive until advanced medical care could take over.

Evolutionary scientists have sometimes interpreted heroic events such as these, along with the vastly more numerous instances of everyday kindness and consideration that members of *Homo sapiens* routinely exhibit to each other, in terms of the principle of *reciprocal altruism* (Trivers, 1971). In that human beings evolved to live in well-coordinated social groups, the argument goes, helping other individual human beings typically meant helping other members *of your group*. Those same group members might be positioned to return the favor sometime down the road. Therefore, it may enhance your own survival and overall reproductive chances—or what evolutionary biologists call an organism's *inclusive fitness*—to help another person, even at some risk to your own well-being, because that other person may in turn help you. Of course, people don't think it through this way before they act. Marine Corporal Carpenter acted on impulse; there was no time to weigh pros and cons. As he looked down onto the subway tracks, Wesley Autrey did not know who the stricken young man was, and he could hardly have expected that his actions would redound to his own advantage later on. There was no time to make a conscious mental calculation; instead, he, too, acted on impulse. Such a prosocial tendency, expressed and felt as a *natural urge to help another person in distress*, might have been naturally selected over the course of evolution to become part of human nature, according to the logic of reciprocal altruism. As Autrey said, "It ain't about being a moral hero." We are just there for each other, often ready to help.

And we are often ready to cooperate, especially when cooperation works to our own advantage as well as the advantage of our group. This is not to suggest that group members always live in peace and harmony. Over the past 200,000 years, members of human groups the world over have regularly competed with each other for limited resources and for status, resulting in endless bickering and jockeying for power within groups, Machiavellian intrigues of all sorts, and the all-too-frequent use of deadly force (Pinker, 2011). In paying obligatory homage to the existence of aggression and violence in human groups, I apologize for stating the obvious. Nonetheless, group members cannot survive without each other, and acts of altruism, kindness, and cooperation reinforce a fundamental design feature for human nature. Within the group, moreover, those individuals who consistently display acts of kindness, care, and cooperation may ultimately obtain an advantage in inclusive fitness *because other group members may appreciate their efforts*. According to the evolutionary logic of reciprocal altruism, group members who distinguish themselves for their overall agreeableness and altruistic tendencies could, in principle, garner more resources in the group than their less cooperative peers, at least in some cases, which would ultimately promote their chances in the game of survival and successful reproduction, perhaps both for themselves and their kin. It may *not* be true, therefore, that nice guys always finish last.

There is yet another way to think about the evolution of human kindness, cooperation, and altruism, but let me warn you now that it remains highly controversial. A small but growing number of evolutionary scientists today explain human cooperation and related features of ultrasocial behavior of *Homo sapiens* to be the result of *multilevel selection* (or what was once called *group selection*). The logic goes like this: Even though cooperative individuals are often appreciated in their groups, they may still lose out in the battle with their more selfish counterparts to obtain maximal resources in the group. Within the group, it may be the case that lazy individuals (freeloaders) and egotists take advantage of the good deeds done by cooperators and altruists, expending less energy for the good of the group while promoting their own selfish interests. Egotists win out over altruists in the group. However, when *groups compete with each other*, the groups that have a preponderance of cooperators and altruists, designed as they are to act for the good of the group, will win out in the battle for resources with groups that are mainly populated by egotists and freeloaders. Put simply, selfish egotists may beat out cooperating altruists *in* the group, but groups of cooperating altruists may beat out groups of selfish individuals when groups compete.

Now, technically, it is individuals, not groups, who pass their genes down to the next generation, which is the main reason that many scientists have always been skeptical of group selection explanations (Dawkins, 1976). And we generally think of natural selection as working at the level of the gene. Still, what benefits the group will benefit its members, and their respective genes. When cooperative groups win out, their members thrive. When egotists are unable to work well together, their groups may suffer, redounding to their potential disadvantage down the developmental road. Proponents of multilevel selection suggest that evolution works at many different levels, leaving room for the possibility that evolved tendencies that directly benefit groups may sometimes trump, or at least exist in tension with, evolved tendencies that directly benefit selfish behavior within the group (Wilson, van Vugt, & O'Gorman, 2008). Still, many evolutionary scientists do not accept the argument for multilevel selection, or else they suggest that the overall idea may be true but only under certain rare conditions. In the current firmament of evolutionary scientists, there are extremely smart people on both sides of the debate regarding multilevel selection. Accordingly, I am not so dumb as to pick a side in this fight given my standing as a humble personality psychologist. And my argument in this chapter regarding the eusocial nature of human nature itself does not really require that you or I take a side in the debate. Either way, human beings appear to have evolved to show extraordinary acts of kindness, care, cooperation, and congeniality, to say nothing of altruism, even as they manifest the competing tendencies of antagonism, aggression, and shameless self-promotion.

E. O. Wilson (2012) articulates an evolutionary reality when he writes: "People must have a tribe. . . . To form groups, drawing visceral comfort and pride from familiar fellowship, and to defend the group enthusiastically against rival groups—these are among the absolute universals of human nature and hence of culture" (p. 57). Put somewhat differently, human beings are naturally endowed with a *need to belong*—a relentless desire for attachment to families, clans, teams, tribes, and all sorts of social groupings (Baumeister & Leary, 1995). To belong to the group, a person must typically engage in some modicum of prosocial behavior. People who do nice things for others in the group are valued by the group, potentially increasing their own inclusive fitness. Their efforts, furthermore, may enhance the group's ability to compete against other groups, which indirectly benefits individual group members. All other things being equal, groups of cooperators typically outperform groups that are populated by antagonistic individualists—a truism that applies to business, sports, and war. When your group wins, you (usually) win, too.

Social scientists have identified a number of mechanisms and processes through which human beings bind themselves together in groups. The simplest is *group identification*. People naturally identify with social groups—nearly *any* social group—and experience the group's triumphs and setbacks as if they were their own. This evolutionary urge may be expressed even in ridiculous ways. In what is called the *minimal group paradigm*, for example, social psychologists assign people to arbitrary groupings, such as "If you were born before noon, you will be in the AM Group, and if you were born after noon, you will be in the PM Group." Under various experimental conditions, the members of the AM Group will begin to believe that they are superior to the members of the PM Group, and vice versa. AMers will favor fellow AMers on all sorts of things, and will show prejudice against PMers. PMers will do the same thing (Tajfel & Turner, 1979). A real-world analogue to the minimal group paradigm is allegiance to particular sports teams, which typically results from random circumstances. I am a devout Chicago Bears football fan only because I happened to grow up near Chicago. Research has shown that people who strongly identify with sports teams will actually lose faith in *their own* mental and social abilities after their team loses a big game (Hirt, Zillman, Erickson, & Kennedy, 1992). This empirical finding is absurdly relevant to my life. Even at age 59, I will sink into a depressive state late on a Sunday afternoon, and conclude that I will never again publish an article or successfully teach another psychology class, when the Bears lose to the Packers. I am not making this up.

When you identify with a group, you adopt the group's goals and attitudes, and you receive from the group a *social identity* (Tajfel & Turner, 1979). The social identity you receive encompasses your own thoughts and feelings regarding how you fit into the group, your role and function in the group, and what membership in the group means more generally for your life. Your identification with the group is more than the specific relationships you have with particular group members. Instead it involves a wholesale incorporation of the group into your self-concept. The group as a whole becomes part of *you*. Identification with one group, moreover, is likely to distance you from rival groups. Whereas you may be a member of many different groups, you will likely reject and even disparage those groups that are in opposition to your own, to the point of rejecting and disparaging members of rival groups. Think about how Tea Party Republicans in the United States feel about liberal Democrats, for example. For any given person, therefore, there exist in-groups (the groups to which you belong) and out-groups (the groups that are in direct opposition to the groups to which you belong). It is important and natural that you cultivate trust within your in-group(s), even as you cultivate distrust of out-groups. When you perceive that your in-group is threatened, you will probably double down on your allegiance to the in-group, while turning up your distrust of out-groups.

For certain eusocial species, such as bees and ants, individual members of the group are so highly similar to each other in their genetic makeup that they may be seen as comprising, in the collective, a superorganism. With that in mind, it should perhaps be no surprise that beehives and ant colonies operate so effectively, for the individual parts are so genetically similar as to be virtually interchangeable. Human groups, by contrast, are not nearly so genetically homogeneous. Even for our hunting and gathering forebears, intermarriage across groups was common, as was migration from one group to another, making for substantial genetic diversity within human groups. This poses an interesting problem for human eusociality: How do you create an effective whole out of a bunch of dissimilar parts? The best answer: *You do it through cultural practices and beliefs*. Comparing bees to humans, social psychologist Selin Kesebir (2012) writes: "Human culture thus functions like a social 'inheritance' mechanism that promotes phenotypical similarity in somewhat the same way that genetic inheritance promotes phenotypical similarity in bees" (p. 243). In other words, the culture of a human group makes the group members more similar to each other than they would otherwise be. You cannot count on the genes to do the trick because everybody in the group is so inherently different. Instead, you have to rely on culture. Group members need to learn the group's culture in order to become good members of the group. Parents, teachers, and other prime socializers in the group teach children the group's customs, traditions, moral codes, valued technologies, and history.

Going back at least 50,000 years (and probably much further), human groups have promoted group harmony, solidarity, and cohesiveness through elaborate cultural practices and beliefs. At the simple end of the cultural continuum is the establishment of group norms and standard procedures for adjudicating disputes in the group. Indeed, even apes and monkeys show rudimentary norms for social decorum and peacemaking (de Waal, 1996). More complicated, and arguably more powerful, are the cultural inventions of moral/legal codes and religious systems, which we examine in more detail in Chapter 7 of this book. Jonathan Haidt (2012) has forcefully argued that human beings evolved to hold strong moral intuitions regarding (1) physical harm, (2) fairness and reciprocity, (3) respect for legitimate authority, (4) loyalty to in-groups, and (5) purity or sanctity. These evolved intuitions promote cooperation among different members of human groups while binding those members more closely to each other, and to the group as a whole. Using culture to magnify human nature, every human society therefore aims to build solidarity and to regulate social behavior by instructing its members to be kind and fair to each other, to respect elders and other authority figures, to show allegiance to the group, and to deem certain things or experiences as sacred.

One of evolution's greatest inventions is human *religion*. You can look the world over, and you will never find a human society that has no tradition or history of religion. Building on what Haidt (2012) characterized as the moral foundation of sacredness, religion fosters group solidarity in *Homo sapiens* while providing group members with a common transcendent meaning for their lives (Durkheim, 1915/1967; D. S. Wilson, 2002). The shared beliefs and feelings of kinship engendered by religion help to persuade individuals to subordinate their immediate self-interests to the interests of the group. In human evolution, such subordination may have promoted cooperative behavior in the acquisition of resources and defense against dangers, which increased the inclusive fitness of group members, as they were better able to reproduce and take care of their kin. From the standpoint of multilevel selection, it may even be true that human groups with stronger religious bonds have tended to outcompete less cohesive groups, which would have the effect of reinforcing religiosity as a fundamental human sentiment.

Even today, religion brings people together and supports their commitment to long-term group enterprises. Human beings will make extraordinary sacrifices in the name of religion, even to the point of martyrdom. At the same time, religion has the power to foment social discord and even war when groups holding different religious persuasions come into conflict with each other. For better and for worse, religion is especially effective in motivating and justifying self-sacrificial acts aimed at promoting the welfare of the in-group. It is the kind of force in human nature—though not the only kind—that might even prompt a person to dive in front of a speeding train in order to save a stranger or give up material riches in order to serve the poor, or agitate for civil rights and world peace. At the same time, religion is powerful enough to motivate kamikaze pilots and suicide bombers. Throughout human history, religion has provided the energy and the justification for some of our species' most praiseworthy achievements, as well as acts of infamy.

## EXHIBIT A FOR A EUSOCIAL SPECIES: CHARLES DARWIN, HIMSELF

Charles Darwin was a highly religious young man. At age 18, he dropped out of medical school and embarked upon a course of study at Christ's College, Cambridge University, designed to prepare him for the ministry. As did many people in the Victorian age, Darwin believed that God had put him on Earth to do good works. He did not doubt the literal truth of the Christian bible. Even in childhood, he held a deep fascination with what he saw to be God's supreme creation—the natural world of rocks, plants, and animals. During the first half of the 19th century, it was possible for an Anglican clergyman to double as a natural historian, so it made good vocational sense that Darwin might supplement his required classes in theology and the classics with the botany lectures given by the renowned Reverend John Stevens Henslow. Darwin admired Henslow for his broad knowledge of science, considering him "quite the most perfect man I ever met with" (Wright, 1994, p. 290). The two became fast friends. They took long walks together to discuss the latest ideas in botany and to collect plant specimens. Darwin also collected beetles and developed a passion for entomology.

When he finished college in 1831, Darwin balked at the idea of becoming a county clergyman but not because he had lost faith. Far from it: He found fascinating and utterly convincing the idea that the natural world was designed by an almighty creator, as espoused in William Paley's enormously influential treatise *Natural Theology; or, Evidences of the Existence and Attributes of the Deity, Collected from the*

*Appearances of Nature*, published in 1802. Darwin desperately wanted to travel and to see the world, not so much to tour the great achievements of human civilization as to explore the natural treasures of exotic lands. Professor Henslow arranged for Darwin to accompany Captain Robert FitzRoy and his crew on the *HMS Beagle*, which would set sail for South America on December 27. Henslow fixed the young Darwin up with his dream internship. The new Cambridge graduate would assist FitzRoy as the ship's naturalist, examining the geology of the South American coast and Australia and collecting various rocks, fossils, plants, seashells, and animal specimens for further investigation. Darwin returned to England 5 years later, a changed man who would forever change the world.

From the standpoints of human nature and personality development, here is the most interesting question about Charles Darwin: Why did it *take him so long* to change the world? Not quite 24 months after he returned from his fateful trip, Darwin was struck with the key insight that provides the theory of evolution with its fundamental coherence and awesome scientific beauty—the idea of *natural selection*. It seems that he came to this idea in the fall of 1838, at the age of 29, a month or so before he proposed marriage to Emma Wedgwood. But then Darwin sat on his secret for *21 years*! And he might have sat on it even longer had not a younger colleague independently come up with the same idea himself. The scientific revolution that Darwin finally launched did not begin in earnest until 1859, with the publication of *The Origin of Species*. By then, Darwin was 50 years old, sickly, and the father of seven living children. Why the long delay?

Darwin artfully constructed a life of humility and rectitude. From early childhood onward, Darwin was viewed by nearly everybody who knew him to be humble and self-effacing. Even as a boy, he would reproach himself when he felt that he had boasted too much about an accomplishment. His father was strict, and he strongly discouraged displays of self-aggrandizement in his children. After his mother died (when Charles was 8 years old), his older sister Caroline assumed the household's moralistic maternal role. Darwin recalled that Caroline was "too zealous in trying to improve me; for I clearly remember . . . saying to myself when about to enter a room where she was—'What will she blame me for now?' " (Wright, 1994, pp. 213–214). After Emma accepted his proposal of marriage, the 29-year-old Darwin, already a celebrity in the scientific circles of London, reported "hearty gratitude to her for accepting such a one as myself" (p. 118), as if to express astonishment that a young woman whose own marriage prospects, if truth is to be told, had dimmed in recent years should accept such a wretch as he.

It is doubtlessly true that Darwin's dispositional humility and recurrent self-doubts were partly responsible for his reluctance to formulate fully and publish his insights about evolution through natural selection. But there were also other good reasons for waiting. Even though he had abandoned his initial belief that immutable species were created through intelligent design, Darwin knew that arguing his point would incur a firestorm of resistance, both in the scientific community and the public at large. Furthermore, his religiously pious wife—devoted as she was to her husband—refused to accept the implications of his theory, and that had to bother him. In 1844, he gave Emma a 230-page sketch of the theory of natural selection and instructed her to publish it should he suddenly die. (Darwin's low self-regard combined with his recurrent ill health to convince him that he was nearly always one step away from death.)

Darwin felt, moreover, that he needed to strengthen the scientific case for the theory before he could effectively present it in prime time. In the 1840s and early 1850s, he worked assiduously to marshal empirical evidence, devoting 8 years, for example, to the exhaustive study of sea barnacles. During this period, furthermore, Darwin continued to burnish his stellar reputation in the scientific community and to amass a large number of devoted friends in science. This strong investment in social and professional relationships was arguably the most important enterprise he undertook during the two decades of delay, for it is likely the main reason that today we credit Darwin with the theory of evolution, rather than one of history's greatest forgotten men, Alfred Russel Wallace.

Poor Wallace! Fourteen years Darwin's junior, the young naturalist quite rapidly and independently arrived at the very same ideas regarding evolution through natural selection. Off on a scientific trip in the Malay Archipelago, Wallace sent Darwin a letter to share the good news. Imagine Darwin's panic when, on June 18, 1858, he read the letter from Wallace. He had been poring over these same ideas ever since the voyage of the *HMS Beagle*, carefully amassing the evidence, biding his time, painstakingly working it all out, step by step, year after year, over 20 years now, and counting. And now some upstart had arrived at the same epiphany after but a handful of naturalistic observations and some hard thinking. Already stricken with anxiety about one daughter suffering from diphtheria and a baby boy who would soon die of scarlet fever, Darwin was having one of the worst summers of his life.

Darwin immediately sent Wallace's letter to a valued colleague, Charles Lyell, suggesting that the young man's theoretical sketch be sent out for immediate publication, so that Wallace would reap the scientific rewards:

> Please return me the MS [the manuscript of the letter], which he [Wallace] does not say he wishes me to publish, but I shall, of course, at once write and offer to send to any journal. *So all my originality, whatever it may amount to, will be smashed*, though my book, it if will ever have any value, will not be deteriorated; as all the labour consists in the application of the theory. (quoted in Wright, 1994, pp. 302–303, emphasis added)

In other words: *Let's give all the credit to Wallace, and my upcoming book will merely provide pedestrian empirical support for Wallace's brilliant insight.*

Although Lyell's response is lost to history, it seems to have gone something like this: *Are you crazy?!* In an astute analysis of this critical moment in the history of science, Wright (1994) suggests that Darwin may have implicitly known that Lyell would come up with a better plan. Many of Darwin's close colleagues were aware of Darwin's ideas on evolution. They rallied to Darwin's defense. Lyell and another eminent scientist, Joseph Hooker, devised a scheme whereby Wallace's short manuscript and an earlier sketch on natural selection that Darwin had privately circulated would be read together at the next meeting of the prestigious Linnean Society. This way, Wallace could not beat Darwin to the punch.

Because Wallace was overseas, Darwin's comrades did not have time even to obtain Wallace's consent. Not to worry. Once Wallace learned of what happened, he wrote proudly to his mother: "I sent Mr. Darwin an essay on a subject on which he is now writing a great work. He showed it to Dr. Hooker and Sir Charles Lyell, who thought so highly of it that they immediately read it before the Linnean Society. This assures me the acquaintance and continued assistance of these eminent men on my return home" (quoted in Wright, 1994, p. 304). The following year, Darwin published the "great work" to which Wallace alluded. Outmaneuvered by Darwin's formidable allies, Wallace never begrudged Darwin the credit that Darwin (mostly) deserved for the full explication of the theory of evolution through natural selection. Indeed, years later, Wallace wrote a big book of his own, entitled *Darwinism.*

How do we reconcile the contradictions in Darwin's personality that seem to come to the fore after the receipt of Wallace's letter? On the one hand, Darwin was truly a modest and principled man, a paragon of Victorian virtue. Many people—then and now—have regarded him as humble and self-effacing *to a fault*. On the other hand, he did not prevent his friends in the scientific community from essentially orchestrating a brilliant coup to assure his preeminence. In a passive-aggressive way, he condoned their plan, rather than releasing Wallace to publish his ideas first. After the presentations were made at the Linnean Society, Darwin boldly and aggressively pushed ahead to finish his magnum opus, to be followed by *The Descent of Man* (1871/1903) and *The Expression of Emotions in Man and Animals* (1872/1965). See Table 1.2 for a timeline of the life of Darwin.

Of all people, it is perhaps fitting that the case of Charles Darwin himself should illuminate a fundamental problem that members of our eusocial species have continuously confronted over the course of human evolution. I suspect it is a problem you have faced in your own life. And if you haven't faced it yet, you will. It is a problem of balance. How do social actors, so dependent as they are on the group, manage to achieve the social acceptance and the social status required for survival and reproduction? How do you win both love and power in your group? How can you *get along* with others while still *getting ahead*?

## GETTING ALONG AND GETTING AHEAD

For the cognitively gifted, bipedal, eusocial species that we call human beings, these two challenges—getting along and getting ahead in social groups—define the primal conundrum. This was true for the *Homo sapiens* roaming the African savannah 100,000 years ago, for the innovative agriculturalists who launched civilization 10,000 years ago, and for Charles Darwin in 19th-century England, and it remains true for you and for me. The first personality psychologist to recognize the importance of this fundamental dynamic was Robert Hogan (1982). In his *socioanalytic theory* of personality, Hogan asserts that human beings are biologically wired to live in social groups that are variously organized into status hierarchies. Group living provided our evolutionary ancestors with advantages in cooperative ventures, such as defense against predators. If you failed to get along with your group members on the African savannah, you were often soon dead. At the same time, having high status in one's group—getting ahead within the group structure—conferred decided advantages on the person who had it, providing the first choices of food, romantic partners, living space, and whatever other desirable commodities and privileges the group afforded, ultimately promoting reproductive success. Therefore, human beings are mandated by human

**TABLE 1.2. The Life of Charles Darwin: A Time Line**

| | |
|---|---|
| 1809 | Charles Edward Darwin is born in Shrewsbury, Shropshire, England, on February 12. He was the grandson of Erasmus Darwin on his father's side and Josiah Wedgwood on his mother's side. |
| 1817 | Develops an interest in natural history and collecting at the day school run by a local preacher. His mother dies. |
| 1825–1827 | Attends medical school at the University of Edinburgh. He neglects his studies and instead pursues hunting and takes taxidermy lessons. |
| 1827–1831 | Attends Christ's College, University of Cambridge, where, with his father's urging, he prepares for a career in the clergy. At Cambridge, he becomes a close friend and follower of the botany professor John Stevens Henslow. |
| 1831–1836 | Travels to South America on the *HMS Beagle*, where he investigates geology, collects natural specimens, and keeps careful notes of his observations and theoretical speculations. Samples of some of the specimens are sent back to England along with a selection of his notes. Henslow publicizes some of Darwin's observations and insights, fostering his pupil's scientific reputation. |
| 1836–1837 | Organizes his collections, writes up his notes, and meets with a number of eminent scientists in England, including the geologist Richard Lyell, anatomist Richard Owen, and the ornithologist John Gould. In his notebooks, he begins to theorize about how one species might change into another over time. |
| 1838 | Darwin continues to immerse himself in his work. His health begins to fail. He reads Thomas Malthus's *An Essay on the Principles of Population*, which seems to catalyze his thinking about evolution. In the fall, he gains the key insight into the idea of natural selection. In December, he proposes marriage to his cousin, Emma Wedgwood. |
| 1839–1858 | Continues scientific work in many different areas, as he develops and refines ideas on evolution. Devotes 8 years to the study of barnacles. Achieves many scientific honors, including the Royal Society's Royal Medal. He and Emma have 10 children, two of whom die in infancy, and one of whom (Annie) dies at age 10. Darwin suffers from poor health throughout. |
| 1858 | On June 18, Darwin receives a paper from Alfred Russel Wallace proposing the idea of natural selection. Friends of Darwin arrange for a joint presentation of Darwin's and Wallace's ideas at the Linnean Society. |
| 1859 | Publication of *The Origin of Species*. Reactions are mixed, but by the 1870s the scientific community accepts the theory of evolution. |

**TABLE 1.2.** (*continued*)

| | |
|---|---|
| 1871 | Publication of *The Descent of Man*, which focuses on the evolution of humans and develops ideas regarding sexual selection. |
| 1872 | Publication of *The Expression of Emotions in Man and Animals*, Darwin's major contribution to psychology. |
| 1882 | Charles Darwin dies on April 19. He is buried in Westminster Abbey. |

nature to seek social acceptance and social status, to seek to be liked and to be powerful. As Hogan, Jones, and Cheek (1985, p. 178) put it, "Getting along and getting ahead are the two great problems in life that each person must solve."

Drawing from sociological role theories, Hogan envisions group life as social performance. *Each of us is an actor on the social stage of life, playing our roles and managing the impressions of others in our group.* "Self-presentation and impression management are not trivial party games," Hogan and colleagues (1985) write. Rather, "they are fundamental processes, rooted in our history as group-living animals. They are archaic, powerful, compulsive tendencies that are closely tied to our chances for survival and reproductive success" (p. 181). Of prime importance in managing group impressions is a social actor's *reputation*. How are you generally perceived by your group? Do you have a reputation in the group as a reliable and trustworthy social actor? Are you generally viewed by your fellow group members to be honest, stable, friendly, aggressive, neurotic? Each social actor in the group has a slightly different reputation.

Reputations are transmitted from one group member to another through a variety of means. Group members observe each other as social actors and make attributions about each other based on those observations. They convey the conclusions of those observations to others. One powerful form of conveyance is *gossip*, a cherished social practice for human actors that likely goes back as far as the advent of human language (Dunbar, 2004). Gossip is actually a good thing (mostly) in group life, for social actors anticipate what others will say about them behind their backs and, therefore, try to display their best behaviors and keep their antisocial tendencies in check, so as to burnish a positive reputation in the group. Indeed, research in social psychology conclusively shows that gossip promotes cooperation in groups (Feinberg, Willer, & Schultz, 2014). When people spread reputational information about others through gossip, the recipients use the information to guide their future social interactions. They will avoid or threaten to ostracize group members who are the objects of negative gossip—selfish, egotistical, obnoxious people. They will cooperate instead with those whose reputations suggest high levels of agreeableness and conscientiousness. The threat of receiving a negative reputation through gossip, moreover, motivates would-be egotists to move their behavior more in the altruistic direction, or at least to be perceived as doing so.

The quality of one's reputation in the group goes a long way in determining the social actor's ultimate success in getting along and getting ahead. And this brings us back to Darwin. As he kept the world away from his great idea for over 21 years, Charles Darwin artfully cultivated a reputation in his social groups as a man of impeccable honor and humility. People were drawn to him for his mild manner and overall agreeableness. His scientific colleagues, even when they did not accept his views, respected his achievements as a naturalist and admired his hard work. Darwin labored for 21 years to build a convincing scientific case for evolution through natural selection. When the greatest professional crisis of his life was suddenly upon him, he cashed in his social capital. After receiving the letter from Wallace, he went immediately to his influential friends—Lyell and Hooker, for starters—to help him resolve the conundrum. True to the uniquely human brand of eusociality, Darwin craved social acceptance and social status, yet in his own inimitable way. He wanted to get along with others, for sure, but he also wanted to get ahead. He had strong ambitions, even as he enjoyed high status in the scientific community. When the chips were down, he leveraged the status and the social acceptance to meet his ambition's need (Wright, 1994). He was the nicest guy on the planet, but Darwin could not let Wallace win.

*Personality begins with the different reputations that human actors achieve as they strive to get along and get ahead in social groups.* In the beginning, natural selection developed (and continues to develop) an overall design for human nature. But each individual human being is a unique variation on the design. Personality is about the variation. Not all variations matter, however. For example, I don't really care if you chew your food mainly on the left side of your mouth or the right side. But if I am to interact with you on a regular, or even occasional, basis, I do care about how *nice* you are, and how honest, conscientious, and needy. The variations that matter most are the ones that observant social actors have been monitoring ever since *Homo sapiens* first walked on the African continent, and the very same variations we have been gossiping about ever since language entered the scene. These are variations that matter for getting along and getting ahead in social groups. In the long run, they are variations that inform our prospects for survival and reproductive success.

It makes consummate evolutionary sense that a eusocial species like ours would evolve to take careful note of variations in personality. If we were not to notice these differences, then, ipso facto, these differences would effectively cease to exist—that is, they would not matter for social life—and personality encompasses only those differences that matter. In its most basic sense, personality depends on recognizable variation in social performance (McAdams & Pals, 2006). It depends on there being different kinds of social actors on the theatrical stage of human life. It depends not only on variation in the group but also the group members' taking note of the variation, considering the variation important, worth gossiping about.

As human groups grow in size and complexity, social actors must process more and more information about each other. With increasing group size comes increasing variation within the group, more social stuff to keep track of, more reputations to monitor and sort out. The evolutionary biologist Robin Dunbar (2010) contends that human beings are capable of having social relationships with no more than about 150 other human beings at any given time in their lives. Beyond 150, the human brain has trouble keeping track of who is who. Dunbar speculates that among our hunting and gathering ancestors, groups of approximately 150 individuals constituted *clans*. Clans lived together and claimed ownership of certain sites and territories. Related clans would be linked in broader groupings called *tribes*. Tribes might range anywhere from 500 to 2,500 men, women, and children. Within clans, and even more so within tribes, social actors would be able to know each other mainly through shorthand reputations. There is too much variation and social complexity for an in-depth, intimate understanding of all the individuals in a person's clan—a fact that is set in even starker relief when we consider the tribe. In order to get along and get ahead in this complex social milieu, what does a group member need to know about his or her fellow social actors?

Answer: the same things you and I need to know today if we are to get along and get ahead in the complex social groupings that contextualize our modern lives. We need to know things like this: Who are the Darwins out there? Who are the subway heroes? Who are the really nice guys (and girls) who will be sweet and agreeable in your presence and help you out when you are in need? Who is honest? Who can be trusted?

Who is dutiful and conscientious? Who will always work hard? Who will dominate you in social relationships? Who will be aggressive and mean? Who are the outgoing people? Who are the introverts? Who are the emotionally volatile people? Who is calm and serene? Who is open-minded and ready to learn new things? Who is rigid and uncompromising? You and I need answers to questions like these because we are both card-carrying members of a eusocial species—which means we are stuck with our group(s). If you are to cooperate and compete with group members, as befits *Homo sapiens*, you need to know and respond effectively to the variations on the general design for human nature that you will repeatedly encounter as you move through life in groups, the differences in personality that make a difference in social life.

You need to know these things about your fellow social actors, the group members whom you regularly encounter in social life. And you also need to know what kind of a social actor *they* perceive *you* to be. For you *as a social actor*, personality consists mainly of those broad behavioral attributions that other people consistently make about you as they observe your social performances. And it consists of the attributions you make about yourself as you observe yourself in social action, and as you observe others observing you.

## CONCLUSION

Human evolution is a 2-million-year sprint toward a unique brand of eusociality, featuring the processing power of big hominid brains and increasingly complex social groupings. Along the way, our bipedal evolutionary ancestors learned to use tools; developed an appetite for meat; tamed fire (which enabled them to cook the meat); organized themselves together around campsites (our primordial homes); and eventually developed the habits of mind, the technologies, and the elaborate cultural practices and belief systems that sustain complex social life even today. Throughout it all, human beings identified strongly with their groups, and continue to do so, for survival and reproductive success have always depended on the support of the group. The man who first worked out the details of evolution through natural selection—Charles Darwin, himself—experienced a primal tension in his life that may, in fact, be endemic to members of our eusocial species: How does a person *get along* and yet still *get ahead* in the social group? Darwin's personal dilemma is indeed our own, and it is the starting point for considering the development of human personality.

Personality begins with the different reputations that human actors achieve as they strive to get along and get ahead in social groups. Social actors take careful note of individual differences in social acting—how it is that some actors are more effective than others, more trustworthy, more emotional, more self-controlled, more socially dominant, and on and on, keeping track of the consistent and consequential variations they perceive in social behavior, the differences that make the biggest difference. As it comes to be construed in the social group, each personality is a unique variation on the evolved design for human nature.

As common members of a eusocial species, we are all much more alike than otherwise. Don't forget: We are all human beings. From a viewpoint located in a distant galaxy, we might all look pretty much the same. But *we* see the differences up close. We see the individual variations on the general pattern of human nature *because we evolved to see them*. And we evolved to see them because these are the differences that make the biggest difference for adaptation to group life. It is these differences that constitute the basic elements of human personality from the standpoint of the social actor. Let us now consider how these differences develop over the life course of individual human beings, beginning a second time, this time with the beginning of an individual human life, as the innately eusocial infant emerges from the womb, ready to become a social actor.

# chapter 2

# The Actor Takes the Stage

## HOW WE PERFORM EMOTION

When the curtain came down at the Ethel Barrymore Theatre on the night of December 3, 1947, the audience sat for a moment in stunned silence and then burst into a round of wild applause that went on and on—for *30 minutes*. The crowd was overwhelmed by the opening-night performance of Tennessee Williams's play *A Streetcar Named Desire*. The memorable night marked the debut of the 23-year-old Marlon Brando, who played Stanley Kowalski, a Polish American, working-class tough whose volcanic exchanges with Blanche DuBois, a Southern belle with a dark past (played by Jessica Tandy), culminate in brutal violence and Blanche's descent into insanity. In the famous production, Brando and Tandy accomplished what stage and screen actors often achieve, though perhaps not so spectacularly, in their best performances: They conveyed human *emotion* in vivid and convincing fashion. This is fundamentally what actors do. Through their actions on stage, they portray the richness of emotional experience—from joy and excitement to anger, fear, shame, and sadness. In the best performances, the audience comes to feel what the characters feel, or else experiences a strong emotional response to the emotions portrayed on stage, as when the audience feels a mixture of pity and disgust as Blanche puts on airs of superiority, and shock when an enraged Stanley rapes her. On the stage—and, I would submit, in everyday social life—acting is largely about the performance of emotion.

Commenting on the dramatic productions in ancient Greece, Aristotle proposed that each actor should display a particular emotional disposition or outlook that is clearly revealed to the audience through the actor's voice and the action of the play (Merlin, 2010). The audience knows the actor's character only through what the actor *does* on stage. From the perspective of the theater seats, it does not matter what thoughts and desires are in the actor's head. All the audience sees is the action. For the actor, then, *I do; therefore, I am.* Effective "doing," Aristotle maintained, depends on the actor's ability to convey emotion through behavior. Accordingly, established regimens for stage performance, such as Stanislavski's (1936) approach to method acting, aim to train professional actors to experience and convey authentic emotion. Actors scrupulously monitor their own performance of emotion in order to convey just the right impression for the audience and for the other actors who are with them in the scene. The skilled actor learns how to control the emotions expressed, ultimately perfecting the art of observing the self in order to manage the impressions of others (Mast, 1986).

For the cognitively gifted eusocial species known as *Homo sapiens*, everyday social life is not so different from what happens on the theatrical stage. In *The Presentation of Self in Everyday Life*, sociologist Erving Goffman (1959) famously described human social behavior as a series of *performances* through which actors play roles and enact scripts in order to manage the impressions of other characters in the social scene. During a performance, the social actor may enact a *routine*—"a pre-established pattern of action which is unfolded during a performance and which may be presented or played through on other occasions" (Goffman, 1959, p. 16). Everyday life is filled with routines—eating lunch with friends, attending meetings, arguing with your mother, working out at the gym, going to the supermarket, and on and on.

In everyday social life, each routine has its own predictable course, but there is still plenty of room for *improvisation*. Actors are not mere automatons who simply read their lines and follow the director's instructions. They personalize the performance; they make it fit their own unique nature and lived experience. Goffman (1959) wrote that each actor brings a unique manner or style of acting to the routine, what he termed a *personal front*. The personal front consists of clothing, age, posture, speech patterns, facial expressions, and other cues that signify the actor's position in the performance and, by extension, his or her status and identity in the group. The personal front, furthermore, includes those idiosyncratic behavioral features by which others repeatedly *recognize* the character. There he is! I know him by that curious smile, or that scowl. There she goes again! She is so alluring, and so disdainful. As Stanley and Blanche, Marlon Brando and Jessica Tandy each expressed a distinctive personal front by which the audience came to know them.

And so do each of us, Goffman (1959) asserted, in our everyday social performances. What Goffman called a "personal front," I will call the rudiments of *personality*. It is the basic dispositions of our respective personalities that we each bring, as social actors, to each and every one of our social performances. From the first day of life onward, these basic dispositions provide each of us with a unique and recognizable style of social display and deportment. The most recognizable and socially compelling features of the style, furthermore, are those that concern how we artfully perform emotion, the unique manner in which we convey and control our feelings of love, hate, joy, anger, fear, and all the other sentiments and affects that are subsumed within the rich array of human emotional experience. Therefore, the *art* of personality development involves, among other things, the expression and refinement of a uniquely personal and recognizable style of emotional performance. On Broadway and in everyday social life, the best performances convey just the right emotional feel. They win the wild applause of the audience, and the respect and admiration of the other actors in the group.

## ACTING, EMOTION, AND THE SELF

By virtue of membership in a eusocial species, human beings move onto the stage as social actors the moment they emerge from the womb, and they do not exit the stage until they die. There is no developmental period in normal human life when the individual is *not* a social actor—not even the first minutes after birth. Yet it may seem odd, at first blush, to think of the human newborn in this way. Goffman's (1959) characterization of role playing and impression management in everyday social life is easy to imagine among human adults. But infants seem so primitive—so far away, developmentally speaking, from Marlon Brando as he plays Stanley Kowalski, or from a normal human teenager as she navigates her way through the treacherous complexities of high school social life. Infants do not seem to have much awareness of themselves as actors in a social setting. Indeed, they do not have an awareness of themselves as much of anything at all. But from the standpoint of the social world into which they are thrown at birth, infants' actions are interpreted in pretty much the same way that human beings interpret social actions expressed by any other animate actor. We watch our babies the way we watch the characters in a movie. We observe every movement in order to make sense of what they are trying to express, especially eager to decode their emotions.

Babies are social actors long before they realize they are social actors. They are social actors *because that is what we, the social audience, observe them to be.* Ask mothers to tell you what they see when they observe the actions of their 1-month-old babies. They will report that they see signs of at least five basic emotions: interest, surprise, joy, anger, and fear (Johnson, Emde, Pannabecker, Sternberg, & Davis, 1982). Nonbiased researchers who observe infants in the laboratory tell a similar story, but with more detail. They report that newborns appear to express the emotions of general distress, general contentment, interest, and disgust; they also report that between 2 and 7 months of age, clear signs of joy, surprise, anger, sadness, and fear are readily observable (Izard et al., 1995). From an evolutionary standpoint, the expression of basic emotions would appear to hold substantial adaptive value, as Darwin (1872/1965) first suspected. The expression of disgust, for example, may originate in the baby's rejection of distasteful foods, which themselves may be toxic. A cry of distress may signal to the caregiver, and to the social group writ large, that the baby senses danger and is in need of comfort and protection.

As social actors, babies communicate information to the group through emotional displays. The main organ for this expression is the face. Across different human cultures, people recognize in human infants the facial expressions of fear (mouth retracted, brows level and drawn up and in, eyelids lifted), sadness (corners of mouth turned down, inner portion of brows raised), joy (bright eyes, cheeks lifted, mouth forms a smile), interest, anger, and disgust (Eckman, 2003). Caregivers and other actors in the infant's social world respond eagerly and in earnest to these facial expressions, with emotional displays of their own. And babies respond in turn, in dynamic, face-to-face interactions, sharing emotional states and engaging in elaborate conversations about emotion, without using a word (Stern, 1985). When mothers are instructed in the laboratory to respond to their 4-month-olds by simply staring at their babies and adopting a still, expressionless face, the babies will react with anger or sadness (Van Egeren, Barratt, & Roach, 2001). The babies seem to expect that other social actors will respond to their emotional displays in socially appropriate ways. Sadly, mothers suffering from serious depression are known to show blunted facial expressions in responding to their infants, which may affect their infants' emotional development in negative ways. Research suggests that babies of depressed mothers eventually stop trying to engage their mothers. Indeed, when psychology experimenters put depressed mothers into the still-face condition, their infants show little response.

The first scripts for social actors, therefore, are not verbal, but facial (Tomkins, 1987). In ancient Greek drama, actors wore masks to provide vivid facial portrayals of emotion. It is no accident, moreover, that many of the most heralded screen actors and actresses of all time—think Meryl Streep and Anthony Hopkins, for instance—are masters of facial expression. Thankfully, one need not have extraordinary talent to convey a wide range of emotions through facial display. The ability seems to be part of human nature for our eusocial species, though individual differences are readily apparent, and some children, such as those with autism and related disorders, may find it very difficult to express and decode facial cues. The psychological limitations that autistic children experience are most clearly evident in the *social* arena. One of the earliest potential signs of the disorder is avoidance of interpersonal eye contact. Peculiarities in facial display, therefore, may sometimes foreshadow the profound disabilities that autistic children will ultimately confront as social actors.

In the first 2 years of life, the social actor's emotional development plays out against the backdrop of an evolving *attachment* relationship. Over time, infants develop a relationship of love and security with their primary caregivers, in the context of which both powerfully positive and negative emotions are experienced, displayed, and negotiated. At 2 months of age, babies begin to display broad *social smiles*, in direct response to particular events in their environment, which indicate to the social actors present that the infant is experiencing joy or happiness. By age 3 months, these smiles appear brighter and stronger in response to real human beings in the infant's environment than to other interesting and animated objects, such as puppets that beckon to them (Ellsworth, Muir, & Hains, 1993).

By age 6 or 7 months, infants save their biggest smiles for their primary caregivers, with whom the attachment bond is beginning to solidify. By contrast, they begin to show facial expressions indicative of fear or wariness in the presence of strangers, a phenomenon known as *stranger anxiety*. Around the same time, they will also express fear, anger, or sadness in response to prolonged separation from their primary caregivers, a phenomenon known as *separation anxiety*. The evolutionary function of attachment is to protect the infant from threats in the environment by ensuring that the caregiver(s) stay(s) in close physical proximity to the infant (Bowlby, 1969). The negative emotional expressions of stranger anxiety and separation anxiety therefore signal to the group that the infant is potentially in danger. Caregivers respond accordingly, doing what they can to calm the baby down and reestablish a sense of security.

In the ideal scenario of secure attachment, the 1-year-old infant implicitly apprehends the caregiver to be a *safe haven* during periods of emotional distress, and to be a *secure base* from which to explore the world when emotions feel more positive. Infants with less secure attachment bonds enjoy less confidence in their caregiver's ability or willingness to assuage their negative emotions during moments of threat and to reinforce their positive emotions when the social world seems less threatening.

As they move into their second year of life, human infants carry with them the implicit (unconscious, inchoate) memory of significant attachment experiences. Developmental psychologists describe this memory as an internalized *working model* of attachment. The working model details the infant's emotional history of attachment and sets forth expectations about how experiences of love and trust may transpire in the future. The working model may be updated and changed as the infant accumulates new experiences with attachment relationships. As social actors, then, 1-year-olds have already accumulated a wealth of emotional experience, which gives them expectations about emotional life in the future. Through their relationships with attachment objects, moreover, they have also developed considerable social expertise. Early socioemotional development occurs without any conscious awareness, however, which is mainly why you remember virtually nothing from the first 2 years of your life.

Self-awareness begins to dawn shortly before the second birthday. Numerous studies in developmental psychology have shown that human infants begin to recognize themselves in mirrors and through recording devices (e.g., video) around 18 months of age. When children begin to realize that the images they see in the mirror are themselves, they literally see themselves acting in reflection, and recognize their actions as their own.

It is also around 18 months of age that children typically begin to utter self-referential words, such as *me* and *mine*, and begin to express certain kinds of self-referential emotions, such as pride and embarrassment (Tangney, Stuewig, & Mashek, 2007). To feel pride or shame in response to one's actions presupposes a sense of the self as an actor whose performances are viewed and evaluated by others in the environment. What William James (1892/1963) first identified for psychologists as the subjective sense of selfhood—the sense that "I" am, that I exist—emerges toward the end of the second year of human life, in the form of a self-conscious actor who recognizes himself when he appears on stage. In a reflexive sense, moreover, the "I" begins to develop an image of the "Me," as the child begins to take note of her own social actions and other actors' reactions to those actions. Over time, I learn more and more about Me, based largely on observing myself as I act and taking note of how other people respond to Me, based on their observations of My performances.

The child's initial sense of herself as a social actor, nonetheless, is surprisingly unstable and inconsistent following her debut. As one indication of the confusion that sometimes occurs, take this charming example of the 3-year-old Jennifer, who participated in a research study on self-awareness. Observing a video taken 3 minutes earlier in which she appears with a sticker on her head, Jennifer says, "It's Jennifer . . . it's a sticker," and then adds, "but why is *she* wearing my shirt?!" (Povinelli, 2001, p. 81). Indeed, 3-year-olds will reach for a large sticker they see on top of their own head while viewing a live video of themselves, but they will not necessarily reach for it, even though it is still there, when viewing a replay of the same video taken only 3 minutes earlier (Povinelli, 2001). Furthermore, when asked who was on TV in the video made minutes before, it is only by 4 years of age that the majority of children will say "Me" rather than their proper name, suggesting a first-person rather than a third-person stance. Even though the young child is aware of himself as an actor on the social stage, he may fail to realize that the actor *continues to be Me* over time. It is not until age 3 or 4 years that the child consolidates a clear sense of self as a continuous social actor extended in time and across successive social scenes.

## PERFORMING POSITIVE EMOTION: THE DEVELOPMENT OF EXTRAVERSION

Long before children become consciously aware of themselves as social actors, they exhibit characteristic acting styles. Parents, older siblings, doctors, and other members of the audience immediately notice that some babies seem consistently cheerful and smiley, while others appear to be more inhibited, tense, or cranky. Differences in the overall quality of the baby's mood, the baby's energy level, behavioral tempo, and alertness appear early on in human development, reflective of inborn differences in physiological makeup. Developmental psychologists refer to these stylistic differences as the infant's *temperament*. The most notable features of temperament are about the actor's *performance of emotion*—how the infant *expresses* and *regulates* the feelings that well up inside.

Emotions come in two broad categories. The positive emotions feel good; the negative emotions feel bad. Scientific research on temperament reinforces what nearly every parent knows: *Some babies feel good much of the time, and other babies don't.* As members of the newborn actor's observing audience, parents and researchers readily detect individual differences in *positive emotionality*, which is the basic temperament tendency to *feel* positive affect such as joy, excitement, and pleasure, and to *act* in such a way as to suggest a positive emotional engagement with the social world (Shiner & De Young, 2013).

Infants and young children who show high levels of positive emotionality are consistently more cheerful, lively, and high-spirited than their peers. They show more pleasure, joy, and excitement, and they seem to experience greater positive emotion in response to rewards. At 2 months of age, they smile and laugh more frequently and with more intensity compared to infants who are rated by others as showing lower levels of positive emotionality. Their expressions of positive emotion reflect eagerness to approach potentially rewarding situations, especially situations that promise social reward. For example, one research study showed that 4-month-old infants who tend to smile and show positive emotion in response to pleasant pictures and sounds in the laboratory were more likely, months later, to show positive approach behavior in response to novel situations (Hane, Fox, Henderson, & Marshall, 2008). Moreover, as they move beyond infancy, children's positive emotionality spills over into social relationships. Children high in positive emotionality appear to enjoy and to seek out social interaction to a greater extent than do children lower in positive emotionality. Accordingly, those who observe their performances describe such children as especially sociable, energetic, ebullient, and socially potent. By contrast, children tending toward the lower end of positive emotionality are viewed to be shy, reserved, and socially lethargic.

Positive emotionality, however, may not always look 100% positive. Sometimes anger gets into the picture. Infants and children who exhibit high levels of positive emotionality are especially eager to seek and experience social rewards. As such, when their efforts to obtain rewards are thwarted, they sometimes exhibit anger, and even aggression. Even though it is not viewed to be "positive" in tone, the emotion of anger plays a major role in reward-seeking behavior across the life course (Harmon-Jones & Allen, 1998). Indeed, infants who experience more anger in response to frustration tend to be seen as more outgoing and sociable in grade school (Rothbart, Derryberry, & Hershey, 2000). Unlike the negative feelings of, say, sadness and fear, anger can be an energizing emotion, motivating social actors to ramp up their efforts to achieve social rewards.

Research in the neuroscience of emotion suggests that some of the same brain processes that are involved with the experience of *positive emotion* itself are also implicated in human *sociality*. There may be a deep connection in human nature between *feeling good* and *being social*. To capture the connection, contemporary neuroscientists invoke the concept of a *behavioral approach system* (BAS). Distributed across many different brain areas and involving a host of different neural processes, the BAS motivates the individual to approach potentially rewarding situations, which themselves are often social in nature, and to experience the positive emotion that is associated with the pursuit and attainment of rewards. Among other things, the BAS encompasses various pathways and structures in the brain that are implicated in the release of the chemical *dopamine*. In the brain, dopamine serves as a "neurotransmitter," a chemical released by neurons to send signals to other neurons. Dopamine has different functions with respect to different systems in the brain, but one of its prime roles concerns reward seeking. Dopamine is released in certain brain regions, such as the nucleus accumbens and prefrontal cortex, as a result of rewarding experiences such as eating food, having sex, and ingesting stimulant drugs such as cocaine. Importantly, dopamine is also released in response to stimuli that are associated with strongly rewarding experiences. You don't have to experience transcendent sex to reap the benefits of dopamine release. BAS circuitry in your brain may stimulate dopamine activity even when you merely think about the object of your sexual desire. As far as dopamine goes, anticipation can be as good as consummation.

Actually, anticipation may trump consummation, when it comes to dopamine. Some scientists believe that dopamine is more about *wanting* it than getting it—more about the pursuit, the chase, the hunt, the longing, and the seeking than it is about the enjoyment that may come when you finally achieve the desired goal. After all, seeking feels good, too. Pursuing the reward is rewarding in itself. Drugs that increase dopamine activity (e.g., methamphetamine and cocaine) tend to increase seeking behavior (and the positive emotions associated with that) but do not necessarily produce spikes in pleasure upon receipt of the reward. By contrast, opiate drugs such as heroin and morphine produce increases in pleasure but do not necessarily motivate approach behavior.

Accordingly, a growing number of scientists argue that the BAS and its attendant dopaminergic circuitry may work in concert with a second broad system in the brain, sometimes called the *opioid system* (Depue & Fu, 2012). The opioid system releases endogenous neuropeptides such as beta-endorphin when the organism achieves rewards, producing feelings of joy and pleasure. If the BAS, then, is mainly about *wanting* rewards (and therefore approaching rewards, seeking them out), the brain's opioid system may be more involved in the *liking* that actors experience once they have achieved the desired reward. With respect to basic emotional experiences, then, the BAS links more naturally to the excitement and anticipation that actors feel when they are pursuing rewards, and the anger or frustration they may feel when their pursuit is blocked. By contrast, the opioid system is more closely linked with the positive emotions of joy and pleasure that come with the attainment of the reward itself.

Early in their acting careers, infants and children whose BAS and opioid systems are set up to produce high levels of positive emotionality may find themselves on a yellow brick road to the enchanted land of *extraversion*. Of course, the road is not straight, and it is *not* inevitable that the actor will indeed get there, though the actor will get *somewhere*. Dimensions of infant temperament do *not* morph naturally and predictably into corresponding personality traits in mature adults. The *artful* nature of personality development tells us instead that each individual journey is unique, influenced as it is by myriad forces inside the person and in the person's environment. Each individual person fashions his or her own singular variation on the evolved design of human nature. Nevertheless, individual differences in positive emotionality in the early years of life are a harbinger of a broad dispositional continuum that becomes clearer and more articulated as children mature into adolescence and beyond. The continuum captures differences in what personality psychologists call extraversion–introversion, or simply E.

E is the all-time rock star for personality—the greatest (and most obvious) idea about individual differences in socioemotional performance ever imagined. When it comes to individual differences, what could, after all, be more fundamental for our eusocial species than a dimension that distinguishes those of us who are more "social" from those of us who are less "social"? We are all social actors, of course, but you could say people who line up on the high end of extraversion are more so: more sociable, more oriented toward social interaction, more inclined to find reward in social situations. Poets and philosophers have distinguished between extraversion and its opposite (introversion) for thousands of years, and behavioral scientists have studied the same continuum for almost 100 years. We know more about extraversion than about nearly anything else in personality.

Figure 2.1 summarizes some of what we know. At its center is a box depicting the developmental sequence for this basic personality trait. In some lives, early temperament differences in positive emotionality may gradually expand and articulate into a bundle of related dispositions that comprise the super trait of extraversion–introversion. Think of people as being arranged on the E continuum to form a bell-shaped curve, with higher numbers of people clustered toward the middle of the distribution (moderate levels of E) and fewer and fewer as you move to the extreme poles. Despite popular notions, people are not either–or when it comes to E. It is all a matter of degree, like height or weight. We don't say that people are either "tall people" or "short people," as if there are only two types when it comes to height. Similarly, we should not speak of people as either pure extraverts or pure introverts—two discrete personality types. Instead, people are arrayed on a continuum, from the extreme extraversion pole to the extreme introversion pole. By definition, most people are not extreme (but a few are).

To measure individual differences in E in adolescents and adults, psychologists rely mainly on self-report questionnaire scales. Paul Costa and Jeff McCrae have developed an especially influential self-report measure (the Revised NEO Personality Inventory [NEO-PI-R]), which breaks E down into six related but separable subtraits, or facets, listed in Figure 2.1. These are excitement seeking, activity, assertiveness, gregariousness, positive emotions, and warmth (Costa & McCrae, 1992). Taken together, six facets assessed on the NEO-PI-R reflect a basic socioemotional distinction that appears on other scales and throughout the scientific literature on E (De Young, 2010). This is the distinction between those properties of E that connote (1) drive and social dominance (expressed in the facets of excitement seeking, activity, and assertiveness; and captured in the idea of a strong *approach* toward rewards) and those that connote (2) sociability and positive interpersonal experiences (expressed in the facets of gregariousness, positive emotions, and warmth; and captured in the idea of *enjoying* the rewards that one has obtained). Extraversion, then, is fundamentally about (1) seeking and (2) enjoying rewards, especially social rewards.

Studies show that extraverts get "more bang for the buck" when it comes to opportunities for social reward. In a recent set of experiments, for example, extraverts (compared to introverts) responded with greater intensity of positive emotion when presented with scenarios that explicitly detailed the *pursuit of rewards*, even when the scenarios were not especially pleasant or happy (Smillie, Cooper, Wilt, & Revelle, 2012). In the same set of experiments, merely presenting emotionally pleasant scenarios did not evoke stronger positive reactions for extraverts, compared to introverts. However, other studies have shown that extraversion is associated with positive emotional responses *even in the absence*

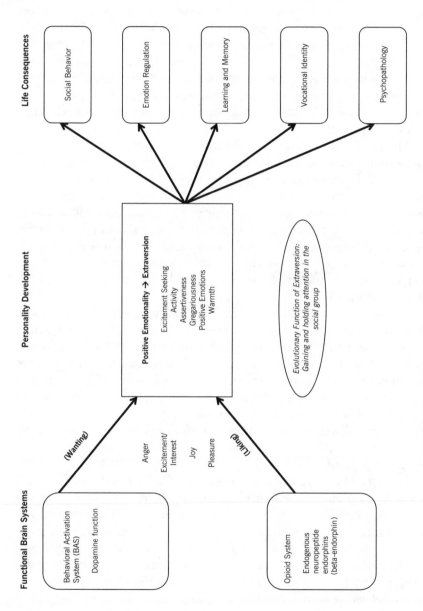

**FIGURE 2.1.** The architecture of extraversion.

*of reward pursuit.* For example, Richard Lucas and Ed Diener (2001) asked students to imagine how much positive emotion they would feel in response to a range of hypothetical scenarios, some pleasant and others unpleasant. Compared to introverts, students high in E tended to show higher ratings on positive emotion for pleasant interpersonal situations, including those that did not involve the active pursuit of social rewards, such as having a conversation with good friends. Interestingly, those high in E showed higher positive emotion ratings, compared to those low in E, even for pleasant *nonsocial* situations, such as sitting alone reading a book on a nice summer day.

Moving from the left to the right in Figure 2.1, we move from the brain systems that are presumed to underlie extraversion—the BAS and opioid system—to E's manifest expression in the social world. Decades of research on extraversion–introversion show that individual differences in E have profound implications for the lives of social actors. Hundreds of scientific studies reveal that consistent variations in E are associated with important differences in (1) social behavior, (2) emotion regulation, (3) learning and memory, (4) vocational interests and identity, and (5) various indices of risk and psychopathology. Table 2.1 lists a handful of the more noteworthy empirical findings.

On balance, scoring toward the high end on E tends to bring more advantages than disadvantages. Compared to introverts, social actors who score high on extraversion enjoy broader and more fulfilling friendships, greater social support, greater social competence, higher levels of societal engagement, better performance as leaders, more optimism and resilience in the face of challenges, and higher levels of happiness and psychological well-being. This is not to say that scoring toward the introversion pole will make you miserable. The findings are statistical generalizations, and there are many exceptions to the general rule, as is usually the case in psychological research.

Nonetheless, there are a few negative correlates of E, as Table 2.1 shows. For example, research suggests that extraverts sometimes fail to take negative feedback into consideration and may therefore not learn as much as they should from their mistakes. E is also modestly associated with certain risky behaviors that sometimes get people into trouble, such as gambling and alcohol consumption. When problematic behavior patterns ascend to the level of what the mental health profession deems to be psychopathology, extraverts are more likely than introverts to exhibit *externalizing* kinds of disorders, such as those associated with aggression, narcissism, and substance abuse. Having said all that, if I could pick my dispositional traits (which I can't), I

**TABLE 2.1. Selected Correlates of Extraversion**

Social Behavior

- More social interaction on a daily basis (Srivastava, Angelo, & Vallereux, 2008)
- Greater popularity (Paunonen, 2003)
- More sexual behavior, more sexual partners (Nettle, 2005)
- Creating more positive social environments for others (Eaton & Funder, 2003)
- Higher levels of social competence (Argyle & Lu, 1990)
- More social goals, greater striving for intimacy (King, 1995; Roberts & Robins, 2004)

Emotion Regulation

- Greater happiness and subjective well-being (Costa & McCrae, 1980; Lucas, Le, & Dyrenforth, 2008)
- Maintaining positive emotional balance (Lischetzke & Eid, 2006)
- Tendency to expend more effort to increase happiness (Tamir, 2009)
- Savoring emotionally positive experiences (Hemenover, 2003)
- Tendency to disregard negative feedback (Pearce-McCall & Newman, 1986)
- Tendency toward anger (Carver, 2004)

Learning and Memory

- Stronger conditioning for rewards and incentives (Matthews & Gilliland, 1999)
- Better performance at speeded tasks, but poorer for accuracy (Wilt & Revelle, 2009)
- Superior performance in divided attention tasks, multitasking (Lieberman & Rosenthal, 2001)

Vocational Interests and Identity

- Interest in sales, marketing, and people-oriented professions (Diener, Sandvik, Pavot, & Fujita, 1992)
- Economic goals, strong interest in making money in business (Roberts & Robins, 2000)

Psychopathology risk

- Less depression and less anxiety (Trull & Sher, 1994)
- Fewer personality disorders (Widiger, 2005)
- Alcohol consumption (Paunonen, 2003)
- Externalizing symptoms, conduct disorder (Krueger, Caspi, Moffitt, Silva, & McGee, 1996)

*Note.* Extraversion is positively associated with each of the behavioral, emotional, and cognitive patterns listed. (Put differently, higher introversion is *negatively* associated with each.)

would go for a relatively high ranking in the broad area of extraversion and positive emotionality.

And why do I want to be high in E? Not only because of what the data show but also because I like the idea, expressed provocatively by the evolutionary psychologist Michael Ashton and his colleagues, that extraversion's prime evolutionary function is to *attract and hold the attention of other social actors* (Ashton, Lee, & Paunonen, 2002). For the particular kind of eusocial species that human beings have evolved to be, social actors show remarkable individual differences in their abilities to get along and get ahead in social groups. Social actors compete with each other to garner the limited resources that are available in the group, with the long-term aim (implicit though it may be) to pass copies of their genes down to the next generation. Whether we consider our ancestral environments of evolutionary adaptedness or modern social life today, actors *need to get noticed* if they are ever to get along and get ahead. They need to attract and to hold the attention of their audiences. Of course, infants enjoy some of that much-needed attention merely by being in the presence of their caregivers. But even in infancy, a temperament of positive emotionality attracts more positive attention from others than does one that suggests inhibition or shyness. For adolescents and adults, moreover, extraversion is a valuable psychological resource for its power to attract the notice and capture the limited attention of others in the group. All other things being equal, I would rather be noticed than ignored.

## THE LIFE AND CAREER OF AN EXTREME EXTRAVERT

George W. Bush never decided to be a rambunctious 1-year-old. He never sat down one day, as a child, and said to himself: "I think I want to be an extravert." He never made a strategic choice to adopt this temperament over that one. Without any conscious deliberation, he burst onto the stage of human relations with a tremendous amount of social energy and good cheer, or at least that is how everybody described it back then, in the late 1940s. In a letter to a friend, his father described his firstborn, just 13 months old, in this way: "Whenever I come home, he greets me and talks a blue streak, sentences disjointed, of course, by enthusiasm and spirit boundless"; "He tries to say everything and the results are often hilarious" (G. H. W. Bush, 1999, p. 64). Family members and friends affectionately called him "Georgie," and described him as energetic, enthusiastic, gregarious, and very funny. In later years, his brother Marvin noted that George W. Bush functioned as the "family clown" (Schweizer & Schweizer, 2004, p. 371). It was largely a compliment. People appreciated the comic role and the enthusiastic way he played it.

Think about the social role of the clown. What is the role's main purpose? It is to make you laugh, to lift your spirits. How does the clown do it? By coming at you, with jokes and outrageous behavior. There is no room in this role for shyness or timidity. The clown is outgoing, gregarious, over the top, in your face. There is something a little bit aggressive about him, and something very physical, how he pushes and prods to get an emotional response. Biographers of the Bush family single out Georgie's "innate aggressiveness" as a key temperament trait (Schweizer & Schweizer, 2004, p. 371), by which they mean to suggest an exuberant social dominance and positive emotionality. In the campaign autobiography he wrote in order to launch his run for the U.S. presidency, George W. Bush (1999) attributed the very same traits to himself: "I am restless"; "I am impatient"; "I am outgoing"; "I've always invaded other people's spaces, leaning into them, touching, hugging, getting close"; "[I] am perpetual motion"; "I provoke people, confront them in a teasing way"; "I will tease" (pp. 80–81). As one journalist once put it, George W. Bush "moves toward conviviality like a heat-seeking missile" (Suskind, 2004, p. 260). The metaphor perfectly captures the idea of rapid approach toward social reward.

By age 5, Georgie had "grown to be a near man," in his father's words, "talks dirty once in a while and occasionally swears"; "he lives in his cowboy clothes" (G. H. W. Bush, 1999, p. 70). Armed with their BB guns, the little cowboys in Midland, Texas, took potshots at the frogs populating a gully behind the Bush property. Georgie was the ringleader. He rode his bike all over town. He played baseball. He also played pranks, got into more trouble than less timid boys might. Georgie was something of a roughneck, full of swagger, known for clowning around. To his classmates' delight, he played the role of clown in the schoolroom, too. You remember boys like him—the ones who made rude noises with their armpits, farted when the teacher left the room and then blamed it on the little girl sitting across the row, or mimicked the teacher when her back was turned. The other kids said, "Good morning, Mrs. Weatherspoon," when they greeted their Sunday school teacher. Georgie, on the other hand, would shout, "Hiya little lady. Lookin' sexy!" (Andersen, 2002, p. 43).

From grade school through middle adulthood, George W. Bush was always one of the most popular guys around. He was elected president of his seventh-grade class at San Jacinto Junior High School. Around the same time, he began to bestow nicknames on his many friends, a practice that would follow him all the way to the White House. For high school, his parents sent George W. to the exclusive Andover Academy, outside of Boston. The New England winters were cold, and George W. was lonely at first. But in short time he made many friends. He organized what was to become a wildly popular stickball league at Andover, wherein players used broomsticks to hit old tennis balls into goals. He appointed himself High Commissioner of the League, and for the year's final contest, his cheering classmates carried him onto the field on their shoulders. Despite his mediocre grades and subpar athletic abilities, George W. Bush flourished at Andover, mainly by dint of his overwhelming gregariousness, his good spirits, his uncanny proclivity to find new ways to make fun mischief, and his ability to forge relationships with different groups of students from different backgrounds and social classes. The art of young Bush's personality development—the recognizable uniqueness of his social presentation—stemmed from his signature way of expressing extraversion:

> Young Bush's particular genius—the facility for wiping out in milliseconds the distance separating himself from total strangers—would more than compensate [for the challenge of living far away from home]. What drew the other boys to him was that instant familiarity: remembering their names (or, if one's surname twisted the tongue, assigning a nickname), flipping arms around shoulders, acute eye contact, a gruff yet seductive whisper. (Draper, 2007, p. 39)

Following in his father's footsteps, George W. Bush graduated from Andover and enrolled at Yale University. Throughout college, this highly effective social actor repeatedly expressed all the cardinal features of extraversion—excitement seeking, ceaseless activity, strong assertiveness (though more so at parties than in the classroom), gregariousness, high levels of positive emotion, and interpersonal warmth. He showed an uncanny ability to accumulate friends and to assemble a wide net of social acquaintances, and then to remember everybody's name. As a freshman, Bush joined the Delta Kappa Epsilon fraternity. As part of the fraternity hazing ritual, the 54 DKE pledges were paddled, verbally assaulted, and given a variety of distasteful tasks to perform. Sleep-deprived and disoriented, they were dragged into a room and told, one by one, to name all the other pledges in their class. The DKEs abused their pledges in this way every year. Going back as far as anybody knew, no victim had ever been able to provide full names for more than a handful of fellow pledges. A typical score might be 6 or 7. When it came to Bush's turn, he made history: He named all 54.

Research suggests that highly extraverted people tend to drink more alcohol and take more risks than do more introverted people, opening up the possibility of substance abuse. George W. Bush's 20-year career in alcohol abuse began with the DKE fraternity parties. The

DKE house was known to have the biggest bar and the best parties on the Yale campus. Years later, one fraternity brother remembered the DKE house as very much like the movie *Animal House*, with George W. Bush playing the role made famous by John Belushi. Before football games, young George would mix up batches of screwdrivers in garbage cans. He was a star participant in the fraternity's beer-chugging contests. Although no photograph has ever surfaced to confirm the story, he was once rumored to have stripped off his clothes and danced naked on the top of the bar.

After Yale and through his 20s and 30s, Bush continued to drink to excess, even during the years when he attended Harvard Business School (his late 20s), launched a career in the oil business, married Laura Welch (age 31), began to raise two daughters (age 35), exercised and ran regularly, and experienced a conversion to evangelical Christianity (age 38). Around his 40th birthday, however, he gave it up cold turkey. Looking back from the stance of sobriety, Bush explained his former drinking as an extension of his extraverted temperament. Drinking was fun; it enhanced the lively social settings that an extravert like George W. Bush found so rewarding. After a tough day of work, he enjoyed kicking back with friends and having a few beers and a few shots in the evening. Well, maybe more than a few. Alcohol made him even more outgoing and gregarious than he was when he was sober, Bush maintained. And that was not always a good thing, he realized, for when he drank too much he could become overbearing and aggressive. What functioned initially to enhance social interactions eventually came to slow him down, Bush said. About to turn 40 years old, Bush saw that excessive drinking ultimately worked to undermine the good times and the positive emotions that he usually experienced in social settings. It also threatened his marriage. Laura enjoyed a good drink, too, but she was increasingly frustrated with her husband's intemperance, and she threatened to leave him. Once upon a time, alcohol was extraversion's best friend, but it became extraversion's enemy. Bush cut the enemy off at age 40, and he never looked back.

George W. Bush brought his extraversion with him as he successfully met new challenges in his midlife years. Along with his priceless pedigree as the firstborn son in a prominent American family, extraversion was arguably Bush's greatest psychological resource during his years as part owner of the Texas Rangers baseball team, governor of Texas, and in the run-up to the 2000 presidential election. His privileged family background combined with his extraverted temperament to open up many opportunities and helped him to garner the extraordinary amount of social capital that a social actor needs to run for public office in the United States. As president, his greatest strength—and a significant weakness as well—may have been his relentless drive and unflagging optimism. It provided him with positive motivation, but it also contributed to his being overly confident at times, to the point of cockiness, and consistently oblivious to negative feedback.

In a book I wrote about Bush, I identified a suite of psychological factors that shaped his controversial presidency and informed, for better and for worse, some of the most fateful decisions Bush made during the years he occupied the Oval Office (McAdams, 2011). Among the key factors were an alarmingly low level of openness to experience (a concept that appears in Chapter 4 of this book); the powerful life goal to defend his beloved father against all enemies (Chapter 6); and a redemptive life story, constructed and internalized in his 40s, that liberated George W. Bush to pursue his greatest dreams, while ultimately imprisoning him, as President, within a tragically limited worldview (Chapter 9). Beneath and behind it all, however, lay the basic temperament trait of extraversion, the simple core melody around which he composed his life symphony. Historians have rated all of the U.S. chief executives, going back to George Washington, on a series of basic personality traits (Rubenzer & Faschingbauer, 2004). As shown in Table 2.2, George W. Bush scores very near the top on the trait of extraversion.

When it comes to the artful way in which a personality trait may express itself in a person's life, a story is often worth more than a statistical table or an empirical result. In the case of extraversion and George W. Bush, I can think of no story about his life that better exemplifies just how outrageously extraverted this social actor could be than the Bob Bullock incident. In this memorable scene, we find the prime actor—George W. Bush—playing the esteemed social role of governor of the state of Texas. The governor is attending a breakfast meeting with political officials and the press, in 1997 (from Andersen, 2002; Weisberg, 2008). Bob Bullock—the 250-pound leader of the political opposition in Texas—stands up to announce that he is not going to support the governor on a particular piece of legislation.

In a gravelly voice, Bullock announces: "I'm sorry, Governor, but I am going to have to fuck you on this one."

The room goes silent, tense. It is an awkward moment. Governor Bush gets up, walks over to Bullock, grabs him by the shoulders, and plants a huge wet kiss on his lips.

"What the hell'd you do that for?!" Bullock blurts out, wiping his mouth in disgust.

**TABLE 2.2. A Ranking of U.S. Presidents on Extraversion, from Highest to Lowest**

| | |
|---|---|
| 1. Theodore Roosevelt | 18. Barack Obama[b] |
| 2. Bill Clinton | 19. Ulysses Grant |
| 3. Warren Harding | 20. Jimmy Carter |
| 4. Franklin Roosevelt | 21. Millard Fillmore |
| 5. George W. Bush | 22. Woodrow Wilson |
| 6. John Kennedy | 23. George Washington |
| 7. Lyndon Johnson | 24. Benjamin Harrison |
| 8. Andrew Jackson | 25. Thomas Jefferson |
| 9. Ronald Reagan | 26. James Polk |
| 10. Harry Truman | 27. James Buchanan |
| 11. Gerald Ford | 28. John Adams |
| 12. George H. W. Bush[a] | 29. Richard Nixon |
| 13. William Howard Taft | 30. James Madison |
| 14. Martin Van Buren | 31. Herbert Hoover |
| 15. Franklin Pierce | 32. John Quincy Adams |
| 16. Abraham Lincoln | 33. Calvin Coolidge[c] |
| 17. Dwight Eisenhower | |

*Note.* Based on Rubenzer and Faschingbauer (2004, pp. 25, 302).

[a]Rubenzer and Faschinbauer (2004) do not include George H. W. Bush (George W. Bush's father) in their rankings of extraversion. I have inserted him into the list where I think he might go.

[b]This is my estimate for President Obama.

[c]It has been reported that a woman seated next to the introverted President Calvin Coolidge at dinner one evening said to him, "Mr. Coolidge, I've made a bet against a fellow who said it was impossible to get more than two words out of you." His famous reply: "You lose."

The governor shoots back: "If you're going to fuck me, you better kiss me first."

For a brief moment, everybody is stunned. And then the room erupts in riotous laughter and applause.

## NEGATIVE EMOTION AND NEUROTICISM

For human beings, there is more to social life than laughter and positive social rewards. Negative emotions, such as fear and sadness, inevitably find their way into human experience, from the first days of life onward. Newborns show clear signs of distress and disgust; by 6 months of age, babies exhibit anger, fear, and sadness; and by age 2, toddlers typically express the more complex social emotions of shame, embarrassment, and guilt. Human beings have evolved to experience negative emotions because negative emotions signal that something is not right in the world. Negative emotions warn that there is a problem, and inclusive fitness demands that actors solve problems, so that they can continue to get along and get ahead in social life, reinforcing their prospects for survival and reproductive facility. For social actors, bad feelings may signify a threat in the social environment or the presence of obstacles in the path to successful social performance, or they may follow (or even anticipate) a poor social performance as a form of (real or anticipated) critique, a censure delivered by a disapproving or disappointed audience or by the self-conscious actor him- or herself, who now knows (or believes) that he or she has failed in some way (or is likely to fail).

Human nature mandates that we will invariably experience negative emotions. But personality comes into play in the readily observed fact that some of us experience negative emotions with more frequency and intensity, and under a wider range of social conditions, than do others. Life is not fair in this way, and in many others. Some people experience a great deal of misfortune over the course of their lives, and others seem to be luckier. But even when exposed to the same or similar events, people vary dramatically in *how they react* to the events, especially negative or potentially negative events, with some people showing much higher levels of negative affect than others. The unfairness, then, is evident not only in the different things that happen to different social actors but also the different reaction tendencies that social actors bring to events in the first place. Each social actor performs negative emotion in a unique and socially recognizable way. We are known to each other by the characteristic manner of our laughter, and our tears.

In the realm of the negative, as in the positive, the rudiments of personality appear to reside in infant temperament. Developmental psychologists have identified a cluster of temperament tendencies that differentiate babies and young children along a dimension of *negative emotionality* (Shiner & De Young, 2013). Those on the high end of this dimension are described as generally more fearful, inhibited, irritable, and prone to frustration, compared to those on the low end. Infants high in negative emotionality are more easily upset, and parents find it more difficult to soothe them, compared to infants low on negative emotionality. On temperament questionnaires, parents of children high in negative emotionality endorse items like these: "Gets quite frustrated when prevented from doing something s/he wants to do"; "Tends to become sad when the family's plans don't work out"; and "Is quite upset by a little cut or bruise" (from Shiner & De Young, 2013, p. 122). Children high in negative emotionality appear to be especially vulnerable to stress and more prone to worry and guilt. Others describe them as especially tense and moody.

As contradictory as it may sound, *negative emotionality is not the polar opposite of positive emotionality*. It is, instead, simply *different*, at least on a conceptual level. A social actor who scores low on the temperament dimension of positive emotionality does not necessarily experience more negative emotions; he or she simply experiences less positive emotion—less joy, less positive approach, but not necessarily more fear, anxiety, and sadness. Similarly, low scores on negative emotionality do not necessarily indicate more positive emotion, but rather simply less negative emotion. Compared to those high in negative emotionality, social actors low on this dimension are described by others as *less* fearful, moody, tense, and stressed out; they are described as especially calm, resilient, and emotionally stable.

In infancy and early childhood, the landscape of negative emotionality divides into at least two regions (Rothbart, 2007). The first is characterized by emotional fearfulness and behavioral inhibition. Infants high on this dimension show great timidity in the face of new events and people. They are consistently inhibited and emotionally subdued in unfamiliar situations. By age 2, they may be especially reluctant to play with an unfamiliar toy. Later, in kindergarten, they may shy away from new activities and people, showing a kind of stage fright in new situations. Compared to less inhibited children, they show intense physiological responses, such as dilated pupils and higher heart rates, when confronted with stressful social situations. In addition, inhibited children show higher levels of morning cortisol in the blood compared to less inhibited children, a difference that is also apparent when comparing shy, inhibited rhesus monkeys to their more sociable peers (Kagan, 2012). Cortisol is a stress hormone that typically signals an increase in overall arousal. Cortisol levels typically rise for all people shortly before they wake up in the morning, as if to prepare the social actor for the challenges of the day's events. The sharper rise for children high in negative emotionality may portend the greater social and emotional challenges that their physiological makeup "expects" them to face.

The second region of negative emotionality encompasses irritability and strong responses to frustration. Especially irritable infants and young children lash out against others when things do not go well in social life. They are easily frustrated and more likely to express agitation, and even hostility, when their efforts to perform well and achieve goals on the social stage meet with challenge, resistance, or failure. The operative emotion here is anger. As we have seen already, anger is a tricky emotion. In some cases, it can signal behaviors that link to positive emotionality and approach motivation, as when actors recruit anger to overcome obstacles and pursue desired goals. In other cases, anger links up with hostility, fear, anxiety, frustration, and overall negative emotionality.

What is called "negative emotionality" in the temperament literature often goes by the name of *neuroticism* (or simply, N) in studies of adult personality. In adolescence and adulthood, individuals who score high on self-report measures of N report greater levels of fear, anxiety, sadness, frustration, guilt, shame, and hostility in daily life, compared to individuals scoring low on N. Social actors high on N suffer from a tendency to be distressed and upset in many realms of their lives. They are chronically worried, nervous, and insecure, and they hold a low opinion of themselves. They report lower levels of life satisfaction and happiness and higher levels of loneliness.

*Neuroticism is a strong risk factor for mental illness.* Recently, Avshalom Caspi and a group of eminent clinical researchers have proposed that high N lies at the center of a single broad factor of psychopathology, forming the underlying structure for nearly all psychiatric disorders (Caspi et al., 2014). Mental disorders predictably plague those social actors who find that their lives demand the repeated performance of strong negative emotion—that they experience and display sadness, fear, anxiety, hostility, shame, and loneliness with great intensity, in great pain, again and again, day after day Not surprisingly, clinical patients suffering from affective disorders such as depression and generalized anxiety show elevated levels of N (Clark, Watson, & Mineka, 1994). Those fortunate social actors who happen to score low on N, by contrast, are generally calm, relaxed, hardy, secure, and self-satisfied. They are *emotionally stable* and less subject to the vagaries of psychopathology.

Research conclusively shows that neuroticism statistically predicts bad interpersonal experiences and negative outcomes in life. Social actors high in N experience a wide range of frustrations and failures on the social stage—from awkwardness in everyday social interactions to problems in decoding and understanding the feelings and intentions of other actors, to debilitating deficits in love and intimacy. High N is associated with higher divorce rates, poorer health, and increased risk for life-threatening illnesses such as heart disease (Ozer & Benet-Martinez, 2006; Smith, 2006). Among older adults, high levels of N combined with high levels of daily stress are especially predictive of poor quality of life (Mroczek & Almeida, 2004). The links to poor life outcomes are partly the result of the wear and tear that attends negative emotions as a response to chronic stress, and the inability to cope with stress and, thereby, to regulate negative emotions. Research suggests that neurotic individuals experience more stress to begin with, are more reactive to stress when it occurs, and are less successful in coping with stress, compared to their emotionally stable counterparts (Bolger & Schilling, 1991).

Deconstructing the everyday emotional experiences of social actors high in N, the personality psychologists Jerry Suls and Rene Martin (2005) describe a *neurotic cascade* of five processes that recurrently cause a big buildup and strong release of negative emotion in daily social life. Highly neurotic actors (1) are more *reactive* to signs of threat and negative emotion in the social world, and thereby (2) are *exposed* to more negative events, which (3) reinforces their tendency to *appraise* objectively neutral or even positive events in negative terms. Heightened reactivity, exposure, and negative appraisals tend to precipitate (4) *mood spillover*, whereby negative feelings in one area of life spill over into others, and negative moods from one day carry over to ruin the next day as well. As a result, highly neurotic individuals often ruminate about bad things, obsessively running negative scenarios over and over in their heads, which makes it very difficult to rid themselves of the negative feelings associated with these events (Nolen-Hoeksema, 2000). Finally, high levels of N are associated with what Suls and Martin call (5) the *sting of familiar problems*. As they depict it, a day's negative events can bring back into psychological play old issues and conflicts that were never resolved, which leads to more negative feelings, thoughts, and actions.

As social actors who perform emotion in everyday life, people high in N tend to experience and convey relatively high levels of negative emotion, most notably *fear* and *anxiety*. Research on animals and human beings reveals that fear and anxiety are very different kinds of negative emotions, however, triggered by different kinds of stimuli in the environment and mediated by different neural pathways and processes. Fear evolved as an adaptive response to immediate and tangible threats in the environment, such as physical attacks from predators or enemies, threats of injury and pain, snakes, spiders, heights, and sudden sounds. The stimuli that elicit fear in animals and human beings are specific, discrete, and explicit, and in turn elicit strong, specific, and usually short-term responses of autonomic arousal. The actor may experience panic and a strong desire to escape. By contrast, anxiety is a more diffuse and typically long-term response to stimuli, situations, and contexts that suggest *potential* risk of danger. The central characteristic of anxiety-provoking situations is *uncertainty*. The actor does not know what is going to happen next. For human beings, the most common contexts wherein anxiety is evoked are social contexts, for social relationships are inherently complex and difficult to predict.

Neuroscientists have hypothesized two different (though somewhat overlapping) systems that may produce experiences of fear, anxiety, and certain other negative emotions, as indicated in Table 2.3. Each of these two systems plays into the development of N over the human life course.

Fear is the primary emotion for the *fight–flight–freeze system* (FFFS; Smillie, Pickering, & Jackson, 2006). When suddenly confronted with an immediate threat to survival, actors likely respond in one of three ways: They may attack the source of the threat in order to overcome it (for which anger may also be a useful emotion to perform); flee in an effort to escape; or freeze in their tracks, which offers the possibility, slim though it may sometimes be, that the source of threat will not notice them or will lose interest. The FFFS serves as the brain's control center for behavioral responses to imminent threat, motivated mainly by fear, but sometimes also anger. The perception of the threat triggers a series of neurophysiological events that ultimately produce fear and the attendant behavioral response of fight, flight, or freezing.

The FFFS plays an important role in the development and expression of negative emotionality. Especially in infancy and childhood, the tendency to experience high levels of negative emotion, particularly fear, may be partly the result of an overactive or especially sensitive FFFS. Among 4-month-old infants, for example, those who react to novel visual and auditory stimulation with strong negative responses, such as crying and agitated leg kicking, are scored as showing high levels of negative emotionality (Hane et al., 2008). These infants appear to show strong fear (and overall distress) responses to stimuli that many other infants perceive to be innocuous or mildly interesting. Their low threshold for alarm and the agitated responses they emit suggest that their corresponding FFFSs are more readily, and perhaps more strongly, activated in everyday life than appears to be the case with infants characterized by lower levels of negative emotionality.

As fear links to the FFFS, anxiety is more closely related to the *behavioral inhibition system* (BIS). The BIS functions to alert the actor to potential threats associated with uncertainty and conflict in the environment, especially conflict about whether to approach or to avoid particular stimuli, situations, people, and events. Faced with uncertainty and/or conflicting possibilities in a given setting, the social actor must survey the environment and decide what to do. The BIS motivates the actor to scan the environment carefully in order to avoid possible danger, to weigh costs and benefits of various behaviors, and ultimately to respond to the situation in a cautious and vigilant manner.

The apprehension of uncertainty and conflict produces the experience of anxiety. Anxiety is the dominant emotional quality for the BIS; sadness may also be involved. Anxiety is what you feel, then, when your BIS is activated in response to a vaguely defined, ambiguous, strange, and/or unpredictable situation—daily life for many of us, it seems! The BIS gets a workout for brainy eusocial creatures like us. As new social situations beckon us toward reward, they may also threaten us with the possibility of punishment. *Will I be good enough? Will they like me? Will I make a fool of myself? How can I ever get through this? I don't know a single soul at this party! I don't know if she loves me. Maybe she hates me!* More often than not, it is the BIS that is summoned forth in those challenging everyday situations involving interpersonal relationships, social conduct, and the limitless array of social challenges that, in one way or another, raise the evolutionary stakes for *Homo sapiens* as we strive to get along and to get ahead in our social groups.

A key brain structure implicated in the experience of both fear and anxiety is the *amygdala*. Named for a Latin word that means "almond," the amygdala is a small, almond-shaped region located deep in the medial (middle) areas of the brain's temporal lobes. Brain researchers believe that certain parts of the amygdala activate emotional and behavioral response to danger. When the amygdala receives a stimulus indicating that the actor senses (or even imagines) a dangerous threat in the environment, it sends signals that mobilize a number of different functions designed to defend the organism against whatever may be threatening it. Signals from the amygdala go to the *hypothalamus*, which stimulates the release of cortisol, elevates blood pressure, and prompts the autonomic nervous system to prepare the actor for the emergency at hand. The physiological responses produce the emotion of fear and motivate the actor to attack the threat, to escape, or to freeze.

In the case of milder threats and the kinds of ambiguous social situations that often produce anxiety, the amygdala sends signals to a large number of brain regions associated with emotion, learning, and memory. These include the *hippocampus*. Resembling a seahorse in shape, the hippocampus is located near the amygdala in the medial temporal lobe of the brain, deep underneath the cerebral cortex. The hippocampus is involved in the formation of memories. It takes information from short-term memory and consolidates it into the longer-term recollections that become part of a person's autobiographical memory. Memories of anxiety-provoking situations can last a lifetime. Stimuli associated with those situations can trigger recollections of similar negative memories, spreading bad feelings across the landscape of consciousness and sensitizing the

**TABLE 2.3. Two Hypothesized Brain Systems Involved in Neuroticism/Negative Emotionality**

| Fight–Flight–Freeze System (FFFS) | Behavioral Inhibition System (BIS) |
|---|---|
| **Function** | |
| To govern responses to immediate danger and threats to physical well-being or survival | To govern responses to potential threats associated with uncertainty and conflict in the environment, especially social risks and uncertainties |
| **Emotions** | |
| Fear, panic (secondarily: anger) | Anxiety (secondarily: sadness) |
| **Behavioral responses** | |
| Active efforts to escape or to overwhelm threat | Passive efforts to avoid social punishments and/or to resolve uncertainty or conflict; vigilance and caution; worry and rumination |
| **Neural circuitry** | |
| In reaction to threat, signals sent to basolateral amygdala, where processed and conveyed to central nucleus, which activates hypothalamus and autonomic nervous system | In reaction to uncertainty, signals sent to certain cells of amygdala, which project to hypothalamus and brainstem structures related to negative emotion; involvement of brain regions associated with learning, memory, and other functions—such as hippocampus, anterior cingulate, and prefrontal cortex |

person to the possibility that more bad things are about to occur. Under the spell of the BIS, the actor typically adopts a vigilant and defensive frame of mind, wary of what may happen next.

Many studies suggest that people who score high on trait scales for N may suffer from an especially overactive BIS. In these experiments, researchers often measure brain activity in response to potentially threatening stimuli. Among the brain areas that are often monitored are the amygdala and the hippocampus. Studies have found that neuroticism is correlated with amygdala activity in response to negative stimuli, such as pictures of angry people, crying people, and cemeteries (Canli et al., 2001). In one study, researchers used functional magnetic resonance imaging (fMRI) of the brain to examine neural activity in the amygdala and hippocampus during a learning task (Hooker, Verosky, Miyakawa, Knight, & Esposito, 2008). Participants learned to associate certain stimuli with anxiety responses displayed on a computer, during which time their own brain activity was measured via the fMRI procedure. The researchers found a positive correlation between N scores, determined on a previously administered questionnaire, and activation of particular parts of the amygdala and hippocampus in response to those stimuli that the participants had learned to associate with anxiety. In other words, the individuals who were especially high in dispositional N in the first place were most likely to show brain activation indicative of negative emotion in response to (previously neutral) stimuli that they had learned to associate with anxiety.

Anxiety is often a *learned* response. Although infants predisposed toward negative emotionality may find novel stimuli to be especially threatening, we are not born knowing what kinds of dangers lie in complex social situations. As social actors move through life and discover the nuances of social situations, they become more astute in recognizing and defending against the perils of social life. Accordingly, the BIS is strongly shaped by learning and personal experience. Early on, actors may not understand or even anticipate the specific threats and contingencies of social interactions. They may not know what social dangers to avoid. As failures and losses accumulate, however, the actor develops an extended network of associations regarding how social relationships can lead to threat, pain, and punishment. As a result, the actor comes to anticipate danger in a broad assortment of social situations, in response to which he or she will now experience and perform the negative emotion of anxiety.

In the production and performance of negative emotion, the BIS often interacts with other brain systems. For example, the infant's early experiences of strong fear, governed by the FFFS, may condense over time into a more generalized anxiousness about life, which may eventually fall under the dominion of the BIS. Experiences of sadness, moreover, may involve both the BIS and the aforementioned BAS (the behavioral approach system, typically associated with *positive* emotionality). When you experience deep feelings of melancholy and lethargy, you may essentially be suffering from both a heightened sensitivity to punishing experiences in life (high BIS) and a *reduced ability to experience reward* (low BAS). In that regard, some research indicates that the intense and prolonged experience of sadness that accompanies depression may be a result of *deficits in positive emotionality* or approach motivation (Nusslock et al., 2011).

Research on the various brain systems that may ultimately feed into neuroticism suggests that the performance of negative emotion across the human lifespan is a complex product of both nature and nurture. Social actors may enter the world with different biological propensities for negative emotionality, but the quality of early experiences also plays a powerful role. The BIS, BAS, and FFFS are sensitive to environmental inputs, and over time their functioning comes to reflect the nature of the actor's accumulated performances. For all of us, the BIS has evolved to detect risks in social relationships, weigh the pluses and minuses of different social actions, and motivate social behavior that aims first and foremost to minimize risk. Modern life presents a host of uncertainties and potential threats to avoid, as well as opportunities to approach social rewards, complex situations that present many options and choices to be made. In a fundamental sense, modern life places tremendous pressure on the BIS. Daily life in modern societies offers relatively few direct threats to life and livelihood but rather a dizzying array of perplexing social situations, and a prodigious amount of uncertainty. This is the stuff of relentless anxiety, more so than outright fear and terror. It is the main stuff out of which neuroticism arises to become such a powerful and sometimes debilitating force in the lives of *Homo sapiens*.

## CONCLUSION

By the time we finally become aware of ourselves as social actors, we have typically been on stage for at least 2 years. As indicated in experiments with mirrors and other reflecting devices, children do not become consciously aware of themselves as separate and recognizable members of a social community until 18 months of age or older, and early awareness is somewhat unstable and fluid until about age 3 or 4. What young children first see and recognize in the mirror is what audiences see as they observe the actor on the stage—an embodied flesh-and-blood entity who moves through space and across a social landscape. As if they had purchased the most expensive seats in the theater, mothers and fathers—and other human members of the infant's social circle—watch the social actor's every move, even in the first days of life, paying special attention, as theater audiences do, to the performance of emotion. Long before they consciously know they are actors, infants and young children perform their roles with characteristic emotional styles—what Erving Goffman conceived to be the actor's unique personal front, and what I have conceptualized here as temperament, the rudiment of human personality.

Temperament is the social actor's characteristic style of *expressing* and *regulating* emotions. When it comes to emotional *expression*, two broad categories are readily observed. In the simplest terms, there is positive, and there is negative.

There is the broad temperament category of positive emotionality, which headlines the performance of joy and excitement, accentuates the active pursuit of reward, especially social rewards, and expands with development to encompass a wide range of behavioral tendencies that fall under the trait rubric of extraversion, including tendencies toward social dominance, assertiveness, gregariousness, and warmth. The activity of the brain's BAS and the opioid system appears to be partly responsible for the origins and development of positive emotionality and extraversion. The personality gradient that runs from extraversion to introversion captures what is arguably the most notable dimension of individual differences for a eusocial species like ours—the extent to which a human being is positively oriented toward *the social*. There has rarely been a more social animal than the 43rd President of the United States, George W. Bush, whose brief case study in this chapter provides a vivid demonstration of one particularly notable career in the artful performance of extraversion.

And there is the equally broad, perhaps even broader, temperament dimension of negative emotionality, synonymous with what personality researchers refer to as neuroticism, headlining the performance of strong negative emotions such as fear, anxiety, and sadness, which all link, in one way or another, to the threats that actors perceive in the environment, which usually means the *social* environment. The neural origins of N appear to reside in the functions of the brain's BIS and the FFFS. Where an actor stands on the gradient running from N to emotional stability has a strong bearing on his or her prospects for getting along and getting ahead in social life, which is, of course, human life: There is no other way for humans to live but to live socially. It is in and through social relationships that actors perform positive and negative emotions; it is in a profoundly social context that variations in actors' extraversion and neuroticism shape the most consequential life chances and outcomes.

Personality development begins with the social actor's performance of positive and negative emotion. Individual differences in the expression of positive and negative emotionality immediately attract the attention of audiences. The audience may come to know the actor first through his or her characteristic manner of expressing emotion. On the theatrical stage, however, skilled actors develop a certain kind of psychological distance on their own performance of emotion. In a sense, they observe themselves as they are acting. They monitor their emotional expressions and work to modify, control, and regulate what they do and the emotions they display. *Good acting involves expressing emotion and controlling the expression.*

And so it is with temperament and the development of personality. Temperament involves both the characteristic expression of emotion and the manner by which the social actor regulates such expression. To this point, we have been mainly concerned with the actor's expression of those emotions that provide life with what Charles Dickens famously characterized as the best of times and the worst of times, those deep feelings we call joy, excitement, anger, fear, anxiety, and sadness. It is now time, however, to step back, as the actor routinely must do, in order to consider how these strong emotions in human life come to be regulated. The next chapter takes up the self's challenge to regulate emotion and the behavior that follows from emotion—that is, how the self regulates itself. The problem of self-regulation—how to control the strong emotions that well up in the hearts and the brains of human beings—presents the most vexing problem that the social actor will ever face.

# chapter 3

# The Problem of Self-Regulation

**M**ary Karr rose to literary fame in 1995, with the publication of her first memoir, *The Liar's Club*, which remained on the *New York Times* bestseller list for over a year. With elegant lyricism and a mordant wit, Karr tells the story of growing up in the early 1960s in a hardscrabble oil town near Port Arthur, Texas. Her mother writes for the local newspaper, drinks heavily, and spends a great deal of time in bed, reading Sartre and Faulkner. Her father is a laborer in the oil industry. On his days off, he regularly sneaks out of the house to join his buddies at the American Legion hall or in the back room of Fisher's Bait Shop, where they drink beer, play dominoes, and tell stories. One of the wives has christened these gatherings "the Liar's Club" because her husband often lies about where he is going on these days, and because the tales the men tell as they drink and play are a wee bit stretched from the ideal of truth. An accomplished little liar herself, the 7-year-old Mary often tags along. She adores her father. But he is scary, and the social world they inhabit is scarier yet.

It is a world where social actors express their emotions in explosive and often destructive ways. On any given day, Daddy could be "spring-loaded on having a fight. For instance, once when we were standing in line to pay the gas bill, he socked a young Coca-Cola driver for saying we shouldn't be in Vietnam" (Karr, 1995, p. 40). On another occasion, he beats a man to a pulp for insulting Mary's mother. When he hears the crunch of broken nose cartilage, Daddy finally stops and stares down at his own bloody hands. "He turned them over like objects of great curiosity, as if they belonged to another man and had been sent to Daddy solely for repair or inspection" (p. 268). Mary's characterization is telling, for it is as if her father's brain has no control over his hands, as if they aren't even his.

On the Shakespearian stage of Mary's social life, the actors have little control over themselves, which means that the audience can rarely predict what will happen next. At age 7, Mary is both audience and actor, observing others and observing herself as she finds her own unique role in the drama. Again and again, what she and her older sister see is the unbridled performance of raw emotion:

> Sometimes we'd hear a crash or the sound of a body hitting the linoleum, and then we'd go streaking in there in our pajamas to see who'd thrown what or who'd passed out. If they were still halfway conscious, they'd scare us back to bed. "Git back to bed. This ain't nothin' to do with you," Daddy would say, or Mother would point at us and say, "Don't talk to me like that in front of these kids!" Once I heard Daddy roar up out of sleep when Mother had apparently dumped a glass of vodka on him, after which she broke and ran for the back door. We got into the kitchen in time to see him dragging her back to the kitchen sink, where he systematically filled three glasses of water and emptied them on her head. That was one of those rare nights that ended with them laughing. In fact, it put them in such a good mood that they took us out to the drive-in to see *The Night of the Iguana* while they nuzzled in the front seat. (Karr, 1995, p. 39)

In a social world where few actors seem able to regulate their feelings and impulses, Mary's mother is the most dysregulated of all. When she feels an emotion, she immediately acts upon it, with little thought as to what the consequences will be. Or else she drowns herself in alcohol, to soften the affective sting. She regularly cusses out doctors and threatens the neighborhood kids. She shoots at least two of her husbands, though poor aim leaves both of them alive. Mary observes that "some kind of serious fury must have been roiling inside of her. Sometimes, instead of spanking us, she would stand in the kitchen with her fists all white-knuckled and scream up at the light fixture that she wasn't whipping us, because she knew if she got started she'd kill us" (Karr, p. 71). She threatened to kill herself as well.

The book's most memorable failure in self-regulation may be the night Mary's mother, in a psychotic rage, stacks up all of her children's toys in the backyard and sets them on fire. Then, she grabs a 12-inch butcher knife and holds it menacingly over her children's heads. Thankfully, a competing impulse breaks through to her consciousness as she summons up restraint and then retreats. The girls are safe now, and their mother has regained a sense of control, though she is still delusional. She picks up the phone and dials the family doctor: "Forest, it's Charlie Marie. Get over here. I just killed them both. Both of them. I've stabbed them both to death" (Karr, p. 157). On other occasions, however, Mary recalls her mother to be caring and loving toward her children. Her emotional volatility is mirrored in many other actors and scenes in Mary's young life as well. Again and again, people act on sheer impulse, as if there were no social constraints. In adulthood, Mary notes that the ancient Greeks explained this kind of behavior as due to *ate*: "In ancient epics, when somebody boffs a girl or slays somebody or just generally gets heated up, he can usually blame *ate*, a kind of raging passion, pseudo-demonic, that banishes reason. So Agamemnon, having robbed Achilles of his girlfriend, said, 'I was blinded by *ate* and Zeus took away my understanding' " (p. 7).

Like Agamemnon, and like her parents, little Mary struggles with her own *ate*. She is suspended from second grade twice, "first for biting a kid named Phyllis who wasn't, to my mind, getting her scissors out fast enough to comply with the teacher, then again for breaking my plastic ruler over the head of a boy named Sammy Joe Tyler, whom I adored" (Karr, pp. 61–62). At recess, she gets into a fight with a Baptist girl and screams that "her Jesus was a mewling dipshit," after which Mary's teacher "picked me up by the waist and carried me wrangling and cussing back to her room" (p. 105). After the night when she burned her children's toys, Mary's mother is hospitalized, and Mary goes on a rampage. "I got my ass whipped three or four times by jumping like a buzz saw into kids popping off this way about her" [mother]. That summer, I bit to draw blood seven or eight times. But the time I took a good chunk out of Rickey Carter's shoulder ultimately led to events that cinched my reputation as the worst kid on the block" (p. 160). The next day, she climbs a tree with her BB gun, waiting for the Carter family to pass by on their way to berry picking. After her first shot misses, Mr. Carter spots Mary in the tree and calls for her to get down. "Eat me raw, Mister!" she screams. "I had no idea what this meant. The phrase had stuck in my head as some mild variant on 'Kiss my ass,' which had been diluted from overuse" (p. 162).

Summing up her temperament, Mary Karr notes, "I was not given to restraint" (p. 227). The understatement is the central theme in her story of childhood. In the broadest sense, the theme is the problem of *self-regulation*. As social actors in daily life, how do we regulate our performances? How do we manage what is inside so that what the audience observes is what we indeed want them to observe? How do we keep ourselves in check so that we do not harm or destroy the world around us, and thereby ruin our own reputations? How do we calibrate the self so that it aligns, more or less, with the social good, or at least the social order? How do we control our emotions and our desires in order to attain the kinds of social reputations that are required in order to get along and get ahead in social life? Mary's problem is ours, too—the greatest problem that social actors ever face.

## ACTORS OBSERVING ACTORS

If you are a member of a eusocial species, the worst thing that can happen to you is to be excluded from the group. At many levels, we human beings all know this, even at the level of the body's immune system: Social rejection triggers inflammation in the body, detectable in blood cells, and correspondingly compromised immune function (Murphy, Slavich, Rohleder, & Miller, 2013). A sure-fire method for endangering your status in the group is to lose control of yourself and thereby violate a norm or value that the group holds dear. Codified in cultural constructions from the Ten Commandments to Emily Post's *Etiquette*, violations range from big things such as killing other people or committing adultery to more minor infractions such as urinating in public or putting your feet up on the table at an elegant dinner party. In order to attain the status and acceptance that human actors need in order to survive, if not to flourish, in everyday social life, we need to *regulate* ourselves—to control our feelings, impulses, and behaviors so that we maximize the chances of positive, and minimize the chances of negative, outcomes. The worst negative outcomes involve social exclusion, such as when we are ignored by those we wish to impress, shunned by our friends or family, fired from a job, excommunicated from society through imprisonment, or put into solitary confinement. That last one is the ultimate punishment for eusocial organisms, short of death.

In the theater and in everyday social life, the greatest challenge for the actor is to learn how to control the performance. As Goffman (1959) suggested, social actors work hard to manage the impressions of others by carefully monitoring and calibrating how they express themselves on the stage. Losing control can sometimes prove disastrous, for not only does the actor thereby ruin the scene, but he or she may also compromise well-being and reputation for the future. Going back to Plato's conception of the Republic, the regulation of the self has proved to be one of the most vexing, if not *the* most vexing, challenge of self-presentation in social life. Indeed, five of the seven deadly sins of Christian medieval thought involved failures in self-regulation—greed, lust, gluttony, sloth, and wrath (Baumeister, 1998). It is therefore not surprising that the most influential social theorists of recent times have typically devoted considerable attention to the problem of self-regulation, articulating its vicissitudes under headings such as "socialization," "social control," "self-control," "impulse control," and the development of "conscience."

For example, Sigmund Freud (1923/1961) imagined the resolution of the Oedipus Complex as the grand solution to the problem of self-regulation. When the 4-year-old unconsciously renounces the sexual feelings he or she has for parents, the child internalizes their threatening authority, setting them up inside the psyche as moral guardians forevermore. The internalized parents become the child's superego, the lifelong functions of which are to *observe* the self and to keep impulses in check. The famous sociologist George Herbert Mead (1934) put his money on the external social world. As the child becomes increasingly aware of how the social world sees him or her, Mead believed, the child will likely monitor behavior more closely and aim to act in ways that meet the approval of the *generalized other*. Like many other theorists, Freud and Mead suggested that self-regulation depends on *the observation of the actor by an audience, be that audience in the real world or in the actor's mind*. Something or someone must keep watch. Actors watch other actors, which means they watch themselves as well. In social life, we each function simultaneously as actors and observers, as audiences for each other and for our own dramatic performances. In this reflective, observing sense, we regulate each other, and ourselves.

As we saw in Chapter 2, members of *Homo sapiens* begin to recognize themselves as actors around the age of 2. In the terms made famous by William James (1892/1963), the "I" begins to recognize the "Me" as an embodied social actor, as reflected quite literally in such things as mirrors and recording devices, and more figuratively in the mirroring appraisals of others. Once the I is aware of and able to reflect upon itself (the Me), the I can begin to control the presentation of self on the social stage. Assisting in its efforts are powerful social–moral emotions, such as embarrassment, shame, guilt, and pride (Tangney et al., 2007). Beginning in the second year, children feel pride when their actions bring the approval of others. In response to the audience's applause, they take a psychological bow. By contrast, they feel shame, embarrassment, regret, or guilt when their actions bring disapproval, when they fail to live up to a socially mandated standard. In general, developmental psychologists assume that children enjoy feeling pride and obtaining social approval, and that they find aversive the experiences of shame, guilt, and fear they may feel when they anticipate punishment and other forms of social critique. Over time, children learn which behaviors bring social approbation and which bring critique. As they seek to maximize reward and the feel-good experience of pride and minimize punishment and the feel-bad emotions of shame and guilt, children should gradually become something like the socialized and self-regulated actors that their ever-watchful audiences—parents, teachers, coaches, rabbis, and superegos—want them to become.

The sense of being observed is a powerful regulating force. Decades of research in social psychology indicate that human beings act in more socially desirable ways when they know, or believe, that other human beings are watching them. The regulating effect of social observation holds even when the other human being is the self. Many studies show that when people find themselves positioned in front of mirrors and other reflecting devices they tend to work harder, show greater levels of kindness and altruism, and more closely comply with social rules and regulations, even when they find such experiences unpleasant. Seeing oneself reflected in the mirror induces a heightened feeling of *objective self-awareness*, whereby the actor becomes explicitly aware of the self as an object of perception (Silvia & Duval, 2001). Such awareness serves as a check on the free expression of impulses, urges, and potentially disruptive emotions.

Cultural factors moderate the effect of objective self-awareness. For example, research shows that Japanese individuals are less influenced by the introduction of mirrors in experimental paradigms than are American research participants (Heine, Takemoto, Maskalenko, Lasaleta, & Henrich, 2008b). Japanese culture more strongly emphasizes the idea that social groups monitor the actor's behaviors, so the state of objective self-awareness may be more the explicit norm, as it were, in Japanese society than in U.S. society. In Japanese contexts, people are said to attend consistently to society's gaze (*seken*), an orientation internalized through socializing experiences that direct attention to how actors appear to authority figures and to society at large. Metaphorically speaking, it is as if the Japanese have mirrors in their heads.

Perhaps Americans rely more on religion for this sort of thing. William James (1902/1958) speculated that human conceptions of an omniscient God serve the same socializing purpose as do the social psychologists' reflecting devices. As the ideal spectator, God sees what actors do—every actor, all the time. Nonetheless, the experience of objective self-awareness exaggerates a state of being that is more or less the norm for our eusocial species, even if some cultures more explicitly emphasize the phenomenon than do others. Most of the time, we do not literally see our actions reflected back to us in mirrors, but we implicitly know, even if we sometimes forget, that others might be watching us and monitoring what we do.

Self-regulation is never easy. Resisting temptations, controlling your emotions, playing by the rules, staying on the diet, staying committed to your spouse, postponing immediate gratification to obtain long-term rewards, keeping those not-to-be-spoken thoughts unspoken, constantly monitoring your effect on other people—it is enough to wear any conscientious actor out. As social psychologist Roy Baumeister has noted, self-regulation is like a muscle that becomes fatigued from overuse. Many studies have shown that as people exert greater and greater efforts in self-control, they eventually slip up or break down, committing social errors and showing poor performance on subsequent tasks (Doerr & Baumeister, 2010).

Intense or prolonged bouts of concerted self-regulation lead to *ego depletion*: The muscle grows weary because an inner resource of self-regulatory energy has been used up. In a related vein, some social psychologists have argued that as people repeatedly attempt to control or discipline themselves, they cannot help but eventually shift their attention toward rewarding cues and thoughts, which makes them more prone to disinhibited behavior (Inzlicht & Schmeichel, 2012). In other words, we cannot keep our eyes narrowly focused on the self-regulatory prize forever because competing thoughts of gratification inevitably rise to the fore. Ego depletion, then, may be a kind of self-observational fatigue. Under social circumstances that invite temptation and indulgence, the social actor observes the self like a hawk, ever ready to tamp down the inappropriate urge. Sooner or later, however, the vigilant, self-monitoring actor gets distracted. You can only look in the mirror for so long.

## EARLY EMOTION REGULATION

The worst grade I ever got in school appeared on my kindergarten report card. Back in 1960, children carried their grade reports home in sealed brown envelopes. After my mother tore open the seal and scanned the contents, she handed the stiff fold-over card to my father.

They both began to laugh. "Danny got an 'N' in *practices self-control*!"

"What does that mean?" I asked.

"It means that you cannot control yourself." At the time, I was puzzled as to why my parents were not taking this issue more seriously. Remembering today the kind of kid I was at age 5, I now think they were laughing because the assessment was ridiculous. Despite occasional flare-ups, I was a pretty cautious and self-controlled child—a temperament characteristic that followed me through high school. Still, at age 5, I had a theory as to why I got the "not satisfactory" grade, and I ran the central hypothesis by my mother. Noting that a particular girl in that class always seemed to get the teacher's attention by bursting out in tears, I decided one day to try the same tactic myself. My strategic self-presentation backfired, however—largely because I was ignorant of gender norms. My mother agreed with my suspicion that teachers may consider crying boys to be sorely deficient in the regulation of emotion. Always the conscientious social actor, I never cried in class again. Next time around, I got an "S" (for "satisfactory") in practices self-control.

By virtue of temperament and circumstances, I was pretty lucky in the realm of early emotion regulation, unlike Mary Karr (1995). As she tells it in *The Liar's Club*, Mary could have been that little girl in my kindergarten class. In the eyes of everybody who knew her, emotion regulation was consistently "not satisfactory" in Mary's grade school years. She writes: "When my big sister pens her memoir, I will always appear as either throwing up or wetting my pants or sobbing" (p. xii). The characterization depicts a social actor who is completely at the mercy of internal forces, such as her digestive system, her bladder, and her uncontrollable emotions. Noted emotions researcher James Gross (2008) observes that "the most important adaptive property of emotions is the degree to which they are (usually) advisory rather than obligatory" (p. 711). What he means is that evolution has designed emotions to provide human beings with fundamental *appraisals* of self and world. Emotions give you advice on how things are going, both inside and outside. They alert you to opportunities for reward, and they warn you of danger. When emotions seize your being, however, and refuse to let go, they become, in a sense, obligatory—you are obliged to follow their dictates. To regulate your emotions is to render them more advisory than obligatory, to use them productively in attaining goals and meeting standards in social life, so that, in the long run, you win acceptance and status in the social group.

In the first few months of life, the human infant has no control over emotions. Thankfully, caregivers step in to fill the regulatory void. Mothers and other caregiving figures regulate the baby's emotional arousal by controlling exposure to events and by rocking, stroking, holding, comforting, and even singing to the baby. Caregivers in all human cultures aim to maintain or increase their infants' positive emotional experiences and to diminish the negative.

Interesting cultural differences may nonetheless be observed very early on. American parents love to stimulate their babies until they reach peaks of delight. By contrast, caregivers among the Gusii and the Aka tribes in central Africa rarely engage in stimulating face-to-face play with their infants and instead seek to keep them calm and contented (Hewlett, Lamb, Shannon, Leyendecker, & Scholmerich, 1998). Research tends to show that in societies that stress *individualism*, such as Northern Europe and the United States, caregivers tend to encourage *high-arousal* positive emotions in their infants, emotions such as intense joy and excitement. They may even encourage young children to vent their anger in order to "get it out of your system." In societies that stress *collectivism*, by contrast, such as many East Asian and African cultures, caregivers may aim to dampen down expressions of exuberance and joy, as well as anger, because strong emotional expressions may be seen as threatening the collective harmony. Instead, parents in collectivist cultures may encourage and reinforce *low-arousal* positive emotions, such as mild joy, relaxed calm, contentment, and serenity (Tsai, Knutson, & Fung, 2006).

By 6 months of age, infants begin to use primitive strategies for regulating their own emotions. For example, they manage to reduce negative arousal by turning their bodies away from unpleasant stimuli or seeking objects to suck, such as their thumbs and pacifiers. By 12 months of age, they will try to calm themselves down by rocking themselves, chewing on objects, or moving away from people or events that upset them (Mangelsdorf, Shapiro, & Marzolf, 1995). By 2 years of age, they can cope with frustration by talking to companions, playing with toys, or otherwise distracting themselves from the sources of their disappointments (Grolnick, Bridges, & Connell, 1996). Toddlers this young have been observed to knit their brows or to compress their lips in efforts to suppress negative emotions such as anger and sadness. By ages 2–3, social actors are becoming more strategic. Rather than express the anger or fear they may be feeling, for example, some actors know to turn to the caregiver and simply *look sad*, which is more successful for eliciting support (Buss & Kiel, 2004).

The quality of attachment bonds established in the first 2 years of life may have a strong impact on the development of emotion regulation (Thompson, 1998). For securely attached infants and young children, caregivers infuse into the social arena a pervasive feeling of trust and safety. In the presence of their attachment objects, securely attached children explore the environment with confidence and aplomb. When they feel fear and sense danger, they readily find comfort in their caregivers' ministrations. In secure attachment, the caregiver functions as both secure base and safe haven (Mikulincer & Shaver, 2007). Emphasizing the comforting, safe-haven function, securely attached toddlers show healthier patterns of daily cortisol production, suggesting better-regulated responses to stress (Gunnar & Quevedo, 2007). In addition, the caregiver in a secure attachment relationship may also play the role of moral guide. Securely attached children check back with their caregivers to determine what kinds of actions are likely to meet their approval or disapproval. Illustrating this point, studies tend to indicate that infants who are securely attached to parents show better regulation of their emotions and their behavior (e.g., Diener, Mangelsdorf, McHale, & Frosch, 2002).

As children develop, they set up in their minds internalized *working models* of attachment relationships (Bowlby, 1969), and they take those models with them from one social situation to the next. As such, actors never enter the stage alone. They come equipped with internalized representations of past relationships. These internal representations or models are like acting coaches in the head. Ideally, they inspire confidence and urge the actor on to better performance and more effective regulation of emotion. (In cases of insecure attachment, however, they may prove nearly useless for self-regulation. Imagine what little Mary Karr's internalized working model of *her* attachment relationship was like.) Effective working models, derived from secure attachment, may also provide constraints and guidelines, much like Freud's superego. Mother was not literally with you every day as you walked into your kindergarten class, but you could still check back with her, in a sense, by unconsciously consulting your mental image of her during times of stress. Consulting a soothing, reassuring, and authoritative source can help to regulate your emotions and behavior. Checking back with your mom, even if she exists for the moment only in your mind, helps to keep you on message, makes it easier for you to follow the socially valued script and to ignore, hold back, put off, or translate into productive behavior a wide range of potentially distracting feelings and impulses.

## EFFORTFUL CONTROL AND THE DEVELOPMENT OF CONSCIENCE

On the campus of Stanford University in the late 1960s, Professor Walter Mischel conducted studies in which children attending the Bing Nursery

School were asked to sit patiently in the presence of a marshmallow. The 4-year-olds were told that if they could refrain from eating the tasty treat for 15 minutes, they would be rewarded with two marshmallows in the end. Most of the children could not delay gratification for such a long time. Some gobbled the treat immediately; others struggled for a few minutes, then gave in. Those who persevered displayed a wide range of cognitive and behavioral strategies. Some covered their eyes so that they could not see the marshmallow. Others started kicking the furniture, or tugged on their pigtails, or stroked the marshmallow as if it were a tiny stuffed animal (Lehrer, 2009). The most effective strategies involved distraction. Children would divert their own attention to some other task, forcing themselves to do other things, such as sing songs from cartoon shows or play hide-and-seek under the desk, trying to avoid thinking about the temptation.

About 30% of the children in Mischel's studies made it all the way to the finish line. Getting two marshmallows to eat on the day of the experiment turned out to be but one of many rewards these children ultimately enjoyed. Follow-up studies showed that the nursery school children who were able to delay gratification for 15 minutes exhibited higher levels of self-control, fewer behavioral problems, better friendships, and even higher Scholastic Aptitude Test (SAT) scores as teenagers, compared to those children who succumbed to the lure of the marshmallow (Mischel, Shoda, & Peake, 1988). The 4-year-olds who were most successful in delaying gratification displayed high levels of what developmental psychologists today call *effortful control* (EC; Rothbart, 2007). They exerted effort to control their impulses, developing a course of action that kept them focused on a long-term goal in the presence of an alluring short-term distraction.

The most famous example of EC in classical literature is the ingenious effort Odysseus exerted, on his long journey home, to resist the temptation of the Sirens. Odysseus knew that the beauty of the Siren songs would lure him into a deadly shipwreck. Therefore, he tied himself to the ship's mast to prevent being seduced into steering toward the dangerous shoals.

Effortful control does not typically require quite so much, well, effort. Moreover, it appears to emerge early in life as a dimension of *temperament*, revealing clear individual differences by the third or fourth year. EC is formally defined as the "child's active and voluntary capacity to withhold a dominant response in order to enact a subordinate response given situational demands" (Li-Grining, 2007, p. 208). It consists of a collection of abilities and inclinations that centrally involve the *executive control of attention* and the *inhibition of potentially distracting impulses* (Rothbart, 2007). As shown in Table 3.1, EC subsumes dimensions of children's behavior such as persistence in difficult tasks, inhibiting urgent impulses in order to complete tasks, focusing attention on long-term goals, and delaying gratification. Table 3.1 also displays a range of laboratory tasks used to measure individual differences in EC. Children with a strong temperament dimension of EC are able to delay immediate gratification to focus attention on longer-term goals to be achieved and rewards to be obtained. In preschool, they are better able to resist candy when told to do so or to focus attention on a game even if they want to do something else at the moment. In grade school, they may be tempted to watch television after school, but if their moms tell them that doing their homework instead will result in their going to the amusement park this weekend, they are able to resist temptation and buckle down.

From early on, girls tend to show better EC than boys (Else-Quest, Hyde, Goldsmith, & Van Hulle, 2006). Differences are also linked to social class and culture. Children from more economically deprived families tend to show lower levels of EC than do children from more affluent families. Studies suggest that Chinese and Korean preschoolers show superior skills in EC, compared to their North American counterparts (Chen, Yang, & Fu, 2012). Chinese and Korean parents appear to emphasize behavioral control for their children to a greater extent than do American parents. The parenting emphasis is in keeping with the East Asian value of *li* (propriety), which is traditionally viewed to be a set of rules for action that aim to cultivate and strengthen innate virtues (Ho, 1986).

Studies conducted by developmental psychologist Grazyna Kochanska show that EC provides a temperament foundation for the development of children's *conscience* during the fourth and fifth years of life (Kochanska & Aksan, 2006). As Kochanska sees it, conscience consists of at least two key components: *rule-compatible conduct* and *moral emotions*. Social actors exhibit an active conscience when they act in ways that are consistent with what group norms suggest to be moral or good behavior. For young children, this typically boils down to doing what Mommy and Daddy say is the right thing to do, which often means putting the brakes on what may seem to be the fun thing to do. Being able to subordinate impulses to longer-term aims in the family paves the way for rule compliance and the ability to cooperate with other authority figures and with peers on the broader social stages of the school and the playground.

**TABLE 3.1. Examples of Laboratory Tasks Used to Measure Effortful Control (EC) in Toddlers and Preschoolers**

| Temperamental dimension | Task name | Description of the task |
| --- | --- | --- |
| Persistence | Bead sorting | Sorting colored beads into different containers |
| | Yarn tangle | Untangling a ball of yarn |
| Inhibitory control | Rabbit/turtle | Maneuvering a turtle (slowly) and a rabbit (fast) along a curved path |
| | Bear/dragon | Performing commands of a bear/suppressing commands of a dragon |
| | Tower | Taking turns building a tower with experimenter |
| | Dinky toys | Choosing a prize from a box filled with small toys without touching or pointing at it |
| | Whisper | Whispering names of popular cartoon characters |
| Focused attention | Shapes | Pointing to small pictures embedded in larger(dominant) pictures of fruit |
| | Day–night | Say "day" to pictures of moon/stars and "night" to pictures of the sun |
| Delay of gratification | Snack delay | Waiting for candy displayed under a transparent box |
| | Gift delay | Waiting for experimenter to return with a bow before opening a gift |
| | Tongue | Competing with experimenter to keep a candy on the tongue without chewing it |

*Note.* Persistence, inhibitory control, focused attention, and delay of gratification are all slightly different dimensions of temperament that fit within the broader temperament construct of EC. Based on Rueda (2012, p. 150).

Key moral emotions for the development of conscience include *empathy* and *guilt,* both of which appear to be highly correlated with EC in the preschool years (Rueda, 2012). Young children exhibit empathy when they express concerns for the feelings of others. EC may promote empathy by clearing away distractions, so that a child can focus attention on the emotions of others. In addition, when a child is able to keep impulses in check, he or she is less likely to be overwhelmed by distress and more able to offer help to another person in need. Guilt is an especially powerful motivator of moral behavior, not just for young children but for social actors across the human lifespan. When 4-year-olds violate a rule regarding moral behavior, they may feel guilt, which may then motivate them to apologize or try to make amends for their mistake. The anticipation of guilt, moreover, serves as a check against immoral behavior for many people. Research consistently shows that the proclivity to feel guilt is negatively associated with immoral behavior. For example, Web-based studies of adults from across the United States have shown that people who score high on measures of guilt-proneness (compared to low scorers) make fewer unethical business decisions, commit fewer delinquent behaviors, and behave more honestly when making economic decisions (Cohen, Panter, & Turan, 2012). *Guilt is good for you* (usually), and good for the group. For the kind of eusocial species we have evolved to be, guilt is one of the most powerful mechanisms ever invented by natural selection to ensure group solidarity and the self-regulation of individual social actors.

EC and the development of conscience in young children rely on a neurocognitive system called the *executive attention network* (Rothbart, Sheese, & Posner, 2007). The network is activated in situations in which a person needs to detect errors in the environment, cope with conflicting cognitive appraisals, overcome habitual or automatic response patterns, or monitor his or her own behavior in the face of competing demands. Successful adaptation to these situations requires an ability to focus attention on the most important stimuli in the environment, while ignoring distractions. The executive attention network works to inhibit thoughts, feelings, and behavioral impulses that potentially cloud one's efforts to analyze a problematic situation. It enables you to step back from the emotional exigencies of the moment—those hot feelings and impulses that might result in a reckless response—to engage in cool deliberation and thoughtful planning, in the service of pursuing a longer-term goal. In order to win my daddy's approval (long-term goal), I may need to resist the desire to pummel my little brother. In order to finish my homework, I may need to postpone my wish to text that cute girl in math class. In order to get that second marshmallow, I may need to distract myself for what seems to be an eternity, until that damn experimenter walks back into the room.

The executive attention network draws upon the functioning of many different parts of the brain, including especially the lateral portions of the *prefrontal cortex* and the *anterior cingulate cortex*. The prefrontal cortex (PFC) itself is the brain region most implicated in planning complex social behavior. Its critical role in self-regulation was most famously illustrated in the tragic case of Phineas Gage, whose left frontal lobe was destroyed when a large iron rod was driven through his head in an 1848 accident. Following the accident, Gage retained many cognitive and motor abilities, as well as his ability to speak. But for the rest of his life, friends and family members insisted that his personality had been dramatically altered. A steady and reliable worker before the accident, Gage became irritable and quick tempered, and he was no longer able to sustain commitment to long-term tasks. In a nutshell, Gage suffered a permanent and profound injury to self-regulation. In the brain's PFC, thoughts and actions are orchestrated for the achievement of self-determined goals. When functioning correctly, the PFC guides the inputs and connections that allow for the executive control of action. With extensive and intricate connections to many other parts of the brain, the PFC exerts a top-down, regulating effect on a wide range of physiological, emotional, and motivational processes.

Forming a collar around the brain's corpus callosum, the anterior cingulate cortex (ACC) plays important roles in a wide range of functions, including regulation of blood pressure and heart rate, mediation of reward-seeking behavior, control of empathy and other social emotions, and governing certain kinds of conscious, rational decisions. On a cellular level, the ACC is unique in its abundance of specialized neurons called "spindle cells." Found only in humans, other great apes, cetaceans, and elephants, spindle cells are well designed to address difficult cognitive problems, especially those that involve the detection of errors in a stimulus array and the adjudication of conflicting cognitions. In such tasks, ACC activation undergirds effortful control by focusing attention on the challenging features of a situation, carefully evaluating the degree or severity of the problem, then guiding the actor's choice of an appropriate behavioral response. The ACC is involved in predicting the outcomes of planned actions before they are performed. It functions to clear a space in consciousness for a rational calculus of future consequences. As one researcher has put it, the ACC appears to "support the cognitive operations by which individuals can 'think before they act' in order to avoid risky or otherwise poor choices" (Brown, 2013, p. 179).

A growing consensus among neuroscientists suggests that the neurotransmitter *serotonin* may be centrally implicated in the development of EC and the broader psychological challenge of self-regulation itself (Carver, Johnson, & Joormann, 2008; De Young, 2010). Prozac and certain other drugs developed to treat depression work through their regulation of serotonin. Labeled selective serotonin reuptake inhibitors (SSRIs), drugs like Prozac essentially slow down the natural processes whereby serotonin is cleared out of the gaps between neurons (synapses), which itself can help to relieve depression symptoms through mechanisms that are not at present fully understood. Serotonin appears to exert effects on thinking, feeling, and behaving as a result of many factors, including the sensitivity and density of different kinds of serotonin receptors in the brain, efficiency of the reuptake of serotonin from the synaptic clefts between neurons, and the recent history of a particular nerve cell's firing. Each of these factors influences what personality psychologist Charles Carver and colleagues (2008) refer to as overall *serotonergic function*. Whereas certain social actors under certain conditions enjoy high (efficient, adaptive) serotonergic function, others suffer from low (inefficient, maladaptive) serotonergic function.

Serotonergic function may influence self-regulation by affecting the relation between two fundamentally different modes of human responding. Carver and colleagues (2008) contend that human beings simultaneously process experiences in two ways, one more basic (and evolutionarily primitive) than the other. Operating largely outside of consciousness, the more primitive mode is impulsive, reactive, implicit, and associative. It calls for the immediate hot response to a stimulus situation. Depending more on conscious thought and rational decision making, the second mode is deliberative, reflective, strategic, and logical. Effective self-regulation often depends on the second mode's ability to override the first mode—the triumph of cool deliberation over impulse. According to Carver and colleagues, high serotonergic function works to enhance the efficacy or power of the secondary system. By contrast, low serotonergic function leads to impulsive responses and resultant deficits in EC that spring from the primitive mode of processing.

Research shows that experimentally increasing serotonergic function reduces responsiveness to negative emotional stimuli, decreases aggression, and increases cooperativeness and social effectiveness (Carver et al., 2008). Experimentally lowering serotonergic function, by contrast, often makes people more impulsive and aggressive because the power of the secondary system has been compromised. Moreover, naturally existing *low* serotonergic function has been linked to behavioral impulsivity, particularly impulsive responses to anger. Low serotonergic function is also correlated with self-reported hostility and sensation seeking. Among children, low serotonergic function is related to externalizing problems, such as conduct disorders and delinquency, as well as attention-deficit/ hyperactivity disorder (ADHD). Among adults, it links to violent aggression, borderline personality disorder, and even suicide. Overall, when serotonergic functioning is poor, actors experience great difficulty in controlling their emotions and regulating their social performances.

## CONSCIENTIOUSNESS AND AGREEABLENESS

It is claimed that when Sigmund Freud was once asked what makes for psychological health in the adult years he answered simply, in German: *Lieben und Arbeiten*. To love and to work. In the art of personality development, there are many different paths that a person can take to arrive at a caring and productive life. Every portrait of psychological health is unique, as is every example of dysfunction. Nonetheless, it seems likely that many successful and loving adults draw upon the powers of EC. Indeed, EC in childhood is probably the most important temperament precursor to two broad dispositional traits of adult personality that are deeply implicated in *Lieben und Arbeiten*: *conscientiousness* (C) and *agreeableness* (A). In the same way that positive and negative emotionality form the temperament basis for the adult traits of extraversion and neuroticism, respectively (Chapter 2), the temperament dimension of EC helps to set the stage for the emergence of C and A.

Conscientiousness encompasses a great many characteristics of personality that center on how hardworking, self-disciplined, responsible, reliable, dutiful, well organized, and persevering a social actor is (Goldberg, 1990; John & Srivastava, 1999; McCrae & Costa, 2008). At the high end of the C continuum, people may be described as well organized, efficient, and dependable. They approach tasks in a systematic and orderly fashion. They analyze problems logically. They perform to exacting standards in their work and in their play. You can depend on them. Self-disciplined and duty-bound, they are reliable and responsible in their dealings with other people. They are rarely late for meetings; they don't miss class. On the other end of the C continuum, actors low in conscientiousness tend to be disorganized, haphazard, inefficient, careless, negligent, and undependable. They may be described as lazy and slothful, indecisive and wishy-washy, extravagant and impractical. People low in C have little regard for the serious standards of work or morality. While their impulsive spontaneity may seem like a breath of fresh air in the face of stale social conventions, their irresponsibility and utter inability to stand *by others* or *for anything* in the long run make them very poor risks in friendship and in love.

Social actors high in agreeableness are really *nice* people. But they are more than nice. Agreeableness incorporates the expressive qualities of love and empathy, friendliness, cooperation, and care. Indeed the very term "agreeableness" may be a bit too meek for a clustering of human traits that includes concepts such as altruism, affection, and many of the most admirably humane aspects of human personality. Social actors at the high end of the A continuum are described as interpersonally warm, cooperative, accommodating, helpful, patient, cordial, empathic, kind, understanding, courteous, and sincere (Goldberg, 1990; John & Srivastava, 1999; McCrae & Costa, 2008). They are also described as especially honest, ethical, and selfless, peace-loving humanists, committed to their friends and their families, and to the social good. Their counterparts on the opposite end of the A continuum, however, get some of worst press in the entire personality lexicon. They are antagonistic, belligerent, harsh, unsympathetic, disingenuous, scornful, crude, and cruel. While low C's may be unreliable, low A's are untrustworthy and malicious. They operate with wanton disregard of others' feelings. They often get in fights. They often hurt other people.

Table 3.2 lists some of the benefits, as well as a handful of costs, for high levels of C and A, as expressed in the realms of love, work, and health and mortality. The two traits are very different, but research shows that they share some common outcomes. For example, C and A are both associated with more secure attachment relationships, better marriages and lower divorce rates, and a stronger personal investment in family roles. Moreover, high levels of C are associated with sexual fidelity in romantic relationships. Social actors high in A tend to be especially adept at resolving conflicts and avoiding serious disputes in friendship and love. They are peacemakers who are especially sensitive to the needs of others. If you are looking for a life partner, then, the research suggests that you should set your sights on one who is industrious rather than lazy, disciplined rather than easily distracted, and warm and caring rather than cold, arrogant, and mean-spirited. Of course, you (and your grandmother) knew that already. Still, the fact that individual differences on both C and A are so consistently predictive of the quality of love relationships, even after controlling for a host of other demographic and social variables, is a rather remarkable empirical finding for psychological science. It shows the power of personality traits in the prediction of important life outcomes (Roberts, Kuncel, Shiner, Caspi, & Goldberg, 2007).

When it comes to work, conscientiousness may be the most valuable psychological asset that a social actor can own. One of the most consistent findings in all of psychological science is that people who score high on C are more successful. Because they work harder to begin with,

**TABLE 3.2. Benefits (and a Few Costs) of Scoring High on the Traits of Conscientiousness and Agreeableness in the Realms of Love and Family, Work, and Health and Mortality, Based on Recent Empirical Studies**

| Conscientiousness | Agreeableness |
|---|---|
| Love | |
| Secure attachment relationships (Noftle & Shaver, 2006) | Secure attachment relationships (Noftle & Shaver, 2006) |
| Better marriages, lower divorce rate (Roberts et al., 2007) | Better marriages, lower divorce rate (Roberts et al., 2007) |
| Investment in family roles (Lodi-Smith & Roberts, 2007) | Investment in family roles (Lodi-Smith & Roberts, 2007) |
| Among college students, close family relationships (Asendorpf & Wilpers, 1998) | Low levels of conflict in personal relationships (Asendorpf & Wilpers, 1998) |
| Sexual fidelity in romantic relationships (Schmitt, 2004) | Prosocial behavior (Graziano & Eisenberg, 1997) |
| | Warm and supportive parenting among mothers (Belsky, Crnic, & Woodworth, 1995) |
| Work | |
| Investment in work roles (Lodi-Smith & Roberts, 2007) | Investment in work roles (Lodi-Smith & Roberts, 2007) |
| Success in nearly every work and occupational setting, especially those requiring autonomy (Barrick & Mount, 1991; Roberts et al., 2007) | Success in customer service and other people-oriented occupations (Hogan, Hogan, & Roberts, 1996) |
| Academic achievement, including higher grades in college (Corker, Oswald, & Donnellan, 2012) | Career stability (Laursen, Pulkkinen, & Adams, 2002) |
| *Difficulty* coping with unemployment (Boyce, Wood, & Brown, 2010) | *Lower* earnings, especially among men (Judge, Livingston, & Hurst, 2012) |
| Health | |
| Longevity (Friedman et al., 1993; Roberts et al., 2007) | Adjustment to life-threatening and traumatic events, such as disability (Boyce & Wood, 2011) |

*(continued)*

**TABLE 3.2.** (*continued*)

| Conscientiousness | Agreeableness |
| --- | --- |
| Healthy lifestyles: less alcohol and drug abuse, lower levels of smoking, healthier diet, safe sex (Bogg & Roberts, 2004; Turiano et al., 2012) | |
| Low levels of obesity (Sutin et al., 2011) | |

because they are more organized and efficient, because they respect the rules and the conventions of the work setting, and for a host of related reasons, people high in C receive better ratings from their supervisors, advance more quickly in their career tracks, and achieve higher levels of pay and prestige at work, compared to their counterparts low in C. When it comes to their work lives, people high in C get along well, and they get ahead. And it does not really matter what kind of work we are talking about—whether one aims to be a concert pianist, an accountant, or an administrative assistant. It is very difficult even to conceive of a niche in the world of work where it does *not* prove advantageous to be self-disciplined, responsible, and achievement-oriented. Research shows that C predicts success in all kinds of jobs. It is an especially powerful predictor, moreover, for jobs that require a good deal of autonomy and responsibility.

For kids, school is the main place where work happens. It should not be surprising to learn, therefore, that conscientiousness predicts academic achievement in school. C is consistently associated with higher grades in high school and college, even after controlling for the effects of standardized tests and socio-economic class. In an effort to tease apart the relationship between C and school success, a team of researchers closely examined the strategies, goals, and academic behaviors of nearly 350 college students over two semesters (Corker, Oswald, & Donnellan, 2012). They found that the path from high C to high grades traveled through behaviors such as completing homework assignments on time, studying hard for tests, and persevering even when the material was boring. Highly conscientious students simply put out more effort, compared to less conscientious students.

People high in C invest a great deal of themselves in their school and work roles. They tend to see work as central to their identity. This may be one of the reasons that serious setbacks in the realm of work sometimes take a significant psychological toll on especially conscientious people.

In one study, researchers tracked measures of work and psychological well-being for 4 years in a sample of over 9,000 adults (Boyce, Wood, & Brown, 2010). When participants in the study lost their jobs, they tended to suffer a decline in well-being, as would be expected. However, those high in C seemed to take the hardest hits. After 3 years of unemployment, individuals who scored especially high in C at the beginning of the study experienced a 120% stronger decrease in life satisfaction compared to those at low levels of C.

Interestingly, people high in agreeableness also invest strongly in work roles. A, moreover, proves to be an asset for certain kinds of work, such as customer service and other jobs that put a premium on being courteous and friendly. People high in A also tend to be trustworthy and reliable employees who can be counted on to help others in the workplace. When it comes to earnings, however, high A is sometimes associated with somewhat *lower* pay. A number of studies have documented a negative association between A and income, especially among men (Judge, Livingston, & Hurst, 2012). One reason may be that people high in A may be attracted to jobs in the helping professions or in the service industries, which may pay less than certain other professions. A may also influence their approach to the job. Motivated to maintain positive relationships in the workplace, social actors high in A may hesitate to ruffle feathers and speak out on their own behalf during periods of conflict. They may be less likely than their peers scoring lower in A to challenge existing practices or to push hard against others in order to get ahead. Their inherent modesty may constrain them from negotiating hard to get a raise or to display with confidence and conviction their superiority to their peers. Because gender norms suggest that men should regularly exhibit dominance, nice guys who seem to care mainly about helping others and maintaining positive relationships may find themselves at a slight disadvantage at work. Sometimes it pays to be at least a little bit disagreeable.

Studies link both C and A to indices of health and well-being, but the stronger case can be made for C. In one of the most influential studies ever conducted in personality psychology, Howard Friedman and his colleagues (1993) tracked the lives and the deaths of 1,500 intellectually gifted men and women who were born in the early years of the 20th century. In grade school, the children were rated by their parents and teachers on a host of personality dimensions, including traits that fall under the broad rubric of conscientiousness. Over the many decades that followed, researchers tested and retested the participants on a range of measures and obtained assessments of family stresses, health behaviors, marriage and work, and many other social and psychological variables. It goes without saying that they noted when each participant died.

Among the strongest longitudinal predictors of mortality in the study were the ratings of childhood C. Those individuals who, as children, were rated as especially responsible and conscientious actually lived longer than did those who were rated lower on this personality dimension. (Ratings on other trait dimensions did not predict longevity.) The statistical effect of C was substantial, comparable in magnitude to the biological risk factors of high blood pressure and serum cholesterol. Friedman and colleagues' (1993) blockbuster finding turned out to be no aberration. Subsequent studies have documented significant relationships between C and longevity, replicated in studies with different cultures, in at-risk samples and healthy community samples, and in studies in which C is measured in childhood or in adulthood. The positive effect of C on longevity, moreover, is statistically independent of, and is as statistically robust as, the well-documented positive effects on longevity of high cognitive ability (intelligence) and high socioeconomic status (Roberts et al., 2007).

Why might conscientiousness be related to mortality? One answer may be risk-taking. People high in C tend to be prudent and cautious, typically avoiding the risks to life and limb that their more impulsive counterparts unwittingly bring on. Indeed, one study revealed that drivers high in C were substantially less likely than those low in C to have automobile accidents (Arthur & Graziano, 1996). They are also less likely to be cited for driving under the influence of alcohol (Hogan & Ones, 1997). Conscientiousness is negatively associated with externalizing problems in youth (acting out, aggression), violent crime in adulthood, and suicide—all of which increase the likelihood of an early death. Even in high-risk groups, C can exert a moderating effect. For example, researchers working with a group of disadvantaged men and women enrolled in an HIV risk reduction program found that individuals higher in C (and lower in neuroticism) were more likely to use condoms and avoid behaviors, such as shared needles in drug use, that are associated with HIV risk (Trobst, Herbst, Masters, & Costa, 2002).

An important factor accounting for the statistical association between C and longevity is health behaviors. In a review of nearly 200 studies, personality psychologists Timothy Bogg and Brent Roberts (2004) found that conscientiousness-related traits were positively related to a healthy lifestyle, and negatively related to an unhealthy one. Across the studies, C was positively associated with exercise and fitness activity, and negatively related to drug use, excessive alcohol consumption, unhealthy diets, and tobacco use. In a study of nearly 1,400 veterans, researchers found that smoking was a key factor linking low C to an early death (Turiano, Hill, Roberts, Spiro, & Mroczek, 2012). C is also related to obesity, itself a major risk factor in health. In a study of nearly 2,000 adults followed over 50 years, low C (as well as low extraversion and high neuroticism) was concurrently associated with higher body mass index (BMI; Sutin, Ferrucci, Zonderman, & Terracciano, 2011). The strongest association was found for the trait of impulsivity, which cuts across both C and N: Participants who scored at the top 10% on impulsivity weighed, on average, 11 kilograms (24 pounds) more than those in the bottom 10% on impulsivity. Over time, furthermore, high impulsivity (and low A) predicted greater increase in BMI.

The many studies documenting significant life benefits for high levels of C and A underscore the idea that these two broad personality dimensions are tied closely to the universal human problem of self-regulation. In order to live well in the realms of love and work, and perhaps even to live long, social actors must be able to control their impulses, avoid distractions, and focus their attention on those social incentives that promise long-term life fulfillment—family, friendships, work, and commitment to the community. In the terms made famous by Freud, C and A are fundamentally about restraining the impulsive *id* and accentuating the rational *ego*, or, put differently, about regulating the self so that good things get done and good relationships get formed. As such, the developmental roots of C and A may be traced back to the emergence of self-regulatory functions in early childhood such as EC, the development of conscience, and the dynamics of moral emotions such as guilt and empathy.

Consistent with this developmental story, recent research suggests that individuals high in C tend to be strongly motivated by apprehension about guilt (Fayard, Roberts, Robins, & Watson, 2012). It is not so much that conscientious people experience more guilt than their less conscientious counterparts. In fact, they may experience *less* guilt. But people high in C consistently act in ways that are designed to forestall, avoid, or alleviate guilt. The prospect of guilt hovers over their daily performances in work and love, like an ideal spectator who is sensitive to the moral ramifications of what social actors do and how they interact with each other in groups.

In the same way that guilt plays a motivating role in C, so may the emotion of empathy motivate behavior that is consistent with high levels of A. The ability to feel what other people may be feeling, and the related cognitive capacity to imagine or understand the world from another's point of view, helps to regulate the self in a social context by focusing on the needs of others. And focusing on the needs of others—caring about what others think, feel, want, and do in a way that approaches how one cares about the self—would appear to lie at the tender but well-regulated heart of A.

## WHEN REGULATION FAILS:
## AGGRESSION AND THE DEVELOPMENT OF ANTISOCIAL BEHAVIOR

The oldest epic story bequeathed to us by the ancient Greeks is a story of unbridled aggression:

> Rage-Goddess, sing the rage of Peleus' son Achilles,
> murderous, doomed, that cost the Achaeans countless losses,
> hurling down to the House of Death so many sturdy souls,
> great fighters' souls, but made their bodies carrion,
> feasts for the dogs and birds,
> and the will of Zeus was moving toward its end.
> Begin, Muse, when the two first broke and clashed,
> Agamemnon lord of men and brilliant Achilles.
> What god drove them to fight with such a fury?
> —FAGLES, 1990, p. 77

Homer wondered what drove the doomed protagonists of the Trojan War to fight with such fury. It was *the gods* who drove them, he concluded. The text suggests that the fighters were motivated to kill each other by forces beyond their control. Unable to summon forth the powers of self-regulation, the brilliant Achilles is ultimately undone by his rage. Indeed, when the gods are on the side of aggression, how can reason ever win out?

Nearly 3,000 years later, Sigmund Freud obsessed over the same question, though he substituted *the id* for the gods. In *Civilization and its Discontents*, Freud (1930/1961) worried himself sick about the ego's impossible task of keeping the id's aggressive instincts in check. For Freud, self-regulation was mainly a matter of repression—holding down our murderous impulses, and casting them into unconsciousness. Still, even when repression works, Freud averred, the social actor is probably going to be miserable. The Freudian scenario goes something like this: Rage and anger are natural responses to frustration; therefore, we often experience strong desires to kill others, or at least hurt them very badly, in order to achieve our selfish ends; but society and the superego strongly abhor the expression of aggression; so the beleaguered ego must find a way to tamp the rage down, hold the aggression back, or channel (sublimate) these potentially destructive impulses into productive actions (e.g., art, work, sensible love) that will benefit society; but the regulatory effort contributes to intrapsychic conflict, which brings on more anxiety and frustration. The price we pay for self-regulation is misery. But the alternative is worse—pure chaos, like the Trojan War.

To be fair, the performance of aggression can sometimes bind together a community of social actors. Ironically, war can sometimes serve this purpose well, at least in the short term. Throughout human history, group members have banded together to wage war on other groups, aiming to resolve disputes regarding territory and resources, sexual partners (the Trojan War), ideology, and numerous other issues. The organized aggression of war may consolidate social bonds within the in-group, as group members mobilize their resources to defeat a rival out-group. (It should be noted that war can also tear a society apart, as when factions within the group square off against one another [civil war], or when the rival group decisively wins the war.) Within the group, moreover, authorities (government, police, the penal system) routinely employ aggression—or the threat of aggression—for the purposes of social control (Foucault, 1995). In this regard, state actions such as imprisonment and (in the case of the United States) capital punishment may be seen as forms of aggression. For tribes of hunter–gatherers and for nation-states, the threat of legitimate (socially sanctioned) force can assure some degree of group stability, even as it reinforces dominance hierarchies in the group (De Waal, 1996). Socially sanctioned aggression may also be displayed in certain sports (e.g., boxing and professional football) and in other activities that enjoy the group's imprimatur.

At the same time, aggression may also pose the greatest threat to a group's well-being, and even its survival. If self-regulation presents the greatest psychological challenge for human social actors, the regulation of aggression is probably the most urgent charge for the group. When group members kill each other, steal from each other, rape each other, destroy each other's property, or create general social chaos through aggressive acts, the group's very existence as a viable human collective, wherein individual actors may survive and flourish (so as to pass copies of their genes down to the next generation), may be gravely threatened. What lawyers, judges, and psychologists call *antisocial behavior* nearly always involves the performance of aggression—committing crimes such as murder, armed robbery, assault and battery, rape, extortion; engaging in subcriminal behaviors that result in injuring other people, such as bullying, stalking, harassing, malicious gossip, and predatory business practices; and acting in ways that directly threaten the health, well-being, and even the lives of other social actors in the group. When children and adolescents engage in aggressive activities such as these, psychologists label it *externalizing behaviors*, for the young social actor is acting out against the external world. When certain adults prove to be hardened and chronic offenders in this regard, expressing absolutely no empathy for other human beings and no remorse for their antisocial behavior, we call them *sociopaths*. For a eusocial species, the word "sociopath" is the worst thing you can say about anybody.

Decades of research in developmental psychology indicate that individual differences in aggressive behavior emerge from a complex interplay of temperament traits, parenting practices, family relations, peer interactions, and the influence of socioeconomic class and culture (Shaffer, 2009). As in nearly all things when it comes to personality development, the developmental trajectory of aggression is unique to each individual person. Nonetheless, research has repeatedly implicated some common risk factors, and together they form a sequence that goes something like this: (1) Early temperament tendencies toward high anger/hostility and low EC combine with (2) ineffective and inconsistent parenting (which often relies on physical punishment for discipline) to produce (3) poorly regulated behavior entailing aggressive outbursts, which may lead to (4) poor school performance and (5) peer rejection in school, which eventually may result in alliance with other aggressive children and teenagers in (6) deviant peer groups, which (7) reinforce and even glorify the performance of aggressive, antisocial behavior. Boys (being more aggressive than girls to begin with) and children from lower socioeconomic strata are especially prone to follow such a trajectory.

Temperament differences that relate to aggression may appear as early as 12 months of age. In one study, researchers measured the degree to which 1-year-old infants used physical force against unfamiliar peers in a highly arousing laboratory situation (Hay et al., 2011). The tendency to push or hit other infants in the laboratory turned out to be positively correlated with the parents' ratings of their infants on dimensions of anger and aggressiveness, suggesting some consistency between aggression in the laboratory and at home. In addition, the tendency to use aggressive force at age 12 months was significantly associated with the mothers' mood disorders during pregnancy and the mothers' own respective histories of conduct problems. Whether by dint of genetic transmission or environmental influences, mothers with a history of dysregulation had babies who, even at age 1, showed deficiencies in regulating their own aggressive impulses.

Temperamental differences in anger have long been documented in infants and young children (Deater-Deckard & Wang, 2012). Yet anger is a tricky thing to categorize, as I noted in Chapter 2. Temperament researchers usually see anger as a component of negative emotionality, along with behavioral inhibition and other expressions of fearfulness. At the same time, anger has also been characterized as an approach-oriented emotion (Harmon-Jones & Allen, 1998) that links it thematically to reward-seeking, the BAS, and even positive emotions such as joy and excitement. Moreover, the overt expression of anger may signal low levels of EC. Whatever its ultimate developmental source, however, "chronic angriness, particularly as it co-occurs with poor self-regulation and frequent exposure to hostile social environments, contributes to growth in aggressive and nonaggressive antisocial behavior problems from childhood to adulthood," conclude two noted experts in the psychology of aggression (Deater-Deckard & Wang, 2012, p. 134). As Homer lamented, rage and the inability to control it are a dangerous psychological mix.

Research clearly shows that deficiencies in EC are associated with the development of aggressive, antisocial behavior (Cale, 2006; Shiner, 2009). As we have seen in this chapter, the broad dispositional traits of conscientiousness and agreeableness germinate best in a temperament soil rich in effortful control and the socializing emotions of guilt and empathy. It should not be surprising to learn, therefore, that low scores on C and A tend to be associated with aggression, conduct disorders, juvenile delinquency, violent crime, and antisocial personality disorders (Widiger & Costa, 2012). As just one example, personality psychologist Colin De Young and his colleagues (De Young, Peterson, Seguin, & Tremblay, 2008) found that low scores on C and A—as well as high neuroticism (N), high extraversion (E), and low levels of intelligence— were strongly associated with externalizing, antisocial behavior among teenage boys. From the standpoint of the broadest psychological traits underlying human behavior, boys and men who are disinhibited and irresponsible (low C) and unempathic and disagreeable (low A), who experience strong negative emotions (high N) and actively seek strong rewards (high E), and whose overall cognitive ability is weak (low intelligence) are most likely to act out against society in violent and destructive ways. They possess a trait profile that is especially resistant to socialization. Therefore, if you want to design a human being who will be trouble for the group, make him male and highly emotional, and deprive him of self-control, empathy, and intelligence.

Some of the most reliable findings in the child development literature are that cold and rejecting parents who apply harsh discipline in an erratic fashion are most likely to raise aggressive children (Dodge, Dishion, & Lansford, 2006; Lee, Altschul, & Gershoff, 2013). The intergenerational effects appear to implicate both genes and environments. Like most traits, individual differences in aggressiveness appear to be partly inherited, as we will see in Chapter 4. Parents with genetic profiles that predispose them to high levels of aggressiveness pass those same genes down to their children. On top of that, however, parents who are cold and rejecting convey the message to their children that they (the children) are not valued, perhaps not even loved. Moreover, the practice of harsh physical punishment models and affirms aggressive behavior for the children. If it is okay for my father to hit me, then it is okay for me to hit my sister—or, later in life, my girlfriend.

Parents from low-income families are more likely than middle-class parents to rely on harsh forms of physical punishment and to endorse aggressive solutions to conflict (Dodge, Pettit, & Bates, 1994). Lower-income parents also experience many other stressors, economic and social, which may make it difficult for them to monitor their children's whereabouts, activities, and choices of friends. Lack of parental monitoring is consistently associated with delinquent activities in children and adolescents, such as fighting, destroying property, drug use, and conduct disorders. More generally, the overall level of hostility and conflict in the family may influence the development of aggression in children. In a study of Israeli and Palestinian families, for example, developmental psychologist Ruth Feldman and her colleagues (Feldman, Masalha, & Derdikman-Eiron, 2010) demonstrated that high levels of aggression among preschool children were associated with higher marital hostility, more difficulty in resolving conflicts in the family, and ineffective discipline. The same findings held for both Israelis and Palestinians.

Antisocial behavior in children typically correlates with poor academic performance and peer rejection. As they move toward their teenage years, aggressive and poorly regulated children, shunned by most of their peers, may begin to associate with each other, forming deviant peer groups. In one longitudinal study, the researchers found that boys from low socioeconomic status who were raised in adverse family environments, and who exhibited low levels of fearfulness, empathy, and self-control as kindergartners, were especially likely to join deviant peer groups as teenagers (Lacourse et al., 2006). Epitomized in urban gangs, deviant peer groups encourage antisocial behaviors of various kinds, typically resulting in crime. Antisocial and criminal behavior increases dramatically in adolescence, peaking out around age 17. Many young people who join these kinds of groups eventually leave the delinquent subculture behind to pursue more socially appropriate life goals. But some stay with it. Those who persist in antisocial behavior beyond their teenage years tend to exhibit especially low levels of impulse control and an inability to plan a more productive future (Monahan, Steinberg, Cauffman, & Mulvey, 2009). They remain the most poorly regulated social actors in the human community. For too many of them, the end game is an adult life on the social margins, failing to get along or get ahead; or it is prison, or an early death.

## CONCLUSION

From the moment they realize they are performing for an audience to the day they exit the stage, social actors struggle mightily to regulate what they feel and what they do. In order to get along and get ahead in the group, human beings must develop effective strategies for controlling themselves as they perform, and thereby controlling the impressions they make among those who are observing them. There is no more daunting task in human social life than self-regulation. As personality develops, thankfully, social actors may be able to recruit psychological allies to assist them in the struggle. Secure attachment relationships, the development of EC, the socializing emotions of guilt and empathy, the consolidation of conscience, the experience of relative familial harmony, the maturation of the brain's PFC, the neural elaboration of high serotonergic function—these are among the better angels of our nature, sent to help us monitor and manage the turmoil within, and cope with the temptations, distractions, and seductions that await us in the outside world. These are the factors and processes that usher in the great socializing traits of conscientiousness and agreeableness.

For Mary Karr, and especially for her parents, most of the angels never descended to Earth. Raised in a tough, working-class environment, Mary experienced high levels of stress and conflict on a daily basis. Her mother's erratic behavior surely undermined any security she might have enjoyed in that attachment bond. And although she claimed to adore her father, she feared him just as much. When it came to EC—well, let's just say that Mary was a little low on that temperament dimension. "I was not given to restraint," she admitted. Whether crying uncontrollably, wetting the bed, cussing out her teacher, or calling Jesus a "mewling dipshit," Mary seemed unable in most instances to keep what was inside of her inside. She found it very difficult to assume the deliberative stance of an observing I who is able to step back from personal feelings and impulses, so as to monitor and control them.

At the same time, Mary Karr seemed to have an uncanny awareness of just how poorly regulated she was, even at age 7, and a clear-eyed understanding of how she and her dysfunctional family were viewed by others in their small Texas town. The uniqueness of her own developmental trajectory—the artful nature of her idiosyncratic personality development—was especially apparent in how keenly aware she seemed to be of her status as a social actor, and supremely cognizant of the observing audience. Moreover, Mary was not without guilt and empathy—harbingers, perhaps, of the hard-won success she managed to achieve in her later years. Despite her compromised powers of self-regulation, despite an untrustworthy and explosive father, and despite a mother who once set fire to her daughters' toys and threatened to kill them with a butcher knife, Mary survived it all, and *she grew up.* As her personality developed, some tendencies remained relatively stable and others showed considerable change. Like most social actors, she probably experienced both continuity and transformation across the human life course.

Mary's case raises a central question in personality development: *What happens to actors as they grow up?* It is the central question to which we turn in the next chapter. As we develop from acting ingenues to experienced veterans of the stage, what developmental patterns may the audience observe in the manner of our social performances? What processes make for the continuity and the change in the reputations that our audiences assign to us? In the broadest terms, what happens to the basic dispositional traits of human personality as we move from childhood and adolescence through our adult years and into old age?

# chapter 4

# The Actor Grows Up

## HOW TRAITS DEVELOP INTO ADULTHOOD

How have you *changed* over the course of your life? Is your personality different than it was when you were a kid? Are you a different kind of social actor today than you were, say, 10 years ago? I think that I am. Although I can't really prove it, I feel that I take things a little less seriously than I did a decade ago. I think I get stressed out less. At the same time, I sometimes observe myself to be more socially dominant than I remember being when I was a young adult. More and more, I will just take charge in a social situation, especially among my colleagues at the university, where I serve these days as the chairman of the Psychology Department. In this case, the role of being chair seems to have made me more extraverted. And I think the increase in extraversion has spread to other domains of my social life, mostly for the better, but sometimes not.

People change over time. But they also remain the same. There may exist a kernel of psychological individuality that remains intact over many decades of life, a kind of stylistic essence to the self. Perhaps you recognize an essential feature of your personality makeup that seems always to have been there, going back as far as you can remember. You've always had a shy streak, you may say. You've always hated to lose. When we meet up with people after years apart, we are often struck by how instantly recognizable their personalities are. *He still has that weird sense of humor. I had forgotten how annoying she could be, but it all came back in an instant.*

If you want to observe change and continuity in personality development on a dramatic scale, go to your high school reunion. Many years ago, I attended the 10-year reunion for my high school graduating class. In my role as a personality psychologist, the reunion gave me an opportunity to observe, in a casual and completely unscientific way, personality change and continuity between ages 18 and 28. Two cases stand out in my memory.

The first was Mary Ann Cromwell (I've changed the names). I hardly recognized her. At age 28, I recalled the 18-year-old Mary Ann Cromwell as painfully thin, poorly dressed, almost pathologically shy, and extremely unpopular in high school. She was the butt of jokes, or else people ignored her. I sat across the row from Mary Ann in trigonometry class. I was never overtly mean to her, like some of my nastier peers, but I didn't talk to her much either—and to exact revenge on an enemy of mine, I once spread a rumor that he and Mary Ann were dating. Well, the 10-year reunion could be labeled "Mary Ann's Revenge." She turned out, by age 28, to be a beautiful and self-possessed young woman at the reunion, attracting a crowd of men who seemed to find her every word fascinating. Basking in her glory, Mary Ann uttered more words at the reunion than she may have spoken in her entire high school career. She described her professional successes and her wide travels. Once an awkward adolescent, she had gone on to complete college, earn an MBA, and land a high-paying job in the banking industry. She now came across as socially poised, confident, friendly, and sophisticated.

My second case was Robert Amundson. He was the high school enemy about whom I had spread rumors. In high school, Robert was generally viewed to be socially dominant, outgoing, spontaneous, and not especially conscientious. He was one of the most popular guys in the class. Ten years later, his social dominance was still on full display. Just like old times, Robert was the center of attention. It seemed to me that he boasted just as much as he always had. He dominated conversations, as he always had. People seemed to accord his opinions especially high status, just as they always had. The only difference I could see with respect to Robert Amundson was his newfound eagerness to talk to Mary Ann Cromwell.

Mary Ann seemed to have changed significantly over the 10-year span. Robert Amundson, by contrast, was a study in personality continuity. Which of the two is the norm? Do people's traits mostly change or remain the same? According to years of research on the development of personality traits, the answer is *both*.

## THE BIG FIVE

In talking about the development of dispositional personality traits across the human life course, I begin by defining our terms. By personality traits, I am considering here those broad and relatively stable individual differences in feeling, thought, and behavior that tend to differentiate one social actor from the next. Once upon a time, personality psychologists despaired about ever being able to map the wide terrain of personality traits. There are simply too many psychological differences between people, many believed, ever to derive a definitive list. Back in the 1930s, Gordon Allport plowed through an English dictionary and found about 18,000 words that seemed to refer to human differences in psychological functioning, of which about 4,500 reflected relatively stable and enduring personality traits (Allport & Odbert, 1936). Of course, many of the 4,500 words overlapped in meaning, as would be the case, for example, with the terms "sociable" and "friendly."

Over the past 75 years, personality psychologists have worked on Allport's list and others. Through advanced statistical procedures and across countless studies, they managed to group common terms and narrow it all down in order to arrive at a short yet comprehensive list. Today, most personality psychologists believe that the entire universe of traits can be grouped into anywhere from two to seven basic regions, each of which may be imagined as a cluster or family of related traits. The most popular current version of trait taxonomies suggests that there are five basic groupings—five superordinate traits, each of which subsumes smaller traits. Personality psychologists call these *the Big Five*.

I have already introduced four of these five basic dimensions. Recall that extraversion (E) and neuroticism (N) track individual differences in the performance of positive and negative emotion, respectively (Chapter 2). At the high end of E, you find social actors who tend to be especially optimistic, energetic, spontaneous, fun-loving, sociable, gregarious, outgoing, and dominant; at the low end, social actors are more reserved, inhibited, quiet, passive, and socially reticent. Neuroticism (N) pertains to broad individual differences in the extent to which people experience strongly negative emotional states, such as sadness, worry, anxiety, fear, and shame. Social actors low in N tend to be emotionally stable and relaxed. Recall that conscientiousness (C) and agreeableness (A) appear to be connected more closely to the social actor's efforts in self-regulation (Chapter 3). C tracks broad differences in how careful, self-disciplined, well-organized, and hardworking people are. A is more concerned with warmth, kindness, empathy, and altruism.

Table 4.1 lists common adjectives used to depict each of these four broad traits (E, N, C, and A), as well as the fifth one: *openness to experience* (O). Adding the fifth factor enables you to spell out the word OCEAN to remember the Big Five. Taken together, the five broad traits comprise the vast *ocean* of psychological characteristics for which people tend to assign broad, dispositional trait labels.

**TABLE 4.1. Adjective Items That Describe Each of the Big Five Traits**

Extraversion (E)

Sociable—Retiring
Fun-loving—Sober
Affectionate—Reserved
Friendly—Aloof
Spontaneous—Inhibited
Talkative—Quiet

Neuroticism (N)

Worrying—Calm
Nervous—At ease
High-strung—Relaxed
Insecure—Secure
Self-pitying—Self-satisfied
Vulnerable—Hardy

Conscientiousness (C)

Conscientious—Negligent
Careful—Careless
Reliable—Undependable
Well-organized—Disorganized
Self-disciplined—Weak-willed
Persevering—Quitting

Agreeableness (A)

Good-natured—irritable
Soft-hearted—Ruthless
Courteous—Rude
Forgiving—Vengeful
Sympathetic—Callous
Agreeable—Disagreeable

Openness to Experience (O)

Original—Conventional
Imaginative—Down-to-earth
Creative—Uncreative
Broad interests—narrow interests
Complex—Simple
Curious—Incurious

*Note.* Based on McCrae and Costa (1987, p. 85).

Openness to experience refers to individual differences in the quality and breadth of a person's thoughts, interests, and values. Persons who score high on the broad trait of O are described by themselves and by others as especially original, imaginative, creative, complex, intellectual, curious, analytical, artistic, nontraditional, liberal, and as having broad interests. Persons low in O are described as more conventional, down-to-earth, simple, incurious, conforming, traditional, conservative, and as having narrow interests. Unlike the other four traits, openness tends to be positively associated with measures of general cognitive ability (i.e., intelligence), though the correlations are *not* so high as to suggest that O *is* intelligence. Openness also encompasses a set of characteristics that pertains to loose boundaries of consciousness and idiosyncratic or odd thinking patterns (De Young, Grazioplene, & Peterson, 2012). In other words, high levels of O may create an interesting mix of "smart" and "weird" features of human personality.

Unlike the other four big traits (E, N, C, and A), O is less about the performance and regulation of emotion in the context of social behavior and more about cognition—how people think rather than how they feel and what they tend to do. Whereas E, N, C, and A seem to trace their origins to emotionally flavored temperament factors such as positive emotionality, negative emotionality, and effortful control (EC), O seems to have a different set of origins. The development of O is likely tied up with the development of general intelligence and with factors that influence one's sensitivity to internal and external sensory stimulation (Caspi, Roberts, & Shiner, 2005). As we see later in this book, O relates in powerful ways to motivation, values, and life narration. O seems to be more important for considering the person as a motivated agent (Chapters 5–7 in this book) and autobiographical author (Chapters 8–10) than it is for informing the daily performances of social actors.

Because O, nonetheless, has traditionally been grouped within the Big Five, I consider it along with its four dispositional partners in pursuing this chapter's central question: What happens to social actors when they grow up?

## RANK-ORDER STABILITY:
## THE REMARKABLE CONTINUITY OF INDIVIDUAL DIFFERENCES

There is an important sense in which people tend to remain the same over time when it comes to broad dispositional traits of personality. The argument for long-term stability in traits begins with empirical findings like these:

- Children rated as especially impulsive and emotionally negative at age 3 tended to show high levels of self-report and peer-report N, and low levels of C and A, as young adults, in an authoritative longitudinal study of about 1,000 individuals conducted in Dunedin, New Zealand. They also exhibited higher levels of criminal behavior and suicidal tendencies as adults. Three-year-olds rated as socially reticent and fearful, by contrast, grew up to show significantly higher levels of inhibition and constraint, lower levels of E, and tendencies toward depression (Caspi, Harrington, et al., 2003; Moffitt et al., 2011).

• Boys and girls who at ages 4–6 were rated by their parents as especially inhibited were more likely in young adulthood (mid-20s) to rate themselves as highly inhibited, to show internalizing problems (e.g., depression), and to be delayed in assuming adult roles regarding work and interpersonal intimacy, in a German longitudinal study of over 200 individuals. In addition, boys rated by their parents as especially aggressive showed higher levels of young-adult delinquency (Asendorpf, Denissen, & van Aken, 2008).

• In a study of over 350 Finnish children, teacher ratings made when the children were 8 and 14 years of age predicted patterns of personality at age 42 in the following ways: (1) Higher levels of behavioral activity in childhood were linked to higher E and higher O in adulthood; (2) ratings of well-controlled behavior in childhood predicted high levels of C in adulthood; and (3) negative emotionality in childhood predicted adult aggression (Pulkkinen, Kokko, & Rantanen, 2012).

• Highly reactive infants at 4 *months* of age were more likely than their less emotionally reactive counterparts to display high levels of social anxiety at age 15 years (Kagan, Snidman, Kahn, & Towsley, 2007). Infant irritability at ages 3–4 months has been linked to shyness in adolescence (Bohlin & Hagekull, 2009).

• Children at age 10 years with high levels of C and A and low levels of N showed better academic achievement and rule-abiding conduct in school, which predicted high levels of competence and resilience at ages 20 and 30 years. Moreover, extraverted 10-year-olds tended to enjoy better friendships and greater success in romantic involvements as young adults, compared to those lower in E (Shiner & Masten, 2012).

Findings like these suggest that early differences in socioemotional functioning—whether we call them "temperament" or "personality"— seem to have staying power. In each case, threads of continuity can be readily traced from particular styles of behavior shown in childhood (e.g., impulsivity, inhibition, negative emotionality) to similar or resultant patterns of behavior observed in adults. More generally, early patterns in traits tend to predict later patterns in traits. Longitudinal findings such as these raise the issue of *rank-order stability* in personality traits—the extent to which individual differences in a given trait hold steady over time.

Think of rank-order stability in terms of the 10-year high school reunion. Imagine that we assigned Big Five trait scores to everybody in my high school graduating class during their senior year. The scores for each trait form a normal distribution, like a bell-shaped curve with the greatest number of people scoring toward the middle of, say, the E continuum and fewer and fewer people out on the extreme ends (the extreme extraverts and the extreme introverts). Let us imagine that Robert Amundson scored near the top in the class on E in his senior year. Let's put me with the many people grouped near the middle of the E distribution—around the 50th percentile. Let us imagine that my very shy and introverted friend named Keith scored near the bottom on E. Now, what does the distribution look like *10 years later*? Does Robert still score near the top at age 28? Am I still in the middle? Does Keith retain his ranking as one of the most introverted people in the group? We can ask the same question for any trait that we measure at two or more time points: *To what extent do people retain their relative positions (their rank orderings) in a distribution of trait scores upon successive assessments?*

The scientific answer to my question is captured in my casual observation that the 28-year-old Robert Amundson seemed very much the same on the trait of E as he was in high school. Many longitudinal studies demonstrate that individual differences in personality traits show *substantial* rank-order stability (Roberts & DelVecchio, 2000). People tend to hold their positions in the rank orderings upon successive trait assessments. This is true for all of the Big Five traits, and equally true for women and men. Not surprisingly, rank-order stabilities are strongest over short time intervals, and they become weaker when the temporal distance between assessments increases. In other words, there is less change in the distribution over a 1-year period (say, between ages 18 and 19) than over a 10-year period (between ages 18 and 28). The overall age of the social actor also matters. There is lower rank-order stability in childhood than there is in young adulthood, and lower rank-order stability in young adulthood than there is in the midlife years. When it comes to dispositional traits, children are still a work in progress; they move around more in the distribution, though they still show modest levels of stability even in their early elementary school years (Durbin, Hayden,

Klein, & Olino, 2007). By the time we reach our 50s, however, trait distributions are remarkably, even stubbornly, stable (Lucas & Donnellan, 2011).

The remarkable temporal consistency in individual differences for personality traits is one of the most important findings in the scientific literature on personality development. It offers definitive proof that individual differences in personality traits have staying power. But we should not get too carried away in interpreting these findings. The research shows that amid the stability in individual differences, there is still plenty of room for change. And even little changes add up over long periods of time. From year to year, people may shift around only slightly on any given trait continuum, but as decades pass the shifts can accumulate to result in substantial change. It is therefore one thing to demonstrate reasonably high rank-order stability between, say, ages 5 and 8, or 50 and 60. It is quite another to suggest that personality traits assessed at age 5 will be highly concordant with those assessed at age 60. The few studies that track individual differences from, say, early childhood to late middle age—over four or more decades of life—show rather modest statistical associations (Fraley & Roberts, 2005; Hampson & Goldberg, 2006). Think about it, though: Over an entire life course, many things can happen, leading to unpredictable shifts in rank-order distributions of trait scores. Rank-order stability may be relatively strong from one year to the next, but *over multiple decades across many individual lives, it is sure to erode.* Strong threads of continuity may be discerned in individual lives. But personality change is also inevitable.

In summary, the evidence for the rank-order stability in the broadest traits of personality is strong. Nonetheless, the path from childhood temperament to the dispositional traits of midlife and beyond is long and winding. A social actor's earliest performances may foreshadow later trends. But an individual human being's unique career in acting is likely to be, we hope, a long one. Over the countless performances that make up the life course, the actor's life and the actor's world will change in countless ways, some expected and many not. Changing relationships, new commitments and roles, unexpected challenges, the failures and losses that will inevitably occur, the peak moments of joy and the deep canyons of despair, the entrances and the exits of other actors and the arrival of new audiences, chance events, luck and serendipity, the cumulative effects of education and social class, the wear and tear of aging—against a life's backdrop of flux and uncertainty and the undeniable influences of external environments, it is perhaps surprising that individual differences in personality traits exhibit any longitudinal stability at all! With all manner of things going against them, traits still manage to show temporal stability. How, then, do they manage to do it?

## THE CONSPIRACY OF GENES AND ENVIRONMENTS

They do it by way of a vast conspiracy. Genes interact with environments on many different levels to drive the development of personality traits. The "environments" within which genes operate run from the proximal cytoplasm of individual cells to the interpersonal dynamics that characterize a human family, and beyond the family to encompass social institutions, religion, and culture—in other words, from the biological micro to the sociological macro. It is difficult to disentangle the influence of genes from the influence of environments, and indeed you could argue that it makes no sense whatsoever to disentangle them, for each—genes and environments—depends on the other for anything to occur at all. Moreover, it is becoming increasingly clear that genes do something much bolder than merely "interact" with environments. Genes and environments seem to *work together* on many different levels and in extraordinarily ingenious ways. The relationship between genes and environments, therefore, is not so much like a meeting of two independent forces (nature vs. nurture) but instead resembles something more like a conspiracy. Nature shamelessly colludes with nurture. In the human case, genes and environments conspire to make a person, and to shape the traits that structure how that person moves through life as an actor on a social stage.

It is no longer controversial to claim that genetic differences between people influence the development of personality traits. The scientific jury came back in about two decades ago. Its verdict was (and remains) that *at least half of the variance in personality traits is accounted for by genetic differences between people.* The finding generally holds for all traits in the Big Five, and it holds equally for men and women (Turkheimer, Pettersson, & Horn, 2014). The strongest evidence for genetic underpinnings of personality traits comes from studies of twins. Identical twins (who share all their genes) turn out to be much more similar to each other on personality traits than are fraternal twins (who share approximately half their genes). Even identical twins who happen, by virtue of adoption, *to have grown up in different families* tend to be highly similar to each other on personality traits (Tellegen et al., 1988), much more similar to each other than fraternal twins and other siblings who grow up in the same families.

It is undeniably true, therefore, that genes are a major factor in accounting for high levels of rank-order stability in personality traits. In simple terms, people's genotypes are different, which leads to different traits. And in that people's respective genetic makeups do not change over time (my genes are the same as they were when I was 5 years old; so are yours), the individual differences in people's traits do not change too much either. There is truth in this simple claim.

But the truth is also complicated in at least three ways. First, saying that 50% of the variance in traits is due to genetic differences between people does *not* mean that 50% of a person's extraversion is determined by his or her genes. The 50% figure refers to the *heritability* of a trait *in a population*. The claim here is that about half of the variation *between people* may be accounted for by the fact that people differ on their genes. The rest of the variation *between people* must be due to the fact that they differ on their environments, too.

Second, heritability can *change* over the life course of a population. This idea seems weird at first, but it is true, and it makes all kinds of sense when you think about it. Research suggests that the portion of trait variation accounted for by genetic differences between people may *decline* as people get older and as environmental influences of all kinds mount (Bleidorn, Kandler, & Caspi, 2014). Heritability is a ratio, so when the environmental effect increases for a group, as it may with the course of time and the accumulation of unique experiences for each unique member of the group, the relative genetic effect accordingly decreases. Even though people's genes do not change, then, the genetic effects on trait variability in a group of people may change over the life course.

Third, and perhaps most important, any particular personality trait is surely influenced by *many* genes, and to date scientists have had very little luck determining which genes they are. Studies that map genome-wide associations to date have not been successful in identifying a specific set of genes that is itself responsible for individual differences in any particular personality trait. There have been some tantalizing leads. For example, many scientists have examined the possibility that a variation on a particular gene partly responsible for regulating serotonergic function—the *5-HTTLPR* serotonin transporter gene—may influence the development of neuroticism and certain other personality characteristics. Some studies have suggested that having a particular form of the *5-HTTLPR* gene may lead to depression and other indices of psychopathology *when combined with* a history of life stress (Caspi, Sugden, et al., 2003; Petersen et al., 2012). Other scientists have failed to replicate these kinds of findings. It is a rapidly changing research area (somebody probably launched a study on the topic this morning, as I write these words), and there are many different opinions out there. What seems likely, however, is that any effect that may ultimately be attributed to the *5-HTTLPR* gene, and other gene candidates like it, will be statistically very small, if indeed there turns out to be any effect at all (Bleidorn et al., 2014).

While scientists will eventually make more progress in their search for genetic determinants of personality, it appears to be increasingly likely that no single personality disposition will be shown to link up with a clear-cut, one-size-fits-all genetic profile. Not only are many genes likely to be implicated in the development of any particular personality disposition, but the strong possibility also exists that there are multiple and perhaps strikingly different genetic ways to get to any single trait. The cognitive scientist Wendy Johnson (2010) makes a parallel argument for the genetics of intelligence. Johnson points out that scientists have yet to find any single gene that accounts for more than a trivial portion of the variance in IQ scores, which themselves are even more heritable than personality traits. In fact, scientists have not even been able to find a gene that predicts how *tall* people will become as adults—and adult height is over 90% heritable in most populations. Johnson concludes that "very different combinations of genes may produce identical IQs or heights or levels of any other psychological trait" (p. 181). It makes obvious sense that no two extreme extraverts would have the same genotype (except for identical twins). But what makes Johnson's claim especially interesting is the assertion that *the particular genes that "produce" the exact same levels of extraversion in two different people are themselves likely to be very different.* You and I may have the exact same level of neuroticism, or conscientiousness, or whatever. But genetically speaking, I got mine one way, and you got yours another.

No single genotype is likely to produce any particular trait profile because traits interact with genes in complicated ways over the course of personality development. And this gets us back to the idea of a conspiracy. Consider the following example: A 4-month-old infant is blessed with a genotype that predisposes him or her to positive emotionality and sociability. As a social actor, he or she smiles more than other babies do in response to social stimuli, and people (the audience) respond in kind. Smiling begets more positive interactions from other people, who themselves *become major features of the developing infant's "environment."* These environments feed back to influence the development of the infant's dispositional traits. A smiley baby will likely encounter more positive environments than a nonsmiley baby will encounter, by virtue of the fact

that social actors *evoke* specific environments. Those evoked environments, in turn, may influence the development of the social actor's traits.

In this simple example of the conspiracy between genes and environments, you might say that the genes make the first move: The genotype expresses itself through behaviors that signal positive emotionality.
Those behaviors then evoke responses that, as environmental influences,
may subsequently exert an effect on the developing social actor. Over a
period of years, positive emotionality shades into extraversion, let us say,
as the smiley baby grows up to encounter environments that reinforce
or strengthen extraversion itself because these environments tend to be
colored by lively positive experiences with other people—environments
that are continually evoked by the actor him- or herself. In partitioning
variance to genes and environments across social actors, the genes may
get a great deal of the "credit" for shaping the extraversion trait, but if
our example of the smiley baby has any validity, the environments may
have done much of the work!

The example of the smiley baby illustrates one psychological
mechanism—let us call it *evocation*—that may express the conspiracy
between genes and environments, and thereby help to explain why
rank-order stability for traits is as high as it is. In Table 4.2, I have listed
six such mechanisms, drawing from the writings of personality psychologists like Avshalom Caspi, Brent Roberts, and other researchers who have
sought to articulate how genes work with environments to produce dispositional traits across the human life course (Roberts, Wood, & Caspi,
2008; Scarr & McCartney, 1983). Among other things, each mechanism
can be seen as potentially reinforcing preexisting tendencies in personality. Through the mechanism of *responsivity*, for instance, actors respond
positively to those features in their environment that are consistent with
their own predispositions, which may work to reinforce those predispositions. Extraverts-to-be may search out environments for stimuli that will
end up reinforcing their extraversion, while ignoring those stimuli that
more introverted actors might find more appealing.

In a related manner, actors are likely to be *attracted* to environments
that are consistent with and to *avoid* environments that are inconsistent
with their preexisting tendencies. As actors grow up, they are likely to
employ with greater and greater skill the mechanism of *manipulation*—
actively altering environments in order to tailor them to their preexisting personality tendencies. A person high in agreeableness may be able
to walk into the most antagonistic kinds of situations and defuse the
conflicts, making peace and love out of what was once an interpersonal
war zone. Peace and love beget more peace and love; the agreeable actor

**TABLE 4.2. Psychological Mechanisms That Reinforce Preexisting Personality Traits**

| Mechanism | Definition | Examples |
|---|---|---|
| Evocation | Actors evoke responses from their audiences that are consistent with or reinforce preexisting tendencies. | A smiley baby stimulates positive emotional responses from parents; a teenager's shyness evokes negative reactions and withdrawal from others, which leads to even more reclusive behavior on the part of the teenager. |
| Responsivity | Actors respond favorably to those features of a social scene that are consistent with their preexisting tendencies, which reinforces those tendencies. | A child high on positive emotionality responds favorably to the exuberance displayed by her older brother, while ignoring her morose older sister; a conscientious college student pays close attention to the professor's lecture, which ultimately pays off via higher grades, which tends to reinforce the trait of conscientiousness. |
| Attraction | Actors are attracted to scenes that are consistent with their preexisting tendencies. | Friendly and caring (agreeable) children are attracted to other agreeable children, such that nice kids make each other even nicer; extraverts are attracted to parties and other potentially lively social scenes. |
| Avoidance | Actors avoid scenes that are inconsistent with or pose problems for their preexisting tendencies. | A child with low self-control refuses to practice the piano or do his homework; introverts avoid parties, which reinforces introversion. |
| Manipulation | Actors alter scenes so that they fit better with their preexisting tendencies. | A conscientious child who prizes order and neatness cleans her room regularly, even though the rest of the house is a mess; a highly neurotic employee repeatedly injects drama into an otherwise quiet workplace, which creates conflict and negative reactions, which in turn reinforces the neurotic employee's neuroticism. |

(*continued*)

**TABLE 4.2.** (*continued*)

| Mechanism | Definition | Examples |
|---|---|---|
| Role selection | Actors select and are selected into social roles that are consistent with their preexisting tendencies, serving to reinforce those tendencies. | A trusting and caring child (high agreeableness) is often chosen by others to be "my best friend," which leads to experiences that reinforce agreeableness; conscientious adults take on leadership roles, which demand even more conscientiousness. |

*Note.* Based loosely on Roberts et al. (2008, p. 384).

creates the kinds of environments that his or her inherent agreeableness finds to be especially, well, agreeable—reinforcing the agreeableness that was operative in the first place.

Across the human life course, the most powerful way whereby genes conspire with environments to undergird stability in personality traits may be *the selection of social roles* (Roberts, 2007). In the theater or cinema, a "role" is the specific part that an actor plays in the performance. Each role comes with its particular affordances and constraints, dictated by the instructions of the playwright and by the expectations that audiences may have about the reality of social life. If an actor plays the role of Brutus in Shakespeare's *Julius Caesar*, therefore, he *must* betray the protagonist in Act III. The role may leave plenty of room for improvisation (Brutus may be resolute or ambivalent, rough-hewn or refined), but if the actor is to be true to the script, he has no choice but to plot Caesar's assassination.

In everyday social life, "roles" refer to highly structured patterns of activity and commitment that are designed to perform essential functions in an ongoing community of human actors. As in the theater, each role comes with a set of expectations regarding how the person who occupies the role should be positioned in social reality, how the person should act and feel, and what goals the person should try to accomplish. Roles may be instrumental (CEO, boss, teacher, student, soldier, quarterback, first-chair oboist, incarcerated prisoner) or expressive (mother, son, lover, mistress, friend, enemy). They may entail formal behavioral protocols (President of the United States) or merely a set of vague expectations (uncle). They may enjoy high social approval (homecoming queen, rabbi) or evoke strong disapproval (class bully, gang banger). For the kind of euosocial species we evolved to be, life without social roles would be so random as to be no life at all. If we did not have roles, most of us would not know what to do with ourselves when we wake up in the morning.

Early in life, we may be selected into roles that are more or less consistent with the dispositional traits that others attribute to us. In these cases, the audience makes the call. Your fourth-grade classmates may have voted you in as the student council representative because they observed you to be an especially conscientious kid, or maybe because you were the most popular one, which was a function of your traits. Or maybe your classmates shunned you and cast you into the horrible role of class scapegoat, perhaps because they perceived you to be arrogant or strange, displaying traits that they did not appreciate. As we grow up, we exert more control over the social roles we play, enabling us to choose roles that feel comfortable, roles that are congenial with our developing dispositional profile. Over time, we may continue to select certain kinds of roles to play, while avoiding others, thereby reinforcing our traits, which may have the effect of contributing to dispositional continuity. In keeping with this claim, research has shown that adolescents who play specific roles in high school, such as being a "jock" or a "brain," tend to adopt similar roles in later life stages, such as in college or in their chosen occupational or leisure interests (Barber, Eccles, & Stone, 2001).

## WHAT CAN PARENTS DO?

It is generally believed that parents are the most important agents of socialization in any child's life. In families across the globe, mothers and fathers aim to keep their children safe and provide them with the resources they need in order to thrive. They discipline their children. They teach them the rules and norms they need to abide by in order to get along and get ahead in the groups that will come to define their children's identities, preparing them for school and, ultimately, life. In accord with cultural norms, parents often receive considerable assistance in their socialization efforts from grandparents, babysitters, aunts and uncles, and other adults in the immediate vicinity who are called upon to be caregivers and to assume other essential roles in raising the children. As such, parents and those who assist them respond to the developing child's personality, and they aim to influence the development of that personality. Parents want their children to be healthy, happy, and successful, which means they want them to be effective social actors. They want their children to have good traits.

What can parents do to promote the development of good personality traits in their children? Parenting manuals and pop psychology books provide all kinds of answers, as do ministers, rabbis, counselors, and many parents themselves. There is no shortage of advice. But what does scientific research have to say about it? Nearly half a century of research in developmental psychology has suggested that an *authoritative parenting style* tends to be associated with many positive outcomes in children's lives (Baumrind, 1971; Darling & Steinberg, 1993; Spera, 2005). Authoritative parenting combines high levels of nurturance with strong parental control. Authoritative parents aim to meet their children's emotional needs on the one hand, but they aim to encourage high standards of behavior for their children on the other. They may shower their children with love, but they also enforce clear rules and employ discipline. In a nutshell, authoritative parents are both *warm* and *strict*. You can contrast the authoritative parenting style to *authoritarian* parenting (which is strict but *not* warm), *indulgent* parenting (warm but *not* strict), and *neglectful* parenting (*neither* warm *nor* strict).

Compared to the other three parenting styles, authoritative parenting tends to predict higher levels of school achievement, moral development, and overall competence in children and adolescents. There is some debate in the scientific literature regarding the generalizability of these findings, for the strongest effects seem to show up in middle-class Western families. Authoritative parenting may resonate well with Western values of autonomy and individual achievement. By providing children with a surfeit of warm affection and, at the same time, articulating clear rules for competent behavior, authoritative parents may be instilling the confidence their children need to pursue their own personal dreams with respect to a societal structure that itself values individual initiative within middle-class conventionality. Other parenting styles may work better in other kinds of cultural contexts. Nonetheless, decades of research on authoritative parenting clearly document ways in which certain parents can have positive effects on their children's development.

But does authoritative parenting directly influence *personality traits* themselves? The positive outcomes that tend to be associated with authoritative parenting seem to fall roughly in the trait domains of conscientiousness (C) and openness to experience (O). Children raised in authoritative households tend to develop the C characteristics of self-discipline and achievement striving as well as the O characteristics of curiosity, intellectual initiative, and personalized moral standards. Many personality psychologists have argued, however, that the positive effects of authoritative parenting on children's personality development may largely be *genetic* effects rather than direct effects of parenting practices themselves. The basic argument goes like this: Authoritative parents are themselves probably high in C and other good traits anyway, and by passing their genes down to their biological children, they are essentially passing down their traits genetically. The parenting practices themselves are incidental.

The evidence for this argument is indirect but compelling. I have already told you that statistical studies of twins (and adoptive children) strongly suggest that about 50% of the variation in observed trait scores is due to genetic differences between people. If heritability is 50%, then we would expect the other half of the variance in trait scores within a population to be due to *environmental* effects. And indeed it likely is. But what do we mean by environmental effects? What most people typically mean, I suspect, is things like overall parenting style and many other factors that all of the children who grow up in a given family share— same parents, same neighborhood, same schools, and so on. Researchers call these things *shared environment* effects because it is assumed that all members of the family share them, and as such these effects should work to make children in the same family *similar* to each other. More-over, shared environment effects should work to make children in the same family similar to each other *above and beyond* the effects of shared genetics. Therefore, my personality should be somewhat similar to the personalities of my biological brother and sister by virtue of our shar-ing half our genes in common. But in addition to that we should be even slightly more similar to each other by virtue of the fact that we grew up in the same family, experienced similar child-rearing practices on the part of our parents, went to the same schools, lived in the same neighborhood, attended the same church, and on and on (shared environment). The shared environment effect should add on to the genetic effect in aligning our personality traits up with each other.

But here is the weirdest thing in all of personality research: *Studies of twins and adoptive children consistently show that shared environ-ment effects are virtually zero.* In other words, once you account for the effects of genes, the shared environmental effects that nearly everybody believes to be so important for the development of personality are vanish-ingly small—effectively nil in most studies. If my last two sentences do not surprise you, then you are not reading carefully enough (or else you took a course in personality psychology once upon a time and you have already wrapped your mind around these surprising findings). According to the research, the reason that identical (momozygotic [MZ]) twins are so similar to each other in personality traits is that they have all their genes in common. The fact that they happen to have grown up in the same family adds nothing to the similarity. (After all, MZ twins raised in *different* families [via adoption] are just as similar to each other as MZ twins raised in the same family.) The reason that biological siblings tend to be *somewhat* similar to each other in personality traits is that they share about half their genes in common. The reason that adoptive children tend *neither* to be similar to their siblings in the same adoptive family (nor similar to their adoptive parents) is that they share no genes in common. With respect to personality traits, then, the conclusion would seem to be this: *It does not matter what parents do.*

But, of course, that cannot be literally true. What parents do *must* matter. I mean, if your parents do not feed you, you will die—and death is really bad for personality traits. There would seem to be a baseline of just good-enough caregiving that is required so that children can have a reasonable chance of surviving to adulthood more or less intact, psychologically speaking. One challenge of parenting is providing an environment that is safe enough and challenging enough that children can find their own way in life, unencumbered by overwhelming burdens and debilitating stress. Even though shared environment effects seem to be small, many researchers still believe that early experiences in the family have long-term effects on personality development. Research on the development of early attachment bonds between parents and their children is partly premised on that expectation. Recent studies showing that the quality of early experience in preschool and kindergarten may have long-term effects on social adjustment and success are similarly based on the expectation that what happens in the environments of young children affects the kinds of adults they will turn out to be (Heckman & Masterov, 2007).

Moreover, because the heritability of personality traits is only 50%, *some sort* of environmental effects *must* be operative in the development of personality traits. Even identical twins are not completely similar to each other in terms of traits, and those differences have been linked to environmental effects. For example, one study has shown that MZ twins who differ in their exposure to stressful life events show correspondingly different scores on neuroticism (Riese et al., 2014). Even though they share all their genes in common, those MZ twins who were exposed to more stress and strain in life (an environmental effect) ended up higher on N than those with less stress. Findings like these implicate what personality psychologists call *nonshared environmental effects*—environmental factors that are unique to one member of a family as opposed to others, presumably working to make members of the same family *different from each other*. Even though my siblings and I were raised in the same family, we each had very different experiences in childhood—different teachers, different friends, different chance events. Those different experiences influenced the development of our respective personalities.

It is well known that parents raise different children differently. They may, for example, issue stricter rules and adopt a sterner approach with a firstborn daughter who has a difficult temperament, compared to their third-born son whose disposition seems sunnier. Their approach to parenting may be driven by their child's temperament, their child's fit into the mix of other children in the family, important events in the parents' own lives, changing economic conditions, and a range of other predictable (e.g., aging of parents themselves) and unpredictable factors. In addition, parents learn things over time, and as a result they may change their approaches to parenting. In many cases, then, parenting styles (authoritative, authoritarian, indulgent, and neglectful) may essentially function as nonshared environment factors in the shaping of traits, in that parents may use one style with one child and another style with another. We should surely not dismiss, therefore, the importance of parenting in the development of personality, even if it is difficult to tease out the complex effects.

It even seems reasonable to suppose that how parents interact with their children—and more generally what happens in children's lives in the early years—may manage to trigger the effects of genes themselves, or to silence potential effects. Research on animals suggests that environmental experiences can essentially *turn genes on and off*, suggesting yet another way in which genes and environments conspire in the making of an organism. The key concept in this work is "epigenetics," which refers generally to factors outside the genome proper that influence how genes are expressed (Cole, 2009). Think of DNA as being like books in a library, precisely ordered and arranged by a meticulous librarian (Champagne & Mashoodh, 2009). Each book contains a wealth of knowledge that becomes available to anyone who reads the book. But until the book is read, no knowledge is conveyed. Likewise, DNA sits in our cells waiting to be "read" by an enzyme called ribonucleic acid (RNA) polymerase, which leads to the production of messenger RNA (a process called "transcription"), which leads to the production of proteins. The active process of reading the DNA triggers the *expression* of a gene. Left unexpressed, a segment of DNA remains like an unopened book, its "knowledge" locked away.

What, then, determines whether the book is to be read? In simple terms, the answer is the *environment*. Factors in the immediate cellular environment involved in transcription influence whether or not a given sequence of DNA will be read. One such factor is DNA *methylation*, whereby a methyl chemical group becomes attached to a particular site in the gene sequence. (The cite is cytosine, which along with adenine, thiamine, and guanine forms the four-letter alphabet of DNA.) The methylation of cytosine changes the configuration of DNA such that the genetic information encoded in that area cannot be read and is nullified: The gene is essentially silenced, or turned off, stopping the production of specific proteins. Two experts in the area of epigenetics put it this way: "DNA methylation reduces the likelihood of transcription much the same way that shifting the furniture in a library can reduce the likelihood that a book will be read. The gene is there, but sits unread, collecting dust" (Champagne & Mashoodh, 2009, p. 128). Conversely, removing DNA methylation can turn the gene back on, as if the furniture in the library were rearranged yet again so that the book we want to read sits prominently on the table in front.

Methylation is influenced by factors such as aging, viral infections, and even processes in the broader social environment. One famous line of research has demonstrated that rat pups whose mothers show low levels of licking and grooming behavior tend to develop more poorly regulated stress response systems, as indicated by lower levels of glucocorticoid receptors in the hippocampus, which appear to be mediated by higher levels of methylation (Weaver et al., 2004). Poor mothering increases methylation, which turns off genes that are designed to build a healthy stress response system. In simple terms, the broad effect of poor maternal care in rat pups affects the expression of genes through methylation. Among humans, analyses of DNA methylation in cells extracted from fetal cord blood suggest that maternal depression and anxiety in the third trimester of pregnancy can lead to increased levels of DNA methylation in infants' glucocorticoid receptors, which may lead to a compromised stress response system (Oberlander et al., 2008).

By exploring the mechanisms through which variations in environments influence the expression of genes, studies of epigenetics suggest yet another way in which genes and environments collude in the making of a person. To date, however, direct and clear-cut effects of epigenetic factors on the development of particular personality traits in human beings have not been firmly demonstrated. Research in this area is still in its very early stages. Nonetheless, the potential implications of epigenetics for explaining continuity in dispositional traits over time, as well as personality change, would appear to be vast (Roberts & Jackson, 2008). Epigenetics may help to explain how individual differences in what happens to actors early in life come to influence the quality of their social performances later on. As such, particular scenes in the actor's life, especially early in development, may ultimately affect gene expression, which, in turn, may affect performance in later scenes, which affects gene expression yet again—and on and on it goes, as the dispositional traits that characterize the actor's unique style of engaging the social world gradually and inexorably take form.

## PORTRAITS OF MATURATION

When human beings talk about the lives of other human beings, and when they talk about themselves, they tell stories that portray long-term stability in personality, as well as dramatic change. Novelists often ascribe to their characters vivid dispositional traits that track continuity over time. Alexei Karamazov, for example, is humble and compassionate throughout Dostoyevsky's longest and greatest novel, whereas his brother Ivan is deeply cynical, brooding, and melancholic. In *The Wizard of Oz*, Dorothy is always sweet and curious. Huck Finn is the paragon of openness to experience. At the same time, novelists are often adept at portraying personal transformation. Alexei attains wisdom and perspective as he grows up, whereas Ivan descends into suicide. Dorothy and Huck learn about the world and about themselves, about the meaning of life, truth, home, and family. They are very different people at the end of their stories than they were at the beginning, even though they have retained many of their self-defining traits. As they grow up, social actors are expected to change. And whereas some changes in some lives are for the worse, the development of personality is generally expected to follow an *arc of maturation.*

One of the earliest and most influential accounts of such an arc appears in the autobiographical writings of Augustine of Hippo (354–430 C.E.). Born to a Christian mother and pagan father in what is now Algeria, the boy who was to become St. Augustine attended school in Madaurus before traveling to Carthage, at age 17, to continue his education in rhetoric. At Carthage, he abandoned his mother's Christian teachings and took up with the Manicheans, who espoused a dualistic religion that pitted the forces of darkness against the forces of light. He also took up with girls. Augustine and his peers boasted of their sexual exploits, as they combined their studies with the lusty pursuit of a hedonistic life style. It is during this time that Augustine was said to have uttered a famous prayer: "God, give me chastity and continence, but not just yet."

Still a teenager, Augustine began an affair with a young woman in Carthage. Because she was below his social class, marriage was not possible. Still, she remained his lover for over 13 years, bearing him a son named Adeodatus. As a young adult, Augustine taught rhetoric in Thagaste (near the place of his birth), Carthage, Rome, and finally Milan. While he enjoyed career success, he experienced considerable conflict in religion and sexuality. His mother urged him to come back to Christianity and to marry a woman of his class. Eventually, he abandoned his long-term concubine (and their son) and consented to a marriage arranged by his mother. But his fiancé was only 11 years old, so he needed to wait 2 years for her to attain the requisite age (and presumably puberty). During the interim, he started up a sexual relationship with another woman, which also ended badly. Eventually, Augustine broke off the engagement, too. He came to believe that his sensuality was distracting him from a life of purpose and high meaning. Responding one day to a child-like voice inside prompting him to read the scriptures, Augustine opened his Bible to a random passage in the book of Romans. He read these words from the apostle Paul: "Not in rioting and drunkenness, not in chambering and wantonness, not in strife and envying, but put on the Lord Jesus Christ, and make no provision for the flesh to fulfill the lusts thereof" (Romans 14:13–14). Thus began his conversion to Christianity.

And thus began a significant transformation in this particular social actor's dispositional traits. Now in his early 30s, Augustine believed that the time was finally right for chastity and continence. He gave up his sexual and material pursuits, sold his patrimony and gave the money to the poor, and began a new life of Christian ministry. In his late 30s, he was ordained as a priest in Hippo Regius. A few years later, he was promoted to bishop. He worked tirelessly to convince the people of Hippo to convert to Christianity. He also wrote game-changing treatises, such as *Confessions* and *City of God*, which shaped Christian practice and doctrine for centuries to come, even to the present day. Drawing partly on his own experiences as a young man, Augustine developed the Christian concept of original sin, arguing that the root of human failings lies in self-centeredness and concupiscence. The church should be like a heavenly city, ruled by love rather than pride, Augustine wrote. Raw sexual desire (concupiscence) separates men and women from God and works against the attainment of Christian maturity. The lust of youth can be tamed and put to acceptable use, Augustine came to believe, only through the Christian sacrament of marriage.

Over 1,500 years later, a young Jewish woman struggled with the same concupiscent desires that St. Augustine learned to control—but then again, who hasn't? Her name was Karen Danielson (later Karen Horney, 1885–1952), and she was to become a famous psychoanalytic theorist who revolutionized how Freudian psychology conceives of women's personality development. Before Horney, Freud argued that young girls come to psychosexual maturity through a variation on what boys experience in the Oedipus complex. Like boys, girls develop an initial attraction to their mothers. But girls unconsciously renounce their attraction, Freud believed, out of the disappointment they feel about the fact that their mothers do not have a penis. Girls want a penis (Freud called this desire "penis envy"), so they switch their affections to the dad (who presumably has one). Eventually, that second attachment also fades, and girls come to identify with their mothers, taking on their mother's sexual orientation and her respect for authority. Nonetheless, girls never lose that sense of envy, disappointment, and incompletion, which stems from their knowledge that they do not have, and will never have, a penis.

Freud's theory sounded almost as implausible in the 1920s as it does today. But it was nonetheless highly influential in psychoanalytic circles. As one of the first women to attain a position of prominence among Freud's followers, Horney reinterpreted the Oedipus complex as a psychological allegory about power. Girls do not want to have a penis, she remarked, but they may envy the power that men and boys enjoy in a patriarchal society. Their attraction to their fathers and their disappointment in their mothers may reflect their desire to have an impact in the world and the frustration they experience when their desire is thwarted. Moreover, women do experience an important sense of power, along with deep fulfillment, in a number of life activities about which Freud seemed to be oblivious. Chief among these is the experience of mothering. Horney believed that Freud did not understand the psychology of women because, in part, he could not empathize with the mothering role:

> I, as a woman, ask in amazement, and what about motherhood? And the blissful consciousness of bearing a new life within oneself? And the ineffable happiness of the increasing expectation of the appearance of a new being? And the joy when it finally makes its appearance and one holds it for the first time in one's arms? And the deep pleasurable feeling of satisfaction in suckling it and the happiness of the whole period when the infant needs her care? (in Quinn, 1988, p. 171)

During the last three decades of her life, Karen Horney was a highly regarded therapist, teacher, and writer. But her psychological road to maturity was a rocky one (McAdams, 1994; Quinn, 1988). As a young woman, she often feared that her sexual desires would rage out of control and thereby destroy her deep longing for psychological freedom. "To be free of sensuality means great power in a woman," she wrote at the age of 20. When a woman is swept away by passion for a man, she "becomes the bitch, who begs even if she is beaten" (Horney, 1980, p. 104). Yet, as Horney's sympathetic biographer has described her youth, she longed to be swept away, to "experience abandon, to be tossed about in the stormy seas of passion, under the sure lead of a man who would be skillful enough to awaken her" (Quinn, 1988, p. 64). With one of her lovers (Ernst), "I feel as a woman only," surrendering to the "elemental passion" and his power (Quinn, 1988, p. 80). Toward another (Oskar), she feels respected as a human being but resents his inability to awaken her passion. She marries Oskar nonetheless but continues to have affairs with other men, even as she raises three young children and provides therapy for her clients. The marriage eventually ends, and the children grow up. Horney's relationships with men never bring her the fulfillment she desires, but she nonetheless seems better able to control her impulses as she moves into midlife, and to devote herself wholeheartedly to her work.

For Jane Fonda, the celebrated American actress and political activist, the arc of maturation is not so much about sexual control as it is about finding self-acceptance. In *My Life So Far*, Fonda (2006) divides her life's drama into three acts: "Gathering" (ages 0–30), "Seeking" (ages 30–60), and "Beginning" (ages 60+). She summarizes the throughline in one sentence: "It is the story of a girl who grew up feeling she wasn't good enough, and this made her especially vulnerable to contracting the Disease to Please; how this affected her adult life (specifically in relation to men); and how she managed—in her third act—to see that she didn't need to be perfect, that good enough is good enough" (p. vii).

Born in 1937 to Canadian socialite Frances Ford Brokaw and legendary American actor Henry Fonda, Jane grew up in privilege, living in southern California and Greenwich, Connecticut, among other places. She was a rambunctious tomboy with a lively and compelling social presence, Daddy's little girl and his favorite. From an early age, however, she feared her father, for his dark moods and sudden bursts of anger. Yet she loved him dearly, too, and always tried to please him. Her parents' marriage was never harmonious, and the family atmosphere was perennially suffused with tension. When Jane was 11 years old, her mother committed suicide while under treatment at a psychiatric hospital. As Fonda tells it from the vantage point of late middle age, her mother's death was one of many factors that arose in adolescence to undermine her faith in her own goodness and cause her to deny the validity of her innermost feelings.

A consummate social actor even before she landed her first Hollywood role, Jane Fonda had no problem channeling her desires and conflicts into effective social behavior. She enjoyed remarkable success as a
fashion model (1960s), actress (1960s–1980s; two Academy Awards for
best actress, in *Klute* and *Coming Home*), fitness guru (1980s–1990s;
countless American households own a Jane Fonda workout video), and
wife (to three husbands: Roger Vadim, Tom Hayden, and Ted Turner—
with all three marriages ending amicably, more or less; she expresses few
regrets). But up through her 50s, Fonda reports, she paid a steep psychological price for success, manifested in 30 years of bulimia and anorexia,
chronically low self-esteem (which she masterfully disguised), and a persistent feeling that she was emotionally divorced from her authentic inner
self. It was not until her 50s, she suggests, that she managed to accept
the fact that she is not perfect, that good enough is indeed good enough.
As part of her personal transformation, she found Christianity and committed herself to improving the lives of underprivileged girls and women,
through advocacy and philanthropy regarding issues of poverty, women's
health, and sexual abuse.

For many people, reaching maturity involves coming to terms with
the mistakes they have made in life. In *My Life So Far*, Jane Fonda
admits to many failings, but she also defends herself vigorously against
her critics. Because of her political activism during the Vietnam War,
she was a lightning rod for American angst during that time. In press
conferences, campus speeches, and visits with the troops, Fonda urged
American servicemen to disobey the chains of command and actively
oppose the war. Even her staunch defenders have conceded that Fonda's
trip to Hanoi in 1972 was a public relations disaster. The most enduring
image from the trip was a photo of Fonda's sitting in a North Vietnamese antiaircraft gun site, as if she were poised to shoot down American
warplanes. In Fonda's (2006) account of how she decided to take the
trip in the first place, she seems reckless and naive. Years later, she still
defends her political activism as motivated by the sincere idealism of a
principled woman in her late 20s and early 30s. But from the standpoint
of middle age, she also expresses profound regrets. In a 1988 interview
with Barbara Walters, Fonda apologized to Vietnam veterans: "I was
trying to help end the killing and the war, but there were times when I
was thoughtless and careless about it, and I'm very sorry." She added: "I
will go to the grave regretting the photograph of me in an anti-aircraft
gun, which looks like I was trying to shoot at American planes. It hurt
so many soldiers. It galvanized such hostility. It was the most horrible
thing I could possibly have done."

As my fourth brief portrait in maturation, consider Shawn Corey Carter, born December 4, 1969, in a housing project in the Bedford-Stuyvesant neighborhood of Brooklyn. Raised by a single mother, along with three other siblings, Shawn never graduated from high school. At age 12, he may have shot his older brother in the shoulder for stealing his jewelry—the facts are uncertain. As a teenager, he sold crack cocaine. He was shot at three times but escaped serious injury. Around the age of 30, he was accused of stabbing an associate in the stomach with a 5-inch blade. He pleaded guilty to a misdemeanor charge and received a sentence of 3 years' probation.

In the first couple decades of his life, poverty and the chaos of the street combined with personal deficiencies in self-control to create a very dangerous situation for Shawn Corey Carter. But he also had a lot going for him. His mother bought him a boom box for his birthday, which sparked an interest in music. After witnessing an older kid put on a street performance of rhyming and rhythm, Shawn started writing rhymes down in a spiral notebook. He began to associate with other talented kids in the neighborhood who competed with each other to develop outrageous lyrics—poetry, really—and the innovative cadences that the world now knows as hip-hop and rap. Shawn became a rapper, and he eventually took on the stage name Jay-Z. Today, Jay-Z is one of the most famous hip-hop artists in the world, as well as a record producer, entrepreneur, and co-creator of a clothing line named Rocawear. Since 2008, he has been married to the R&B singer Beyoncé (Knowles). In early 2012, she gave birth to their daughter, Blue Ivy Carter.

In his remarkable memoir, *Decoded*, Jay-Z (2011) describes how his time as a hustler on the streets ultimately shaped his art. Hip-hop had always described poverty in the ghetto and depicted the violence of thug life, Jay-Z writes, but with his first album onward, he was more interested in exploring "the interior space of a young kid's head, his psychology" (p. 18). "Thirteen-year-old kids don't wake up one day and say, 'Okay, I just wanna sell drugs on my mother's stoop, hustle on my block till I'm so hot niggas want to come look for me and start shooting out my mom's living room windows'" (p. 17). The reality is more complex:

> To tell the story of the kid with the gun without telling the story of why he has it is to tell a kind of lie. To tell the story of the pain without telling the story of the rewards—the money, the girls, the excitement—is a different kind of evasion. To talk about killing niggas dead without talking about waking up in the middle of the night from a dream about a friend you watched die, or not getting to sleep

in the first place because you're so paranoid from the work you're doing, is a lie so deep it's criminal. I wanted to tell stories and boast, to entertain and to dazzle with creative rhymes, but everything I said had to be rooted in the truth of that experience. I owed it to all the hustlers I met or grew up with who didn't have a voice to tell their own stories—and to myself. (pp. 17–18)

Jay-Z has sold over 50 million albums worldwide and received 17 Grammy awards. Two of his albums, *Reasonable Doubt* (1996) and *The Blueprint* (2001), are considered landmarks in the genre. *Billboard* magazine has ranked him the fifth top solo male artist and the fourth top rapper of all time. In January 2009, *Forbes* ranked Jay-Z and Beyoncé Hollywood's top-earning couple, with a combined total of $162 million for that year alone.

Yet artistic and financial success do not necessarily equate with personality development. Skeptics may contend that Jay-Z, now in his mid-40s, is hardly a model citizen. Still, it is hard to ignore the positive changes he has experienced in his life. After being sentenced to probation for the 1999 stabbing incident, Jay-Z expressed public regret for his loss of self-control, and he vowed never to get involved in that kind of situation again. Indicative of the arc of maturation are his midlife ventures into politics and philanthropy. He worked to register voters in the 2008 U.S. presidential election, and he pledged funds to the American Red Cross relief effort after Hurricane Katrina. Developmental trends may also be observed in his lyrics. For example, in the 2012 production of *Glory*, dedicated to his new daughter, Jay-Z details the couple's struggle with infertility, his wife's miscarriage, and the joys of fatherhood.

## DEVELOPMENTAL TRENDS IN BIG FIVE TRAITS

The four protagonists of my portraits in maturation consistently displayed personality traits that distinguished them from their peers. Energetic and curious from early childhood onwards, Karen Horney and Jane Fonda seemed to exhibit sky-high levels of E and O throughout their lives. It seems likely that most everybody in his social world considered Augustine of Hippo to be an exceptionally caring and sensitive person—higher in A than most other people he knew. As we saw earlier in this chapter, the concept of rank-order stability captures the sense in which people may be consistently different from each other over time.

But the four portraits also suggest substantial change in dispositional traits. As they move across the adult lifespan, all four protagonists seem to exhibit gains in self-regulation and to become more socially responsible. In terms of the Big Five traits, Augustine and Horney seem to exhibit increases in various features of C, as they become better able to tamp down or control sexual impulses. Jay-Z appears to become a kinder and more compassionate person, demonstrating increases in A. Jane Fonda's maturation seems to track a decline in N, as she gradually becomes more adept at dealing with negative feelings and accepting her own flaws. And let us add Mary Ann Cromwell to the group—the star of my 10-year high school reunion. Between the ages of 18 and 28, Mary Ann seemed to become more extraverted, less neurotic, and to display more O.

These portraits in maturation show developmental changes in the absolute level of a particular person's traits. When applied to a group of social actors, we may speak of the same idea as referring to *mean-level change* in personality—the extent to which members of the group, *on the average*, tend to increase or decrease on a given dispositional trait as it is tracked over time. Again, my high reunion example proves instructive. Had we given trait inventories to me and my fellow graduates at age 18 and again at age 28, we might have noticed mean-level changes over 10 years for the group as a whole. The entire distribution of scores on the trait of N, for example, might have shifted slightly to the lower end—which would indicate that this sample's young adults *in general* had become somewhat less neurotic over time. The mean-level change would not apply to every person, of course; some individuals might have increased, others might have stayed steady, and still others might have decreased in N. Moreover, the individuals who were highest (or lowest) in N at age 18 might still be highest (or lowest) in N relative to other group members at age 28, indicating relatively high rank-order stability. Still, the group as a whole may have changed, suggesting a general developmental trend for a particular personality trait.

The four cases of personality maturation and my observations of Mary Ann Cromwell convey the gist of what a growing number of empirical studies tend to show. Mean-level changes in dispositional traits are consistently observed—and roughly along the lines noted in the lives of St. Augustine, Karen Horney, Jane Fonda, and Jay-Z. In terms of the Big Five traits, cross-sectional and longitudinal studies suggest that people tend to experience *increases in C and A* and *decreases in neuroticism* as they move across the life course, *from adolescence through late middle age*.

Brent Roberts and his colleagues (2006) published the landmark paper on this topic almost a decade ago. They conducted a statistical review of 92 longitudinal studies, analyzing mean scores on Big Five traits by age decades, from age 10 to age 70. Most of the studies were from North American samples of participants, with largely white and middle-class samples. The mapping of the mean scores showed that scores in C tended to increase gradually and steadily across the age span, but the increase in A was less smooth. Average scores in A crept up slowly to age 50, showed a sharp increase from 50 to 60, then leveled off again. N decreased through age 40, then leveled off. E showed a mixed picture. E-spectrum traits related to social dominance tended to show increases through age 30, whereas E-like measures related to energy and social vitality tended to decrease after age 50. O showed a curvilinear trend: an increase up to age 20, then a decrease after age 50. Women and men tended to show roughly the same developmental profiles, this despite the fact that most studies typically show that women score slightly higher than men on both A and N.

Empirical findings that have appeared since Roberts's authoritative review have tended to show roughly similar age trajectories (e.g., Specht et al., 2014). Not every study shows the exact same trends, of course. Moreover, researchers have been slow to conduct studies in cultures outside of Europe and North America (an exception is Walton et al., 2013). Nonetheless, the developmental trend in these studies is pretty clear: As they move across the adult life course, social actors tend to become increasingly industrious, self-disciplined, reliable, and well organized (C); increasingly courteous, sympathetic, forgiving, caring, and good-natured (A); and *decreasingly* anxious, insecure, nervous, irritable, and vulnerable (N)—at least through late middle age (say, the 60s). The changes are not huge, even from decade to decade, but they do add up. By contrast, patterns in mean-level change for the broad dispositional traits of E and O are ambiguous or uneven. In essence, the arc of maturation is long, and it bends mainly toward A and C, and away from N.

What accounts for these developmental trends? One answer is that people naturally become more agreeable, conscientious, and emotionally stable over time as a result of universal biological changes that accompany aging (Costa & McCrae, 2006). Studies from developmental neuroscience suggest that the brain's PFC may not reach full functional maturity until the 20s. The PFC is intimately involved in rational decision making, long-term planning, top-down impulse control, and various forms of self-regulation. Brain maturation, then, could be partly responsible for increases in A and C, and perhaps even decreases in N.

Whereas some evidence can be garnered for the biological maturation hypothesis, many psychologists argue that the adoption of adult *social roles* is a more important factor (Roberts, 2007; Specht et al., 2014)—in particular, normative social roles related to family, work, and civic engagement. The two arguments are not necessarily inconsistent, in that biological changes could impel people to adopt important social roles, which in turn could impact trait levels. But social role explanations tend to underscore the long-term influences of nonshared environments on the development of personality traits, focusing attention on the social actor's social world.

Research has increasingly demonstrated that changes in social roles accompany, and often seem to cause, changes in dispositional traits. As an example, a longitudinal study of young adults in Germany showed that getting married (or establishing a long-term romantic partnership) led to increases in C and decreases in N over time, whereas those young adults who stayed single over time showed no change on C and N (Neyer & Lehnart, 2007). Research has shown that young men high in A are more likely than those scoring lower on A to engage in community service professions; their involvement in these service roles, moreover, further increases their A (Jackson, Thoemmes, Jonkmann, Ludtke, & Trautwein, 2012).

In another study of German youth, the researchers observed the expected pattern of increases in C and A and decreases in N over time (Ludtke, Roberts, Trautwein, & Nagy, 2011). However, those young adults who transitioned from high school into vocational careers showed *especially sharp* increases in C, compared to those young adults who went from high school to college, who themselves showed *especially sharp* increases in A. The vocational role may call for particularly high levels of C, whereas becoming a college student may require, or produce, increases in A that are even steeper than the norm. Research shows that people who experience more successful and satisfying careers in young adulthood increase disproportionately on C and decrease disproportionately on N over time (Roberts & Mroczek, 2008). Researchers followed 1600 men across 12 years of middle adulthood and found that getting married was associated with above-average increases in emotional stability (in other words, especially sharp decreases in N), whereas the death of a spouse was related to temporary decreases in emotional stability followed by a gradual recovery period (Mroczek & Spiro, 2003). Loss of a job has been linked to decreases in C and increases in N (Costa, Herbst, McCrae, & Siegler, 2000).

In a study that underscores the importance of social roles, German personality psychologist Wiebke Bleidorn and her colleagues (2013) examined Internet responses on a Big Five inventory from over 800,000 young adults (ages 16–40) from 62 different nations. From Argentina to Zimbabwe, scores on A and C increased from the younger to the older participants (along with E and O), and N decreased. At the same time, the researchers observed interesting differences between nations with respect to *when* the developmental trends kicked in. In those societies in which adults are expected to assume the roles of spouse, parent, and employed worker at an earlier age (e.g., Mexico, Ecuador), the researchers observed earlier shifts in the direction of greater A and C, and lower N; by contrast, in those societies in which marriage, childrearing, and paid employment tend to occur later (e.g., Norway, Denmark), the mean-level developmental shifts in traits also came later. Cross-cultural differences in the timing of trait change, as observed in this impressive study, tend to support the idea that the actor's social roles have a significant impact on personality development in young adulthood.

As young adults take on such normative social roles as spouse, parent, and coworker, they typically make commitments and assume responsibilities that may require higher levels of A and C, and lower N, than they have hitherto been accustomed to displaying. Taking on the role of husband usually entails a promise, or at least expectation, of fidelity to one's wife, which may mean that a man needs to exercise more restraint in sexuality than he has in the past. Becoming a parent may call upon new reserves of compassion and care, as well as buckling down at work in order to secure a stable family income. As adults accept more responsibility for the welfare of others (their children, their coworkers, their friends in need), they may shift attention from their own emotional problems to the problems of people who depend on them. You may not be able to wallow in your N when you face important responsibilities in family, workplace, church, neighborhood, and community. In some instances, focusing on the needs of others can itself enhance A and C, and lead to declines in N—as may have been true for Karen Horney. In addition, experiencing success in the normative social roles of adulthood may directly produce psychological benefits. Becoming a good mother or performing well at work may boost your confidence; it may make you feel better about yourself (lower N) and promote a more caring and focused approach to life (higher A and C).

## CONCLUSION

With respect to the first layer of human personality, dispositional traits show both continuity and change over the life course. The performances that determine the extent to which social actors manage to get along and to get ahead in life are decisively contoured by dispositions toward E, N, A, C, and O—fundamental differences between social actors that gradually develop over time. From one performance to the next, one year to the next, the audience cannot help but recognize the characteristic brands of social behavior that individual actors recurrently display—the unique manner in which each actor performs emotion and regulates the performance. But over many performances and many years, the actor is bound to change. If the audience members could watch the bulk of the entire movie—from age 5 to age 75, say—they might leave the theater with the sense that yes, indeed, there was *something essential* about him that *was there all along*, yet he seems to be, at the same time, a *very different person* than he was when he began.

As social actors grow up, the differences between them reveal a remarkable degree of staying power from one year to the next, increasingly so as they get older. Rank-order stability in personality traits is a product of a multifaceted and multilevel conspiracy between genes and environments. Through processes of evocation and manipulation, for example, genotypes afford initial behavioral tendencies that shape and select environments, which in turn shape those very same tendencies whose origins reside in the genotypes, such that environmental influences may ultimately reinforce personality proclivities that were there, in nascent form, near the very beginning. Through epigenesis, certain environmental events or conditions may essentially turn genes off and on. In the midst of the collusion, however, every social actor experiences a unique mix of potentially life-altering events—predictable changes such as puberty and the assumption of age-graded normative roles, and countless experiences and transitions that could simply never have been predicted when the actor was born, and whose effects may be dramatic even as they are difficult to discern, such as particular successes and failures in life, loves and losses, accidents and lucky breaks. The effects of nonshared or unique environments help to account for important changes in personality dispositions as the actor grows up and matures. And as the actor takes on new roles in family life and work, personality traits may change to suit the new role demands.

As explicated in a growing number of research studies and exemplified in this chapter's cameo appearances of a religious saint, a renowned psychoanalyst, a controversial movie star, and a famous hip-hop artist, social actors tend to become increasingly agreeable and conscientious as they move into adulthood and through midlife, and somewhat less neurotic. These maturational trends are good news for personality development—and good news for our eusocial species, for our very survival depends on the effective social commitments of hardworking, caring, and emotionally stable adults who need to step up to the plate, in the prime of their lives, and take on the most daunting adaptive challenges that face the group. There is nothing more important for our eusocial species than the successful performance of adult social roles—caring for our children as parents, finding a productive niche that contributes to the common good, becoming a leader in the group, developing an expertise that contributes to the welfare of the group, cooperating with each other as conscientious and agreeable group members in order to solve vexing problems, and coming together to defend the group when the group faces threats from the outside. Three cheers for personality development!

Having paid homage to the fundamental importance of dispositional traits in the development of personality, one still has to wonder: *Is that all there is?* I mean, sure, it's great that Jay-Z and many of the rest of us manage to meet the demands of normative social roles as we mature, and thereby come to experience higher levels of A, C, and emotional stability. And from the standpoint of personality science, it's great that psychological variations on the evolved design for human nature can be so usefully construed in terms of a handful of dispositional traits, as expressed in the Big Five. Nonetheless, accounting for psychological individuality solely in terms of broad dispositions of social performance, like E and A, seems to leave out so many things that a person might know, or at least suspect, about his or her own psychological individuality. The art of personality development seems to demand more than what we can get from dispositional traits alone.

Over the course of her adult life, Jane Fonda experienced a decline in dispositional N, and perhaps an increase in A, too. But so many other things changed as well. In her late 20s, she took up political causes with a vengeance, but her political activism mellowed in intensity as she moved into her 40s and 50s. Fonda reports that she was late to the party when it came to feminism. Her early Hollywood roles reinforced gender stereotypes, and in her three marriages she tended to assume surprisingly subservient roles. In recent years, however, she has focused increasing attention on women's issues, such as reproductive rights and sexual abuse, and she seems to have found a clearer feminist voice. After a half-century of agnosticism, she became a Christian. In her late 50s, Jane Fonda began to see her life as a drama with three acts—Gathering, Seeking, then Beginning again. She began to discern a new throughline in her life story: about how a girl who always wanted to be perfect eventually came to realize that simply being "good enough" is good enough.

Although Jane Fonda made a career in acting, we are all social actors, striving to get along and get ahead in social groups, even when the camera is turned off. But we are all so much more. Behind our social performances are the recurrent desires, goals, and values that speak to what we, as *motivated agents* in the world, aim to accomplish in our lives—how we want to be perfect perhaps, like Jane Fonda, or to experience the heights of power or the most passionate erotic love, how we strive to actualize our most cherished values or put into practice our elaborate philosophies of life. And behind it all are the stories we construct to make sense of our lives as a whole, whether they be comedies, romances, adventure stories, or the kind of three-act drama that Jane Fonda began to tell, and to live, in her late 50s. The stories speak to personality at the level of the *autobiographical author.*

We are born social actors, and we will be social actors until our last breath. But as we become fully human, we become more. Personality development is about more than the actor's dispositional traits. It is also about what we want and value in life, and how we come to understand it all in narrative. Let us now move in personality development from the social actor to the motivated agent. Let us move from the performances that the audience sees to the motivational secrets that reside in the mind of the performer.

# Part II

# Becoming an Agent

A goal is a dream with a deadline.
—NAPOLEON HILL

# chapter 5

# The Age 5–7 Shift

Second grade was my breakout year. At the shining new Kuny Elementary School in Gary, Indiana, Miss Elisha presided over a class of about 25 boys and girls, most of whom would turn 8 by the end of the school year. My memory is that Miss Elisha was what we would categorize today as "totally hot," and I was in love with her, even though I was not too clear back then on what being "hot" was fundamentally about. My ardor was reinforced by the fact that Miss Elisha gave me outstanding marks on my classwork. It was in second grade that I began to excel in school, and when it became apparent to me that some of my peers did not excel. It was in second grade that I first realized that some people consistently excel at certain things and not others, that people are sorted by how well they perform in particular domains, and that it feels so good to excel, to do well at what you like to do, to strive to do well in those areas in which you seem to have talent or interest, and into which you invest so much personal *value*. My classmates chose me to be representative for the Student Council. I attended meetings and prepared simple reports about the meetings, which I regularly recited to the class. It was in second grade that I first had homework to do. I needed to *schedule* time for the homework. I began to keep a schedule in my head. I began to make simple lists. I began to think of my daily life in terms of the *goals* I needed (and wanted) to achieve: finish Student Council report for tomorrow; save allowance to buy more baseball cards; walk home from school with Donna Scott (because she is the pretty blonde); try to become best student in the class, or close to it, by end of year.

Three years after I finished second grade, Harvard psychologist Sheldon White (1965) wrote a famous article in which he identified a transition phase in human development that he labeled *the age 5–7 shift*. White (1965; Sameroff & Haith, 1996) argued that children experience a host of cognitive and social changes in middle-childhood that ultimately result in a newfound sense of maturity and rationality. In 16th-century Europe, children were widely assumed to reach an *age of reason* around their seventh birthday, and were therefore given instruction in civility from that point on. Catholic canon law and English common law, and the several religious and legal practices that have arisen from them, expressed the view that children first know right from wrong and are therefore able to make reasonable moral decisions around the age of 7 or 8. In the evangelical Baptist church I attended throughout my childhood, we were taught that children become responsible for their own Christian status—that is, they become able to make a reasonable *decision* to accept Jesus Christ as their Lord and Savior—around the age of 8. My Sunday school teachers called this "the age of accountability." Therefore, if you died at, say, age 9 and had never gotten around to making your choice for Jesus, well . . .

In societies around the world, children are first given responsibilities for such tasks as babysitting for younger siblings, tending animals, performing household chores, and learning some of the rudiments of the economy—basic farming, fishing, hunting—around the age of 6 or 7 years (Rogoff, Sellers, Pirotta, Fox, & White, 1975). Formal schooling typically starts around age 6, and even when it starts earlier (as in the case of preschool and kindergarten), the level of rigor and academic focus tends to rise sharply in the second and third grades. Before then, teachers offer profuse praise and reinforcement for the efforts little children exert to do well in arts and crafts, school projects, playground activities, and the like. After age 7 or 8, effort is still applauded, but teachers (and parents) become much more interested in results. "I tried really hard on that social studies test, Mom!" "Yeah, well, you still got a C." Perhaps it is not surprising, therefore, that before age 8, children tend to show almost uniformly high levels of self-esteem (Harter, 2006). In second and third grades, self-esteem begins to plummet for many, and consistent individual differences in positive self-regard begin to appear. The age of accountability is a time for sorting it all out. Who is saved? Who is not? Who is on top? Who is on the bottom? Where do you rank? What's your score?

What Sheldon White called the age 5–7 shift is a rough marker for a fundamental transformation in the human life course, a psychosocial transition that has profound implications for personality development. Depending on what features you focus on and whose life you are talking about, the shift may begin before the age of 5 and continue well after the age of 7. Indeed, the ages "5" and "7" are really just proxies for a gradual transformation in psychological functioning that occurs sometime in middle childhood—an age-graded metaphor that I have borrowed from White and others to stand for a group of correlated changes that mark the primary school years. The shift appears to be driven by biological and maturational changes, and by the social conventions of society and schooling. Broad individual differences may be observed in the ways in which this transformation unfolds. And even for those like me who enjoyed their second-grade experience, the developmental move is surely a mixed blessing, for it invariably entails some loss of psychological innocence and spontaneity.

For the cognitively gifted, eusocial creatures we have all evolved to be, it is an essential part of the developmental script that, sooner or later, we become more or less rational, planful, goal-oriented persons. The very survival of the group calls for it. For most of us, the "sooner or later" seems to be temporally situated in our early primary school years. It is during this time that our parents and teachers expect us to develop goals, plans, and projects to structure our daily routines and give meaning to our envisioned futures. It is during this time that society expects us to incorporate values and beliefs regarding ultimate life concerns—what is good, what is true, what is God—and to begin to take responsibility for the moral choices we make. We begin to take ownership of our daily lives and to make decisions regarding what we value. We begin self-consciously to plan for the future, taking stock of where we are positioned in what we now perceive to be an ordered, hierarchical world.

In its deepest and most abstract meaning, the age 5–7 shift pertains to the full emergence of *motivated agency* in the human life course. To be an "agent" in the fullest sense is to take ownership of personal experience and to organize behavior for the future in the service of valued goals. Before I knew Miss Elisha, I was merely a *social actor*, routinely displaying the temperament traits that defined my nascent social reputation and personality. In second grade, I continued to perform as a social actor. But I became a *motivated agent*, too.

## AGENCY AND PERSONALITY

In the theater and in everyday social life, actors have secrets that no observers can see. Actors play their roles on a social stage, but no matter how long audience members watch the performance, they can never know for sure what is going on in the actors' heads. Whether the actors themselves have full conscious knowledge is the question that Freud famously asked, but everybody agrees to this: *Something* is going on in the actors' heads. Something that the audience can only infer. *What does the actor want?* What is the actor *really* trying to accomplish? One answer is this: The actor is trying to accomplish the role. The actor wants to enact the performance the situation demands. This answer is true enough, as Goffman (1959) and other role theorists have traditionally argued, but it may seem trivial or unsatisfying for many observers, and for the actors themselves. The audience is still left wondering about the motivational secrets that presumably lie somewhere inside the performers on stage, beyond the audience's direct gaze. What is interesting here is not so much that observers cannot directly know the secrets inside but rather that they know they cannot know, that observers always expect that there *must* be something beyond their direct observations, something inside the actors' heads, something *motivational*, something about desire, want, goal, and value. We assume that actors want something within and beyond their social performance. We assume that human beings are motivated, goal-directed *agents*. And even when actors are not acting, even when it seems they are doing nothing at all, we assume that, as motivated agents, they still want something.

To be an agent is to make choices and, as a result of those choices, to move forward in life in a self-determined and goal-directed manner (Martin, Sugarman, & Thompson, 2003). Human agency suggests intention, volition, will, purpose, and some modicum of personal control in life. For over 2,000 years, scholars have debated the extent to which human beings have any agency at all. Are we free to choose our own fates? Or are we pawns in a complex chess game wherein factors external to the self—be they God, material reality, social forces, reinforcement contingencies, genes, or dumb luck—make all the moves? What seems clear, however, is that most human beings much of the time *believe* they do have *some* degree of agency, if not in practice, at least in principle and according to prevailing cultural understandings about what agency is (Haggard & Tsakiris, 2009). A belief in personal agency (even if some philosophers consider it to be a belief in an illusion or myth) seems to be a good thing for most people, most of the time.

Nonetheless, agency feelings and beliefs may be fragile and historically contingent. The heroes of Homer's *Iliad* and the patriarchs of the Old Testament made war, sired offspring, and even sacrificed their own children in response to voices in their heads (and other experiences, e.g., visions), which they attributed to external agents such as Athena, Apollo, and the God of the Old Testament. With this in mind, philosopher Julian Jaynes (1976) suggested that the tellers of these tales did not originally understand the actors to be agents, perhaps because they—the tellers— did not understand themselves to be agents either. Jaynes provocatively argued that human beings actually *learned* how to think of themselves as motivated agents—invented the idea of free will—sometime during the millennium before Christ.

Even today, a sense of agency may slip away when we feel that our lives are controlled by powerful external sources. When a capricious or punishing environment fails to support or reinforce goal-directed striving, for example, the person may experience a decrement in what psychologist Albert Bandura (1989) calls *self-efficacy*—the person's belief that he or she can execute goal-directed behavior in a successful manner, especially under challenging or stressful circumstances. Over the course of repeated and uncontrollable punishments, a person may even quit trying to accomplish goals altogether, descending into a kind of learned helplessness (Seligman, 1975). When agency dies, some people simply give up.

The grand theories of personality that were proposed in the 20th century varied widely with respect to the emphasis they placed on human agency. Freud, in his psychodynamic theory, suggested that the prime forces controlling behavior and experience were located in the unforgiving external world (societal norms and laws, physical constraints) and in the unconscious recesses of the human mind. The id and the superego— as opposed to each other as they seemed to be—shared the role of exerting implacable pressure on a beleaguered ego. In the face of the id's sexual and aggressive urges and the moral commands issued by society and the superego, the ego's powers of agency were limited at best. Still, Freud believed some agential control could be exerted, and the ego psychologists who followed in Freud's footsteps (e.g., theorists Anna Freud, Erich Fromm, Erik Erikson, and Robert White) granted the ego greater powers of coping, mastery, and agential control. Early behaviorist views of personality contended that human action, like the movements of rats and pigeons, was nearly 100% controlled by external forces. However, the social-cognitive theories that evolved out of behaviorism, such as theories developed by Albert Bandura (1989) and Walter Mischel (2004), tended to view human beings as potentially rational and deliberative decision makers, endowed with expectancies, values, and social learning strategies.

Throughout the history of personality psychology, those theories that have focused prime attention on the motivational *dynamics* of behavior—the forces that energize and direct what people do—have had to take a stand on the issue of agency. But many personality theories are not primarily concerned with motivational dynamics. For example, theories of dispositional traits and their temperament precursors focus mainly on individual differences in the *structure* of personality. As we saw in Chapters 2–4 of this book, structural theories of personality dispositions tend to ask questions like these: What are the different types of social actors we encounter in daily life? What are the basic traits that differentiate one person from the next in a social group? If a psychological scientist can show that a person high in extraversion tends to engage in highly sociable behavior and experience positive emotions across a range of situations, the scientist does not really need to know *why* the extravert does (and feels) what the extravert does (and feels), in the sense of knowing what happen to be the extravert's goals, plans, and values. Put more generally, you *do not need to know a person as a motivated agent in order to make a reasonable prediction about what he or she will do as a social actor.* If her social reputation is that she is outgoing, lively, and spontaneous, then the reasonable prediction to make is that she will continue to act in this manner, regardless of her motives and goals in life, across many situations and contexts, more so than somebody low on this trait.

It is not that the dispositional trait perspective in personality psychology rules out human agency, or conceives of persons as nonagents. It is rather that the trait perspective takes no position when it comes to the question of human agency. It says: "I refuse to answer on the grounds it doesn't matter." From the standpoint of the trait perspective, extraverts are extraverts, regardless of whether they want to be or not, regardless of what their goals, plans, projects, and values are for the future. People high in agreeableness show friendly and caring behavior across many situations. People high in neuroticism suffer from chronic negative affect. Do people high in neuroticism *want to* suffer this way? Probably not. Did they sit down one day and *decide* to become high in neuroticism? Surely not. The trait concepts that provide critical, invaluable, and incontestable information as to how social actors will feel and behave across different situations and over time can never fully penetrate the mask the actor wears.

*What do the actors want? What are their goals and values?* As members of the audience, we cannot even ask these questions until we switch our epistemological frame and view human beings as motivated, goal-oriented, planful agents, as well as social actors. As we saw in Chapter

2, people do not even know they are social actors until about age 2. It takes longer still before they fully understand the nature of their own motivated agency—until second grade, or even later.

## A PORTRAIT OF THE AGENT AS A YOUNG CHILD

Like all animals, *Homo sapiens* is designed to pursue goals. We must, in some manner, go out into the environment and identify what we need (to survive and procreate), and we must move our bodies in some manner to get it. Even the newborn human infant behaves in a goal-directed fashion, turning its head toward the nipple to suck, positioning its body in such a way as to achieve the goal of nursing. It is fair to say, then, that human beings, like other animals, exhibit a primitive sense of motivated agency from the very get-go. Moreover, much of what we do on a daily basis is in the service of one kind of goal or another, from brushing our teeth in the morning to searching for the car keys in order to drive to the store. In this obvious sense, social actors are nearly always motivated agents, too. The actor always wants something, which makes the actor an agent.

It is one thing, however, to say that human beings typically behave in a goal-directed manner, even as infants, but it is quite another to say that they *conceive of themselves (and others) as motivated agents who pursue valued goals over time*. Agency in the full sense—encompassing self-conscious striving, will, choice, deliberative planning, and purpose—requires years to develop. Human beings take an important step along the developmental path when, toward the end of the first year of life, they exhibit a marked interest in *intentionality* (Tomasello, 2000; Woodward, 2009). At approximately 9 months of age, infants begin to behave in ways suggesting that they understand what others are *trying* to do. They imitate and improvise on adults' intentional, goal-directed behaviors at much higher rates than random behaviors. They attend to objects and events toward which adults express interest and positive emotions, as if to suggest that they, too, may *want* what others want. They decode others' behaviors to determine the extent to which the actions are intended or wanted. For example, 9-month-olds (but not a 6-month-olds) express more impatience (e. g., reaching, looking away) when an adult is unwilling to give them a toy (when the adult refuses to give it) than when the adult is simply unable to give it to them (because she drops or fumbles the toy, according to the script laid out by the experimenter) (Behne,

Carpenter, Call, & Tomasello, 2005). In this clever study, 9-month-olds can tell when the adult intends to keep the toy away from them (which they find to be very annoying) and when the adult unintentionally (it seems) screws up. They are more forgiving in the latter scenario, as if to suggest that trying (agency) is what really counts!

Around the same age, infants begin to engage with adults in scenarios of *joint attention*. For example, they visually follow a caregiver's pointing finger to find the object to which the caregiver is calling attention, then turn back to the caregiver to confirm that they are indeed looking at the intended object. They may also hold up or point to an object for an adult to see, thereby attempting to direct the adult's attention to it. In these scenarios, the infant aims to coordinate its own intentions with those of another agent, as if to say: "Let us both agree that we intend to (want to) look at (make sense of) this particular object." The cognitive scientist Michael Tomasello (2000) argues that this kind of communicative exchange forms the basis of all cultural cognition. In effect, the infant and the adult arrive at a common ground of shared representations regarding external reality. Based on a shared intention, they establish an agreement regarding the meaning of something in the external world.

Long before human beings explicitly know they are agents, they are primed to detect agency in the world. In the second year of life, toddlers often attribute intentionality to behaviors they observe in others and, in some cases, to actions that emanate from nonagents (Luo & Baillargeon, 2010). As an example of the latter, they may do things to suggest that they (implicitly) believe a toy or doll has its own point of view on the world and is motivated to enact its own desires.

In the third and fourth years of life, children develop a more explicit theory of mind (Apperly, 2012; Wellman, 1993). "Theory of mind" is the common-sense, folk-psychological conception that you and I and most human beings have about why people do what they do. We generally assume that people do things *because they want to do them* (desire) and in light of *what they understand to be true* (belief). If I observe Amanda searching for cookies in the cabinet, I naturally assume that (1) Amanda wants cookies (she is hungry; she has desire), and (2) Amanda believes the cookies are in the cabinet (otherwise, she would look for them someplace else). Theory of mind is essentially a formal (and very simple) explication of basic motivated agency: Agents move forward in time (pursue goals) in order to satisfy their desires and in accord with what they believe to be true. In their minds, agents have desires and beliefs, and they are therefore motivated to act upon them.

Developmental psychologists have conducted hundreds of studies on theory of mind. A common methodology they use is the *false-belief task*. In one version, children are told a story about Sally and Andrew (Apperly, 2012). Sally is playing with her toy, then puts it away in the cupboard before going outside. While she is outside, Andrew moves the toy from the cupboard to a chest of drawers. Sally then returns inside to resume play with her toy. Now, the experimenter asks the child: *Where will Sally look for her toy?* If you were the participant (and if you are paying attention to my example), I hope you would say: "In the cupboard." (After all, that is where she left it.) But if you were 3 years old, you might say: "In the chest of drawers." Why would you say such a dumb thing? Because you are not taking Sally's *mind* into consideration. You are imposing your own privileged perspective (you saw Andrew move the toy) on to Sally. But Sally did not see Andrew do it; therefore, she must *believe* the toy is still where she left it. Children ages 2 and 3 years typically flunk this kind of explicit false-belief test. By age 5 or 6, they nearly always pass (Wellman, Cross, & Watson, 2001).

Still, there are broad individual differences in theory of mind development. Research suggests that children develop theory of mind more quickly if they also (1) show high levels of EC and executive function (abilities to suppress impulses and focus on the future; Pelicano, 2007); (2) have parents who engage them in conversations that make repeated reference to mental and emotional states (Astington & Jenkins, 1995); (3) have older siblings with whom they have presumably gained experience in figuring out other minds (Perner, Ruffman, & Leekham, 1994); (4) have more experience with children's storybooks, through which they learn about characters' minds (Mar, Tackett, & Moore, 2010); and (5) are rated by their preschool teachers as more sociable and less aggressive than other children (Astington, 2003). Theory of mind is intimately tied to cognitive development and to the workings of childhood temperament, and these relations may express themselves in different ways in different cultures (Lane et al., 2013).

It is hard to imagine what life would be like for our eusocial species if human beings did not develop theory of mind. If we did not understand ourselves as mindful agents who strive to put our desires and beliefs into action, how would we be able to cooperate on joint ventures, establish alliances, develop commitments to others and to groups, and predict the future? Yet it is just this kind of deficit that may be partly responsible for the odd behaviors and social difficulties shown by some autistic children (Baron-Cohen, 1995; Losh & Capps, 2006). Research has shown that autistic children often perform poorly on theory-of-mind tasks. Case studies of autism, moreover, sometimes suggest a remarkable lack of personal agency, which can border on depersonalization. Behavior may follow performance scripts, but it seems to lack an internally generated purpose, as if it is being performed by a robot. In extreme cases, not only does the autistic child fail to articulate personal goals and desires, but he or she may find it difficult even to take personal ownership of subjective experience. For example, the neurologist and writer Oliver Sacks (1995) tells the story of Stephen Wiltshire, a prodigy with autism, who, despite his extraordinary artistic talents, never seems to develop a sense of personal agency:

> I had the feeling that the whole visible world flowed through Stephen, like a river, without making sense, without being appropriated, without becoming part of him in the least. That though he might, in a sense, retain everything he saw, it was retained as something external, unintegrated, and never built on, connected, revised, never influencing or influenced by anything else. (p. 56)

For most children, however, an early appreciation of intentionality has blossomed, by age 5 or 6, into a full understanding that human beings are fundamentally intentional, purposeful, goal-directed agents. In fact, many children seem to overdo their newfound understanding of agency, imputing purposeful design in most anything they see (Kelemen, 2004). They project agential qualities onto inanimate and even imaginary objects, such as favorite toys and imaginary companions. They conclude that artifacts in the environment are the result of the agential activities of others—all things that exist were made by purposeful agents who self-consciously set forth to make them.

The idea of an ultimate maker makes good sense to a mind primed to detect agency (Bering, 2006). Religious accounts of the creation of the world hold special appeal for children of this age, an appeal that often endures for the remainder of the lifespan if the belief is reinforced by cultural factors. In the words of one developmental psychologist, young children endowed with theory of mind are "intuitive theists" who express a "promiscuous teleology" (Kelemen, 2004, p. 295). God is imagined as a purposeful agent whose own desires, goals, and beliefs are translated into motivated action. Motivated agents perceive the world as populated with and determined by other motivated agents, and all can be traced back to an ultimate Agent, whose own desires, goals, and beliefs set everything into motion.

## BECOMING GOOD: COGNITIVE DEVELOPMENT IN GRADE SCHOOL

In the *Nicomachean Ethics*, Aristotle posed a question that was as important in ancient Athens as it is today: How do we live a good life? Happiness (in Greek, *eudaimonia*) is the ultimate aim of human action, Aristotle wrote, the natural consequence of a life well lived. For Aristotle, life itself was like playing a musical instrument. Like the finest musician who achieves an exalted level of musical *virtuosity*, the happiest man or woman ideally attains a kind of excellence (in Greek, *arête*) in living. But whereas the musician endeavors to create a beautiful sound, the person who lives an excellent and happy life strives to express *virtue*, for human happiness depends on contributing to the common good in some way. Two thousand years before Darwin, Aristotle sensed that ours is a profoundly eusocial species, meaning that the good for the individual has to be tied, though sometimes in complex and nonobvious ways, to the good of the group. At some deep level, we human beings know this, which is why we devote so much time and energy to socializing our young in the arts of virtue. According to Aristotle, socialization and education for virtue require extensive practice, as would be the case for playing a musical instrument or learning a craft. We learn by doing, Aristotle contended. Young children, therefore, must be taught how to behave in ways that are consistent with the virtues that society holds dear, such as courage, temperance, justice, and friendship, even before they are able to comprehend the meanings of these abstract terms:

> The virtues we do acquire by first exercising them, just as happens in the arts. Anything that we have to learn to do we learn by the actual doing of it: people become builders by building and instrumentalists by playing instruments. Similarly, we become just by performing just acts, temperate by performing temperate ones, brave by performing brave ones. . . . In a word then, like activities produce like dispositions. Hence, we must give our activities a certain quality because it is their characteristics that determine the resulting dispositions. So it is a matter of no small importance what sorts of habits we form from the earliest age—it makes a vast difference, or rather all the difference in the world. (Aristotle, 2004, p. 32)

Virtue begins when social actors habitually perform good behaviors, Aristotle believed. For social actors, habits lead to dispositional traits. But habits get you only half the way there. According to Aristotle, habits paved the way for the eventual development of *character* (in Greek, *ethos*). To express a virtuous character, a person must engage in rational and deliberative choice, and then act upon the choice: "Acts that are incidentally virtuous [should be] distinguished from those that are done knowingly, of choice, and by a virtuous disposition" (Aristotle, 2004, p. 37). Aristotle used the example of courage to illustrate the distinction: "The quasi-courage that is due to spirit seems to be the most natural, and if it includes deliberative choice and purpose it is considered to be courage" (p. 72). Translating Aristotle's insight into contemporary terms, a courageous temperament (say, positive emotionality, as described in Chapter 2 of this book) may spur the *social actor* to behave boldly and with great confidence, even fearlessness, which may function as a kind of behavioral or emotional precursor to courage; courage in the fullest sense, however, is manifest only when the *motivated agent* rationally considers various contingencies, then purposively makes a choice. Reality—dictated by nature and society—presents us with the contingencies. Within these constraints, we must deliberate and ultimately exercise our human agency:

> Choice involves deliberation. . . . What we deliberate about is practical measures that lie within our power; this is the class of things that actually remains for the accepted types of cause are nature, necessity, and chance, and also mind and human agency of all kinds. . . . The effects about which we deliberate are those which are produced by our agency. . . . (p. 57)

As we have already seen, research findings trace the development of motivated agency from the infant's early appreciation for intentionality to the emergence of theory of mind. By age 5, most children understand that mindful human agents, themselves included, strive to achieve desires in accord with belief. But if agents are to be successful in achieving the goals they formulate in their minds, they have to proceed in a deliberative and rational manner, as Aristotle knew. As we saw in Chapter 3, temperament can help out. Young children who show high levels of EC are better able (than their more impulsive counterparts) to resist impulses and weigh options. EC and the development of empathy in the preschool years contribute to the development of a conscience (Kochanska & Aksan, 2006). It is fair to say that, by age 5, most children have developed a rudimentary conscience, or what Freud called a "superego." But the kind of rationality required for the exercise of Aristotelian virtue, and thereby the full expression of a good life, may require still more cognitive development and more socialization. What seems still to be needed is exactly what White (1965) argued is ideally achieved in the age 5–7 shift.

With respect to cognitive development, Jean Piaget (1970) proposed that around the age of 7, children become remarkably more rational, systematic, and logical in their thinking about the objective world. In what Piaget considered to be *the* developmental watershed in human ontogeny, children begin to exhibit *concrete operations* in their daily thinking. Piaget's stage of concrete operations marks the ability to think about the concrete world as a logically organized, rule-governed reality. From the perspective of concrete operations, children begin to understand the deep logic of the material world—how the nature of things may remain the same even when surface appearances are changed; how the natural world follows lawful regularities that can be formalized in verbal or mathematical terms; how reality can be quantified, classified, and systematically organized. Although subsequent research has suggested that Piaget may have gotten some of the details wrong about concrete operations and may have underestimated the rational abilities of younger children, the overall developmental shift he observed is widely recognized.

I think that concrete operations erupted in full force during my second-grade year. I suddenly perceived that the concrete world could be known in terms of its logical and systematic properties. This became a huge asset in schoolwork, as much for its motivational power as my newfound skills in cognition. From the standpoint of midlife, however, my clearest recollections regarding the impact of concrete operations pertain to Halloween and baseball. At ages 4 and 5, my immediate aim after finishing trick or treat was to eat the candy I had collected. By second grade, I had discovered an elaborate, concrete operational ritual: Pour all the candy out onto the living room floor and *sort it* into categories; organize the candy by size, chocolate content, perceived value, or whatever; develop rational *plans* to eat the candy over the course of the next week in such a way as to maximize enjoyment; formulate rational schemes to cheat my younger brother out of his best candy (the poor fool—he had not yet attained concrete operations) through devious (but deeply rational) trades, like this one: Jeff, I will give you *two* bubble gums (worth a penny each) for that *one* chunky bar (worth at least 10 cents). Because two is more than one, my brother complied.

On baseball, I had zero interest and knew absolutely nothing about how the game was played, until the spring of 1962 (toward the end of second grade), when I suddenly began collecting baseball cards, to the point of an obsession. I became fascinated with the rules of baseball, the structure of the Major Leagues, the standings, the records, the deep logic of it all. I began to play baseball, too, and my father took me to my first Major League baseball game (Cardinals 15, Cubs 3; I sulked all the way home). I memorized the information provided on the backs of baseball cards (batting averages, home runs, runs batted in [RBIs], earned run averages, win–loss ratios, final team standings), which all pertained to the previous (1961) season. And what a season that was, even though I never saw it directly. The Yankees beat the Reds in the World Series. Maris hit 61 home runs to break Ruth's record, but Mantle might have hit as many had he not sustained an injury in September. Whitey Ford went 25–4 during the regular season. Norm Cash hit .361 to lead the American League (with 41 home runs and 132 RBI's—an extraordinary performance; he should have been Most Valuable Player [MVP]). Vada Pinson was Rookie of the Year in the National League. The Cubs finished seventh (out of eight). To this day, I have retained an astounding amount of useless information about the 1961 season! Ask me anything.

The implications of concrete operations go beyond schoolwork and baseball, and this gets us back to Aristotle. Once a person understands that laws and logic govern the material world, he or she begins to appreciate how the same may also hold true, more or less, for society. Very young children know that there are social rules and conventions, but they do not truly understand why. They do not typically have a broad conception of a social world out there; a world beyond the immediate family or play group; a world made up of school, neighborhoods, organizations, cities, states, and so on—not unlike teams organized into leagues in baseball. But after they make the 5–7 shift, they get it. In *A Portrait of the Artist as a Young Man*, James Joyce (1916/1964, pp. 15–16) describes how Irish schoolboy Stephen Dedalus, upon considering his geography lesson, thinks about his own place in a hierarchically ordered social reality:

> He opened the geography to study the lesson; but he could not learn the names of places in America. Still they were all different places that had those different names. They were all in different countries and the countries were in continents and the continents were in the world and the world was in the universe.
>
> He turned to the flyleaf of the geography and read what he had written there: himself, his name, and where he was.
>
> Stephen Dedalus<br>Class of Elements<br>Clongowes Wood College<br>Sallins

County Kildare
Ireland
Europe
The World
The Universe

It should come as no surprise that Stephen's mind moves next to the topic of God. He wonders: What is the ultimate source of this hierarchical order? And what governs social relations in the world? Whether they think about God in this regard or not, children endowed with concrete operations are now able to consider the laws and norms that pertain to broader social collectives, to society, and even to a moral universe writ large.

In Lawrence Kohlberg's (1969) classic theory of moral development, the emergence of concrete operations helps to catalyze the transition from the *preconventional* to the *conventional* stages of moral reasoning. At preconventional stages, Kohlberg argued, children (and some adults) determine what is good or bad exclusively in terms of the effects of an action upon the self. Moral reasoning is essentially hedonistic and self-centered. At conventional stages, by contrast, older children (and many adults) rely on a broader consideration of interpersonal and societal standards (conventions) to determine what a moral person should do. From the conventional perspective, the child understands the social world as a more or less ordered and rule-governed reality and realizes, at some level, that such a structure *needs to be true* and real, or else there would be chaos. From the standpoint of conventional moral reasoning, it is in the very nature of society that people must play within the bounds of conventional rules. Not to do so would be like disregarding the umpire's call at first base, or refusing to return to the dugout after striking out at the plate. The game would fall apart. Even when 10-year-olds decide to break the rules (as they often do), they typically know that they are violating some kind of social convention. They may not care about the conventions, but they understand why they exist. Going back to my Baptist Sunday school example, older children blessed with concrete operations have reached something like an age of moral accountability. In Aristotle's terms, they are now fully capable of virtue—and vice.

As children become more capable of concrete operational thought, they make parallel advances in the realm of social perspective taking. Developmental psychologist Robert Selman (1980) traced the growth of perspective taking from the relatively egocentric understanding of very young children to the complex societal perspectives exhibited in early adolescence. According to Selman, most children around the age of 5 understand that different people have different perspectives on the world. But they assume these differences are mainly due to the different information each person has. By age 7 or 8, however, children recognize that even when different people have the same information, they may still see the world in different and conflicting ways. Children learn to coordinate their own perspective with those of others and eventually to adopt the objective perspective of a disinterested third party. In early adolescence, they are readily able to assume the broad perspective of society in general. Virtuous, prosocial behavior tends to track advances in perspective taking and role playing. Research has consistently revealed positive associations between prosocial behaviors and highly developed abilities to assume and understand the perspectives of other people (Eisenberg, Fabes, & Spinrad, 2006). Advances in social perspective taking are part of the reason that prosocial behavior itself tends to increase across the years of middle childhood.

In most societies today, the broad institutional context wherein the cognitive and social developments of middle childhood are most clearly expressed and refined is *elementary school*. Educational systems vary widely from one culture to the next, but certain core features of schooling can readily be observed. First, children typically *leave home* to attend school. As a result, their social worlds expand dramatically to encompass teachers, school workers, and a larger set of peers. In the classroom and on the playground, children meet new and more complex challenges in negotiating interpersonal relationships.

Second, schooling blends academic concerns with issues of character development. In the United States, public and private elementary schools focus largely on individual knowledge and skills acquisition. Children develop the basic tools of learning as teachers strive to foster verbal and analytic problem solving. Instruction centers on rules, descriptions, and abstract concepts. Children are exposed to issues and problems in a range of academic areas, from social studies to mathematics. At the same time, however, schools aim to inculcate certain values, such as honesty, cooperation, respect for authority, and citizenship. Ideally children learn to *do well* in their academic studies, but they also learn to *be good*. Different societies prioritize different skills and different character virtues, but all societies want their children to master these skills and virtues; all societies aim to produce good children.

*How can I be good?* Good at what? Good at reading, writing, and arithmetic—and good at sports, video games, music, art, and making stuff. Good at friendship. And, perhaps most importantly (in the minds of many parents and friends) just plain *good*—as in being a good person. The psychosocial environment of elementary school is organized around the question of goodness, the most consequential result of the age 5–7 shift. As motivated agents, children set for themselves goals about doing well and being good. Equipped now with concrete operational skills, children systematically compare themselves to each other on a range of dimensions and qualities, sorting it all out as I used to sort my candy on Halloween night. Alex is good at sports, but not math. Courtney exhibits unsurpassed talent in the visual arts, but she is an average student otherwise. Nicole's marks on the fourth-grade standardized tests put her at the 85th percentile—pretty good, indeed! Sam is the most popular kid in the class; everybody likes him. Jeffrey is a bully. In the minds of his classmates, he is *not* good. In his own mind, he is better than they are.

The question of goodness lies at the heart of Erik Erikson's (1963) characterization of the grade school years. According to Erikson's famous model of psychosocial development, middle childhood comprises the fourth of eight stages in the life cycle, the stage that pits *industry* against *inferiority*. To exhibit "industry" is to work hard in order to master the academic and interpersonal tasks that middle childhood sets forth. To experience "inferiority" is to fall behind, to finish low down in the standings. As Erikson saw it, schooling teaches children how to use the *tools* and assume the *roles* that society deems to be central for becoming a productive member of the adult world. The tools may be not only pencils, protractors, and art supplies; or computers and iPads; but also baseball gloves, hockey sticks, musical instruments, and even hunting rifles. The roles are the structured scenarios for social relations that will prove to be as important as anything else for getting along and getting ahead in the group—how to be a good friend, for example, a good daughter, a trusted team player. Children are challenged to do well and to be good when it comes to mastery of skills, tools, and roles. In one domain after another, some do well, and others do poorly. And everybody is keeping track.

## SELF-ESTEEM

The development of motivated agency reaches a critical threshold for personality when children begin to formulate and systematically pursue long-term goals in school, social relationships, and family life. It is

difficult to identify a discrete moment when this psychological phenomenon breaks through, but it is rare before the age of 5 and increasingly
common after age 7. At any given moment, preschool children may have
goals; but they do not commonly wake up in the morning with an agenda
in their conscious minds about what they will achieve today, this week,
and this year, and how they will systematically go about trying to achieve
it, what obstacles they will need to overcome, whom they will need to
influence, how they will need to use their skills, and so on. They don't
typically have a plan. As they move through elementary school, however,
children become increasingly purposeful, strategic, and future-oriented.
As they become self-conscious and planful motivated agents, *a second
layer of personality begins to form,* layered over the dispositional traits
that continue to develop and to shape their performance as social actors.
For motivated agents, *personality is more about goals and values than it
is about traits.* If an observer, therefore, wishes to characterize the personality of an older child (say, a 10-year-old), the observer must consider
more than the 10-year-old's dispositional personality traits. To understand an older child's unique adjustment to the world, one must inquire
into his or her motivational agenda. What does the older child want and
value? What goals does the older child recurrently pursue? What plans
does the older child have for the future? And how well is the older child
doing, compared to others and in the older child's own mind, regarding
progress toward achieving valued goals?

Research in developmental psychology suggests that older children
and preadolescents strive for many different kinds of social goals. Among
the most important goals for social adjustment in school and interpersonal relationships are those that can be grouped into the two superordinate categories of *affiliation* and *power* (Ojanen, Grönroos, & Salmivalli,
2005). These two categories roughly parallel the evolutionary challenges
of getting along and getting ahead in human groups. Thus, affiliation
goals involve being liked by and feeling close to peers, and power goals
are about social dominance and status. Interestingly, preschool children
do not seem to distinguish these two aims (Hawley, 2002). By the time
children are 8 or 9 years of age, however, they not only recognize the
difference between affiliation and power but they also demonstrate consistent motivational tendencies in prioritizing and pursuing goals related
to these two domains (Rodkin, Ryan, Jamison, & Wilson, 2013). From
grade school onward, girls appear to care somewhat more about affiliation, and boys about power, but both are considered to be very important
by nearly all children, even when they feel that they are not faring well in
attaining goals in these two domains.

In an illuminating study of 980 Finnish children in third, fourth, and fifth grades, researchers found that the motivational domains of affiliation and power break out into three factors: social development goals, demonstration–approach goals, and demonstration–avoid goals (Rodkin et al., 2013). Mapping directly onto affiliation, *social development goals* aim at improving relationships and social skills, as in gaining insights into friends or learning how to get along with others. Social relationships are formed, maintained, and developed for the inherent positive qualities they provide. With respect to the power domain (demonstrating social status), a basic distinction was observed between the goal of achieving dominance on the one hand and the goal of avoiding being dominated on the other. *Demonstration–approach* goals aim at attaining status and garnering positive feedback from others. *Demonstration–avoid* goals involve avoiding negative judgments from others (e.g., not being seen as a "geek" or "loser").

The findings from the study showed that children who consistently pursued social development goals tend to engage in more prosocial behavior and to be seen by their peers as nice and caring. But they were *not* the most popular kids in the class. Popularity was positively associated with demonstration–approach goals and negatively related to demonstration–avoid goals. The most popular children were those who pursued goals aimed at attaining status; the least popular were those whose main aims were to avoid being rejected and dominated, perhaps as a function of their self-perceived lower status. Interestingly, demonstration–approach goals were also positively associated with *aggression*. In a finding that distresses many teachers and parents, numerous studies have shown that popularity among older children and adolescents (both boys and girls) is often linked to at least a moderate degree of aggressive behavior, as well as to social dominance, athleticism, and physical attractiveness (Hartup & Abecassis, 2002). Prioritizing goals related to improving relationships and expressing care for others (social development goals) may buy some degree of intimacy and likability, but it is not the best ticket to popularity among older children and adolescents. Getting along and getting ahead are not exactly the same thing.

The extent to which older children and adolescents achieve valued goals appears to have a substantial impact on their *self-esteem*. Self-esteem is the overall evaluation—from highly positive to highly negative—that a person makes of the self. Before the age of about 8 or 9, most children see themselves in a brightly positive light, showing nearly uniformly high levels of self-esteem (Harter, 2006). Around second and third grade, however, something rather dramatic happens. Marked individual differences in self-esteem begin to appear, with some children maintaining high levels, others dropping to very low levels of self-esteem, and many falling somewhere in between. Self-esteem may also be domain-specific (Marsh & Hattie, 1996): A child may feel good about him- or herself in sports but feel inferior in schoolwork. Roughly tracking the age 5–7 shift, it is as if self-esteem suddenly becomes a relevant issue in the mind of children once they have, in turn, consolidated a theory of mind, developed cognitive skills linked to concrete operations, and begun to pursue temporally extended personal goals.

The idea that self-esteem may be tied closely to human agency goes back at least as far as the seminal writings of William James. James (1892/1963) defined self-esteem with a famous ratio: Self-esteem = "success" divided by "pretensions" (p. 175). What James depicted as "pretensions" includes the goals, values, and expectations that people seek to achieve; success is what people feel when they achieve them, or at least make good progress toward achieving them. The implication in James's simple formula is that if people did not have pretensions—if they never held out valued goals to pursue—they would never have to worry about self-esteem. In other words, self-esteem is strongly linked to the concept of a motivated agent, a goal-oriented striver, a decision maker who exerts his or her will in order to achieve valued ends in the future. Indeed, self-esteem's appearance on the psychological scene, around age 8 or 9 years, signals the culmination of the development of motivated agency in the childhood years, as indicated in Table 5.1.

Many researchers suggest that the emergence of individual differences in self-esteem around the age of 8 or 9 results in part from increasing expectations for achievement coming from parents and teachers and from cognitive-developmental changes that enable older children to compare their own goal-based achievements in various domains—from sports to academics to moral behavior—to the achievements of others. Of course, self-evaluations appear even in areas in which it occasionally feels as if little can be done by way of goal attainment. For example, relative judgments of physical attractiveness play into self-esteem, especially for girls (Harter, 2006). Even in this domain, however, young people (and older people) strive for improvement, through clothing, hairstyles, and the like early on, and in later years through dieting, exercise, plastic surgery, and on and on. For some people, improving physical appearance can become an overriding life goal and a key element in determining overall self-esteem.

For the motivated agent, then, a central issue is this: How well are you doing? To answer the question, you take stock of your valued goals

**TABLE 5.1. Developmental Steps in Becoming a Motivated Agent**

| Age (years) | Developmental emergence |
|---|---|
| 0 | *Goal directedness.* Even newborn infants respond to the world in a goal-directed manner. For example, the baby moves its head toward the nipple in order to suck. Human behavior is rarely random. |
| 1 | *Intentionality.* Toward the end of the first year, infants show a preference for observing and imitating the intentional, rather than unintentional, behaviors of others. They show a rudimentary understanding of the fact that people intend to do things. |
| | *Joint attention.* When attending to an object, an infant may check back with the caregiver to determine if the caregiver is also attending to the same thing as a way of gaining information on the caregiver's intentions and point of view. |
| 2 | *Agency projection.* In the second year of life, toddlers attribute intentionality to other people and to many objects in the world, such as toys and dolls. They may reveal an implicit assumption that these objects possess their own agency (e.g., desires, beliefs). Some researchers argue that children as young as 18 months therefore show a primitive, implicit "theory of mind." |
| 3–4 | *Theory of mind.* Children develop an explicit theory of mind: They come to understand that people are motivated agents in the sense that they have desires and beliefs in their minds upon which they act. Goal-directed behavior is motivated by what an agent wants (desire) and what an agent believes to be true. Children apply this understanding to themselves. |
| 5–7 | *Schooling and socialization.* In most societies, children leave home to begin school around age 5 and/or they begin systematic training in social and technical practices that contribute to the economic and moral well-being of the group. Children take on increased responsibilities, such as minding younger siblings and helping out with domestic tasks. |
| 7–8 | *Concrete operations.* Thinking about the concrete world becomes more systematic, rational, and logical. Children become experts in classifying and organizing the material world; they are able to apply rational cognitive operations to make sense of reality. The powers of concrete operations enable an understanding of moral and social conventions while enhancing skills in planning and goal-setting. |
| 8–9 | *Self-esteem.* Children begin to evaluate themselves in terms of how well they are doing with respect to achieving valued personal goals, often linked to concerns about peer acceptance and status. When goal attainment is high, they experience high levels of self-esteem; failure in goal pursuit leads to low self-esteem. |

and evaluate your progress toward achieving them. Social comparison facilitates the evaluation. You may look around and conclude that you are doing quite well compared to others. In James's (1892/1963) terms, your pretensions may be high, but social comparison suggests that your successes are also substantial. Or you may see that you are not doing so well, compared with others in your social environment. In this case, social comparison tells you that the discrepancy between your successes and your pretensions is quite large, leaving you with a distressingly tiny fraction for self-esteem.

As soon as individual differences in self-esteem begin to show up in middle childhood, girls show lower scores than boys (Harter, 2006). The sex difference persists in varying degrees across much of the rest of the lifespan, with the largest advantages for males typically showing up in middle and late adolescence (Harter, 2006; Robins, Trzesniewski, Gosling, Tracy, & Potter, 2002). Children and adolescents from East Asian societies, such as China and Japan, tend to show somewhat lower scores on self-esteem than their American and Canadian counterparts (Harter, 2006). Still, warm and supportive parenting in both Eastern and Western societies tends to predict high self-esteem in offspring (Gutman & Eccles, 2007). From adolescence onward, African Americans tend to score higher on self-esteem than do European Americans (Twenge & Crocker, 2002). Following adolescence, self-esteem scores tend to rise gradually, reaching a peak around age 60 years, then beginning to decline around age 70 (Robins et al., 2002).

Social psychologists have conducted a wealth of research on the vicissitudes of self-esteem (Baumeister & Bushman, 2008). What factors enhance or undermine self-esteem? How do people maintain high levels of self-esteem, even when they receive negative feedback? What benefits follow from having high self-esteem, and what negative ramifications follow from low self-esteem? For example, high self-esteem tends to be associated with greater initiative in the pursuit of goals and greater enjoyment of success in goal attainment. Low self-esteem is associated with fear of failure, higher levels of internal conflict and ambivalence, and with a cautious, prevention-focused orientation toward life's challenges. At the same time, there is considerable evidence to suggest that high levels of self-esteem may not be all that they are cracked up to be. It is not clear that boosting self-esteem actually improves people's performance on challenging tasks. What seems more likely is that success on challenging tasks boosts self-esteem. Cross-national comparisons suggest that many Americans report unrealistically high levels of self-esteem compared to citizens of other countries. Bullies, violent criminals, and narcissists often show very high levels of self-esteem. Furthermore, pursuing self-esteem as an end in itself can be counterproductive, leading to lower levels of well-being and diminished commitments to other people (Crocker & Park, 2004).

## NARCISSISM: A PROBLEM OF UNMITIGATED AGENCY

In the ancient Greek legend, the beautiful boy Narcissus falls so completely in love with the reflection of himself in a pool that he plunges into the water and drowns. The story provides the mythical source for the modern conception of *narcissism*, which is conceived as excessive self-love and the attendant qualities of self-centeredness, arrogance, and a lack of regard for other human beings. Empirical efforts to assess individual differences in a tendency toward narcissism consistently identify two central features: *grandiosity* and a *sense of entitlement* (Brown, Budzek, & Tamborski, 2009). Grandiosity is self-importance: The narcissist believes that he or she is an exceptional human being, more important than anybody else, destined for greatness. Sense of entitlement is the expectation that other people will also see the narcissist in the same way and therefore shower admiration and attention upon the narcissist. They will love and adore the narcissist as much as he loves and adores himself, or herself, though men tend to be more narcissistic than women. In their self-absorbed minds, narcissists are entitled to the admiration of others, highly deserving of praise and esteem. On self-report measures of narcissism, such as the Narcissistic Personality Inventory (NPI; Raskin & Hall, 1981), they tend to endorse items such as these: "I really like to be the center of attention"; "I will never be satisfied until I get all that I deserve"; "I think I am a special person"; and "I like to look at my body."

Among other things, narcissism typically entails *excessively high self-esteem* (Back, Schmukle, & Egloff, 2010). Some theories of narcissism suggest that the excessively high self-esteem is a cover-up for an underlying (even unconscious) deficit in self-worth. For example, the great psychoanalytic theorist Heinz Kohut (1977) believed that the origins of narcissism could be traced back to the parents' failure to affirm their child and to build up a secure sense of a core self. Other theories suggest that narcissists have never really suffered from lack of affirmation, yet they still crave more and more anyway, to feed their insatiable need to be esteemed. Either way you look at it, the research shows that manifest narcissism is often linked to social problems. People who score high on measures of narcissism express more hostility and are more likely to behave aggressively when they are insulted compared to those who score low in narcissism (Rhodewalt & Morf, 1998). Narcissism has been linked to extreme mood swings and intensity of emotional experience in daily life (Emmons, 1987), and to problems in inhibiting negative social responses (Vazire & Funder, 2006).

Yet narcissists are also often capable of garnering positive attention from others, especially early on in a relationship. Studies show that narcissists can be charming and attractive on first sight, and can even attain high levels of popularity in the short term (Back et al., 2010). Their dynamic social demeanor, often fueled by high levels of extraversion, can attract positive attention. They also tend to wear flashy and attractive clothing. Perhaps you wanted to know that young female narcissists wear more makeup and tend to show more cleavage, compared to their less narcissistic counterparts (Vazire, Naumann, Rentfrow, & Gosling, 2008). All other things being equal, narcissists also tend to be rated as significantly more physically attractive than less narcissistic people (Holtzman & Strube, 2010). Being a physically beautiful human being, like Narcissus himself, may breed narcissism: When people consistently notice your good looks (and when you notice the same every time you look in the mirror), you may begin to believe that you are indeed a really special person.

Most narcissists eventually wear out their welcome. Over time, people become increasingly annoyed by the self-centeredness that narcissists relentlessly display and by their relative inattention to the needs of others (Back et al., 2010). In the long run, the social costs of narcissism can be high, leading to social rejection rather than the admiration that narcissists crave. Nonetheless, some highly narcissistic people attain positions of high esteem in the arts, sports, politics, and other domains (Corry, Merritt, Mrug, & Pamp, 2008; Wink, 1992). Moreover, people may put up with a narcissist, or be forced to put up with him or her, if the narcissist is gifted with other redeeming qualities, such as leadership skills or creative genius. Take, for example, the case of Steve Jobs.

Steve Jobs (1955–2011), the charismatic chairman and CEO of Apple, Inc., revolutionized personal computing. At age 21, he teamed up with Steve Wozniak to invent and market the Apple I computer, assembling machines in his parents' garage. When Apple went public just a few years later, Jobs was suddenly worth $256 million. By the time he introduced the Macintosh to the world in a famous 1984 Super Bowl commercial, Jobs had proven himself to be the industry's leading innovator in computer technology and a marketing genius.

His stupendous rise was followed by an even more precipitous fall when he was ousted from a leadership role at Apple during a 1985 coup. After Jobs left, the company fell on hard times, but Jobs himself recovered gainfully to found NeXT computing and to produce animated films, such as *Toy Story* (1995) and *Finding Nemo* (2003), through the Pixar partnership and the Disney company. Jobs returned to Apple as a conquering hero in 1996. He took the company from near bankruptcy to profitability by 1998. Over the next decade, Jobs famously orchestrated the development and marketing of the iMac, iPod, iPhone, and iPad. The magical powers and sleek designs of these products gave Apple a cachet that no company has ever been able to match. When Jobs died from complications of pancreatic cancer at age 56, Apple had become the world's most valuable publicly traded company. More importantly, Jobs changed the world forever. He dramatically impacted how hundreds of millions of people carry on their daily lives, how they work, how they spend their leisure time, how they listen to music and communicate with each other, and even how they shop. His cultural influence was on a par with such great 20th-century innovators as Thomas Edison and Henry Ford.

As a devotee of all things Apple (I am typing this book on a new iMac), I would love to tell you that Steve Jobs was also a really nice guy. But I would be lying. To use one of Jobs's favorite appellations (with all due apologies), he was truly an "asshole." He called himself that on occasion, but as I read fair-minded accounts of Jobs's life (e.g., Isaacson, 2011), I would say that those were occasions of understatement, for he was often much worse. Jobs brutalized employees, demeaned and humiliated them on a daily basis. If he did not like somebody's work, he might scream at them in a rage: "These charts are bullshit!"; "This deal is crap"; "You are a fucking idiot." As Isaacson noted, Jobs operated with "an almost willful lack of tact. . . . It was more than just an inability to hide his opinions when others said something he thought was dumb; it was a conscious readiness, even a perverse eagerness, to put people down, humiliate them, show he was smarter" (p. 223). "Under Steve Jobs, there was zero tolerance for not performing," a CEO of a supplier remarked. When VLSI Technology failed to deliver computer chips to Apple on time, "Jobs stormed into a meeting and started shouting that they were 'fucking dickless assholes'" (p. 359). At the same time, people were drawn to Jobs for his genius and charisma. "He would shout at a meeting, 'You asshole, you never do anything right,'" recalled Debi Coleman, who was in charge of Macintosh manufacturing in the 1980s. "It was like an hourly occurrence. Yet I consider myself the absolute luckiest person in the world to have worked with him" (Isaacson, 2011, p. 124).

The same mixture of repulsion and attraction characterized his relationships with friends and lovers. When Jobs was happy with what a friend could provide him, the friend became the prized object of his attention. But once the friend failed to deliver or disappointed Jobs in some way, Jobs simply severed the tie. There was no loyalty. A girlfriend from high school described Jobs as "an enlightened being who was cruel." It was "a strange combination," she said (Isaacson, 2011, p. 32). In his 20s, Jobs struck up a romantic relationship with Chrisann Brennan. In 1978, she gave birth to their daughter Lisa. Jobs denied paternity and refused to offer any financial support. Chrisann and Lisa lived off of welfare for a time, in a tiny dilapidated shack in Menlo Park, California. Finally, the County of San Mateo sued, and Jobs agreed to pay $385 a month in child support, just before Apple was to go public. He eventually named one of his NeXT computers after his daughter, Lisa. But Jobs rarely exercised his visitation rights.

Another girlfriend, who came close to marrying Jobs, was "entranced by him, but she was also baffled by how uncaring he could be." Tina Redse recalled, "I couldn't abide his unkindness" (Isaacson, 2011, pp. 264–265). While Jobs was dating Redse, he was also courting the woman who would ultimately become his wife, Laurene Powell. Not surprisingly, both were beautiful women. Which one should he marry? Jobs "surprised a wide swath of friends and even acquaintances by asking them what he should do. Who was prettier, he would ask, Tina or Laurene? Who did they like better? Who should he marry?" (Isaacson, 2011, p. 272). It was as if the two women were nothing more than competing commodities. Which one should Jobs buy? Although he eventually settled into a more or less happy marriage with Laurene, raising three children and reconnecting with Lisa, Jobs never matured out of his manipulative and objectivizing orientation to interpersonal relationships. Jobs claimed to love his children, but even Laurene admitted that he rarely paid them much attention. She thought he might change his priorities when health problems arose: "After two years of him being ill, he finally gets a little better, and they [the kids] expected he would focus a bit on them, but he didn't," she remarked (Isaacson, 2011, p. 543). In contrast to Bill Gates and many other wealthy entrepreneurs, Jobs gave almost nothing to charities.

Years after they broke up, Tina Redse happened to read a psychiatric description of *narcissistic personality disorder*. She was amazed at how closely the label captured the personality of Steve Jobs: "It fits so well and explained so much of what we had struggled with, that I realized expecting him to be nicer or less self-centered was like expecting a blind man to see" (Isaacson, 2011, p. 266). Although the assignation of a clinical diagnosis to Jobs is beyond our expertise here, there is little doubt that he would be placed at the high end of any narcissism continuum one might imagine. And we would likely place him there even if I never mentioned that Jobs threw a tantrum in 1982 (age 27) when he learned that *Time* magazine had not chosen him to be Man of the Year. Or that he expressed outrage that President Barack Obama, in office for only a few months in 2009, had not yet given him a phone call.

For the purposes of this chapter, Jobs's case is instructive for many reasons. First, it illustrates how an insatiable drive to enhance one's self-esteem can shade easily into narcissism. Second, it shows how narcissism cannot be fully understood from a Layer 1 trait perspective in terms of personality. Like many narcissists, Steve Jobs was high on extraversion and low on agreeableness when it comes to dispositional traits (Chapters 1–4 in this book). But the nature of his narcissistic engagement of the self and the world was less about his emotional and behavioral traits as a social actor and more about his pursuit of valued goals as a motivated agent. The dynamics of a narcissistic personality require a consideration of Layer 2 in personality—the motivated agent's goals, plans, and values (Chapters 5–7 in this book). The second layer of personality—the layer of motivated agency—begins to manifest itself after the age 5–7 shift, when the person begins to conceive of him- or herself as a full-fledged motivated agent who strives to attain valued goals in the concrete world. Third, and relatedly, the problem of narcissism may stem from an uncontrollable proliferation or expansion of agency, as if agency itself were like a cancerous tumor whose unrestrained growth ultimately threatens the host. Becoming a motivated agent is a good thing. But agency needs to be held in check, mitigated, or softened in some way if a person is to enjoy conventional psychological health and adjust to the demands of group life.

As a *social actor*, Steve Jobs consistently displayed characteristics suggestive of grandiosity and a sense of entitlement. But the key to his narcissism, for better and for worse, was the way in which he moved through life as a *motivated agent*. In a comment containing more insight than she may have realized, Laurene Jobs hinted at the distinction between Jobs as actor and Jobs as agent: "Like many great men whose gifts are extraordinary," his wife said, Steve Jobs is not "extraordinary in every realm. He doesn't have social graces, such as putting himself in other people's shoes, but he cares deeply about empowering humankind, the advancement of humankind, and putting the right tools in their hands" (Isaacson, 2011, pp. 543–544). Put differently, Laurene asserted that Steve Jobs may have been sorely deficient as a social actor, but what really matters is the power of his personal agency—his *desire* to empower, his *belief* in the advancement of humankind, his *goal* to put the right tools in people's hands, his indomitable *will* to change the world.

At its core, narcissism is an expression of what the great philosopher/psychologist David Bakan (1966) called *unmitigated agency*. Bakan argued that healthy psychological adjustment typically requires that a person's will to assert the self over and against the world needs to be mitigated or softened by countervailing concerns for community and interpersonal relatedness. Agency tends to run amok in the absence of communion, and when agency runs amok, narcissism may result. In a similar line of reasoning, social psychologist Keith Campbell (1999) developed an *agency model of narcissism*, which depicts narcissism as resulting from a strong and abiding motivational emphasis on pursuing goals of power, status, personal perfection, and the like, to the exclusion of communal concerns, and a relentless focus on enhancing self-esteem. People who score high on measures of narcissism fantasize about power and status to a greater extent than do people low in narcissism (Raskin & Novacek, 1991). Importantly, their fantasies involve an imagined audience. For the narcissist, it is not enough to be successful in achieving goals. One must be widely recognized for the achievement, glorified and honored by others. The narcissist needs other people, not as communal companions so much as fawning admirers, who serve to affirm the narcissist's agency and boost self-esteem.

Narcissists endeavor to bend reality so that it conforms to their indomitable will. Borrowing a term from a famous episode of the television show *Star Trek*, one colleague invoked the term "reality distortion field" to describe how Jobs refused to accept limitations to his vision, aiming to bend the laws of physics or logic to make impossible things possible. In unmitigated agency, physical and social facts must be bent to accommodate the agent's plan. The colleague considered the expression to be both a compliment and a caution: "It was dangerous to get caught in Steve's distortion field, but it was what led him to actually be able to change reality" (Isaacson, 2011, p. 118).

Jobs was famous for demanding perfection in Apple products, especially with respect to product design. He obsessed over the tiniest details of every product, in an effort to achieve a perfect look and feel. Paying little heed to physical and financial constraints, to say nothing of interpersonal niceties, Jobs relentlessly pushed suppliers, engineers, designers, and marketers to do exactly what had to be done to actualize his vision.

Agency run amok. Yet the tangible results were sometimes awe-inspiring. By the end of his life, the reality distortion field, and Jobs's animating agential vision, had become the defining mythos for Apple, Inc., as expressed in the company's motto, "Think different." You may think that the narcissist is crazy, but sometimes crazy can pay off, as expressed in a tone poem developed for the Apple brand:

> Here's to the crazy ones. The misfits. The rebels. The troublemakers. The round pegs in the square holes. The ones who see things differently. They're not fond of rules. And they have no respect for the status quo. You can quote them, disagree with them, glorify or vilify them. About the only thing you can't do is ignore them. Because they change things. They push the human race forward. And while some may see them as the crazy ones, we see genius. Because the people who are crazy enough to think they can change the world are the ones who do. (Isaacson, 2011, p. 329)

## CONCLUSION

Beyond the realm of dispositional traits such as extraversion and conscientiousness lies the land of motivated agency—the goals, plans, projects, and values that fill in many of the details of psychological individuality. If human beings begin (literally) to see themselves as social actors around the age of 2 years, an understanding of oneself as a motivated agent awaits the age 5–7 shift. In middle childhood, then, a second layer of personality begins to form, even as temperament tendencies continue gradually to develop into full-fledged personality traits. *Personality thickens over time.* We begin with an initial layer of temperament, morphing gradually into dispositional traits. In middle childhood, we start to add a second layer that comprises nascent goals and values. As we see in the next two chapters, goals and values develop toward greater depth, articulation, and coherence over time, as motivated agents move into adolescence and beyond. The first and second layers of personality, therefore, continue to develop over time, sometimes in tandem and other times with surprising independence or asynchrony. The social actor's traits sometimes relate in predictable ways to the motivated agent's goals, and other times traits and motivations have little to do with each other. It is a cliché to say that personality is complex. But it is nonetheless true. Personality is complex and multilayered, increasingly so with increasing development.

The age 5–7 shift is a rough marker, as well as a deep metaphor, for the emergence of motivated agency in the human life course. Yet the line of personality development described in this chapter, and summarized in Table 5.1, runs back to the first year of life and well beyond the age of 7. Like all animals, human infants are born to be motivated agents in the primitive but crucial sense that their behavior is directed toward the achievement of goals. The newborn orients itself toward the breast in order to take in nutrition. The newborn is not conscious of the goal, but the goal is there to give guidance and structure to behavior. By 9 months of age, human infants recognize intentionality in others, expressing a special interest in the goal-directed nature of other agents' behavior. Around the same time, they engage in scenarios of joint attention with caregivers, monitoring the reactions of others in response to objects or events in the environment and coordinating their own intentions with the assumed intentions of others. Young children are agency detectors. By age 4, most of them have developed an explicit theory of mind, which tells them that human agents (themselves included) are endowed with minds, within which reside desires and beliefs. By the time they hit kindergarten, most children have developed a folk psychology of human motivation. People act upon their desires and beliefs, children reason. Motivation is fundamentally about what agents want and what agents believe to be true about the world.

Cognitive development and schooling catalyze the growth of motivated agency in middle childhood. The emergence of what Piaget called concrete operations confers upon children's thought a more systematic and logical quality. Equipped with concrete operational thought, children are then able to organize and make rational sense of the concrete world and the conventions that structure social relations. As potentially rational agents, children in third and fourth grade can construct reasonable plans and scenarios for the achievement of personally valued goals. When they make good progress toward achieving their goals, children enjoy a boost in self-esteem. Failures in goal pursuit reduce self-esteem. From age 8 or 9 onward, we all covet high self-esteem. But the relentless quest for stratospheric self-esteem can sometimes become an overriding preoccupation, as in the case of narcissism. When the pursuit of valued goals, especially those related to power and status, crowds out any concerns for positive social relatedness, motivated agents may begin to display the grandiosity and sense of entitlement that we all recognize as narcissism.

The narcissist is a motivated agent on steroids. The narcissist wants too much and believes too strongly in his or her animating agential vision. Still, it is good and proper for personality development that we all want *something*, that we all begin in middle childhood to transcribe our wants into valued goals upon which we stake our esteem. Our goals and our values orient us toward the future and provide structure and meaning to our agential strivings. They urge us to make plans and develop strategies, so as to turn our wants into realities over time. Motivated agency begins with what we want. And this, of course, raises a timeless question for personality development: What *do* we want?

# chapter 6

# The Motivational Agenda

## WHAT AGENTS WANT

The question of *motivation* is the question of what *moves* behavior—what sets behavior into *motion*. By the time we are in kindergarten, we intuitively sense that motivation is about what we *want* and what we *believe* to be true in the world. The child's theory of mind asserts that agents have desires (wants) in their minds and that they act upon them, guided by belief. By second or third grade, moreover, we understand that we may need to formulate a *plan* in order to get what we want. Plans help us achieve our *goals*. The full sequence of motivated agency eventually becomes clear: We want something. We set forth the goal of getting what we want. We develop a plan in order to get it. We execute the plan. We achieve the goal.

But what determines what we want in the first place? What are those particular desires that set the goal-directed sequence into motion? Pleasure and pain, you might say. We seek to obtain pleasure and avoid pain. We want to feel good, and to avoid feeling bad. Fair enough. But what gives us pleasure? What makes us happy? And what makes us feel really bad?

Over the past 100 years, psychologists who study human motivation have answered these questions in many different ways. One general perspective argued that the prime motivations for human behavior are essentially no different from the forces that drive and shape the lives of all other animals. In order to survive and reproduce, human beings need food, water, shelter, and other basic resources. When all is said and done, then, human behavior is motivated by basic physiological *needs*, which give rise to specific and socially contoured *wants*, which human beings

170

translate into conscious and unconscious life *goals*. Following this line of thought, American behaviorists of the 1930s and 1940s, such as Clark Hull and Kenneth Spence, argued that all behavior—whether displayed by rats or humans—can be reduced, or traced back to, the organism's efforts to satisfy basic drives such as hunger, thirst, and sex.

For the most part, mid-20th-century behaviorists focused on simple behaviors emitted by rats and pigeons. Writing at the same time, psychoanalysts such as Sigmund Freud and his followers focused their attention on the dreams and fantasies of their all-too-human patients. But the clinical psychoanalysts shared the same general outlook on motivation promulgated by many animal behaviorists. For Freud, the ultimate motives in human life were sex (Eros) and aggression (Thanatos). Like hunger, drives for sexual expression and the release of aggressive energy build up over time, Freud argued. Within the constraints set up by society and the superego, people act upon their unconscious sexual and aggressive urges, often disguising and sublimating these drives into more or less socially acceptable behaviors, and into symptoms.

If the behaviorists and Freud likened us humans to beasts, a countertrend elevated us to angels. In a clash of intellectual titans, Carl Jung broke with Freud, his mentor, over the topic of human motivation. Sex and aggression should never be ignored, Jung conceded, but the most important motive for human behavior across the life course is to develop or actualize the self, what Jung called *individuation*. Each of us strives to become the authentic person we were uniquely designed to be. The same general idea became the cornerstone for 20th-century *humanistic psychology*, as developed in the seminal writings of Carl Rogers and Abraham Maslow. The inspiring motivational messages of humanistic psychology eventually found their way into countless volumes of American self-help, 12-step programs, and New Age therapies, leading to psychospiritual best sellers such as *The Road Less Traveled* (Peck, 1978) and *The Purpose Driven Life* (Warren, 2002). The general idea running through this tradition of thought is that human beings strive to fulfill deep and ennobling motives for self-actualization, spiritual completion, personal salvation, and the like. We become who we are by discovering and making manifest our good inner potential.

Yet another line of thinking has it that there are many different kinds of human motivations, and no single motive reigns supreme. Harvard personality psychologist Henry Murray (1938) developed a famous list of about 20 "psychogenic needs" that regularly energize and direct human behavior. These include the motivations for achievement, affiliation, dominance, nurturance, order, play, and avoiding harmful situations. In a similar vein, evolutionary psychologists such as David Buss (1995) propose that there are as many fundamental motives as there are fundamental problems that human beings have evolved to solve. Therefore, we need and want to fulfill motives involved with mate attraction, mate selection, procreation, child rearing, forming alliances in social groups, defending ourselves against attack, finding food, obtaining shelter, and on and on.

Buss (1995) makes a strong case for multiplicity in human motivation. But the evolutionary perspective is instructive in another way, too. As cognitively gifted eusocial organisms, we *Homo sapiens* distinguish ourselves from all other species on Earth for our talents in group organization and planning. As motivated agents, we are extraordinarily adept in working together to develop the most elaborate and sophisticated plans, programs, schemes, and strategies to achieve our goals. It requires a tremendous amount of brain power and interpersonal cooperation to achieve any of the following quintessentially human aims: harvest crops, educate children, establish a government, rob a bank, travel across continents, attain financial security, win a football game, smuggle drugs, worship God, go to war, regulate an economy, purchase a computer, fulfill a life dream.

There are so many different goals that we brainy human agents, living together in complex social groups, set our minds to achieve. But we would never be able to achieve them if we did not believe in our innate power to do so. The evolution of the human PFC enables us to make more or less rational decisions and engage in all manner of plotting, scheming, and planning—often in the company of others whose respective human brains work in the same way. The same evolved capacities enable us to reflect upon our strivings and evaluate how well we are doing. Imagine, however, if upon reflection we concluded that none of our efforts were doing any good. Imagine that we had no faith in the power of our individual and collective wills, no faith in the individual and collective decisions we make to enact plans in order to attain goals. Upon reflection, we would conclude that nothing we plan or do really matters, for the power to generate our own goals and to achieve them is completely outside our purview. If we were ever to come to such a conclusion, then we would also have to conclude that we are indeed *not* motivated agents at all. We would have to conclude that we have no agency.

What do agents want? More than anything else, they *want to be agents*. Behind the many goals and motives that we human beings pursue may lie a fundamental need to exert our agency in the first place. As motivated agents, we want many things. But we want agency first and foremost, even if we do not always consciously realize such, because if we did not experience the power of agency in the first place—if we were unable to exert our autonomous wills in order to achieve self-determined goals—all of our striving would be useless.

In a deeply ironic sense, we have no choice when it comes to motivated agency. Human evolution has made us into schemers and plotters, and we could not be otherwise even if we wanted to be. As brainy eusocial creatures, we *have to have a plan*. And we have to believe that the plan *will work*. And the plan *has to* work, at least now and again. In the human case, motivated agents have no choice but to want to exert their agency. Psychologically speaking, then, there is no more compelling desire in all of life than the desire to be a motivated agent. The desire is so ingrained and so pervasive that we usually take it for granted—until somebody or something tries to take our agency away.

## SELF-DETERMINATION THEORY AND THE NEED FOR AUTONOMY

When people identify intensely pleasurable activities in their lives, they often point to moments when they are doing something that they *really* want to do. In these peak experiences, the joy or satisfaction in the moment seems to well up from within. The activity itself—be it making love, playing chess, watching a great movie, conversing with close friends, skydiving, or sipping a margarita by the pool—is experienced as enjoyable for its own sake. When people tell you about the activity afterwards, they don't typically need to explain why indeed they were motivated to do what they did. The conversation rarely goes like this: "Oh, so the two of you had fabulous sex on the beach. In the moonlight. With the waves gently washing over you. Gee, why would you want to do that?"

Certain activities in life derive their reinforcing quality by tapping into the wellspring of *intrinsic motivation*. The rewarding power of the activity is intrinsic to (inherent in) the activity itself. People who engage in intrinsically motivated behavior do not need an outside reason for doing the behavior. They do what they do because they like doing it, not because they will receive an external reward down the road. Over winter break in seventh grade, why did I play ice hockey in a local park for hours and hours every day, to the point of risking frostbite? Because I loved to play hockey back then. Why am I writing this book right now? God knows it cannot be for the money! The truth is that I have *always wanted to* write a book on personality development. As weird as it may sound to you, I actually like doing this. It is intrinsically motivating, even when I have difficulty in formulating just the right way to convey an idea, as I am experiencing this very moment. I hope there are numerous activities in your life that you do because you really want to do them. These intrinsically motivated behaviors may link to love, friendships, family, work, play, leisure, religion, spirituality, civic engagement, or any other valued realm of human life. Psychological research shows that people who pursue intrinsically motivating goals in their daily lives tend to enjoy especially high levels of happiness and well-being (Kasser & Ryan, 1996). In addition, studies in developmental psychology show that children and adolescents will devote more effort to homework and other arduous tasks when they feel intrinsically motivated (Trautwein, Lüdtke, Kastens, & Köller, 2006).

It is the nature of human existence, however, that much of what we do in daily life is motivated by external contingencies, at least in part. *Extrinsic motivation* is aimed at obtaining rewards from the environment, or avoiding punishments. Many of our activities are motivated by the anticipated rewards of social approval, prestige, money, material gain, and the like. There is no shame in this, for as a eusocial species we have evolved to be especially sensitive to social rewards and punishments. Only the most idealistic dreamer believes that human beings should pursue intrinsically motivated goals to the exclusion of everything else. We live in groups; groups regulate our behavior; there is no way to escape extrinsic social forces if we belong to the species called *Homo sapiens*. Moreover, the anticipation of external rewards can make us do some really good things—things we would never do if left to our own intrinsic devices. At the same time, life may lose vitality and meaning if we come to believe that nearly *everything* we do is dictated by the bitch goddess of extrinsic motivation. Even if we enjoy success with our extrinsic goals, even if we obtain the fame, the money, and the approval we have been striving to obtain all our lives, we may still feel *unsatisfied*. We may even feel that our very agency is compromised. At the end of the day, if I cannot do what I really want to do, at least some of the time, and pursue the goals that I really (intrinsically) want to pursue, then what kind of a motivated agent am I?

The distinction between intrinsic and extrinsic motivation is the conceptual starting point for *self-determination theory*. Developed by Edward Deci and Richard Ryan in the 1980s, self-determination theory has become a dominant theoretical perspective in personality and developmental psychology for making sense of how motivated agency works (Deci & Ryan, 1985; Ryan & Deci, 2006). As Deci and Ryan see it, intrinsically motivated behavior is self-determined in that the driving forces for the behavior reside within the self rather than the external environment. When behavior is fully self-determined, the motivated agent pursues a goal with "a full sense of choice, with the experience of doing what one wants, and without the feeling of coercion or compulsion" (Deci & Ryan, 1991, p. 253). As motivated agents, we feel free to pursue the goals that we find to be intrinsically valuable and rewarding.

By contrast, we tend to experience behavior that is *not* intrinsically motivated as either *controlled* or *amotivated*. Controlled behavior occurs when we strive to meet the demands of an external force, or an internalized force that was once external (e.g., harsh demands of the superego). Controlled behaviors may feel "intentional" in that we intend to do them, but we still feel that we are doing them to satisfy an end that is external to the behavior itself. In the case of controlled behavior, then, motivated agency has been compromised somewhat. We make plans to achieve goals. We put the plans into action by doing what needs to be done. But we feel constrained because the behaviors that are required to achieve the goal bring no rewards themselves. In the more extreme case of amotivated behavior, motivated agency breaks down completely in the face of overwhelming external demands. Amotivated behaviors are unintentional and often disorganized because the person cannot exert choice or will. For example, under the stress of an imminent writing deadline, a journalist may wander around her office in a daze. She cannot bring herself to do what she needs and wants to do. She feels that she cannot possibly complete her project in the short time allotted, so her behavior becomes random and amotivated.

Deci and Ryan argue that self-determined behavior stems from three basic psychological needs. First, the need for *autonomy* involves the agent's desire to feel a sense of independence from external pressures. It is indeed the very need to feel that one is a free and autonomous agent, able to make decisions according to one's will. When the need for autonomy is being satisfied, the agent feels that personal goals line up with deep values and interests. Second, the need for *competence* encompasses the agent's striving to control the outcomes of events and to experience a sense of mastery and effectiveness in dealing with the environment. When the need for competence is being satisfied, the agent feels a sense of accomplishment, achievement, and even power. Third, the need for *relatedness* encompasses the agent's strivings to care for others, to feel that others are relating to the self in authentic and mutually supportive ways, and to feel a satisfying and coherent involvement in the social world more generally. When the need for relatedness is being satisfied, the agent feels love for others and a secure sense of belonging to the group.

Intrinsically motivating activities often find their reinforcing sources in the three big needs of self-determination theory. Behaviors that stem from the needs for autonomy, competence, and relatedness often feel intrinsically rewarding. Moreover, acting and striving in accord with the three needs may promote psychological growth, according to Deci and Ryan (1985). In support of these claims, research shows that when people are pursuing goals that tap into the needs for autonomy, competence, and relatedness, they tend to experience higher levels of self-esteem and psychological well-being (Milyavskaya, Phillipe, & Koestner, 2013). Pursing intrinsic goals also appears to promote a general sense that one is growing and changing in a positive direction for the future (Bauer & McAdams, 2010). Moreover, studies show that when people feel deprived of autonomy, competence, and relatedness, they experience strong desires to compensate for the loss and ever stronger urgings to meet these basic needs (Sheldon & Gunz, 2009).

Although Deci and Ryan give the three needs equal billing in their writings on self-determination theory, it seems to me that *autonomy* is the most basic of the three. As I read self-determination theory, the need for autonomy lies at the very heart of motivated agency. If your need for autonomy is squelched, you feel that you have lost control of your own motivations. Gone is any semblance of free will or self-efficacy. When the need for autonomy is squelched, you lose the power of autonomous choice and decision making, and you feel instead that forces beyond your control—forces external to the self—ultimately determine your behavior. You feel like a dispensable pawn in a game of chess. You feel helpless. It seems to me that if you cannot experience some form of rudimentary satisfaction with respect to the need for autonomy, then your needs for competence and relatedness are essentially moot. As I see it, you cannot effectively *strive for* mastery or love if you cannot *strive*. Experiencing some rudimentary satisfaction of the need for autonomy is essential for agentic striving—striving for *anything*, be it competence, relatedness, or becoming President of the United States.

Becoming an effective motivated agent, then, requires the nurturance, cultivation, and satisfaction of the need for autonomy. Parents in all cultures seem to know this, even if broad cultural differences in raising children may be observed. Parents know that children need to be able to exert some modicum of control in the world. They know that children ultimately need to be able to make self-determined choices and enact behaviors aimed at accomplishing self-determined goals. Children also need to learn the *limits* of autonomy. They must learn how to mesh their intrinsic desires with society's norms, rules, and requirements. For all human beings, the world plays out as a complex dialectic between agency and constraint. If children are to do well in the world, they need to experience a social environment that both nourishes autonomy and channels motivation into socially constructive ends.

From the standpoint of self-determination theory, then, the social world presents motivated agents with a mix of opportunities and constraints for self-determined behavior. In this regard, Deci and Ryan (1991) identify three especially important dimensions of the social environment. First, the social environment may offer what they call *autonomy support*. In other words, parents and teachers may be encouraging of choice and innovation in behavior. Environments that discourage choice undermine the need for autonomy. A large body of research shows that parents and other socializing agents who provide high levels of autonomy support tend to promote psychological adjustment and mental health in children (Ryan & Deci, 2006).

Second, the social environment may provide *structure* for goal-directed striving. Highly structured environments provide clear guidelines about what kinds of behaviors lead to what kinds of outcomes, and they give the motivated agent explicit feedback regarding how well he or she is doing in achieving goals. Too much structure is bad, however, for it runs the risk of promoting extrinsic goals. There is a sweet spot here, a balance between structure and indulgence that is probably different for each culture, and perhaps even for each child.

Third, the social environment may offer interpersonal *involvement*. Involvement describes the degree to which significant others are interested in and devote time and energy to the development of children. The more involvement, the better for everybody. All in all, social contexts that provide high levels of autonomy support, *moderate* structure, and many highly involved socializing forces (parents, teachers, mentors, etc.) are optimal for encouraging self-determined behavior and the positive development of motivated agency.

## COMPETENCE: ON GETTING AHEAD IN SOCIAL GROUPS— MOTIVES FOR ACHIEVEMENT AND POWER

Deci and Ryan (1985) were not the first psychologists to propose that a broad-based need for competence qualifies as a fundamental motivational tendency in human lives. A generation before, the personality psychologist Robert White (1959) wrote a famous paper critiquing the midcentury notion that all behavior is ultimately motivated by biological drives.

White documented numerous examples found in humans and other animals of behavior being driven, or pulled along, by factors such as curiosity and exploratory instincts. What biological drives are being satisfied, White asked, when monkeys play with puzzles (as they are wont to do in laboratory situations) or when 8-year-old humans, living in Brazil, kick a soccer ball around for hours on end? While there is no denying that biologically based drives for food, water, and sex occupy important roles in human motivation, White argued that wide swathes of behavior have nothing to do with these drives and are instead energized and directed by a broad desire to master the environment. White called this desire "effectance"—the drive to be an effective agent in the environment, any environment. He asserted that satisfaction of the effectance drive leads to the experience of competence.

Members of *Homo sapiens* want to be competent, by nature. The reason should be obvious. The most competent agents are likely to be the victors in that long(est)-running movie we call human evolution. All other things equal, they are more likely to survive and pass copies of their genes down to the next generation than their less competent peers. For our brainy eusocial species, competence involves mastering both the physical/material and the social environment. It means learning how to use the *tools* to which the group has access in order to further individual and group aims—be those tools weapons, implements for food preparation, or high-speed computers. It also means mastering the social *roles* that are available in the group, in order to get things done for the group and exert influence in the group. Although self-determination theory does not make this link explicit, it would seem that the broad-based drive toward competence ultimately serves the general evolutionary challenge of *getting ahead* in human groups.

It is part of human nature to want to get ahead; it is part of human nature to strive toward competence. Personality enters the picture when we observe variations on the general design for human nature—in this instance, when we note individual differences in the *strength* of a motive toward competence. Self-determination theory tends to downplay individual differences in such a motive, as did Robert White (1959) when he proposed the concept of effectance (Sheldon & Schuler, 2011). Deci and Ryan prefer instead to think of the need for competence as a fundamental design feature of human life. We all have the need, they point out, and it beckons to be assuaged. Moreover, our tendencies toward competence can be nurtured, cultivated, reinforced, and refined by parents, teachers, social institutions, religion, and other aspects of culture. As a portrait of human nature, I find their account to be appealing.

Nonetheless, everyday observations and research both suggest that people *do* differ in the strength and salience of motives and goals seemingly linked to a general tendency toward competence. If these motives and goals are not direct expressions of the need for competence itself, they seem to be derived in some way from it. At minimum, they look and sound like competence, mostly. The prime example in personality psychology of just such a dimension of individual differences is the *achievement motive*.

The story of achievement motivation goes back to the 1930s, when Henry Murray and his colleagues at the Harvard Psychological Clinic developed a personality theory centered on individual differences in a couple dozen psychological needs. Each of Murray's needs orients the person *to the future* by generating personal goals aimed at satisfying the need. Murray was skeptical about the idea that people truly know what their strongest needs are. Unlike dispositional traits, Murray argued, needs reflect *desires* that prompt motivated agents to pursue future ends, but the desires themselves may not always be conscious. In order to tap into unconscious motivational trends, Murray developed a procedure called the *Thematic Apperception Test* (TAT), in which people tell imaginative stories in response to picture cues. Murray believed that respondents project their strongest desires and concerns onto the pictures and into the fantasy stories they tell. A person with a strong need for dominance, therefore, should construct imaginative stories that feature powerful protagonists who aim to dominate others. A person with a strong need for affiliation, by contrast, should imagine stories of love and friendship.

Looking to focus research attention on one of Murray's needs, David McClelland and his colleagues (McClelland, Atkinson, Clark, & Lowell, 1953) chose the need for achievement (abbreviated *n*Ach, and most often termed the "achievement motive"), defining it as a recurrent desire to *perform well and strive for success* whenever one's behavior can be evaluated against a *standard of excellence*. It was a good choice. Like White (1959), McClelland realized that most people want to be effective and competent in their dealings with the real world. We want to do well. But some people appear to have a stronger and more salient desire in this regard than do others. McClelland (1961) observed that consistent differences in *n*Ach appear first around the age of 8 or 9 years. As I suggested in Chapter 5, children begin to sort themselves out as motivated agents in the elementary school years, after the age 5–7 shift. Some kids put their motivational eggs in the achievement basket. Others invest in different goals.

Modifying the TAT for standardized research purposes (today the procedure is commonly called the *Picture Story Exercise*, or PSE), McClelland and his students developed a coding system to determine the relative strength of achievement themes in imaginative stories. People showing a higher density of achievement themes in their stories were deemed to score high on achievement motivation, compared to those telling stories with fewer achievement themes (i.e., those scoring lower in achievement motivation). Research conducted since the 1950s has consistently shown that adults who score high on *n*Ach tend to behave in recurrently different ways than those who score low. For example, people high in achievement motivation tend to prefer and to exhibit high performance in tasks that pose optimal (not too hard, not too easy) challenges, especially when they receive immediate feedback concerning success and failure; they tend to be persistent and highly efficient in many kinds of performance, even cutting corners when necessary to maximize productivity; they tend to exhibit high self-control and a future time perspective; they thrive on personal challenge; and they tend to be restless, innovative, and drawn toward change and movement (McClelland, 1985; Schultheiss & Pang, 2007). People high in achievement motivation are often drawn to careers in business. McClelland (1985) argued that business is a good match for *n*Ach because business requires that people take moderate risks, assume personal responsibility for their performance, pay close attention to feedback in terms of costs and profits, and find innovative ways to make products or provide services. These hallmarks of entrepreneurship closely match the goals, values, attitudes, and behaviors of people high in achievement motivation.

Murray and McClelland both believed that motives are, for the most part, *learned*. Reflecting the behaviorist precepts of the day, McClelland posited that children come to associate positive emotions with certain kinds of incentives as a function of the rewards and punishments administered by their parents. When children are consistently rewarded for doing well on instrumental tasks, he reasoned, they develop stronger achievement motivation. He also argued that achievement motivation is shaped by the values that families, schools, religious institutions, and society writ large aim to convey. Values may be transmitted in many ways, but McClelland reasoned that one especially influential mechanism for passing values on to children is the books and stories children read in school. Treating these texts like the PSE stories used in motivational research, McClelland endeavored to estimate the relative importance of achievement motivation *for an entire society* based on the density of achievement themes in children's readers. In a famous book called

*The Achieving Society*, McClelland (1961) reported analyses showing a strong correlation between the salience of achievement themes in a society's textbooks and the economic output of that society a generation or two later. Anticipating an argument made today by some economic historians (e.g., Clark, 2007), McClelland surmised that a strong emphasis on meeting standards of excellence as conveyed in children's schoolbooks promotes the development of higher achievement motivation, which itself can become an engine for economic growth years later, when those same children grow up to become entrepreneurs and economic innovators. Other studies have shown that achievement motivation changes as societal values change. For example, the rise of the women's movement in the United States paralleled a significant increase in American women's achievement motivation between the years 1957 and 1976 (Veroff, 1982).

Also derived from Murray's (1938) original list, a second motivational variable that seems to fall somewhere within the broad domain of competence is *power motivation* (Winter, 1973). "Power motivation" is the general desire to feel strong and have a forceful impact on one's environment. Like the achievement motive, power motivation is usually viewed to be a line of general desire in a person's life that can be assessed through the PSE (Schultheiss & Pang, 2007). Power motivation also expresses itself in more specific personal strivings, projects, and goals (Little, 1999). But whereas achievement motivation is about doing well and achieving success in relation to a standard of excellence, power motivation is about feeling strong, wielding influence, and expressing social dominance. People who score high on the PSE measure of power motivation tend to seek power and influence in many different situations. Compared to their counterparts scoring lower on the power motive, they are more likely to hold elected offices, pursue careers that involve exerting strong influence on others (e.g., teacher, therapist, CEO), take large risks in order to attain visibility, collect prestige possessions such as fancy cars and credit cards, enjoy large friendship groups in which they can attract broad attention, and be seen by others as especially influential and forceful leaders (Schultheiss & Pang, 2007; Winter, 1973, 1987).

Power motivation is associated with positive behaviors, such as helping others and doing volunteer work, as well as negative behaviors, such as aggression and (among men only) profligate sexuality (Zurbriggen, 2000). In a sense, power is like fire—it can be productive or destructive. There are a number of studies that point to the downside of high power motivation. For example, when people high in power motivation find themselves in situations of low status, they experience dramatic increases in the stress hormone cortisol and decreases in testosterone (Josephs,

Sellers, Newman, & Mehta, 2006). Over time, repeated experiences of defeat or submission in dominance contexts may take a heavy toll on people high in power motivation, leading to increased susceptibility to illness (Schultheiss & Rohde, 2002). When people are asked to list their personal goals, moreover, those who show a predominance of power-related goals and strivings in their lives tend also to report lower self-esteem and lower overall happiness (Emmons, 1999).

## ACHIEVEMENT GOALS IN THE LIFE OF HILLARY RODHAM CLINTON

In any given life, motives like achievement and power develop and operate in a complex system of personal desire and belief, ultimately translated into *goals* (Elliot, Conroy, Barron, & Murayama, 2010). Goals are the specific end states that people try to attain. People orient themselves toward the future by projecting a motivational agenda—a set of personalized goals—that they hope to attain. The agenda is constrained by the opportunities available in the motivated agent's environment, societal norms and expectancies, gender, class, and a wide range of variables in the agent's world. The motivational agenda changes over time, as goals evolve and as life circumstances change. In the art of personality development, every individual person follows a unique career in goal pursuit.

Over the course of her life and career, Hillary Rodham Clinton has pursued a variety of personal goals, many of which seem to link up with the achievement motive. As a lawyer in Little Rock, Arkansas (in the 1980s), the First Lady of the United States (1993–2001), a New York senator (2001–2009), and Secretary of State under President Barack Obama (2009–2013), Hillary Clinton projected an ambitious motivational agenda that combined personal goals with the means and ends of public policy. Doing well, demonstrating competence, striving for effectiveness, getting ahead—these seem to be the major themes.

During her husband's two terms in the White House, Hillary Clinton became a lightning rod for American ambivalence regarding the appropriate goals, values, and strivings that women should project. Vilified by the political right, Clinton won admirers among Democrats, women, and minorities for her (ultimately failed) efforts to initiate national health care reform and her (generally effective) advocacy for women, children, and military families. She also won praise for the stoic way she managed to weather the storm created by her husband's philandering. Her colleagues in the U.S. Senate admired her hard work on policy issues and her strong political skills. She proved to be a tireless campaigner in her unsuccessful run for the Democratic presidential nomination in 2008. As Secretary of State, she was at the forefront of the U.S. response to the Arab Spring uprisings in Tunisia, Libya, and Egypt, advocating strongly for military intervention in Libya. Her overall foreign policy philosophy asserted that American power could be leveraged best through a combination of military strength and increased U.S. capacity in global economics, development aid, and technology. Clinton viewed women's rights and children's rights to be critical for U.S. security interests. By the time she finished her tenure in the Obama cabinet, Clinton had visited 112 countries, making her the most widely traveled Secretary of State in history. As I write this (summer of 2014), speculation is rampant that she will run again for President in 2016.

Hillary Rodham began to pursue achievement goals in her elementary school years. From about the age of 7 or 8 onward, she evidenced a remarkably robust desire to perform well and strive for success within contexts that provided clear standards for excellence. Despite adhering to the traditional gender norms that prevailed in the 1950s, both parents encouraged their daughter's achievement striving. "They believed in hard work, not entitlement; self-reliance not self-indulgence," Clinton (2003, p. 2) recalled. Her father was a strict disciplinarian who expected his daughter to excel in school and adhere tightly to the rules of decorum that prevailed in middle-class, God-fearing, Republican families in the late 1950s. Her mother modeled high achievement motivation in her role as homemaker: "When I think of her in those days, I see a woman in perpetual motion, making the beds, washing the dishes and putting dinner on the table at precisely six o'clock" (Clinton, 2003, p. 9).

Hillary loved schoolwork. She found intrinsic interest in academic learning, and she relished the immediate positive feedback, in the form of good grades and high praise, that she typically received. In the classroom and outside it, she organized her life according to achievement goals: "As a Brownie and then a Girl Scout, I participated in Fourth of July parades, food drives, cookie sales and every other activity that would earn a merit badge or adult approval. I began organizing neighborhood kids in games, sporting events and backyard carnivals both for fun and to raise nickels and dimes for charities" (Clinton, 2003, p. 13).

At the First United Methodist Church in Park Ridge, Illinois, Hillary learned that God wants little girls and boys to pursue achievement goals. The 18th-century founder of the Methodist Church, "[John] Wesley taught that God's love is expressed through good works, which he explained with a simple rule: 'Do all the good you can, at all the times you can, in all the ways you can, in all the places you can, to all the people you can, as long as ever you can'" (Clinton, 2003, p. 22). In exploring the historical and cultural roots of achievement motivation, McClelland (1961) linked nAch to the Protestant work ethic, a variation of which animates Wesley's words. In addition to reinforcing and morally validating the *desire* to achieve, the ethic encourages motivated agents to *believe* that effort, more so than ability or luck, is what counts in God's eyes.

For a sixth-grade autobiography assignment, Hillary Rodham wrote that she planned to be a teacher or a nuclear scientist someday. Instead, she became a lawyer. From grade school through law school, she exhibited many of the characteristics that research has shown to be associated with high achievement motivation: (1) high aspirations combined with moderate (not too high, not too low) risk taking; (2) a preference for situations in which personal responsibility can affect results; (3) a pragmatic approach to problem solving, with emphasis on efficiency; (4) self-control and delay of gratification; (5) a future time perspective; (6) upward social mobility; and (7) a penchant for travel (McClelland, 1985; Schultheiss & Pang, 2007). Over time, her achievement goals became more fully articulated and specific. She aimed to do well in the arena of public policy and politics. She became fascinated with politics, campaigning in high school for the conservative Republican Barry Goldwater in the 1964 Presidential election. She shifted rather dramatically toward a more liberal political position at Wellesley College, when she supported Eugene McCarthy's efforts to obtain the Democratic nomination for President in 1968.

At Yale Law School, Hillary Rodham developed expertise in children's issues. She volunteered at New Haven Legal Services to provide free legal advice for the poor. She was awarded summer grants to work on policy issues in Washington, D.C., where she was assigned to Senator Walter Mondale's Subcommittee on Migratory Labor. She researched migrant workers' problems in housing, sanitation, health, and education. And at Yale she began dating a fellow law student named Bill Clinton.

As motivated agents, each of us pursues a wide variety of goals over the course of a life. The same has always been the case for Hillary Rodham Clinton. During her years as a partner at the Rose Law Firm in Little Rock, Arkansas, and as wife of the Governor, Clinton took on many different projects and aspired to attain many different objectives in her public and personal life, pursuing goals related to friendship, intimacy, power, leisure and entertainment, financial security, and parenting, among others. She has written that the most important goal in her life was to raise her daughter Chelsea.

As a motivated agent, therefore, Hillary Clinton has always been much more than a case study in high nAch. The *art* of personality development defies simple categorizations of people's lives. Moreover, even in the realm of achievement motivation, she encountered unique obstacles and took advantage of unique opportunities. Never content to stay home and bake cookies, as she famously noted in one press interview, she needed to channel her achievement strivings into paid (or volunteer) *work* in the public realm. She had to have a job to do.

Beginning with the job of reforming health care, Hillary Clinton took on countless projects during her years in Washington, D.C., from initiating and shepherding through Congress laws regarding adoption and foster care to promoting nationwide immunization against childhood illnesses. When things got really tough, she threw herself ever more deeply into her work. After her health care initiative failed to win support and Republicans took over Congress in the 1994 midterm elections, a chastened Hillary Clinton recalled the words of another First Lady who would have surely scored high on achievement motivation: "Eleanor Roosevelt once said, 'If I feel depressed, I go to work.' That sounded like good advice to me" (Clinton, 2003, p. 262).

## RELATEDNESS: ON GETTING ALONG IN SOCIAL GROUPS— MOTIVES FOR AFFILIATION AND INTIMACY

Let us shift gears now, moving from work to love, and consider the following two evocative passages as they pertain to the nature of human relatedness:

> Only connect! That was the whole of her sermon. Only connect the prose and the passion, and both will be exalted, and human love will be seen at its height. Live in fragments no longer. Only connect, and the beast and the monk, robbed of the isolation that is life to either, will die. (Forster, 1910, pp. 174–175)

> When I confront a human being as my Thou and speak the basic word I–Thou to him, then he is no thing among things nor does he consist of things. He is no longer He or She, a dot in the world grid of space and time, nor a condition to be experienced and described, a loose bundle of named qualities. Neighborless and seamless, he is Thou and fills the firmament. Not as if there were nothing but he; but everything else lives in his light. (Buber, 1970, p. 59)

The first passage comes from E. M. Forster's celebrated novel *Howard's End*. One of the characters in the story is describing a philosophy of life that underscores the value of human communion. Human beings need to connect with each other in order to feel individually whole. We need to break down the barriers between us, and break through the rigid categories that may exist in our minds, so that we can come together with those who initially seem so different from us. Live in fragments no longer, Forster says. Find enhancement in human community.

The second passage, from Jewish theologian and philosopher Martin Buber, bores in on the intricate dynamics of interpersonal intimacy. What happens between two people when they focus unswervingly on each other? One possibility is what Buber calls an encounter of *I* and *Thou*. In an I–Thou moment, two completely separate individuals apprehend each other in their full otherness, and in so doing discover a common bond. If I apprehend you as a Thou, I do not analyze you or subject you to any preconceived notions I may have about who you are. You are not a dot in the world grid of time and space; instead you are unique and whole, like nobody else I have ever known, or will ever know. And I am like that to you, if you, in turn, encounter me as a Thou. In the relationship of I and Thou, each partner fills the other's phenomenological world, if even for but a split second in time. As a theologian, Buber believed that human beings find God in interpersonal relationships, and only there. It is what happens *between us* that most matters. In another passage from *Howard's End*, Forster (1910) seems to be echoing Buber's radical sentiment about human relatedness when he writes: "It is the private life that holds out the mirror to infinity; personal intercourse, and that alone, that ever hints at a personality beyond our daily vision" (p. 78).

In self-determination theory, the need for relatedness encompasses strivings for love, friendship, community, and all manner of warm and caring relationships that human beings can form with each other. The need for relatedness runs from the kind of intensely personal encounters—one on one—that Buber depicts in the I–Thou relation to the group-based positive connections that human beings build up in families, neighborhoods, organizations, social institutions, and even nation-states. The motives and goals that may be subsumed within the broad category of relatedness would appear to serve the evolutionary mandate of *getting along* with others. We have evolved to get ahead and get along in social groups. If competence presumes the former, relatedness evokes the latter.

In the field of personality psychology, the motivational variables that appear to track individual differences in the realm of relatedness are the *affiliation* (Atkinson, Heyns, & Veroff, 1954) and *intimacy* (McAdams, 1980) motives. Affiliation concerns connections people feel to groups, whereas intimacy is more about the quality of one-on-one relationships. But in research studies, the two turn out to be very similar; both assess individual differences in the strength of a motive to pursue warm, close, and communicative interactions with other people. As with achievement and power motivation, researchers have tended to measure individual differences in affiliation and intimacy motivation through thematic content analysis of imaginative stories (the PSE). As with achievement and power, moreover, individual differences are also indicated in people's open-ended descriptions of their personal goals, projects, and strivings in life.

Compared to their peers who score lower, people high in intimacy motivation show more nonverbal signs of intimacy (e.g., smiling and friendly eye contact) when interacting with friends, spend a great deal of time thinking about friendships, and are seen by others who know them as especially sensitive, sincere, and caring (McAdams, 1989). They are good listeners. People high in intimacy motivation value sharing and warmth in small groups. High levels of intimacy motivation are also associated with greater happiness and overall psychological well-being. Relatedly, pursuing more goals associated with friendship, intimacy, and compassion is associated with self-esteem, life satisfaction, and better coping with stressful life transitions (Crocker, Canevello, Breines, & Flynn, 2010). Research shows that women and girls consistently score higher than men and boys on intimacy motivation, a difference that shows up as early as the third grade (McAdams, 1989).

## PROMOTION VERSUS PREVENTION

Cutting across the broad motivational domains of competence and relatedness runs another basic distinction with considerable psychological influence. It is the simple difference between moving toward a desired end state and moving away from an undesired one. Psychologists have long recognized the difference between pursuing a goal in order to obtain a reward (approach motivation) and pursuing a goal in order to avoid a punishment (avoidance motivation). In the early achievement motivation literature, the distinction translated into that between *n*Ach (striving to do well in order to attain success) and fear of failure (striving to do well in order to avoid defeat) (Atkinson, 1964).

Beyond achievement, researchers have examined approach and avoidance goals in many different ways. The research tends to show that pursuing goals aimed at avoiding or escaping negative situations is associated with higher levels of the trait neuroticism and lower psychological well-being (Little, 1999). Having many avoidance-oriented goals may be a sign that life is not going so well. You may feel that the world is full of dangers that you need to avoid. Motivated agents who focus mainly on avoidance goals may feel that they are always playing defense, rather than offense, in the game of life.

Social psychologist E. Tory Higgins (1997) has tweaked and refined the distinction between approach and avoidance goals in his *regulatory focus theory* of human motivation. Higgins argues that as people orient themselves to the future, they regulate their actions according to two fundamental principles. According to the *promotion focus* principle, the motivated agent aims to promote the self by approaching situations that promise reward, growth, expansion, and the like. When the agent is successful in promotion, he or she feels *joy* in achieving the goal; when the agent is unsuccessful, he or she feels *sadness* or disappointment. According to the *prevention focus* principle, the motivated agent aims to protect the self by preventing harm, actively avoiding situations that threaten the self. When the agent is successful in prevention, he or she feels *relief* in achieving the goal of safety or security; when unsuccessful, the agent feels *anxiety* and fear because the threat remains. Over the course of a day, a person shifts from prevention to promotion focus and back again, in response to perceived opportunities and threats in the environment. At the same time, some people may consistently tend toward prevention, in that their striving tends to focus on achieving safety and security, and minimizing threat. Other people may tend toward promotion, consistently prioritizing personal goals that aim to expand, assert, and develop the self while pursuing self-relevant rewards.

Seeking to prevent negative outcomes sometimes means preventing your own *mis*behavior. In other words, you can focus prevention efforts on the self, scanning the self for its shortcomings and staying vigilant lest the self do something that is *wrong*. According to Higgins (1997), prevention focus goals may sometimes work to diminish the discrepancy between the actual self and what he calls the *ought self*. By keeping your impulses in check, by disciplining and restraining yourself so as to prevent negative outcomes, you may become closer to the (morally, ethically) good person that you feel you ought to be.

In a parallel sense, promotion focus goals may seek to decrease the discrepancy between the actual self and what Higgins calls the *ideal self*. By pursuing opportunities that promise to reward and expand the self, you may eventually come closer to being the (instrumentally) ideal person that you have always longed to be. Prevention goals and the ought self therefore seem to link up more closely with the social and moral demands of family, government, religion, and society. By contrast, promotion goals and the ideal self aim to fulfill the agent's personal desires and dreams. Going back to the distinction that gave rise to self-determination theory, it may sound as if prevention goals are usually *extrinsic* and promotion goals are *intrinsic*. But that is not necessarily true. For example, a promotion focus desire may be intrinsic or extrinsic—you may want to master a skill or form a more loving relationship with your husband (intrinsic goal) or become the richest entrepreneur in Silicon Valley (extrinsic goal). As shown in Table 6.1, the distinction between promotion and prevention is conceptually independent of other important distinctions drawn in this chapter, as is that between extrinsic and intrinsic and that between the needs for competence and relatedness.

## PURSUING GOALS ACROSS THE LIFE COURSE: THE DEVELOPMENT OF MOTIVATIONAL AGENDAS

Whether they are about achieving against a standard of excellence or about power, friendship, or simply having fun, personal goals orient the motivated agent toward the future. Whereas dispositional traits such as extraversion and agreeableness convey how a social actor performs emotions and interacts with other people on a daily basis, goals translate the person's inner desires and beliefs—the agent's specific motivational agenda—into projects of sustained activity aimed toward accomplishing particular future ends. Your traits are about *how you act today*; your goals are about *what you want for tomorrow*. At any given moment in the life course, a person projects many different goals into the future. Some goals may be simple and concrete: "I want to get my hair cut this week"; "I aim to get a high grade on Friday's math test"; "I need to apologize to my sister for insulting her husband." Others may suggest more abstract, long-term aims: "I want to figure out the meaning of my life." Your most important and psychologically absorbing goals in life are likely to become incorporated into your personality, filling in a second layer of psychological individuality. The goals and aims of the motivated agent, then, layer over the dispositional traits of the social actor.

From middle childhood through old age, motivated agents face many psychological challenges when it comes to establishing and pursuing the goals that comprise their respective motivational agendas. Foremost for many of us is the challenge of setting up a goal in the first place. It is not always easy to know what you want, and even if you do know, you may have trouble figuring out how to translate what you want into an

**TABLE 6.1. The Geography of Goals: Three Dimensions of Human Motivation**

Intrinsic versus extrinsic

The pursuit of *intrinsic* goals is inherently satisfying; the motivated agent enjoys the activity associated with goal pursuit in and of itself, as an end rather than a means to another end. According to self-determination theory, intrinsic goals meet basic human needs for autonomy, competence, and relatedness. *Extrinsic* goals are aimed toward obtaining external rewards or meeting social demands; the motivated agent views the goal-directed activity as a means to another end. Extrinsic goals promise the rewards of money, material possessions, praise, fame, and the like.

Competence versus relatedness

Building on the basic need for autonomy, the needs for competence and relatedness constitute a fundamental distinction in self-determination theory. Goals falling under the rubric of the need for competence aim to develop and demonstrate the agent's mastery of the environment. Included within this category are goals related to achievement motivation, power motivation, and other tendencies that promote the development of the individual as an effective force in the world. Such aims may enable the agent to *get ahead* in social groups. Goals falling under the rubric of the need for relatedness aim to connect the person to others in bonds of love, friendship, and community. The motivated agent pursues goals related to establishing close relationships with others, helping others, providing care for others, allying with others for the common good, and the like. In personality research, individual differences in the intimacy motive roughly track the relatedness dimension. Aims that line up with the need for relatedness may enable the agent to *get along* in social groups.

Prevention versus promotion

Goals focused on *prevention* aim to avoid pain, punishment, and threats in the environment; they orient the motivated agent toward safety, security, and self-control. When prevention goals are successfully met, the person feels relief; when striving for prevention fails, the person feels anxiety or fear, because the threat has not been removed. According to regulatory focus theory, prevention goals often aim to decrease the discrepancy between the actual self and the *ought self.* Goals focused on *promotion* aim to approach positive incentives, obtain rewards, and experience growth or expansion of the self. When promotion goals are successfully met, the person feels joy; when striving for promotion fails, the person feels sadness or dejection. Promotion goals often aim to decrease the discrepancy between the actual self and the *ideal self.*

---

actionable goal. Research and common sense both suggest that simply identifying a personal goal that you plan to pursue makes it much more likely that you will engage in behavior that is commensurate with that goal (Oettingen & Gollwitzer, 2010).

Once you set up the goal, you need to focus time and effort on achieving it. If you run into persistent obstacles in goal attainment, you may need to figure out how and when to give up, so that you can move on to other goals. And you need to organize your different goal pursuits within a more or less efficient and manageable life program, so that you do not wear yourself out (Oettingen & Gollwitzer, 2010). You may get overwhelmed if you find you are pursuing different goals that conflict with each other, or if your goals are too grandiose. Having said that, if your goals are nothing more than trivial pursuits, you may get bored and sense that your life lacks meaning. Research suggests that goal conflict leads to frustration and unhappiness (Emmons & King, 1988). People seem to be happiest when they are pursuing goals that are both meaningful and manageable—grand enough to give their lives a sense of purpose and satisfaction but humble enough that they can actually be achieved (Little, 1999).

Grounding his ideas in self-determination theory, personality psychologist Kennon Sheldon (in press) views the selection and pursuit of goals over the life course as a processing of *becoming oneself*. We learn who we are, Sheldon asserts, by figuring out what we want and how we may go about getting it. It is not a simple matter, however, to figure out what we want. In any individual life, it is better to pursue some goals than others. The pursuit of goals that line up with intrinsic needs for competence and relatedness is good in general terms, but figuring out how to do this in a unique individual life can be a daunting challenge. According to Sheldon, becoming ourselves involves *self-concordant goal selection*. We need to select goals that are consistent with our underlying motivations and with the skills and talents we have. Some people appear to be more adept in self-concordant goal selection than others. Moreover, social contexts that support autonomy and encourage self-reflection may help a person to develop the unique, personally tailored motivational agenda that will bring maximal fulfillment and satisfaction in life.

With respect to personality *development*, the move into adolescence and young adulthood nearly always ramps up the prospects and the perils of goal pursuit. Erik Erikson (1963) argued that the prime psychological challenge during this time in the human life course is to formulate an identity. "Identity" means many things, but from the standpoint of the person as a motivated agent, identity is mainly about exploring and ultimately committing to specific life goals and values *for the long haul*. It is about choosing what sorts of career goals to pursue, and deciding what the most important values are in your life, now that you are on the brink of becoming an adult. Where is your life going? Who do you wish to become? When it comes to identity, there may be many different kinds of goals you might pursue. But you cannot pursue them all. You cannot be everything. In a famous passage, William James (1892/1963) described the identity choice that must be made:

> I am often confronted by the necessity of standing by one of my empirical selves and relinquishing the rest. Not that I would not, if I could, be both handsome and fat and well dressed, and a great athlete, and make a million a year, be a wit, a *bon vivant*, and a lady-killer, as well as a philosopher; a philanthropist, statesman, warrior, and African explorer, as well as a "tone poet" and saint. But the thing is simply impossible. The millionaire's work would run counter to the saint's; the *bon vivant* and philanthropist would trip each other up; the philosopher and lady-killer could not well keep house in the same tenement of clay. Such different characters may conceivably at the outset of life be alike *possible* to a man. But to make any one of them actual, the rest must more or less be suppressed. So the seeker of his truest, strongest, deepest self must review the list carefully, and pick out the one on which to stake his salvation. All other selves thereupon become unreal, but the fortunes of this self are real. Its failures are real failures, its triumphs real triumphs, carrying shame and gladness with them. (p. 174)

As James saw it, committing the self to the goal of becoming a particular kind of adult in the world is an agential choice of profound psychological significance—a decision upon which to "stake" your "salvation." James may have projected more drama into identity goals than is typically the case, for people are often able to change their professional and interpersonal goals over the course of adulthood when things don't work out. Moreover, the stakes may not be quite as high as salvation versus damnation. Still, the consequences and implications of identity formation in young adulthood are considerable. Perhaps, a better metaphor is that of the investment banker: The motivated agent strategically infuses capital into those life strivings, projects, and goals that promise a good return in the future. The relative success of the investments may be measured by how much they ultimately pay back in personal meaning and self-esteem. The banker may be able to modify the investment portfolio over time, as circumstances change. Still, failed investments produce sunk costs. Psychologically speaking, we are talking real money here.

During adolescence and young adulthood, the life goals that pertain most directly to the issue of identity gather around the topics of occupation, ideology, and personal relationships. For over 40 years now, James Marcia (Kroger & Marcia, 2011; Marcia, 1966) has studied how young adults explore identity options and make commitments to identity goals.

Marcia's research shows that at any given point in a young adult's life, he or she may be categorized into one of four different *identity statuses*, each corresponding to where he or she is, psychologically speaking, when it comes to exploring identity options and committing to identity goals.

Young adults in *moratorium* are in the midst of exploring occupational goals and ideological values but have not as yet committed themselves for the long run. As motivated agents, they are still trying to figure out what they truly want (and value) in life. They are eager to know themselves better, and they look forward to resolving the identity challenge. Their counterparts who have graduated to the status of *identity achieved* have explored various options already and have now committed to particular occupational goals and ideological values for adulthood. As motivated agents, they know what they want (and value), for now at least. As such, they tend to enjoy high levels of self-esteem and greater overall psychological maturity, compared to the other three statuses.

Young adults who show the status of *foreclosure* never fully explored and questioned the goals and values that were available to them in adolescence and young adulthood. Instead, they settled on occupational and ideological commitments that were reinforced in childhood. As motivated agents, they certainly know what they want (and value), but there is a sense in which they have failed to exercise their full agency. As a result, their life goals may be more extrinsic than intrinsic, and likely to center more on prevention than promotion. Finally, those who are categorized as having *identity diffusion* seem unable to embrace the perspective of the motivated agent. They are not exploring, and they have made no commitments. Perhaps they have decided not to decide, or have simply not been able to get it together, psychologically speaking, to focus on occupational goals and ideological values to be considered for the future. They do not know what they want (or value) in adult life, and they are not, at the moment, looking to know.

From young adulthood through old age, people change their goals, plans, programs, and life projects in response to normative developmental challenges, such as marriage and retirement, and unpredictable events (e.g., divorce, or winning the lottery). Historical factors such as war, economic recessions, social movements, and changing social mores may exert significant effects on the personal goals and strivings that occupy prime positions in identity (Elder, 1995). In their midlife years, many people may reassess their goal priorities. Although very few people experience a full-blown "midlife crisis," studies suggest that many people in their 40s and 50s engage in what lifespan psychologist Abigail Stewart calls *midlife reviews* and *midcourse corrections* (Stewart & Vandewater,

1999). Although few adults may overthrow the entire panoply of choices, values, and commitments that structure their motivational agendas, it is quite common for midlife men and women to review where they are going in life, develop new pursuits and shed old ones, change priorities, and alter the direction of their strivings to accommodate the changing social ecology within which their agency is embedded. Regrets about goals not pursued in the past may motivate significant changes in direction.

Research has revealed developmental trends in the content and structure of personal goals, as well as changes in the ways people think about, draw upon, pursue, and relinquish goals as they get older. For young adults in modern societies, goals related to education, intimacy, friendships, and careers are likely to be especially salient. Middle-aged adults tend to focus their goals on the future of their children, securing what they have already established, and property-related concerns. Older adults show more goals related to health, retirement, leisure, and understanding current events in the world (Freund & Riediger, 2006). Goals indicative of prosocial engagement—caring for the next generation, civic involvement, improving one's community—become more pronounced as people move into midlife and remain relatively strong for many adults in their retirement years (Peterson & Duncan, 2007). Goals in early adulthood often focus on expanding the self and gaining new information, whereas goals in late adulthood may focus more on the emotional quality of ongoing relationships (Carstensen, Pasupathi, Mayr, & Nesselroade, 2000).

As adults move through midlife and beyond, their goals tend to shift gradually toward intrinsic motivation, and away from extrinsic motivation (Morgan & Robinson, 2013). They tend to invest more heavily in aspirations that satisfy enduring, endogenous needs such as autonomy, competence, and relatedness. They tend to pull back from motives that promise future rewards, fame, money, and the like. Compared with younger adults, older adults derive greater meaning from self-transcendent goals that emphasize religious activities, social causes, altruism, maintaining traditions and culture, and preserving cultural values (Reker & Woo, 2011).

The ways in which people manage multiple and conflicting goals may also change over time, as indicated in Table 6.2. Young adults seem better able to tolerate high levels of conflict among different life goals, but midlife and older adults manage goals in ways to minimize conflict. In trying to reconcile their goals to environmental constraints, young adults are more likely to engage in what motivational psychologist Jutta Heckhausen (2011) calls *primary control strategies*, which means they

**TABLE 6.2.  Developmental Change in Goal Pursuit**

Young adulthood

- Establishing an identity: Exploring range of life goals (and values) and committing to subset that aims to provide life with meaning and purpose.
- Promotion focus greater than prevention focus.
- Goals related to education, jobs, friendships, love and marriage.
- Tolerance for contradictory and conflicting goals.
- Primary control strategies: Actively changing the environment to accomplish goals.

Middle adulthood

- Midlife reviews and midcourse corrections: Reassessing goals and making changes.
- Goals related to raising children, running a household, civic engagement, passing on cultural traditions.
- Ability to manage goals in order to minimize conflict.
- Increase in intrinsic motivation.

Later adulthood

- Prevention focus greater than promotion focus.
- Goals related to health, retirement, leisure, passing on cultural traditions.
- Winnowing of goals down to most important and meaningful concerns, often related to family.
- Even more increase in intrinsic motivation.
- Relatedness goals greater than competence goals.
- Secondary control strategies: Modifying expectations to accommodate and compensate for limitations.

*Note.* In broad-brush terms, this table summarizes the main findings from empirical research on age differences regarding the content of personal goals and the ways in which adults experience and pursue their goals. Although age estimates are inexact, think of "young adulthood" as roughly equivalent to ages 20–40, "middle adulthood" as ages 40–65, and "later adulthood" as ages 65 and above.

try actively to change the environment to fit their goal pursuits. By contrast, midlife and older adults are more likely to employ *secondary control strategies*, which involve changing the self to adjust to limitations and constraints in the environment. With some exceptions, older adults seem to approach goals in a more realistic and prudent manner, realizing their limitations and conserving their resources to focus on those few goals in life that they consider to be most important (Ogilvie, Rose, & Heppen, 2001; Riediger & Freund, 2006). Compared to younger adults, they are often better able to disengage from blocked goals and to rescale personal commitments in the face of lost opportunities. As adults move into and through their midlife years, they become more adept at selecting goals that offer the best chance for reward, optimizing their efforts to attain the best payoffs for their projects and strivings, and compensating for their own limitations and losses in goal pursuit (Haase, Heckhausen, & Wrosch, 2013).

In old age, people become increasingly focused on how much time they have left to live. As such, recalibration of future-oriented aspirations becomes a key factor in successful aging (Riediger & Freund, 2006). Older adults need to scale back some of their goals and invest most of their agency in priorities that are most immediate and urgent—mainly health, family, and close social ties. In the later years, then, the motivational pendulum continues to swing further and further in the direction of relatedness, and away from competence goals. As the ratio of gains to losses in one's life becomes increasingly negative, moreover, older adults shift their investments of resources toward the maintenance of functioning and counteracting loss, as opposed to personal growth and expansion of the self. As such, prevention-focused concerns trump promotion as people get older. Secondary control strategies come to predominate over the more active primary strategies as older adults recalibrate their expectations and their hopes so that they can carry on as well as possible in the face of mounting losses and inevitable decline.

## MOTIVATION AND CULTURE

Developmental psychologists generally believe that people's motives and goals are decisively shaped by the kinds of environments they experience as they move across the life course. Parents, teachers, and other role models encourage children to pursue certain goals and avoid others. Peers and the media exert powerful influences as well. As McClelland (1961) emphasized in his studies of achievement motivation, the socialization of motives and goals occurs within particular cultural contexts that shape individual desire and belief. Social scientists define "culture" as an organized body of rules and norms that binds people together in a group (LeVine, 1982). Cultural factors provide strong guidelines regarding what goals are worth pursuing in life, when they should be pursued, and why.

In contemporary psychological science, researchers have expressed a great deal of interest in the distinction between *individualist* and *collectivist* cultures (Markus & Kitayama, 1991; Triandis, 1997). Identified often with the United States and certain Western European societies, individualism exalts the autonomy of the individual person over and against the interdependence of the group. Members of an individualist culture are generally expected to give priority to their own personal goals, even when those goals conflict with the goals of family, work group, or country. Individualism valorizes personal choice and individual agency. By contrast, collectivism privileges the goals of the group, over and against the individual. Identified often with China, Japan, and certain East Asian societies, collectivism says that individual agents should modify their striving so as to be in accord with the group. Collectivism valorizes group harmony and social conformity. Members of a collectivist society are certainly expected to develop their own personal goals and values. But their aspirations should be tempered by the recognition that the good of the group usually trumps individual goal expression.

It does not take much thought to realize that the characterizations of cultural individualism and collectivism are exaggerations, even caricatures. No human society could survive for long if its members paid no attention to the collective good. Therefore, a purely individualistic culture is a myth. Likewise, pure collectivism, without any allowance for the vicissitudes of individual agency, is equally unrealistic, for human beings are stubbornly agential, evolved to be that way in fact, and individual desires and beliefs will always motivate agents to find ways to do what they want to do. Instead, the individualism versus collectivism distinction is a matter of degree, or relative emphasis (Oyserman, Coon, & Kemmelmeier, 2002). Moreover, individual human agents often rebel against the cultural norms that prevail in their own society (Gjerde, 2004). In other words, some of the greatest advocates for individual expression may live in collectivist cultures, and zealous collectivists may live in individualist cultures as well.

Having said all that, research does support the general idea that cultural individualism and collectivism influence personal goals and motives. The cultural differences in goals appear strongest with respect to the dimension of prevention versus promotion (Higgins, 2008). For example, goals aimed at *avoiding negative states* seem to be rather more common and salient among East Asians and Asian Americans, compared with European Americans (Elliot, Chirkov, Kim, & Sheldon, 2001). By contrast, European Americans privilege goals aimed at *approaching positive states*. Avoidance goals suggest a prevention focus, in that the motivated agent seeks to be vigilant and cautious, lest he or she do something that would harm others or damage the well-being of the group. As Higgins (1997) describes this dynamic in his regulatory focus theory, the prevention focus encourages the motivated agent to set goals that aim to decrease the discrepancy between the actual self and the *ought self.* The agent knows that he or she ought to place prime importance on the good of the group. Accordingly, the agent is careful to avoid doing harm. By contrast, approach goals suggest a promotion focus, glorified in individualist cultures as the uninhibited pursuit of self-fulfillment. The person is impelled to promote his or her own unique motivational agenda. Under the regime of cultural individualism, it is important to stand out and maximize the expression of your own *ideal self*.

We all live in many different cultures at the same time. For example, I am an American, so I have deep familiarity with the ethos of cultural individualism. At the same time, I work within an academic community that values education and the pursuit of intellectual ideas over nearly everything else. I grew up in the Baptist church, and I married a Lutheran woman, each of which has immersed me in a particular religious culture. In the Baptist church, the most important goal in life was to attain personal salvation; the second most important was to win others to Jesus. The Lutherans offer a very different motivational agenda, as do Catholics, Jews, Buddhists, and Muslims. I endured a difficult childhood in a tough, working-class neighborhood in a city that was in economic decline, and when I visit my mother and siblings for holidays and family gatherings, I am reminded of that particular culture, too—the one I spent much of my adult life trying to ignore. Looking good and making money were the prime extrinsic goals I noted when I was a child, though emphasis was also placed on getting a good education in order to move up and out. Each of these cultures has likely influenced my personal goals, plans, and projects in many ways, some of which are probably beyond my conscious understanding.

The same is probably true for you. The motivational agendas you have pursued over the course of your life probably reflect a range of cultural influences, derived from family life, school, religion, work, personal relationships, social class, and gender norms. David McClelland (1961) was surely right when he claimed that motives are learned in society and culture. Let us not forget, however, that you were the one who learned them, and you continue to learn. Motivated agents bring their own inimitable will to the game of goal pursuit. They selectively absorb what their culture has to offer, appropriate it all in a way that works for them.

Dispositional personality traits have some influence, too. For example, people high in agreeableness tend to prioritize relational goals, whereas those high in conscientiousness tend to find achievement and power goals more to their liking (Bleidorn et al., 2010). Openness to experience tends to be associated with hedonistic and aesthetic goals, whereas extraversion predicts having many goals of many different kinds (Roberts, O'Donnell, & Robins, 2004). Still, the research reveals that correlations between traits and goals are quite modest. You cannot reduce your goals to the operations of your dispositional personality traits. Or, to put it all in the terms of this book, the social actor and the motivated agent represent two very different lines or layers of personality development.

With respect to that second layer, then, we employ our agency to appropriate personal experience and process the many influences upon us in order to create a motivational game plan, translating desire and belief into personal goals, and thereby decisively orienting our lives to the future. Our parents, teachers, friends, and cultures may help to shape what we want and what we believe. But at the end of the day, we are the ones who translate our own desires and beliefs into the goals we choose to pursue. As motivated agents, we make our own choices, and we alone are responsible for the choices we make.

## CONCLUSION

Members of *Homo sapiens* project themselves into the future by setting up goals in their minds and working to attain those goals. Personal goals translate desire and belief into purposeful striving. As such, goal pursuit is the primary mechanism through which human motivation manifests itself, expressing how we all endeavor to do what we *want* to do, and avoid doing what we do not want to do, as we move forward into the future.

Self-determination theory provides a useful psychological rubric for organizing many of the prominent goals that make up motivational agendas in human lives. The theory asserts that intrinsic goals tap into deep sources of human satisfaction, whereas extrinsic goals aim for external rewards such as wealth and social recognition. Many intrinsic goals derive their force from the three basic organismic needs for autonomy, competence, and relatedness. The need for autonomy is arguably the most fundamental factor in motivated agency, for it goes to the person's sense that he or she can exert some degree of control in setting and striving for goals, that the source of motivation is indeed the self. In this sense, the need for autonomy is the very need that motivated agents feel *to be motivated agents*.

The need for competence pertains to the desire to experience mastery in interacting with the world. In terms of evolution, competence recalls the timeless human challenge of getting ahead in social groups. Research on achievement motivation and on power motivation tracks individual differences in broad motivational tendencies that cover some of the same ground that the idea of competence covers. The chapter's case of Hillary Rodham Clinton illustrates the pursuit of achievement goals across the life course. Going back to her grade school years, she exhibited many of the behaviors, attitudes, values, and characteristics that research suggests are associated with high achievement motivation. Clinton seems to be higher in achievement motivation than most people, consistently aiming to do well and achieve success relative to standards of excellence. But like everybody, she has also pursued many other kinds of goals in her lifetime, including those related to power, intimacy, friendships, entertainment, and health.

The need for relatedness pertains to the desire to connect to other people in warm, caring, and productive ways. As such, relatedness captures the timeless evolutionary challenge of getting along in social groups. Research on individual differences in affiliation and intimacy motivation tracks motivational tendencies subsumed within the relatedness category.

Although people sometimes show consistent motivational trends over many decades in life, as seems to be the case for Hillary Clinton, they also demonstrate significant developmental change. As people get older, they change their goals, and they change the ways in which they pursue and engage their goals. For example, intrinsic goals appear to increase with aging, as people move from young adulthood through midlife and beyond. In our later years, prevention goals (aimed toward avoiding negative outcomes and assuring security) typically outweigh promotion goals (aimed toward approaching positive outcomes and enhancing growth), and concerns regarding relatedness are usually stronger than those concerning competence. Younger adults juggle many different kinds of goals, even when the goals conflict with each other. Midlife and older adults are more adept at managing conflict between goals, and they often develop strategies for maximizing efficiency and compensating for weaknesses in goal pursuit. In our last years, goals related to health and family typically dominate the motivational agenda.

Personality and developmental psychologists have made good progress in charting the development of motives and goals over the human life course. But they still know very little about the ultimate developmental sources of individual differences in goals. Why do some people focus most of their agency on achievement goals, while others show strong goals in the areas of intimacy, power, or security? In adolescence and young adulthood, goals coalesce around the problem of identity formation as young people struggle to understand who they are by sorting out what valued life goals they want to pursue. Dispositional personality traits such as extraversion and conscientiousness may exert some effect, too, but traits and goals do not seem to line up in a straightforward manner. Gender, ethnicity, and social class help to shape our motivational agendas. Cultural factors are also important, as research on individualism and collectivism continues to show.

Nonetheless, psychological scientists still do not understand well why some people want some things and other people want other things. And if each of us is completely honest, we probably have to admit that we do not truly understand why we want what we want either, and why we want it more, whatever it is, than other people want it. Motivation remains one of the great mysteries in personality development—so much so that the topic itself motivates many people to begin thinking seriously about personality more generally, and about how we each come to be the persons we are.

# chapter 7

# How Values Shape Agency

## MORALITY, RELIGION, AND POLITICS

W hen Americans were asked in a 1999 Gallup poll to name the one person of the 20th century they most admired, they gave the most votes to Mother Teresa. Recipient of the 1979 Nobel Peace Prize, the Blessed Teresa of Calcutta, M.C. (1910–1997), founded the Missionaries of Charity, a Roman Catholic religious order that operates hospices and homes in over 100 countries for people with HIV/AIDS, leprosy, and tuberculosis. The order also staffs soup kitchens, counseling programs, orphanages, and schools. Members adhere to vows of chastity, poverty, and obedience. Following Mother Teresa's example, they pledge to give of themselves fully and wholeheartedly to the poorest of the poor.

From the age of about 9 onward, Mother Teresa's moral and religious values formed the nucleus around which her personality revolved. Born to wealthy Albanian parents in the city of Skopje (now in Macedonia), Agnes Bojaxhiu attended daily Mass and accompanied her mother on regular excursions to distribute food and money to the local poor. The family prayed together every evening. Her father was a city counselor. When Agnes was 9 years old, her father unexpectedly died as a result (most likely) of being poisoned by political opponents. His death seemed to catalyze the young girl's moral development and intensify her religious fervor. Agnes became fascinated by stories of the lives of missionaries. With the encouragement of her mother, she left home at age 18 to join the Sisters of Loreto as a missionary in India. Eventually, she took her vows to become a nun, receiving the name "Teresa." Through her mid-30s, her main duties centered on teaching children at the convent schools.

On September 10, 1946, Teresa was traveling by train from Darjeeling to Calcutta when she received what she later described as a message from God: "I was to leave the convent and help the poor while living among them. It was an order. To fail would have been to break the faith" (Clucas, 1988, p. 35). Shortly thereafter, she shed the traditional nun's habit for a simple white cotton sari decorated with a blue border. She ventured out into the slums of Calcutta to care for "the hungry, the naked, the homeless, the crippled, the blind, the lepers, all those people who feel unwanted, unloved, uncared for through society, people that have become a burden for society and are shunned by everyone" (her words, in Williams, 2002, p. 62). In order to minister to the dying, she opened ecumenical hospices, where Catholics were given last rites, Muslims were read the Quran, and Hindus received water from the Ganges River. "A beautiful death," she once said, "is for people who lived like animals to die like angels—loved and wanted" (Spink, 1997, p. 55).

A common view regarding the religiously devout is that their strong faith quashes all doubts. Mother Teresa, however, defies the stereotype. From her mid-30s onward, she expressed grave doubts about the existence of God. Looking inside herself for signs of conviction, she often found profound emptiness and darkness instead. In these moments she wondered why she ever chose a religious vocation for life. Yet some observers have suggested that her questioning and her sense of abandonment may have led to a deeper form of faith. Mother Teresa "reframed her feeling of being abandoned as her experiencing the abandonment Christ felt on the Cross," concluded two scholars who studied her life (Scarlett & Warren, 2010, p. 654). Whereas religious faith provides many people with a sense of security and joy, the results for Mother Teresa may have been exactly the opposite. Paradoxically, the dread and the loneliness she experienced in her relationship with God may have solidified her identification with Jesus, who bore the sins of the world, according to Christians, and suffered mightily as a result. In the crucifixion story, a dying Jesus cries out: "My God, my God, why have you forsaken me?"

As motivated agents, human beings often draw on religious values to guide their future actions, especially when those imagined actions are tinged with moral meaning. But moral motivation may also stem from values that are not themselves derived from religion. Consider, for example, the case of Andrei Sakharov (1921–1989), one of the 20th century's most celebrated human rights activists and winner of the 1975 Nobel Peace Prize. The Norwegian Nobel Committee called him "a spokesman for the conscience of mankind." Although baptized in the Russian Orthodox Church, Sakharov was an atheist for his entire adult life. Unlike

Mother Teresa, he never struggled with religious faith because he had none. He did not believe in God. But he did believe that people possess human rights, and that society should ensure that those rights are given expression. The sources for Sakharov's animating values were moral and political rather than religious.

Born in Moscow to a well-educated family, the young Andrei Sakharov excelled in schoolwork, especially science. The behavior of protons and neutrons was much more interesting to him than was the behavior of people. Unlike Mother Teresa, he was not moved as a child by the suffering of the oppressed. After receiving a PhD in theoretical physics, he researched cosmic rays, then joined a team of Soviet scientists who developed nuclear technology for warfare. Sakharov played a key role in designing the first Soviet hydrogen bomb. By the late 1950s, he had become one of the most prominent scientists in the Soviet Union. Around the same time, he began to voice concerns about the moral and political implications of his scientific work.

In a study of Sakharov's career as a moral activist, developmental psychologists Anne Colby and William Damon (1992) traced how Sakharov's initial concerns regarding nuclear weapons morphed gradually into a broader critique of the Soviet political system. As his moral agenda expanded, the range of people and institutions with which Sakharov had contact, and which worked to enrich his developing moral perspective, expanded as well. By the mid-1960s, Sakharov and a small group of fellow scientists were urging their peers to reform scientific practices that were too beholden, they believed, to the Cold War agenda of Soviet leaders. In an open letter to the Soviet Congress, Sakharov and colleagues warned against authoritarian strains in the Soviet political system, as exemplified in new antislander laws and other government efforts to silence protest. In 1967, he wrote a letter to the Soviet leader, Leonid Brezhnev, pleading the case of two political dissidents who had received harsh sentences under Soviet law. The following year he published a book titled *Progress, Coexistence, and Intellectual Freedom* (Sakharov, 1968), which argued for a reduction of nuclear weapons and détente between the Soviet Union and its archenemy, the United States. The book introduced Sakharov to many Western readers and greatly expanded his sphere of influence. As a result, the Soviet leadership stripped Sakharov of his state clearance for research, effectively ending his career as a scientist. Shortly thereafter, his first wife died.

In the 1970s and 1980s, Sakharov became the most influential Russian critic of the Soviet political system and an ardent advocate for political freedom and human rights. By 1973, Sakharov and fellow dissidents were reaching out to the United Nations and other international agencies for help. Sakharov began to conduct interviews with foreign journalists, asking Westerners to intervene on behalf of Soviet dissidents who had been confined in psychiatric hospitals and exiled to prison camps.

Finally, the authorities had had enough. On January 22, 1980, Soviet police arrested Sakharov and exiled him to the remote city of Gorki, where he was kept under tight surveillance and isolated from the press for 6 years. When his second wife, Yelena Bonner, sought to travel to the United States for heart surgery, the Soviet authorities denied her request. Sakharov launched a hunger strike to protest the restriction. He was taken to a hospital and force-fed, then held in isolation for 4 months.

Sakharov was finally released from exile in 1986, after Mikhail Gorbachev assumed power in the USSR and initiated epic political reforms. In 1989, Sakharov was elected to the new parliament, the All-Union Congress for People's Deputies, where he co-led the democratic opposition to the communist regime. A few months later, the Berlin Wall came down, signaling the beginning of the end for the Soviet Union. Just a month after that, at age 68, Sakharov died of a heart attack.

If personality is a person's unique variation on the general design for human nature, then what features stand out as the most prominent variations from the norm in the lives of Mother Teresa and Andrei Sakharov? Their dispositional traits are important, for sure. As a social actor, Mother Teresa seems to have been especially high on the trait of agreeableness, particularly with respect to the facets of humility and altruism. Sakharov was probably pretty high on conscientiousness, like many of his peers in science, and very high on openness to experience. I suspect they were both in the medium range on neuroticism. But these kinds of personality attributions seem almost beside the point in the face of extraordinary moral commitment. What seems to stand out in sharper relief in the unique and artfully constructed lives of Mother Teresa and Andrei Sakharov is their moral motivational agenda—the values and goals they pursued as they sought to exert a transformative effect on their worlds. It is nearly impossible to talk about either one of them without talking about moral, religious, and political values.

As moral exemplars, Mother Teresa and Andrei Sakharov may be extreme cases. But they are not so different from many other people, perhaps even you, the reader, in developing and displaying their moral, religious, and political values as foundational principles in their lives. We all have values and beliefs, and for many of us, these ideological dimensions seem to assume as much importance in our personality, if not more, than our dispositional traits. To understand the personalities of many, if not most, people in the world today, therefore, you must consider how they address fundamental value questions such as these: *What is good? What is God? How should society work?* It is part of human nature, I would argue, to ask questions like these, questions that go to the heart of what it means to live as a member of our peculiar eusocial species. The answers we formulate to these questions shape our lives as motivated agents. They say as much as does anything else about who we are and why we do what we do.

## MORALITY AND PERSONALITY: WHAT IS GOOD?

Human groups are always moral groups. In order to live together and adapt to the challenges of group life, human beings must adhere to some kind of moral code, even if it is no more exalted than the code that prohibits killing your neighbor, then stealing his wife. Groups may differ widely with respect to what they consider to be good and bad, right and wrong. But no human group can function without some shared agreement regarding moral conduct. Even schoolchildren playing soccer at recess must adhere to a code of conduct that prescribes what is right and wrong in the game. Without the rules, the game falls apart.

And so it is in the game of life, at least for *Homo sapiens*. It is certainly possible to imagine a human society somewhere and someplace—say, hunting and foraging on the African savannah 200,000 years ago—wherein group members developed no *religious* or *political* sensibilities whatsoever, no belief in God and no clear consciousness of how a complex society should be governed. Organized religion and complex political structures are probably recent human achievements, emerging after the advent of language and the subsequent explosion in cultural innovation that began 50,000 years ago. It is, however, impossible, I would submit, to imagine a human society, should it hope to be viable, without a moral code of some sort, without a shared understanding—even implicit and prelinguistic—of what constitutes right and wrong conduct in the group. "What is good?" is a natural human question to ask, a primal and preverbal question that evolution has prepared us to ask and to answer through group life. Morality is primary for our eusocial species because *without morality we cannot be a eusocial species.* Like food and water, we cannot live without it.

In *The Descent of Man and Selection in Relation to Sex*, Charles Darwin (1871/1903) theorized that human morality evolved naturally out of social instincts that human beings share with certain other animals. Early humans, Darwin imagined, were endowed by natural selection with social proclivities that may "lead an animal to take pleasure in the society of its fellows, to feel a certain amount of sympathy with them, and to perform various services for them" (p. 95). For primates and certain other eusocial species, basic social instincts should predispose individuals to express rudimentary forms of care and consideration for other group members (De Waal, 1996). The social affinity might serve as a check on aggression within the group, a natural restraint on ruthless exploitation. It also paves the way for cooperative activities, such as food sharing among chimpanzees and other great apes.

Sharing behavior and other collaborations may depend on a rudimentary sense of *fairness* in the group. Chimpanzees and capuchin monkeys respond negatively when resources are distributed in a grossly inequitable manner (Brosnan, 2006). As juveniles, social canids (wolves, coyotes, and domestic dogs) refuse to interact with individuals that violate rules regarding fair play in the group. Those that play too roughly are ostracized. One researcher has observed that when coyotes mature, those that are rejected from play sessions are much more likely to leave the pack than those that are included, which more than doubles their risk for an early death (Bekoff, 2004). Among coyotes and humans, then, fair play appears to have its advantages.

By age 6 months, human infants prefer good guys to bad guys in simple moral scenarios (Bloom, 2012). By 2 years of age, humans show a strong preference for fairness in the allotment of rewards and punishments (Sloane, Baillargeon, & Premack, 2012). Eventually, we humans go much further. With development, we display moral sensibilities that are vastly more expansive and nuanced than anything found elsewhere in the animal kingdom. Compared to our primate cousins, for example, human beings (1) exhibit considerably more respect for other group members' property and possessions (articulated in the notions of "ownership" and "property rights"); (2) cooperate more extensively in child care and other prosocial activities; (3) use communication to educate and socialize others rather than merely to issue commands; and (4) develop norms that codify moral behavior, and institutions that aim to cultivate and enforce it (Tomasello & Vaish, 2013). To become socialized in human groups is to become moralized—to learn the rules and norms of the group; to learn how to control yourself so that you do not violate the rules and thereby disrupt the well-being of the group or members in it; to learn how to be nice, play fair, help others, share resources, respect authority, and demonstrate loyalty to the group. Moral emotions such as guilt and empathy contribute to the development of conscience in the preschool years and the eventual articulation of morally freighted dispositional traits such as conscientiousness and agreeableness.

Many psychologists believe that the elaborate moral codes that human beings construct to govern social behavior have developed out of primitive moral intuitions, or gut reactions that human beings automatically experience regarding right and wrong. In a highly influential formulation, Jonathan Haidt (2012) has suggested that human beings are endowed with strong moral reactions to violations in at least five different areas of social life: care/harm, fairness/cheating, loyalty/betrayal, authority/subversion, and sanctity/degradation (see Table 7.1). According to Haidt, you don't need to have learned the Ten Commandments or to have taken a college class on ethics to recoil at the sight of a person being harmed, especially if that person appears to be innocent of any wrongdoing. Even young children know it is generally wrong to inflict pain on a sentient being, such as another child or a puppy. They know that the right thing to do is to care for somebody in pain rather than to inflict pain. Young children react negatively to violations of fairness and reciprocity, too. They respond negatively when resources are allotted in an inequitable manner, when one member of the group does not play fair, or when somebody receives a benefit from another and does not reciprocate in kind. They do not like cheaters.

The Golden Rule—do unto others as you would have them do unto you—formalizes a doctrine about care/harm and fairness/cheating that most young children instinctively know to be true. According to Haidt (2012), care/harm and fairness/cheating undergird a basic *ethic of autonomy* in human groups. The gut reactions that people feel in response to violations in these two areas provide the evolved emotional material out of which conceptions of human rights are derived. The authors of the American Declaration of Independence could never have argued that human beings are "created equal" and "endowed by their Creator with certain unalienable Rights" if they had not been endowed themselves, by evolution it turns out, with moral intuitions regarding harm and fairness.

Intuitions regarding ingroup loyalty and hierarchy serve to bind autonomous agents together within the group, reinforcing what Haidt (2012) describes as an *ethic of community*. Human groups cannot function well if individual members feel no loyalty to the collective. As a result, evolution has shaped human beings to respond with anger and even moral outrage when somebody betrays the group. Traitors are reviled in all societies; in some nation-states, treason constitutes a capital crime. Even on the more mundane level of interpersonal relationships, those who betray others—in friendship, in love—are widely viewed to have violated a moral principle.

In a related vein, most human groups require some degree of hierarchical structure, some stabilizing authority. In families, parents are authority figures, and children are expected to respect and obey them. In larger collectives, authority is distributed across various roles and offices. Different individuals are "in charge" of different domains and functions, ranging from law enforcement to teachers to those assigned the role of defending the group against outsiders. The individuals who occupy these roles—the authorities themselves—must enjoy some level of respect or deference. When authority is repeatedly subverted, chaos will ensue, as we have seen in recent years for failed states such as Somalia and (as I write this chapter) Syria. In the course of human evolution, it is likely that when groups descended into chaos, individual group members suffered grievously—they died, failed to reproduce, suffered malnutrition, were taken captive by rival groups, and so on.

A fifth moral intuition regarding sanctity/degradation—involving feelings of disgust, revulsion, and anger in response to violations of purity—may have its evolutionary origins in experiences with pathogens and toxins. Analogous to how the body reacts with disgust to spoiled food, human beings react to certain social phenomena—certain forms of sexuality, for example, certain behaviors of out-group members—with disgust, moral indignation, and other negative responses. On the other side of the moral ledger, people (women, mainly) who treat their bodies as temples of purity are praised in many cultures for the virtues of temperance and chastity. Sanctity/degradation may feed into religious sentiments by elevating certain practices to the level of the sacred, while degrading others as vulgar. A shared sense of sacredness may bind group members together under a moral banner, solidifying loyalty to the group and respect for authority.

As social actors, then, we respond instantly to violations of care, fairness, loyalty, authority, and purity. As such, we are moral *actors* from very early childhood onward. But we do not become moral *agents* until we are at least capable of deliberating about our actions and consciously forming goals and values as a result.

The first step in becoming a moral agent is to make an explicit moral judgment. Rather than merely act in a purely reflexive manner, a moral agent must (at minimum) make a conscious decision, must deliberate

**TABLE 7.1. Five Moral Foundations**

| Foundation | Description | Common expressions |
|---|---|---|
| Care/harm | Reacting negatively to harm of other sentient beings; knowing that inflicting pain is wrong; desiring to care for others, especially when they are in need; valuing love, nurturance, kindness, mercy. | • Thou shalt not kill.<br>• Do no harm (Hippocratic oath).<br>• Love thy neighbor as thyself.<br>• *Ahisma* (Hindu: do not injure).<br>• Be nice. |
| Fairness/cheating | Reacting negatively to inequity or breaches in fairness; expecting reciprocity in relationships; sharing and working for the common good; valuing justice, equality. | • Do unto others as you would have them do unto you (Golden Rule).<br>• Cheaters never prosper.<br>• An eye for an eye; tit for tat.<br>• The social contract.<br>• Play fair. |
| Loyalty/betrayal | Reacting negatively to failures in commitment, breaking promises, or undermining trust; staying true to the ideals of the group, pledging oneself to the well-being of the group; valuing commitment, fidelity, martyrdom. | • Until death do us part.<br>• I pledge allegiance to. . . .<br>• "I only regret that I have but one life to give for my country" (Nathan Hale, American martyr).<br>• Stand by me. |
| Authority/subversion | Reacting negatively to disrespect of legitimate authority and efforts to subvert the established order; showing respect, deference, or obedience to authority; valuing order, hierarchy, the rule of law, and other authorities or authoritative institutions. | • Thou shalt have no other gods before me.<br>• Honor they father and thy mother.<br>• Filial piety.<br>• Law and order.<br>• Obey the rules. |
| Sanctity/degradation | Reacting negatively (often with disgust) to violations of purity or sacredness; being sensitive to pollution or corruption from foreign elements; valuing purity, chastity, temperance. | • Remember the Sabbath day, to keep it holy.<br>• Cleanliness is next to Godliness.<br>• Purification rites.<br>• Be holy. |

*Note.* Based on Haidt (2012).

over what is right and what is wrong, even if the deliberation is short-lived. How do moral agents do this? According to social psychologist Kurt Gray, people make moral judgments by casting characters within an imagined dyadic scenario (Gray, Young, & Waytz, 2012). Whether we are talking about situations that invoke care/harm, fairness/cheating, loyalty/betrayal, authority/subversion, or sanctity/degradation, Gray maintains, people tend to think of the moral scenario as involving at least one intentional *agent* and one suffering *patient*. Morality = Agency + Patient. In the simplest case of a moral violation, an agent intentionally causes the suffering of the patient: A rapist assaults his victim; a cheater deprives another of his fair share; a disloyal husband betrays his wife (or a traitor betrays his country); a disrespectful daughter insults her father; a sexually promiscuous woman brings dishonor on her family. Because they have intentionality, agents are *responsible* for what they do; because they are capable of experiencing suffering, patients have *rights* that should be maintained. In making moral judgments, people evaluate the quality of the agent's intentionality ("Did he mean to do it?" "Did she understand her responsibilities?") and the quality of the patient's suffering ("How much pain did he experience?" "How serious was her suffering?").

In making moral judgments, people typecast characters according to their respective qualities of intentionality and experience. Some characters who are high on both intentionality and experience (adult humans) may therefore be cast as either agents or patients. Some characters are high on agency and low on experience (God, Google). They can be cast as agents, but they do not fit the role of patients (God does not experience suffering the way human beings do, many people would say, though Christians may site the odd example of Jesus Christ). Some characters are low on agency and high on experience (infants and young children, puppies). They are readily cast as patients because they are capable of experiencing suffering, but they do not make appropriate agents because we do not hold them responsible for their actions. Finally, some characters have neither agency nor experience, such as dead people or inanimate objects. In most cases, characters who lack both agency and experience do not qualify for moral scenarios. I can kick a rock with all my might, but I will never be accused of a moral transgression because the rock feels no pain.

In that agents have responsibilities, moral considerations come into play for both bad behavior (violations) and good behavior (intentional acts of benevolence). When an agent is intentionally helpful (good), he or she is cast in the role of the *hero*. When an agent is intentionally harmful (bad), he or she becomes the *villain* in a moral scenario. Similarly, when patients are helped by a good agent, they become *beneficiaries*.

When patients are harmed by a bad agent, they become *victims*. Moral judgments, then, involve assigning characters to the roles of hero, villain, beneficiary, and victim (Gray et al., 2012). Stories of moral heroism evoke emotions of inspiration and elevation—we may feel inspired or transported to a higher plane when we witness a scene of heroic altruism, as in the case of the subway hero in Chapter 1 of this book. Stories of moral villains, however, elicit emotions of anger and disgust. We want the perpetrators to be punished. When we hear about beneficiaries (patients who receive help from agents), we tend to feel happiness and relief. By contrast, we respond with sympathy and sadness when we hear the story of a moral patient who suffers (the victim), and we may feel the urge (as agents) to right the wrong.

Here is the key developmental point in all of this: *Becoming a motivated agent with respect to moral judgment involves knowing what moral intentionality and experience are all about.* Put differently, you cannot be an agent until you really understand what an agent is (and what a patient is). Children cannot engage in moral typecasting until they understand that other people have minds within which reside intentions, thoughts, and feelings. With the development of theory of mind and the age 5–7 shift (Chapter 5 in this book), children can weigh the answers to these questions: What did the agent intend to do? What did the patient experience?

As children master theory of mind and develop the perspective-taking skills that come with the age 5–7 shift, they graduate from being mere moral actors to becoming moral agents themselves, capable of moral decision making and eventually responsible for the moral decisions they make. Having said this, I must also acknowledge that children (and adults) show wide individual differences with respect to their apprehension of the moral agent and moral patient positions. Some autistic individuals, even as adults, never develop a full sense of human agency, showing persistent deficits in theory-of-mind skills. In a parallel fashion, some psychopaths fail to experience the degree of empathy and perspective taking that is required to comprehend fully another person's suffering. According to Gray and colleagues (2012), autistic individuals may be compromised in moral decision making because they do not fully "get" agency, and psychopaths may be compromised because they fail to appreciate what it means to be a moral patient.

The development of moral agency paves the way for the articulation of values, virtues, personal ideologies, and other cognitive expressions of moral sentiment. What a person believes to be his or her moral values typically refers to social arrangements that the person imagines to be especially good and praiseworthy, such as a world in which all people are created equal, a world wherein people obey the law, a world where God's love reigns supreme, a world in which people honor their commitments, a just society, a caring community, freedom, liberty, salvation, wisdom, enlightenment, interpersonal harmony, peace, and happiness for all (Rokeach, 1973; Schwartz, 2009). Moral values articulate visions for what a good life might be, projected ideals that expand upon and give cognitive meaning to gut intuitions regarding care, fairness, loyalty, authority, and sacredness. These imagined end states may be projected into the future, like goals. Indeed, values and goals share a teleological quality in that they project the agent into the future, oriented toward a desired end state. A person's goals and values frame his or her plans for future striving. They specify the good and desirable end states with respect to which a motivated agent organizes his or her motivational energy. They identify what a motivated agent is motivated to achieve in the future, what the agent considers to be worthy of motivational pursuit.

## RELIGION AND PERSONALITY: WHAT IS GOD?

In Chapter 5, I stated that, psychologically speaking, I became a motivated agent around second grade. A couple of years before, probably during the summer between kindergarten and first grade, my brother and I were abducted by a church lady. As Jeff and I were sitting idly on our front lawn one Sunday morning, Mrs. Pelke drove by and asked if we wanted to go to church. We did not know what church was, but because we were bored out of our minds that morning, we decided to run inside and ask our mom if we could go. She said okay, which began my lifelong love/hate relationship with religion. Mrs. Pelke hauled us over to the First Baptist Church in Merrillville, Indiana, where we learned Bible verses and worked on the various sorts of Sunday school arts and crafts projects that little Baptist kids worked on in the 1960s. Jeff and I also attended the afterschool Bible Club that Mrs. Pelke ran once a week out of her living room. Mrs. Pelke encouraged all the kids to pray to Jesus and ask Him to come into our hearts. He would be our Lord and Savior, and we would go to heaven as a result. My memory is hazy, but I am pretty sure I did that prayer. Later, around sixth grade, I formally affirmed my faith and was baptized at Glen Park Baptist Church.

As I matured into motivated agency during my grade school years and came to perceive my life in terms of goals and values to be pursued in the future, I imported religious ideas into my sense of self. I saw myself as a Christian whose life was to be guided by Christian values and beliefs. At the same time, competing points of view (from school, from friends, from the media) also came to hold sway in my life, and I was never really able to reconcile the contradictions. My Baptist pastor truly believed that God created the world in seven 24-hour days, yet high school biology class proved (to me, at least) that such a literal belief was ridiculous. I was okay with the Baptist idea that all people are sinners ("For all have sinned and come short of the glory of God"; Romans 3:23). But it was never clear to me why a man named Jesus needed to be killed 2,000 years ago in order to save others from their sins. *Does that make sense?* People who never had a Mrs. Pelke in their lives, or who grew up outside the orbit of the Christian church, can surely be forgiven for thinking that Christian ideas are downright absurd. Indeed, many Christians have thought the same thing—see Søren Kierkegaard (1813–1855) for one of history's best examples, and maybe Mother Teresa.

Nearly 50 years later, I am now no longer sure that I am a Christian, if Christianity is equated solely with *belief.* I don't think I believe in God even, though sometimes I feel that I do. Still, my wife and I drive 35 minutes nearly every Sunday morning to attend services at a Lutheran congregation. She sings in the choir. I have served on the church council. Why do we do this? Because we always have, perhaps. Because she is the daughter of a Lutheran minister, and her faith is less ambivalent than mine. Because we love the music and appreciate the dynamic pastor, who is also a good friend. Because, in America, if you want to do good works, religious institutions are often the places where you can do them. Churches, synagogues, mosques, and other religious institutions typically provide an alternative discourse and way of thinking about life in America, one that elevates morality and service over the extrinsic goals of wealth, beauty, sexiness, and success.

One of the biggest reasons we still attend a church is *the community.* We like the people there and feel a strong bond to the group. The great sociologist Émile Durkheim (1915/1967) argued that the prime function of religion is to build community. Religion brings people together under a common sociomoral banner, or what the sociologist Peter Berger (1967) characterized as a *sacred canopy.* Within the group, people learn stories about why the world exists and what place human beings may assume in an ultimate cosmic order. In a multigenerational and socially diverse context, religiously observant people receive and provide instruction on values, virtue, and moral development. Religion functions to bind people from different generations and walks of life into caring moral communities (Graham & Haidt, 2010).

*Homo sapiens* seem peculiarly drawn to religion. Anthropologists have observed that religion is pervasive across human cultures; all known human societies have, or have had, some kind of religious tradition. Because religion appears to be a human universal, scientists have speculated on its evolutionary roots. Some argue that religion is itself an evolved adaptation for human life. In *Darwin's Cathedral*, David Sloan Wilson (2002) contends that religion has evolved to promote cooperation in groups, which strengthens the group's ability to compete against other groups, which indirectly promotes the inclusive fitness of individual members of the group. When the group flourishes, its members are better able to survive and reproduce. Religious sentiment creates solidarity, Wilson argues, supporting long-term enterprises among group members, such as raising children, defending the group against invaders, building alliances, and creating culture.

Other scientists have argued that religion is more of a by-product of other evolved adaptations, having developed across different human cultures and ecologies because it happens to assist other mechanisms in meeting many different human needs (Kirkpatrick, 2005). For example, religion can function like an attachment system, promoting feelings of security by assuring people that God or some other supernatural force cares for them (Granqvist, Mikulincer, & Shaver, 2010). Religion can enhance good feelings about the self (Sedikides & Gebauer, 2010) and reinforce a sense of control in life (Kay, Gaucher, McGregor, & Nash, 2010). Religion can promote self-regulation. Indeed, many studies show that church attendance and other indicators of religious observance in the United States are positively associated with physical and mental health, and negatively associated with substance abuse, tobacco use, delinquency, crime, and divorce (Seybold & Hill, 2001). By sustaining the idea that life retains ultimate meaning, moreover, religion may shield people from the terror of death and relieve anxiety in the face of uncertainty (Berger, 1967; Vail et al., 2010). Religious sentiments and norms may also contribute to hierarchical stability in human groups by providing a sacred imprimatur for group standards and laws (Kirkpatrick, 2005). If group members believe that moral norms in the group derive their authority from an otherworldly source, they may be less eager to violate those norms, fearing retribution from beyond.

Belief in supernatural deities, moreover, may be grow naturally out of the peculiar way human beings think about nature and about other people (Bering, 2006; Gervais, 2013). Research by developmental psychologists suggests that young children reliably distinguish between animate and inanimate objects in the natural world. When an inanimate object is seen to move with no visible external cause, young children will often assume that an invisible force of some kind made the object move. If the force is imagined to be inside the object, then children (and adults) imagine the object to be alive in some sense—an active *agent* who *intends* to move. If the force is imagined to be outside the object, then children (and sometimes adults) may invoke notions of God or some other external *agent* whose *intention* is to make the object move. The human mind seems to have evolved to detect agents in the natural world, tuning perception and cognition toward vigilance in order to protect the individual from potential threats from other intentional beings, such as animal predators and hostile human beings.

As children come to impute mindful activity in others, they may imagine ultimate agents whose minds reside in otherworldly beings, such as gods, angels, devils, saints, ghosts, dead ancestors, and the like. Cultural learning plays into cognitive development here. Religious instruction from parents and other authorities reinforces a natural tendency to perceive agency nearly everywhere and to assume, therefore, that what happens in the world is largely dictated by the minds of agents, be they human or divine. In most religious communities, the ultimate agents are divine agents, whose intentionality establishes a sacred order in the universe (Berger, 1967). It seems that many human beings feel that they understand the nature of the world deeply only when they are able to construe an ultimate agentic cause (Gray & Wegner, 2010). Otherwise, life seems random. Knowing that there is an ultimate agent behind it all, moreover, may reinforce the value of moral behavior. Even when you are bereft of human company, God is there, many believe. You are never alone. God watches, and God knows who you are:

> O LORD, you have searched me and you know me.
> You know when I sit and when I rise; you perceive my thoughts
>     from afar.
> You discern my going out and my lying down; you are familiar
>     with all my ways.
> Before a word is on my tongue you know it completely, O LORD.
>                       —PSALM 139: 1–4, New International Translation

For any given person, the development of religious beliefs and values depends on the kind of religious community to which the person belongs.

In contemporary modern society, many people receive no religious instruction at all. But many more still do, whether formally through Sunday school, catechism, confirmation classes, and the like, or informally via influences from parents, peers, the media, and other socializing agents in the person's environment. Many children are exposed early on to religious images and stories—accounts of ancient floods and plagues, stories of betrayal and redemption. In Western religious traditions, they learn about the main characters and plotlines of religious narratives, such as the agential exploits of God, Abraham, Moses, David, Mohammed, the Virgin Mary, Jesus, various saints and martyrs, distinguished rabbis and prophets, and the Mormon pioneers. They are told that simple lessons about morality, such as the Golden Rule, owe their authority to a religious source. As they move toward adolescence, they may learn specific creeds and abstract doctrines that are associated with particular faith traditions. Reflecting the advance of cognitive development, religious instruction becomes more systematized and scholarly as children grow older, moving from a focus on emotionally laden symbols, images, and narratives to a consideration of formal rules and underlying principles (Fowler, 1981).

Still, even the most religious Americans today appear to pay much less attention than they did, say, 50 years ago, to doctrinal differences among faith traditions (Wolfe, 2003). Most Christians, for example, don't care so much anymore about whether God is unitary or a trinity (Father, Son, and Holy Ghost), or whether salvation comes through good works or grace (the signal dispute that set off the Protestant Reformation 500 years ago). Instead, many American Christians develop religious values within a loose set of fuzzy ideas about who God is and what it means to be a good, religious person. Moreover, these values often reflect secular society as much as they do religion. Sociologists Christian Smith and Melinda Denton (2005) conducted an in-depth study of religious beliefs and values among American teenagers who profess an affiliation with Christianity. They found that most American teenagers ascribe to a watered-down, generic brand of religious belief, reflecting common themes in American culture more generally. Smith and Denton identified five basic tenets that undergird religious value systems for many American adolescents:

1. A God exists who created and orders the world and watches over people.
2. God wants people to be good, nice, and fair to each other, as taught in the Bible and by most world religions.

3. God also wants people to be happy and to feel good about themselves.
4. People should call upon God during times of need because God helps people solve problems.
5. Good people go to heaven when they die.

Teenagers and adults show huge individual differences in the extent to which they exhibit religious beliefs, values, and practices in their lives. These differences reflect different childhood experiences, for sure, but perhaps surprisingly, variation in religiosity also shows a substantial genetic component (Koenig, McGue, & Iacono, 2008). Indeed, the heritability of religiosity appears to *increase with age* into adulthood, probably because as people grow older, they are better able to ignore what other people want them to do and to follow instead the promptings of their genotypes. In a genetic analysis, two researchers recently provided evidence that the heritability of religion is tightly connected to the heritability of personality characteristics that specify concerns for (1) community integration and (2) existential certainty (Lewis & Bates, 2013). Religion functions to consolidate community and to provide answers to ultimate questions of existence, and people for whom these two issues play a central role in personality—being close to others in community and endeavoring to find ultimate meaning in life—may be (genetically) drawn to religion.

In a similar vein, other studies have shown that religiosity is connected to the dispositional traits of agreeableness (A) and conscientiousness (C) (Saroglou, 2010). People high in A and C tend to be more connected to religion than people who score low on these two traits, all other things being equal. In the Big Five trait taxonomy, A and C are the two great socializers, intricately involved in self-regulation. Among its many functions, religion works to promote self-regulation for many people. Religion may resonate well with especially agreeable people, who take great joy in close interpersonal relationships and altruistic strivings, and with people high in C, who appreciate order in the world, respect rules, and work hard to control impulses so that they can achieve conventional success. The development of religious values, furthermore, may promote the development of dispositional traits themselves. A recent study shows that high school sophomores who profess strong religious values tend to show larger increases in A and decreases in antisocial traits over the next 3 years (assessed again when they are seniors), compared to less religious sophomores (Huuskes, Ciarrochi, & Heaven, 2013).

## POLITICS AND PERSONALITY: HOW SHOULD SOCIETY WORK?

The opening lines of the First Amendment to the U.S. Constitution read like this: "Congress shall make no law respecting an establishment of religion, or prohibiting the free exercise thereof." In other words, the U.S. Congress is prohibited from making laws that directly *support or prohibit* the expression of religion among American citizens. This text is widely regarded as establishing a constitutional principle commonly referred to by Americans as *separation of church and state*. The principle asserts that religion (the church) and politics (the state) are two independent realms in American life.

The fact, though, that the framers of the U.S. Constitution made such an explicit point of separating the two suggests that religion and politics may often be conflated in the minds of *Homo sapiens*, and in the groups wherein they live. The framers achieved a radical departure from traditional human practice. Before the advent of modern democracies, religious authority and political authority were typically conjoined in nation-states, principalities, and other sovereign human communities. For centuries, Europeans conceived of government in terms of the divine right of Kings, and before that, very few human societies likely even considered the possibility that the exercise of political power should be separated from religious life. Hunting and gathering societies never got around to composing constitutions, of course. But even if they had (let us pretend for a moment that they were literate), they would have found no need to make separate rules for *divine* influence and *social* power.

Religion and politics are linked closely in the human mind because both spring from *moral* considerations regarding how people *should live together in groups*. Even today, religious authority and political authority play off each other, as if each derives its psychological and social meanings from a common source. Recruiting participants from many different societies, East and West, a team of researchers has shown that when people begin to lose faith in the government, they increase their adherence to religion, and vice versa (Kay, Shepherd, Blatz, Chua, & Galinsky, 2010). The researchers characterize the relation between religion and politics as hydraulic: As one begins to ebb, the other flows. Both provide human beings with a sense of structure and order in the world, and people look naturally to both for guidelines regarding how to live together and what to value in life.

Political values and beliefs may be characterized in many different ways. The most common contemporary frame, however, pits a conservative political orientation against a liberal one (Jost, 2006). Ever since the French National Assembly of 1789 seated the nobles to the right of the presiding officer and the representatives of the common people to the left, the distinction between right (conservative) and left (liberal) has proven to be an efficient and useful way to categorize political viewpoints. In late-18th-century France, the nobles were the privileged class, and their political persuasion favored *conserving* the status quo. The common folk were more inclined to value societal change, which they imagined might improve their lot in life.

Although the particular beliefs and attitudes associated with the right and the left respectively have varied dramatically over the past two centuries, conservatives have tended to place greater emphasis on traditional sources of order and wisdom, sometimes harkening back to an imagined golden age when social life was better than it is today, whereas liberals have tended to agitate for progressive change. Of course, everybody realizes that change must occur; human life is dynamic, and societies are always in flux. But when conservatives imagine positive change, they often couch it in terms of *restoration*—the urge to restore something good that has been lost. By contrast, liberals typically imagine change in terms of progressive *reform*. Whereas conservatives may sometimes long for something good from the past, or seek to conserve something good in the present, fearing it may be readily lost, liberals tend to distrust the past and look eagerly to establish a new and better world in the future (Allit, 2009).

The conservative–liberal continuum tracks the different values and goals for social life that motivated agents project onto their self-governing social groups. Over the past 200 years, it has tracked how human beings who live in modern societies believe their respective societies should be governed. With the establishment of democratic institutions and the rise of industry, technology, science, urbanization, international markets, and globalization over the past 200 years, people living in modern societies have witnessed dramatic changes in social relations and arrangements. Invoking two German terms, sociologists have described a resultant tension that modern people feel between the promptings of *Gemeinschaft* and the demands of *Gesellschaft*.

Translated roughly as "community," *Gemeinschaft* refers to traditional patterns of social relations based on shared blood, shared place, and shared beliefs, the prototype for which is the extended family or clan. *Gesellschaft* refers to the more modern, impersonal arrangements of "civil society" reflected in modern markets, urban settings, and complex bureaucratic states, wherein individuals are more or less free to pursue their own destinies. The conservative sentiment often seems to bend toward the traditional community of *Gemeinschaft*, whereas liberal sensibilities often value the autonomy that motivated agents may enjoy within the frame of *Gesellschaft* (Haidt & Graham, 2009). This is not to suggest, of course, that conservatives reject the modern world, or that liberals have no concern for traditional social institutions, like the family. These kinds of gross caricatures are unfair, even if political campaigns often use them. I am talking instead about *subtle but deeply felt differences in agential inclinations*, experienced by different motivated agents, conservative and liberal, who develop correspondingly different political values, beliefs, and goals.

Running from right to left, the broad dimension of political conservatism versus liberalism organizes a wide array of beliefs, attitudes, and values that adults living in modern democracies tend to hold. It is also a strong predictor of voting patterns. Although many voters claim that they cast their ballots for "the best person," people who espouse strong conservative viewpoints tend to vote for conservative candidates, and liberals reliably vote for more liberal candidates (Jost, 2006). In the United States, one's self-reported position on the conservative–liberal continuum is a powerful predictor of one's standing on a range of social and political issues, from abortion rights to gun laws to environmental regulation. A visitor from another planet might find it difficult to explain why the same people who strongly oppose restrictions on the ownership of firearms in the United States would also strongly support laws to punish people who burn the American flag. Or why those who believe that taxes should be sharply raised on the rich and on large corporations should also favor same-sex marriage, stem cell research, and affirmative action for racial minorities. Social and political attitudes group together into clusters, even if people believe that they carefully consider each issue on its own terms. Any given person may show an idiosyncratic pattern—say, a devout Catholic who opposes both birth control (a politically conservative position) and capital punishment (a politically liberal position). But the many exceptions still prove a powerful rule: Political orientation is a robust construct for predicting and organizing the beliefs, attitudes, opinions, and values people hold about key societal issues of the day.

Political orientation predicts so well because it involves what social psychologists call *motivated social cognition* (Jost, Glaser, Kruglanski, & Sulloway, 2003). As motivated agents, human beings formulate social attitudes and values that meet underlying needs and goals. In this sense, political cognitions bear a great deal of psychological heat. They express underlying fears, hopes, desires, and wishes regarding social life. They also reflect deep moral (and often religious) concerns regarding how people should live and what society should do to promote a good life in the future. For many people, the political is deeply personal, even if they profess little conscious interest in current events and the nightly news.

Across many studies, research indicates that political conservatives score higher than political liberals on death anxiety, fear of threat and loss, need for order, and self-esteem. Political liberals score higher than political conservatives on tolerance for uncertainty, sensation seeking, and openness to experience (Carney, Jost, Gosling, & Potter, 2008; Jost, Federico, & Napier, 2009). Conservatives often describe themselves, and are described by others, as especially cautious, inhibited, self-controlled, fearful, tough, loyal, conventional, decisive, moralistic, and concerned with rules and norms. Liberals often describe themselves, and are described by others, as especially sensitive, open, tolerant, flexible, impulsive, curious, and emotionally expressive.

Social and political psychologists explain these observed differences in many different ways. John Jost and his colleagues (2003) argue that conservative political values function to manage uncertainty and threat by justifying the system's status quo. Conservatives are more resistant to change and more accepting of prevailing norms in society because, Jost argues, they harbor stronger fears than do liberals about things running out of control. Craving order and stability, conservatives invest in the system, even if current conditions are unfair to many people, even unfair to themselves. By contrast, liberals are impatient with perceived inequalities and injustices, and they welcome change. More open to new experiences and less invested in tradition, liberals are more willing than conservatives to question the status quo and to upend conventions when they see an opportunity for progress. Conservatives view them as reckless and disrespectful; liberals view conservatives as rigid and moralistic. Both sides have a point.

Recalling a motivation idea I introduced in Chapter 6, social psychologist E. Tory Higgins and his colleagues suggest that political conservatism reflects a *prevention focus* approach to life, whereas liberalism stems from *promotion focus* (Cornwell & Higgins, 2013). Prevention focus motivation aims to avoid negative outcomes and minimize risk. When a motivated agent senses threats in the environment, he or she must adopt a vigilant pose in order to detect and fend off the source of danger. Research shows that conservatives see the world as a more dangerous place than do liberals. Moreover, many people—conservative or liberal—*become more conservative* when they are faced with serious threats or when they are reminded of their own mortality (Landau et al., 2004). By contrast, a promotion focus orientation motivates an agent to seek out rewards in the environment, in order to maximize positive emotions. When people feel secure, they are more inclined to take risks. In agitating for social change, liberals may express their dissatisfaction with current conditions in society. But their discomfort may be premised on a felt security about life more generally, a sense that the world is safe enough to support a promotion focus orientation to political life.

If political conservatism reflects a prevention focus orientation to motivation, then conservatives should be more concerned than liberals with *protecting* the group from danger. If liberalism comes from promotion focus motivation, then liberals should be more concerned than conservatives with *providing* resources for the group. According to social psychologist Ronnie Janoff-Bulman (2009), the fundamental motivational difference between conservatives and liberals recalls the most primal psychological needs in human development—protection and provision. Think of the helpless human infant in the care of its parents. What must caregivers provide for the infant? The caregiver must protect the infant from dangers in the environment, and the caregiver must feed the infant. Nothing is more basic than protection and provision. Now imagine that the government in a democratic society is like the infant's caregiver. What must the government do for us? It must protect us from harm, and it must provide us with some modicum of resources.

Accordingly, sociolinguist George Lakoff (2002) contends that conservatives imagine government as a strict father, who provides rules in order to protect his children (citizens). Liberals imagine government as a nurturant caregiver, more like a mother who provides her children (citizens) with the nourishment they need in order to grow. At least one study suggests that political conservatives tend to recall important experiences in their own lives in which authority figures established rules and guidelines for them, in an effort to protect them from trouble, while liberals recall more personal experiences of nurturance and the provision of resources (McAdams et al., 2008).

Yet another interpretation comes again from Jonathan Haidt (2012) and his colleagues (Graham, Haidt, & Nosek, 2009). Recalling the five moral foundations, Haidt suggests that political conservatism may stem mainly from deep intuitions regarding loyalty–betrayal, authority–subversion, and sanctity–degradation. By contrast, liberalism stems more directly from concerns regarding care–harm and fairness–cheating. All five moral foundations are important for all people, Haidt maintains, but

conservatives and liberals differ in the prioritizations of these foundations, or perhaps in how salient each of the foundations is in decision
making.

Conservatives think it is wrong to hurt others, and they believe in
fairness, but what really gets them going, morally speaking, are the issues
of loyalty to the group, respect for proper authority, and veneration of
that which is sacred or holy. Liberals are simply less concerned about
loyalty, authority, and sacredness, even if they see the value in these considerations, but what keeps them up at nights are violations of harm and
fairness. It drives liberals crazy that the richest 1% of the American population holds something like 40% of the nation's wealth. It is just not *fair*,
liberals say. Conservatives tell the liberals to chill out (nobody said life
was fair, and rich people may create jobs for others), but they (conservatives) get really hot and bothered when people disrespect authority, such
as when immigrants enter the United States illegally, and then clamor for
citizenship. Liberals counter that illegal immigrants were simply trying
to make a better life for themselves when they entered the United States
(seeking provisions, as it were). And they worry about the *harm* that may
come to the innocent children of these immigrants. Conservatives don't
really want to harm the children either, but they cannot let go of the fact
that the immigrants broke the law, and thereby defied legitimate *authority*, in the first place.

## OVER THE COURSE OF LIFE

As motivated agents, most human beings eventually develop moral, religious, and political values of one kind or another. By the time they reach
adulthood, most can formulate personal answers to questions like these:
What is good? What is God? How should society work? These questions
feed into an even more fundamental question in the psychology of human
personality: *Who am I?* As the great psychoanalytic theorist Erik Erikson
(1963) suggested, many people begin to question who they are in their
adolescent and young adult years, as they embark upon a search for *identity*. Erikson believed that identity is tied up with personal ideology. To
know who you are, he contended, you must have a clear understanding
of what you believe to be good and true in the world, which invariably
brings to mind issues of ethics, faith, and the nature of society. Many
adolescents are drawn to these issues, partly because their newfound
powers of abstract reasoning enable them to appreciate the nuances of
philosophical thought, and partly because their own search for identity

brings these issues to the psychological forefront. Ideology and identity, therefore, are two sides of the same coin for many people in their teens and 20s, and beyond.

As they began to establish their respective identities, one a missionary and the other a scientist, Mother Teresa and Andrei Sakharov staked out their initial moral, religious, and political positions in their teens and 20s. After Jesuit missionaries visited her church to tell of their work in India, the 12-year-old girl who would become Mother Teresa began to imagine her vocation as a servant of God. In her teens, she discussed her developing religious identity with her mother and friends, and with the fellow Catholics she encountered on religious pilgrimages. Shortly before her 18th birthday, she resolved to join the Sisters of Loreto as a missionary, while praying to the shrine of the Black Madonna of Letnice. During his teenage years, Andrei Sakharov immersed himself in scientific studies. His adolescent idealism ran toward rationalism and the promise of a better society through science and social engineering. While he never wavered in his moral commitment to the scientific enterprise, his political values changed markedly after the development of the hydrogen bomb. In his early 30s, he began to agitate for political change. His initial criticisms were aimed at the role of government in science. As he moved into midlife, Sakharov expanded his political ideology to encompass a critique of the Soviet government writ large and to embrace the international cause of human rights.

While the outlines of their moral commitments began to become apparent in the teenage years, the determinants of personal ideology in the lives of both Mother Teresa and Andrei Sakharov can be traced back much further. In both cases, family influences seem to have been paramount. Agnes Bojaxhiu grew up in a religiously devout family. The family prayed together every night and read the bible. On many days, her mother took the little girl out into the streets to provide food for the poor. In Sakharov's case, his father taught physics at the high school and college levels. His grandfather was a prominent lawyer who advocated for humanitarian principles in Russian society. Early experiences with religion, science, and social issues shaped the unique motivational agendas that Mother Teresa and Andrei Sakharov established and pursued. And surely, genes played a role, too.

I have already told you that genetic endowments appear to play an important role in the development of religious values. Studies of twins suggest that "religiosity"—the tendency to take on religious beliefs and practices—is at least moderately heritable (Koenig et al., 2008). Political attitudes also reveal genetic influence. People are not born Republican or Democratic in the United States, but their positions on certain social and political issues show surprisingly robust heritabilities (Alford, Funk, & Hibbing, 2005). For example, monozygotic (MZ; genetically identical) twins often match each other closely on their opinions regarding the death penalty and progressive taxation, more closely than is the case for dizygotic (DZ; fraternal) twins. Given that both MZ and DZ twins experience respectively similar childhood environments, the fact that MZ twins show higher similarities on political values than do DZ twins would seem to point to the power of genes.

In a study of nearly 2,000 Germans, including many MZ and DZ twin pairs, personality psychologist Christian Kandler and his colleagues have shown that variation on the conservative–liberal continuum is linked to the heritability of personality traits, as well as certain environmental influences (Kandler, Bleidorn, & Riemann, 2012). Kandler argues that the prime determinants of variation in political values among adults are (1) genetic differences between people, (2) the effects of assortative mating (politically like-minded people marry each other, reinforcing their political values), and (3) big environmental events that impact an entire cohort, such as war or economic depression. Dovetailing with the genetic interpretation, at least two longitudinal studies also suggest that early-developing temperament traits may predispose people to adopt either conservative or liberal political positions later on (Block & Block, 2006; Fraley, Griffin, Belsky, & Roisman, 2012). The findings suggest that more inhibited and fearful preschool children show a slight but significant tendency to become conservatives in adulthood. By contrast, children who are more restless may be slightly more likely to become liberals. Still, the statistical effects in these studies are quite modest. The dispositional traits of young social actors may exert small but nonetheless noteworthy effects on the kinds of values that motivated agents eventually develop. In the same sense, though, that being a social actor is not exactly the same thing as being a motivated agent, your temperament is not your values.

Within the Big Five taxonomy of personality dimensions, the one trait that bears most direct relevance for personal values is *openness to experience* (O). As I suggested in Chapter 4, O differs from the other four dispositions in the taxonomy—extraversion (E), neuroticism (N), agreeableness (A), and conscientiousness (C)—in its emphasis on *cognitive* features of psychological individuality. O is less about how people, as social actors, perform emotion on the social stage of life and more about how people *think about* their goals and values (the person as motivated agent) and about the stories they construct to make sense of who they are (the person as autobiographical author). O taps into the extent to which a person approaches experience with an open and curious mind, ready to change in response to events that challenge prevailing conceptions. People who score high on measures of O are consistently described as intellectually curious, creative, original, complex, artistic, and interested in change; those scoring low are viewed to be more conventional, down-to-earth, incurious, conforming, traditional, and somewhat resistant to change.

The importance of O may be observed in the moral, religious, and political realms. O is positively associated with *higher stages of moral reasoning, greater religious searching or quest*, and *liberal political attitudes*. With respect to Lawrence Kohlberg's (1969) stages of moral development, people high on O are more likely than those scoring lower on O to question accepted societal norms and to develop in their place more nuanced and principled postconventional perspectives on morality. Importantly, high O is not associated with higher levels of moral behavior per se but rather with more mature and sophisticated ways of *thinking about* moral issues. People high in O hold less traditional moral values, and they are more likely than those low in O to invest moral meaning into values about exploring the self, developing their potential, and achieving self-actualization or transcendence in life (Schwartz, 2009).

Religious people high in O are more likely to view religion as a personal journey or quest and, thereby, to experience more change and development in their religious beliefs. For example, in a large study of religious development among Germans and Americans, researchers identified O as the strongest predictor of "migration in the religious field" (Streib, Hood, Keller, Csoff, & Silver, 2009, p. 28). People high in O tended to move away from the religious traditions they grew up with and to sample new faiths and alternative religious perspectives. Some even left the religious field completely and became agnostics or atheists. Those low in O, by contrast, tended to move around less, typically remaining faithful to the traditions of their youth.

High O is also associated with involvement in *spirituality* and "New Age" expressions of religious experience (Dillon & Wink, 2007). These relatively nonconventional manifestations of religious sentiment in American society serve as alternatives to regular church attendance. Sociologist Robert Wuthnow (1998) has described Americans who look for religious fulfillment in spirituality as *seekers* and those who look for it in conventional religious practice as *dwellers*. The distinction between seekers and dwellers—those who seek out new meanings in life versus those who dwell comfortably within conventions—captures perfectly an essential difference between people who score high and people who score low on O.

When it comes to politics, people high in O are reliably found on the liberal end of the continuum; conservatives tend to be low in O (Jost et al., 2003). One of the most conservative U. S. Presidents in recent times was George W. Bush. Historians who rated all of the American Presidents for individual differences on the Big Five personality traits, going back to George Washington, gave Bush the lowest rating of all on O (Rubenzer & Faschingbauer, 2004). In a psychobiography of George W. Bush (referred to in Chapter 2 of this book), I identified high E and low O as the two cardinal traits of his personality makeup (McAdams, 2011). The combination produced a bold and energetic leader (high E) who tended to see the world in black-and-white, us-against-them terms, and who rarely questioned conventional dogma or his own gut instincts (low O). In times of war, low O may be useful in promoting allegiance to the national cause, but it can also prove an obstacle to compromise and peace making.

Low O fits well with an ethic of loyalty and duty, resonating with conservative attitudes regarding respect for authority and commitment to the ingroup. By contrast high O fits well with the more liberal sentiments of self-exploration, development, growth, and the restless pursuit of new knowledge. These radically different value agendas find their parallels in two venerated societal institutions that have always aimed to mold the minds of young Americans—the *military* and the *university*. Think of the military as exemplifying the conservative focus on commitment to God and country. Think of the modern American university, especially the liberal arts college, as exemplifying the ethic of critical thinking and self-development. The stark institutional distinction tracks value differences that line up with (1) conservative versus liberal and (2) low versus high O. The result is an imagined moral contrast between, say, West Point or the Naval Academy on one side and University of California, Berkeley or Wellesley College on the other.

Whether conservative or liberal, religious or secular, case studies of people who have distinguished themselves for moral commitment, like Mother Teresa and Andrei Sakharov, consistently underscore the importance of parents and other role models in the development of values. For example, researchers have examined the lives of men and women who rescued endangered Jews during the holocaust (Fogelman, 1994; Oliner & Oliner, 1988). Common to nearly all of these morally exemplary individuals were reports of a nurturing and loving home life, parents who modeled altruism or religious values, learning tolerance for people who are different, and early experiences of loss or suffering that helped to build a resilient character. In recalling their own childhoods, those adults who risked their lives to save others during World War II tended to describe their parents as loving disciplinarians. Their parents made them feel special and valued, while at the same time providing them with clear standards and guidelines regarding how to live in the world as a moral agent. Rather than punish their children with physical reprisals, the parents endeavored to provide moral lessons and explain the reasons why a particular behavior or decision might be good or bad.

The memories these moral exemplars reported about family life point to the power of what I described in Chapter 4 as *authoritative* parenting. The authoritative parenting style combines a loving emphasis on the value of children with the establishment of clear norms and standards. Authoritative parents invest a great deal of energy in making their children feel that they are valued and loved. At the same time, they hold their children to high standards in schoolwork, peer interactions, athletics, and other domains in which children's performance is evaluated. Decades of research in developmental psychology has shown that, in most middle-class samples, authoritative parenting produces children who display a wide range of psychological and social advantages. In the moral domain, authoritative parenting is consistently associated with higher levels of empathy, conscience, moral development, and prosocial values among children and adolescents (Pratt & Hardy, 2015).

When parents make it clear to their children that they are both loved and accountable, children tend to respond in a favorable manner. They are more likely, therefore, to accept the validity of the values that their parents urge them to accept. At the same time, they are also likely, especially as adolescents and young adults, to review those value positions in a critical manner. In some cases, they may end up departing radically from the positions their parents hold. Still, they are likely to maintain respect for their parents' viewpoints. At the end of the day, authoritative parents do not reliably produce moral clones of themselves. But they are more likely than parents with less effective parenting styles to produce offspring who become effective moral agents in the world, able to think for themselves as adults and act in accord with self-chosen moral, religious, and sociopolitical principles.

Over the life course, personal values continue to evolve. In adolescence and young adulthood, many people devote considerable energy to questioning and reformulating their moral, religious, and political values. The teens and 20s mark a zenith in ideological fervor. Things seem to settle down a bit thereafter. For example, political orientation tends to remain pretty stable after young adulthood. People who are highly conservative at age 25 tend to express conservative values at age 50; young liberals tend to remain relatively liberal as they grow into midlife.

Still, dramatic transformations do occasionally occur. For example, former U.S. President Ronald Reagan held relatively liberal, pro-union views when he was a young actor in Hollywood. After he met Nancy Davis, the woman who was to become his second wife, he moved sharply to the right. As Governor of California and later as President, he became a champion for American conservatism. Political values may also change in response to societal change. People often become more conservative during times of war. Certain other historical events, such as the Great Depression in the United States in the 1930s, may shift values strongly to the left. With respect to viewpoints on individual social and political issues, moreover, dramatic changes can sometimes occur in relatively short order, as a society's overall ethos evolves. The best recent example is Americans' attitudes toward same-sex marriage, which have become dramatically more positive and accepting in the past 10 years.

Moral, religious, and political values may change in response to changes in family and work roles. The birth of a couple's first child may shift the focus from self-promoting to family-oriented values. New mothers and fathers may become more prudent in their spending patterns, hoping now to save money for their child's education and future well-being. Along with the shift in financial priorities, they may also shift their personal values in the direction of stability and security concerns. They may decide to attend church again, after a long furlough, and to expose the baby to the faith traditions they may have known growing up. Politically speaking, they may move in a conservative direction, now more concerned with law and order in society, or toward the liberal side, more affirming now of tax increases to support local education.

When career trajectories change, people's values may follow suit. A woman who leaves the teaching profession to start up a business may decide that she no longer supports government oversight of the private sector. Her political values may move in a more conservative or libertarian direction. A man who loses his job in a recession may lose faith in the values that he previously embraced. He no longer believes that the world is fair and just, and he descends into bitter cynicism. The unexpected death of a loved one may undermine religious faith—turn a believer into an atheist, for how could a loving God allow something so horrible to happen? Or the reverse may occur: Grief may bring the bereaved closer to God.

In Chapter 4, I reported that average levels of C and A tend to rise gradually from young adulthood through late midlife, and N tends to fall. Research has revealed clear developmental trends in adulthood for dispositional traits. By contrast, it is more difficult to discern predictable patterns of change in adulthood when it comes to moral, religious, and political values. Compared to traits, goals and values show more variability in mean-level change. However, some evidence does suggest that older adults may prioritize altruism values over financial gain, more so than younger adults. In a recent study of Swiss adults ranging in age from 18 to 85 years, the developmental psychologist Alexandra Freund found that age was positively related to prosocial values and inversely related to material values. The younger adults expressed stronger values aimed at becoming rich and accumulating material possessions compared to older adults. In comparison, older adults expressed stronger values aimed at promoting the public good (Freund & Blanchard-Fields, 2014). Strictly speaking, the results from this cross-sectional study could be explained by what psychologists call "cohort effects"—how people raised in one generation (e.g., those who grew up in the 1940s) differ from those from another generation (e.g., those who grew up in the 1990s) as a function of different historical experiences. A stronger case for development change might be made with a longitudinal study that follows the same people over time. Nonetheless, the findings from Freund's study are suggestive of a developmental trend in values that may parallel the expected increase in the trait of agreeableness.

We would all like to believe that people's moral, religious, and political values change for the better over time—that we all move in the direction of wisdom and enlightenment as we move across the adult life course. With a few notable exceptions, however, the research data are ambiguous. There is little empirical evidence to support the idea that people's values follow a clear upward trajectory over the life course. While some people, like Andrei Sakharov, steadily build and broaden their moral principles over time, many others show very little moral development after, say, the age of 25 (Westenberg, Blasi, & Cohn, 1998). Longitudinal studies of religious belief and practice tend to show that religious values decline in significance from adolescence through late midlife, but they tend to rebound as people move into their retirement years (Dillon & Wink, 2007; Koenig et al., 2008). Political participation is low among young adults, but it picks up again as people become stakeholders in society. Values seem to develop in fits and starts, as motivated agents confront new challenges in life and develop new goals.

Complicating any developmental trends that might be observed are historical cohort effects, as we saw above in the study by Freund. In the United States, the generation that grew up during the Great Depression and World War II internalized a strong sense of patriotism and traditional religious values. As adults, many attended religious services regularly, and they voted in record numbers. Their children—the Baby Boomers—came of age in the 1960s, amid the excitement of the Civil Rights and Women's Movements and the national turmoil created by the Vietnam War. They also experienced a dramatic liberalization of sexual mores. As a group, Baby Boomers do not enjoy the kind of pro-American, optimistic ideology that their parents knew. They are less religious but perhaps more spiritual; they are less likely to vote than their parents were, though they often hold strong political views; they tend to divide readily into polarized camps, such as liberals versus conservatives. The children of Baby Boomers witnessed the rise of the Internet and the trauma of 9/11. Many have had difficulty finding good jobs in the wake of the Great Recession of 2008–2009. How these events, and others shard by this cohort, may shape their values over the life course remains to be seen.

## CONCLUSION

We *Homo sapiens* are unfailingly social. As cognitively gifted members of a eusocial species, we come into the world ready to perform as social *actors*. Because we are social actors, we are moral actors, too, for no social group can survive for long without norms for moral conduct. These norms may be codified extensions of primitive moral intuitions— intuitions we have evolved to feel in our bones regarding violations of care, fairness, loyalty, authority, and sanctity. Indeed, by 6 months of age, babies show a primitive moral sensibility. But they are not moral *agents* yet. They do not make conscious moral decisions; therefore, we adults do not hold babies morally accountable for the "choices" they make. Babies do not articulate moral values and moral goals. They do not wake up in the morning with a detailed plan as to how they will accomplish morally worthy ends today. In the terms developed in Kurt Gray's theory of moral typecasting, human infants are moral *patients*, like puppies and other sentient beings to whom we ascribe *experience*, but they are not yet moral agents. They may be beneficiaries or victims in moral scenarios, but they cannot be moral heroes or villains.

It takes a relatively long time and a wealth of human experience before the cognitive gifts that confer moral agency upon human beings are able to take full effect. By 4 years of age, most children understand that other people have minds, like their own, endowed with desires and beliefs. Their internalized theory of mind provides children with a folk conception of human motivation: People pursue goals in accord with their desires and their thoughts. The same conception is readily projected onto imagined otherworldly agents, such as God, angels, saints, devils, and dead ancestors. These personified projections, decisively shaped by family and cultural influences, feed into religious faith. With further cognitive development, elementary schoolchildren become more planful and future-oriented in thinking about their own behavior, and in considering the desires, thoughts, plans, and goals of others. Correspondingly, their parents and teachers begin to accord them a greater degree of moral responsibility. Gradually, we human beings become full-fledged moral agents as we develop conscious, cognitive constructs—personal values—that articulate what we believe to be good, right, and praiseworthy. Like goals and personal projects, a person's moral, religious, and political values contribute to a motivational agenda, while orienting the motivated agent to the future with direction and purpose.

Personal values address the big questions that we moral agents cannot help but ask as we strive for desired ends in complex human groups: What is good? What is God? How should society work? The beliefs and values that adolescents formulate in response to these questions come to comprise a personal ideology. One's ideology feeds into one's identity in the adolescent and emerging adult years, for the big questions about morality, religion, and society frame the even bigger question for identity: Who am I? Over the adult life course, individual differences in personal values tend to show a reasonable degree of stability. But significant change can also be observed. Moral, religious, and political values evolve in response to changing roles and life circumstances. Getting married, having children, getting a new job, losing a job, divorce, retirement, failing health—these kinds of life transitions may result in significant value change, or they may not. Historical events, such as wars and economic depressions, can affect the values of an entire society, exerting trickle-down effects in individual human lives. Amid relentless societal change in the modern world and the idiosyncratic trajectories of individual biographies, it is difficult to predict how personal values will develop over the life course. I would love to report that people's moral, religious, and political values tend to "improve" with age, tend to develop in the direction of greater tolerance or wisdom or some other imagined enlightened state. But scientific evidence for such a romantic view is sparse.

Like goals, personal values layer over dispositional traits in the development of human personality. Goals and values differ from dispositional traits, just as the motivated agent differs from the social actor. But goals and values may be related to and interact with dispositional traits in the development of personality. After all, the motivated agent is a social actor, too—the very same developing person whose personal goals and values shape and are shaped by social roles and social behavior. The dispositional traits C and A are laden with moral meaning; their development is deeply implicated in the development of moral agency. Moreover, individual differences in O show strong relationships with many different value dimensions. High O is positively associated with higher stages of moral reasoning, more change and growth in the development of religious values, and political liberalism. Lower scores on O are statistically linked to more conventional moral perspectives, less value change, and political conservatism.

Moral, religious, and sociopolitical values project downward to dispositional traits and upward to the integrative stories that people formulate in the process of developing identity. As Erikson (1963) suggested, personal ideology is part and parcel of identity: Knowing what you believe in is key to knowing who you are. And knowing who you are involves developing a meaningful *story* for your life (McAdams, 1985). Imagine a person's ongoing life as a story. It has a beginning in the temporal past and an imagined ending in the future. The story contains a main character (the protagonist) who, as a motivated agent, pursues valued goals over time. The pursuit of goals over time drives the story's plot. The plot is situated in a particular historical moment—in a specific time and place. We think of that time and place as the *setting* for the story. But there is a sense in which the story plays out within another setting as well, a backdrop of personal beliefs and values. Let us call that backdrop an *ideological setting*—the protagonist's fundamental beliefs and values about the good, about God, and about how society should work. A person's moral, religious, and political values situate his or her life story within an ideological context or frame. The story makes sense only if the reader understands the background values and beliefs.

As autobiographical authors, we human beings construct stories for our lives that are framed within the ideological context produced by our most cherished values. In personality development, then, values serve as a bridge from the motivated agent to the autobiographical author. As we move into our adolescent and young adult years, we begin to construct life stories—narrative identities—that provide our lives with a full sense of meaning, purpose, and temporal continuity. As autobiographical authors, we reflect upon and remake the past, then connect the past to imagined scenarios for the future. The stories we tell are layered over our values and goals, which are layered over our dispositional traits. Let me now turn your attention, then, from the social actor and the motivated agent to the autobiographical author. Let us turn from traits, and from goals and values in the development of personality, to stories.

# Part III

# Becoming an Author

We tell ourselves stories in order to live.
—JOAN DIDION

# chapter 8

# The Stories We Live By

About 300 years ago, a peculiar new form of literary expression emerged in Western Europe. It was called the *novel*. In early examples such as Daniel Defoe's *Robinson Crusoe*, novelists created extended prose narratives that imaginatively depicted the experience of being human—human feelings, thoughts, desires, and behaviors—through a sequence of events involving a particular group of persons living in a particular time and place. The power of the novel lay in its ability to explore subjective human experience with extraordinary breadth, depth, and authenticity. By tracking over time how people perform as social actors and what they want and value as motivated agents, the novel expresses how characters change, as well as how they remain the same, over the course of seconds, minutes, days, years, and decades. Increasingly through the 20th century and up to today, moreover, the modern novel aims to convey what William James (1892/1963) described as the stream of human consciousness flowing over time (Langbaum, 1982). The modern novel asks: How do self-conscious human beings make sense of themselves from one moment to the next and over the long haul? How do people make meaning out of their social performances and motivated projects extending over time? How do these meanings shift, evolve, and interact across the sequence of moments, episodes, chapters, and epochs that comprise a human life?

Many scholars believe that the rise of the novel parallels and reflects changes in how modern human beings have come to think of themselves (Taylor, 1989). The Industrial Revolution, the spread of democracy, advances in science and technology, the proliferation of capitalism and free markets, increasing urbanization and globalization, the extension of the expected human lifespan, and other social and cultural developments have, over the past few centuries, resulted in the emergence of a *modern sense of selfhood.* In the modern world, people tend to see themselves as multifaceted, complex entities who develop over time and who are responsible, in a fundamental sense, for their own development. Modern people perceive themselves and their lives as *projects* that they must *work on*, seeking to explore, develop, fulfill, control, regulate, improve, and understand themselves over time. The social demands of modern life, moreover, require that modern people play many different roles, pursue many different goals, and interact with others in many different ways across a wide range of different social contexts. To be a modern person, then, is to be many different things in many different situations and, at the same time, seek to understand how the many different and evolving features of one's being come to comprise a single, integrated, whole person. The question of identity reaches a crescendo of urgency in the modern world: *Who am I?*

One answer is this: *You are a novel.* You are an extended prose narrative featuring a main character. As a social actor, the protagonist of your story plays many different roles and displays many different traits across a range of social situations. As a motivated agent, the main character pursues personal goals over time, driven by value and necessity, constantly changing yet remaining somehow the same, moving across a temporal landscape of consciousness. You are the entire novel itself, and you are the novelist; you live the story as you write it.

Beginning in the adolescent years, many people living in modern societies today become storytellers of the self—*autobiographical authors* who try to make sense out of the confusion of modern life by constructing integrative self-narratives, complete with settings, scenes, characters, plots, and themes. Regarding the identity challenge of figuring out *who we are* in the modern world, the eminent sociologist Anthony Giddens (1991) writes: "A person's identity is not to be found in behavior, nor— important though this is—in the reactions of others, but in the capacity to *keep a particular narrative going*" (p. 54, original emphasis). "We tell ourselves stories in order to live," writes American essayist Joan Didion (1979, p. 11). The most important story we ever tell is the story of our lives.

## STORYTELLING

Long before the advent of the novel, of course, human beings told stories about their experiences. Indeed, human beings are storytellers by nature. In a multitude of guises, as folktale, legend, myth, fairy tale, history, epic, opera, motion picture, television sitcom, biography, joke, personal anecdote, and the modern novel, the story appears in every known human culture. We expect much of stories. We expect them to entertain, educate, inspire, and persuade; to keep us awake and to put us to sleep; to make us feel joy, sadness, anger, excitement, horror, shame, guilt, and virtually any other emotion we can name; to help us communicate with each other; to explain things that are difficult to understand; to cause us to wonder about things that seem so simple; to clarify and to obfuscate; to make the mundane sacred and the sacred mundane; to help us pass time; to distract us; to get us focused; and to tell us who we are.

Stories are universal. But *what are they*, exactly? Are they anything a person says? No, they are not! I can say this to you: "Two plus two equals four." Is that a story? I can describe the theory of evolution to you. I can tell you how an engine works—well, *I* can't, to be honest, but *somebody* surely could! You might tell me why you think the American economy sank into a deep recession in the summer and fall of 2008. You may tell me what the capital of Maryland is. All of these examples of things that people might say to each other are positively and categorically *not* stories. They are instead what the great cognitive psychologist Jerome Bruner (1986) called *paradigmatic* expressions of human thought. When we think and talk in the paradigmatic mode, we are trying to explain how the world works through logic, empirical proof, theories, and carefully crafted arguments—the kinds of analytic strategies we learn in school. Paradigmatic thought is not only the stuff of science and philosophy, but it is also the stuff of auto mechanics, everyday engineering, and nearly every other successful effort to figure out how things work in the physical and chemical world. How do computers work? Why is my microwave oven broken? How did *Homo sapiens* evolve? What will the weather be like tomorrow? Why is it usually colder in Alaska than in Hawaii? We answer questions like these by appealing to logical discourse, scientific reasoning, and other analytic strategies that aim to give us the one right answer. Paradigmatic inquiry aims to reveal *the truth*.

But stories are different. In what Bruner (1986) calls the *narrative* mode of human thought, people create stories about intentional agents who pursue goals over time. A story begins with an intentional, motivated agent—be the agent Little Red Riding Hood (who intends to deliver cakes to Grandma) or Jane Austen's Emma, who intends (even though she may not realize it at first) to find a good husband. For the most part, people use the narrative mode to *explain why people do what they do*. If I want to understand why earthquakes occur more often in California than in Indiana, I need to engage in paradigmatic analysis. But if I want to explain why my family moved from California to Indiana in 1955, I have to engage in narrative thought—that is, I have to tell you a story.

The story I would need to tell about why my family made the cross-country pilgrimage would feature motivated agents—my father and mother—who were unable to find work in Los Angeles and who missed their respective families back in the Midwest. They had hoped to strike it rich in sunny California, but their dreams were dashed; they found it impossible to pay the bills, their new baby was a lot of trouble and very expensive, and they longed for the social support that they had once had, before they moved west in the first place. I can tell you a sensible story about why my family moved, and you will likely be satisfied with my narrative explanation. The narrative mode works for this kind of explanation to the extent that the story I tell exhibits *verisimilitude*—which means "lifelikeness," or human plausibility. Listening to the story, you may say, "Yeah, that makes sense. That is the kind of thing that human beings might have done, back then and there. Their motivations are understandable to me, knowing what I know about people and motivation. It is a reasonably convincing story." The narrative mode usually works pretty well for explaining why people do what they do, for humans typically feel that they understand what other humans do when they understand their motivations (Gray & Wegner, 2010)—and stories are fundamentally about motivations, about intentional agents who pursue goals over time (Bruner, 1986).

Stories do not typically work well, however, to explain the physical and chemical world. If my car mechanic tries to explain what is wrong with my engine by appealing to intentional agents (the carburetor hates the drive shaft and, therefore, intends to sabotage all upcoming excursions), I will take my car somewhere else. Engines, geological faults, atoms, molecules, and the laws of physics do not have intentions; therefore, the narrative mode is not up to the task of explaining how the physical and chemical world works. It also fails to provide an adequate explanation for ultimate causes in the biological world, at least from a scientific perspective. The religious creation stories that have fascinated *Homo sapiens* for at least 3,000 years are beautiful examples of the narrative mode in action: A motivated agent (i.e., the Old Testament God) *intends* to create the world; a curious woman (i.e., Eve) intends to disobey her creator, seduced as she is by a wily serpent; an angry God *decides* to destroy what He has created by bringing on a flood; and so on. By contrast, the theory of evolution gets a failing grade in the narrative mode. *Where is the intentional agent? There is none, only blind natural selection.* Horrible story! From a paradigmatic standpoint, however, it is one of history's greatest masterpieces, maybe its greatest. An extraordinarily elegant theory, Darwin's thesis is—a paradigmatic expression for explaining how the biological world came to be, a theory that seems, based on current evidence, to be profoundly true even if it fails to satisfy most people's yearning for a good story.

The narrative mode fails miserably in most realms of explanation. This is why it is so important to develop critical thinking skills, analytic strategies, and the like—increasingly so in the modern world. But stories are really good for understanding people, which may be one of the reasons that parents read stories to their children at bedtime, and why people the world over love novels and movies. A good story engages our emotions and functions to entertain us for sure. But beyond the entertainment, much of the inherent appeal of narrative may lie in its ability to abstract and simulate social experience (Mar & Oatley, 2008). When we read a good story or watch a good movie, we observe social interaction up close. We witness the clash of human intentions and the timeless social conflicts and motivational dilemmas that characterize so well what it is like to be a member of our eusocial species. *Stories teach us how to be human.* They provide condensed accounts of fundamental social dynamics in human life, and they do so in a way that deeply engages our emotions.

My claims regarding the power of narrative go beyond my lifelong love of great fiction, from Dostoyevsky to Ian McEwan. There is empirical support—paradigmatic evidence for the efficacy of the narrative mode. For example, the cognitive scientist Raymond Mar has shown that lifetime exposure to good fiction is positively correlated with social skills and empathy, controlling for education and intelligence (Mar, Oatley, Hirsch, dela Paz, & Peterson, 2006). By contrast, reading nonfiction books—expressions of paradigmatic thought—turned out to be unrelated to social skills in Mar's research. Reading stories, moreover, appears to activate neural representations of social experiences. The same brain regions that track visual and motor activity in social interaction are recruited to process the information that stories provide about how characters move in the physical world and how they pursue goals (Speer, Reynolds, Swallow, & Zacks, 2009). We may think of reading a good novel as living *vicariously.* We may imagine that reading is akin to escaping from the real world. But this may be largely wrong. If stories are condensed simulations of real life, and if our brains treat them as they treat real life itself, then the line between fiction and reality becomes blurred. Stories are so much about human life that they are, for many intents and purposes, life itself. Put differently, it is hard to imagine what human life would be like if we did not have stories to convey it.

## CHILDREN'S STORIES

Shortly after my daughter Ruth began to talk, she told her first story. It went like this: "Garby truck hit car-go. Broke. Daddy fix." (To understand the story, you need to know that "garby" was her word for garbage, and "car-go" = car.) Ruth's story displays many of the cardinal features of narrative, found in all human cultures. First, note that the story portrays a sequence of events spread out over time. Ruth had heard my wife and me talking about a car accident. A garbage truck had indeed hit our 1979 Ford Fiesta, parked in an alley near our house. It tore off the front bumper and did some damage to the driver's side. The trash collection company had left a written message with a phone number on my windshield, so after talking with them, I called my insurance agency and worked out the procedure for getting the damage repaired. Second, note that the story involves an intentional agent—the hero, her father! The story's dashing protagonist saves the day by carrying out self-determined plans and intentions. Third, note how Ruth manages, even in seven words, to build up a kind of suspense and then to resolve the tension in the end, just as Aristotle and psychological research (Mandler, 1984) suggest good storytellers should do. The story begins with an unusual event, a deviation from the canon of mundane daily life (Bruner, 1986): A runaway garby truck has crashed into a parked car-go. The car is "broke." Oh my goodness, what will happen next? The hero "fixes" the car—well, he called the insurance company, but I still find great drama here! Fixing the car resolves the tension and returns the listener to where the listener was before the story began. In some stories, resolution comes with the characters' "living happily ever after," or with the death of the protagonist. In this case, Daddy fixes the car. Problem solved. Trouble averted. End of story.

Children's stories, like Ruth's, are often based on lived experience. Things happen in their lives, or they hear about (or imagine) things happening. Then they construct stories to tell others what they did or what they witnessed. The stories they tell about events in their lives contribute to their evolving *autobiographical memory* (Howe & Courage, 1997). With the development of language and the emergence of self-recognition behavior in the second and third years of life, children begin to encode, store, and retrieve little stories about their lived experience. Across the preschool years, they make significant advances in their ability to recall particular episodes from the recent past and to describe those events to others. They remember and describe what role they had in the event, and they come to consider the memory of the event as their own—*my* memory about *me*.

The development of autobiographical memory piggybacks on their growing understanding of human agency, from the early (age 1 year) preferences they display for imitating intentional (as opposed to accidental or random) behaviors to the maturation of theory of mind in the third, fourth, and fifth years. *Autobiographical authorship depends on (and derives from) motivated agency.* Stories are accounts of what motivated agents (characters) strive to do over time (Bruner, 1986). Narrative plots track how agents pursue intentions over time. If a child does not "get" the idea that people are motivated agents, then he or she will not be able to tell good stories about lived experience. For that reason, among others, autistic children often display deficits in both theory-of-mind abilities and self-storytelling skills (Losh & Capps, 2006). They cannot tell good stories (authorship) because they do not fully understand or appreciate human motivation (agency).

Autobiographical memory and self-storytelling develop in a social context. Parents typically encourage children to talk about their personal experiences as soon as children are verbally able to do so (Fivush, 2011). Early on, parents may take the lead in stimulating the child's recollection and telling of the past by reminding the child of recent events, such as this morning's breakfast or yesterday's visit to the doctor. In this sense, parents provide children with what developmental psychologists call *scaffolding* for the development of memory and narration. In the construction of an office tower, scaffolding supports the various workers, tools, and materials that are required to raise the edifice. So, too, parents' conversational interactions with their children help to build children's memory skills and their facility in sharing their memories and experiences with other people. Taking advantage of this initial conversational scaffolding provided by adults, the young child soon learns to take more initiative in sharing personal events. By the age of 3 years, children are actively engaged in co-constructing their past experiences in conversations with adults. By the end of the preschool years, they are able to give a relatively coherent account of their past experiences, independent of adult guidance.

Children show broad individual differences in their inclinations and abilities to tell stories about their experiences. Studies of parent–child conversations show that the particular ways in which mothers and fathers talk to (and with) their young children have a strong impact on the development of autobiographical memory and self-narration. For example, mothers tend to encourage daughters, more than sons, to share *emotional* experiences, including especially memories of negative events that produced sadness (Fivush & Kuebli, 1997). Early on, and perhaps as a result of parental reinforcement, girls use more emotion words than boys in their autobiographical recollections, and their stories tend to be richer in context and meaning (Haden, Haine, & Fivush, 1997).

A key parental variable in the research literature on children's stories is conversational *elaboration.* Parents with an elaborative conversational style ask their children to reflect and elaborate upon their emotions, thoughts, and desires. They provide many opportunities for their children to describe what they are feeling in their experiences. By contrast, parents who show a more restricted conversational style focus more on the description of behavior rather than the exploration of inner experience. They may dismiss their children's feelings or show relatively little interest in pursuing the emotional dynamics of their children's experiences. Studies have consistently shown that mothers who employ elaborative conversational styles with their children do indeed encourage their children to explore their experiences in greater depth, resulting in the children's development of richer autobiographical memories and more detailed stories about themselves. Conversely, a more restricted style of conversation on the part of mothers is associated with less articulated personal narratives in children (Fivush, 2011).

Research also shows that mothers of securely attached children tend to use more elaborative and evaluative strategies when reminiscing with their children, compared to mothers of insecurely attached children. Securely attached children may in turn be more responsive than insecurely attached children in the conversations they have with their mothers about personal events (Reese, 2002). Importantly, intervention programs designed to teach mothers how to use more elaborative strategies in conversations with their children show significant effects on how mothers do indeed interact and, as a result, significant increases in children's self-storytelling skills and the psychological richness of their autobiographical memories (Peterson, Jesso, & McCabe, 1999; Reese & Newcombe, 2007).

By the time children are able to generate their own narrative accounts of personal memories, they also exhibit a clear understanding of the canonical features of stories themselves. Five-year-olds typically know that stories are set in a particular time and place, and involve characters (agents) who act on their desires and beliefs over time. They expect stories to evoke suspense and curiosity and will dismiss as "boring" a narrative that fails to live up to these emotional standards. They expect stories to conform to a conventional *story grammar* or generic script concerning what kinds of events can occur and in what order. In a simple, goal-directed episode, for example, an initiating event may prompt the protagonist to attempt some kind of action, which will result in some kind of consequence, which in turn will be followed by the protagonist's reaction to the consequence (Mandler, 1984). Stories are expected to have a definite beginning, middle, and end. The ending is supposed to provide a resolution to the plot complications that developed over the temporal course of the story. If a story does not conform to conventions such as these, children may find it confusing and difficult to remember, or they may recall it later with a more canonical structure than it originally had.

## BECOMING THE AUTHOR:
## THE EMERGENCE OF NARRATIVE IDENTITY

> There is a story, always ahead of you. Barely existing. Only gradually do you attach yourself to it and feed it. You discover the carapace that will contain and test your character. You find in this way the path of your life.
> —MICHAEL ONDAATJE (2011, p. 181)

It is one thing to tell stories about discrete experiences in your life— a day at the zoo, a visit to Grandma's, a mishap on the playground, a moment of love or betrayal that you will never forget. It is quite another, however, to fashion a narrative for your life as a whole, so as to "discover the carapace that will contain and test your character," and thereby reveal the "path" your life may take. As children, we learn how to tell the little stories in life to prepare us, as adolescents and young adults, to tell a much larger and more significant one. In modern Western societies and increasingly across the world, human beings confront the daunting challenge of self-authorship as they move through the second and third decades of their lives, a period encompassing adolescence and the early-adult years and now often referred to as *emerging adulthood* (Arnett, 2000). It is the same challenge that the great psychoanalytic theorist Erik Erikson, writing in the 1950s and '60s, first described as the psychosocial problem of *identity*.

Who am I? How do I fit into the adult world? Answering these identity questions in your teens and 20s involves, among other things, rethinking the social roles and dispositional traits that shape your characteristic performances as a social actor. Like Holden Caulfield in J. D. Salinger's *Catcher in the Rye*, you may begin to notice glaring discrepancies between how you typically behave in one set of social contexts versus another—say, how you act around your close friends versus your parents. It is almost as if you are two different people—wild and uninhibited with your friends, say, and ridiculously demure around parents and other authority figures. Which one is the real you? Identity calls for sameness and continuity in life (Erikson, 1963), which suggests some degree of authenticity in social behavior. You don't want to be a "phony," as Caulfield famously proclaimed. From the standpoint of the *social actor*, having a coherent identity means that people can count on you to display a characteristic pattern of feeling and behavior from one situation to the next. There should be a real you there, an authentic social actor whose dispositional signature is recognizable across a range of social performances.

Erikson's concept of identity also brings to the fore those features of your developing personality that connect to the *motivated agent*: What are your values in life? What goals do you aim to achieve in the long run? As I suggested in Chapter 6, a venerable line of research in developmental psychology has examined how emerging adults explore and commit to various life goals and values as they aim to formulate purposeful identities (Kroger & Marcia, 2011). At any given point in time, this research tradition suggests, young people may exhibit different *identity statuses*, each of which marks a developing person's position as a motivated agent. To be in the status of *identity achieved* is to have thoroughly examined different options available to you, then committed yourself to self-chosen values and goals for the future. Young people in the status of *moratorium* are still exploring ideological and occupational options; they have yet to commit. By contrast, those in the status of *foreclosure* never really explored their options but instead committed themselves to values and occupational goals that were presented to them early on in life, perhaps by their parents. Finally, those young people who have yet to explore or commit, who seem indeed to have skipped over or ignored the challenges posed by identity in the emerging adulthood years, exhibit the status of *identity diffusion*. When it comes to self-defining values and goals in life, they do not know who they are, and they are not trying to find out.

In his classic case study of identity formation, Erikson (1958) examined the life of Martin Luther (1483–1546), the 15th-century church reformer who launched the Protestant Reformation. Between the ages of about 18 and 35, Luther underwent a series of dramatic personal transformations on his way to consolidating a coherent personal identity. His father wanted him to pursue legal studies or to go into business, but the young Martin felt a religious calling. During a violent thunderstorm in the summer of 1505, a bolt of lightening struck nearby, hurling Luther to the ground and precipitating a kind of convulsion. He screamed out: "Help me St. Anne . . . I want to be a monk!" (Erikson, 1958, p. 38). After entering the monastery in Erfurt, the young novitiate threw himself into his studies with fanatical fervor. He would become the most learned and obedient monk, Luther believed. But 2 years later, he experienced another religiously inspired convulsion, falling to the floor of the church choir during the reading of a biblical passage and roaring like a bull: "Ich bin nit! Ich bin nit!" ("I am not! I am nothing! I do not know who I am!") (p. 23). He wrestled with doubts and other personal demons for years thereafter. But by 1512, Luther emerged from an extended moratorium with new theological insights and a clear sense of his own vocation as a reformer in the church. He became a doctor of theology and began to deliver sermons at the University of Wittenberg. In his preaching and his voluminous writing, Luther expressed a new understanding of the Christian concept of salvation, describing it as something that is given to human beings by grace rather than earned through good works. He also envisioned the Christian God as a directly accessible being. Rather than rely on the church hierarchy and the dictates of the pope, common folk might encounter God, Luther believed, through reading the scriptures, which Luther himself translated into German, and through prayer, meditation, and song.

In working through his identity struggles, Martin Luther confronted features of his own personality that were directly tied to his roles as a social actor and to his personal values and goals as a motivated agent. As a social actor, he went from being an obedient monk to a rebellious agitator, though Erikson also shows that Luther's dispositional traits (high neuroticism, as evidenced in lifelong bouts of depression; high conscientiousness, as expressed in a fierce sense of duty) remained remarkably stable throughout. As a motivated agent, Luther took on new goals in his 20s and early 30s, and revised his own personal ideology, though Luther felt that he had always stayed true to God's word and that he had no choice—no agency—to strive for anything different. Therefore, Luther's identity crisis and resolution certainly seem to have expressed themselves at the levels of the social actor (traits and roles) and the motivated agent (goals and values). The most psychologically noteworthy changes, however, seem to have occurred at the level of *life narrative* (McAdams, 1985). In developing a new understanding of how people might relate to God, Luther formulated a new story for his own life, a narrative carapace that contained and tested his character. It was a story in which he, God's chosen protagonist, would do daily battle with the devil and the devil's agents, the greatest of whom was, in Luther's narrative, the Pope himself, and the church hierarchy surrounding the Pope. It was a story in which a hero who, once upon a time, wanted so desperately to become an obedient part of the system now felt he had no choice but to turn the system on its head.

In Erikson's (1963) view, formulating an identity marks a person's psychosocial transition into adulthood. To know who you are is to be an adult. In *Young Man Luther*, Erikson (1958) hints at the possibility that achieving an identity, and thereby assuming an adult status in the world, centrally involves the construction of a self-defining story:

> To be adult means among other things to see one's own life in continuous perspective, both in retrospect and prospect. By accepting some definition as to who he is, usually on the basis of a function in an economy, a place in the sequence of generations, and a status in the structure of society, the adult is able to selectively reconstruct his past in such a way that, step for step, it seems to have planned him, or better, he seems to have planned it. In this sense, psychologically we *do* choose our parents, our family history, and the history of our kings, heroes, and gods. By making them our own, we maneuver ourselves into the inner position of proprietors, of creators. (pp. 111–112, original emphasis).

Since the mid-1980s, scholars across the social sciences and humanities have expanded upon the idea that identity is, in part, an *integrated life* story (e.g., Gregg, 1991; McAdams, 1985; Ricouer, 1984). The idea that people have stories for their lives and that they live according to narrative assumptions has seeped into the popular imagination in many Western societies. In television and radio shows, such as *This American Life* and *StoryCorps*, in magazine articles, blog posts, on Facebook and other forms of social media, and in many other popular venues, people not only tell stories about themselves, as they always have, but they also self-consciously fashion, market, and brand their own life narratives.

In psychological science today, investigators use the term "narrative identity" to refer to the *internalized and evolving story of the self that a person constructs to provide his or her life with unity, purpose, and meaning* (McAdams & McLean, 2013). In formulating a narrative identity, you reconstruct the past and imagine the future in order to explain how you have become the person you are becoming. In Erikson's terms, the story manages to "selectively reconstruct" the past "in such a way that, step by step, it seems to have planned" you, or better, you "seem to have planned it." At some level, we all know that life is pretty chaotic and unpredictable. Technically speaking, life does not "plan" you, and you are likely to have a very difficult time "planning" it. If we were purely objective about it all, we would see that life rarely goes according to anybody's plan.

*But we are not objective.* We seek a pattern in life; we need a narrative to explain how we came to be and where we may be going. Therefore, we construct life stories—narrative identities—that provide our lives with a sense of temporal continuity, stories that show how our past, as we now selectively recall it, gave birth to the present situation, which will ultimately lead to the future as we now imagine it will be. Narrative identity is a *personal myth.* As such, it provides meaning and verisimilitude, more than it provides objective truth. We humans need meaning, perhaps even more than we need truth. We need to know that our lives mean something and that our own development as persons conforms to some recognizable and meaningful pattern. Therefore, as *autobiographical authors,* we come to construe our lives as ongoing narratives of the self. Our narrative identities are the stories we live by. In the structure of the developing personality, these stories layer over our values and goals, which layer over our traits.

The cognitive skills and personal experiences required for the development of a narrative identity begin to come online in the adolescent years. A key factor is the emergence of "autobiographical reasoning," which refers to a wide set of interpretive operations through which *people derive personal meanings from their own autobiographical memories* (Habermas & Bluck, 2000). For example, a person may trace a particular passion in life back to an early event "where it all began," or may designate a specific episode from the past as a "turning point"—"I was never the same after *that* happened." In another form of autobiographical reasoning, a person may tell how a particular episode conferred upon the self a lesson learned or an insight gained (McLean & Pratt, 2006). In this regard, research on narrative identity suggests that people are especially eager to derive lessons and insights from negative emotional scenes in life, searching for redemptive meanings in suffering and adversity (McAdams, 2013c).

Autobiographical reasoning also encompasses the ways in which autobiographical authors string together multiple events to draw a conclusion about the self. On college admissions essays, candidates may arrange important episodes from their past into a narrative that explains how they came to hold a certain value or aspiration in life, or why their admission to the particular college represents the logical, even inevitable, endpoint in a sequence of personal events defining who they were, are, and hope to become. Although they may not explicitly define their task as such, admissions officers may be judging not only the quality of an applicant's autobiographical experiences but also the reasoning the applicant uses, as an author of self, to make narrative sense of those experiences. In a similar vein, research on psychotherapy patients who experience successful therapeutic outcomes indicates that they tend to organize memories of particular therapy sessions to tell a heroic story of individual triumph over an implacable foe (Adler, 2012; Adler, Skalina, & McAdams, 2008). In these instances, autobiographical reasoning serves to arrange the memories of individual sessions into a recovery narrative that illustrates the protagonist's steadily accelerating individual agency.

As summarized in Table 8.1, developmental research shows that autobiographical reasoning skills begin to emerge in early adolescence and continue to grow through the teens and 20s. Older adolescents and young adults show more facility than their younger counterparts, for example, in deriving organizing themes for their lives (thematic coherence) and in sequencing personal episodes into causal chains in order to explain their development (causal coherence). They are more likely than their younger counterparts to articulate how they have grown from their experiences. They are better able than younger adolescents to identify clear beginnings and endings in their life narrative accounts, and to incorporate foreshadowing, retrospective reflection, and other markers of mature self-authorship (e.g., Pasupathi & Wainryb, 2010).

From the early teens through the 20s, furthermore, autobiographical authors develop a more detailed understanding of the typical or expected events and transitions that mark the human life course—when, for example, a person leaves home, how schooling and work are sequenced, the expected progression of marriage and family formation, how careers develop, what people do when they retire, and so on (Thomsen & Bernsten, 2008). In modern societies, moreover, emerging adults often spend many years in advanced schooling, job training, and other programs and contexts through which they obtain specific knowledge about the kinds of lives and life course expectations—professional and personal—that may prevail in a given line of work or particular subculture or community. These expectations provide an overall developmental script for the life story, within which the author can construct his or her personalized narrative identity.

Authoring a self-defining life narrative is a process embedded in the social ecology of everyday life. From adolescence through young

**TABLE 8.1. Milestones in the Development of Narrative Identity**

| Age (years) | Developmental emergence |
|---|---|
| 2–3 | *Autobiographical memory.* Young children begin to remember personal events as things that have happened to them, or as things they have done. These episodic memories become attached to the self—"my" little memories about "me." Parents often encourage children to talk about these memories, and through conversation, the memories may become solidified or elaborated. |
| 3–4 | *Theory of mind.* Children come to understand that people are motivated agents who have minds containing desires and beliefs, and who act upon those desires and beliefs. Stories are fundamentally about the exploits of motivated agents (characters) played out over time. Therefore, the folk psychology of motivation provided by theory of mind lays the cognitive groundwork for telling intelligible stories. |
| 5–6 | *Story grammar.* By early grade school, children have a clear, albeit implicit, understanding of how a story should be structured. A story should begin with a motivated agent who seeks to accomplish goals; the goal striving is thwarted or complicated in some manner, revealing a conflict and ushering in suspense; the story should build to a climax, and then it should be resolved. Stories should have a clear beginning, middle, and ending. |
| 10–14 | *Cultural script.* Children and adolescents learn what a human life typically contains and how the life course is typically sequenced and structured. They come to understand that there are periods or stages in life—birth, schooling, leaving home, getting a job, marriage, having children, retirement, and so on. Different cultures offer different scripts for living a life. |
| 12–25 | *Autobiographical reasoning and advanced storytelling skills.* Adolescents and emerging adults gain proficiency in deriving personal meanings from autobiographical events. For example, they may string together events to explain a development in their own lives (*causal coherence*: Habermas & Bluck, 2000), or they may derive a theme that organizes their life as a whole (*thematic coherence*). They may come to understand particular scenes in their life stories as providing *lessons* or *insights* (McLean & Pratt, 2006). Over time, they may use sophisticated narrative devices to make sense of their lives, such as foreshadowing and flashbacks. |

adulthood, people construct narrative identity through a process of experiencing events, narrating those experiences to others (e.g., friends and parents), monitoring the reactions of others to those narrations, editing the narrations in response to the reactions, experiencing new events, narrating those new events in light of past narrations, and on and on. As personality psychologist Kate McLean describes it, selves create stories, which in turn create new selves, all in the context of significant interpersonal relationships and group affiliations (McLean, Pasupathi, & Pals, 2007). Narrative identity emerges gradually, through daily conversations and social interactions, through introspection, through decisions young people make regarding work and love, and through normative and serendipitous passages in life, such as when a student meets with a vocational counselor to discuss "What do I want to do with my life?" or a young couple sits down to write wedding vows.

Gender, ethnicity, race, and social class shape the process of constructing a narrative identity. Women tell different stories about their lives than do men, based both on different experiences and different cultural expectations regarding the kinds of narratives women and men are supposed to tell. Culture provides a menu of images, metaphors, and plots for the construction of narrative identity. As storytellers of the self, we sample from the menu in making our lives into stories, aiming to find narrative forms that capture our own lived experience, allow for the limitations and constraints we know we face, and convey our best aspirations for the future. We appropriate models for living that prevail in our culture. In this sense, autobiographical authorship rarely feels like freedom—we simply cannot make up any old story and call it ours. Instead developing a narrative identity usually mean cobbling together a story, or set of stories, that seems to work for us now (and going forward) given where we are right now in our lives in society and in history, and given limitations we face in life and the opportunities that come our way.

## IN SEARCH OF SELF: THE CASE OF BARACK OBAMA*

By the time Barry Obama arrived as a freshman at Occidental College in the fall of 1979, he had already formulated a set of questions that would ultimately structure his narrative identity: *Who is my father? What is my calling in life? What does it mean for me to live as a black man in America?* His biological father—Barack Obama, Sr.—left his wife and infant son behind in Hawaii to attend Harvard, then returned to his homeland in Kenya. Therefore, Barry met his biological father only once, when Barack, Sr. flew back to Hawaii for a short visit in 1971. Yet his mother regaled her firstborn with heroic stories of his father, whom she described as a great scholar and a distinguished man of the world. Growing up with

*This section on Barack Obama draws heavily from McAdams (2013a).

his white maternal grandparents in Hawaii and Indonesia, Barry Obama enjoyed many friendships and happy times. He was an easygoing kid—think extremely low neuroticism, mild introversion, and moderately high agreeableness. At the exclusive Punahou School in Honolulu, the teenager did well in his studies and played on the varsity basketball team. Punahou enrolled students from many different ethnic and racial groups, including native Hawaiians and students of Asian and European descent. There were, however, only a handful of African Americans. As a result, Barry earnestly studied up on African American culture—he learned how to be black—through watching television, listening to African American music, and reading magazines and books featuring African American icons such as Ralph Ellison, Langston Hughes, and Malcolm X. Born to a white mother and black father, he struggled to reconcile the racial polarities he experienced in high school, as described in this passage written nearly two decades later:

> I learned to slip back and forth between my black and white worlds, understanding that each possessed its own language and customs and structures of meaning, convinced that with a bit of translation on my part the two worlds would eventually cohere. Still, the feeling that something wasn't quite right stayed with me, a warning that sounded whenever a white girl mentioned in the middle of a conversation how much she liked Stevie Wonder; or when a woman in the supermarket asked me if I played basketball; or when the school principal told me I was cool. I did like Stevie Wonder, I did love basketball, and I tried to be cool at all times. So why did such comments set me on edge? (Obama, 1995, p. 82)

At Occidental, Barry took classes in politics, history, and literature mainly, and he made friends with the more politically active black students on campus. He wore leather jackets, drank beer, and smoked marijuana. He began to use the name "Barack" to signify a stronger identification with his mythic father and a newfound sense of worldliness and sophistication. After his sophomore year, he transferred to Columbia University, desiring a more urban and diverse social environment. He did not, however, take as much advantage of the social environment as expected. Obama found it difficult to make close friends at Columbia. For the first time in his life, he spent significant chunks of time alone. During his senior year, he received a phone call from Africa telling him that his father had died in an automobile accident. After graduation, he stayed in New York for 2 more years, working for the Business International Corporation and the New York Public Interest Research Group. In an interview years later, Obama looked back on his time in New York (ages 20–24) as an especially intense period of identity search. In New York, he saw that

> a whole bunch of stuff that had been inside me—questions of identity, questions of purpose, questions of, not just race, but also the international nature of my upbringing—all those things [were] converging in some way. And so there's this period of time when I move to New York and go to Columbia where I pull in and wrestle with that stuff, and do a lot of writing and a lot of reading and a lot of thinking and a lot of walking through Central Park. And somehow I emerge on the other side of that ready and eager to take a chance in what is a pretty unlikely venture: moving to Chicago and becoming an organizer. So I would say that's a moment in which I gain a seriousness of purpose that I had lacked before. Now, whether it is just a matter of, you know, me hitting a certain age where people start getting a little more serious—whether it was some combination of factors—my father dying, me realizing I had never known him, me moving from Hawaii to a place like New York that stimulates lots of new ideas—you know, it's hard to say what exactly prompted that. (in Remnick, 2011, p. 114)

At age 24, Obama moved to Chicago to take a position as a community organizer under the direction of Jerry Kellman. A white Jewish activist from New York, Kellman headed a coalition of churches and community groups on the far South Side of Chicago, an area of abandoned steel mills, dilapidated housing, high crime rates, and bad schools. Because the far South Side was predominantly African American, Kellman needed a black organizer to work the churches and the streets. By dint of complexion and vocation, Barack Obama fit the part perfectly. Obama worked in various capacities with neighborhood groups, churches, the police, and politicians in Chicago. He organized neighborhood cleanups and crime-watch programs, sponsored career days for area youth, and worked to secure agreements from city aldermen to improve sanitation services.

Community organizing was grueling work, and Obama experienced many failures and made many mistakes. One persistent problem was that others often perceived him to be distant and aloof, even when they admired the work he was doing. Aware of the problem, Obama set out to become a better listener. He came to value small talk and moments of idle conversation, wherein people opened up to tell the *stories of their lives*. In the process, Obama began to open up, too. As Obama later described it, he learned that "beneath the small talk and sketchy biographies and received opinions people carried within them some central explanation of themselves. Stories full of terror and wonder, studded with events that still haunted or inspired them. Sacred stories" (1995, p. 190). This realization "finally allowed me to share more of myself with the people I was working with, to break out of the larger isolation that I had carried with me to Chicago" (p. 190). Over time, Obama found that "those stories, taken together, helped me bind my world together." They gave me "the sense of place and purpose I'd been looking for" (p. 190).

Obama spent 3 years in Chicago as a community organizer (ages 24–27). Then he attended law school at Harvard. Upon completion of his legal studies, he returned to Chicago, where he worked briefly as a lawyer, taught classes at the University of Chicago Law School, met and married Michelle Robinson, and eventually launched a political career. Back in Chicago, he began to work on an autobiographical book, titled *Dreams from My Father* (Obama, 1995). *Dreams* chronicles Obama's childhood years and provides a vivid description of his search for identity. Indeed, the book itself, structured as a narrative of ascent and redemption, is a detailed externalization of the personal myth he constructed in his 20s to provide his life with meaning, purpose, and temporal continuity. In other words, Obama's first autobiographical book *is quite literally his narrative identity*, transcribed into the written word, as he understood his narrative identity to be around the age of 30. As Erikson (1958, p. 111) would have it, *Dreams* tells the story of a man who now "sees his own life in continuous perspective, both in retrospect and prospect," such that "step for step, [the story] seems to have planned him, or better he seems to have planned it."

In writing *Dreams*, Obama provides answers to the three key questions of his identity search (McAdams, 2013a, 2013c).

*Who is my father?* The author of *Dreams* tracks the long evolution of his beliefs and feelings about the complex man who abandoned him as an infant. In turn, an accomplished scholar and a charlatan, a generous patriarch and a drunk, an instigator for African democracy and an unreconstructed authoritarian, resolute and feckless, Barack Obama, Sr., was a bundle of contradictions. His American son sought to comprehend and internalize all those contradictions when he traveled to Kenya to interview distant family members during the summer before he attended Harvard. The trip helped Obama understand his roots, even though he had never lived in Africa. It helped him formulate the opening chapter of his life. It gave his story the kind of beginning that he, the author, demanded it should have.

*What is my calling in life?* His years as a community organizer on the South Side of Chicago convinced Obama that his calling was public service. Despite the frustrations and setbacks, Obama felt irresistibly drawn to community organizing for what he described as its "promise of redemption" (Obama, 1995, p. 135). The gritty and thankless work he performed in the Chicago streets aimed to *deliver people from their miseries to an enhanced status or state*, which itself is the fundamental meaning of the idea of redemption (McAdams, 2013c). Moreover, Obama came to link community organizing to a broader political vocation that he associated with a grand narrative of African American liberation and social progress. The broad narrative tracked what Obama (quoting Martin Luther King, Jr.) often referred to as the long arc of history that bends toward justice, running from the Emancipation Proclamation to King and encompassing women's suffrage, civil rights, and the expansion of freedom and equality in the United States. Obama began to see himself as a character in this historical narrative. His narrative understanding of self would later find its ultimate reinforcement when Obama became the first black President of the United States.

The same grand redemptive narrative helped Obama answer the third identity question: *What does it mean for me to be a black man in America?* For Obama, it came to mean continuing the pursuit of expanded freedoms and rights for African Americans themselves, building on the legacy of the black heroes he read about in high school, from Frederick Douglass to the civil rights heroes of the 1960s. It meant living on the South Side of Chicago with other African American men and women, attending a black church, and identifying wholeheartedly with Chicago's black community. Finally, it meant marrying a black woman from Chicago, which Obama did at age 31. Beyond an act of love and commitment, his marriage to Michelle helped to solidify Barack Obama's narrative identity as he moved into the new roles and positions he would assume in his 30s and beyond. The marriage marked the end of his emerging adulthood period.

In Shakespearian comedies, happy stories often end with a wedding. Obama's story had not reached an ending, of course, but with his completion of law school, his return to a public life in Chicago, and his union with the African American woman of *his own dreams*, rather than the dreams from his mythic father, Barack Obama had completed a concerted period of identity search. He had a story now, a narrative carapace to contain and test his character. He would now endeavor to live it out.

## WHAT LIFE STORIES LOOK LIKE, AND HOW THEY RELATE TO OTHER FEATURES OF PERSONALITY

There are at least two very different ways to conceive of a life story. The more common way is to think of it as the full history of a person's life. In Barack Obama's case, his life story would encompass all of the major facts of his life, such as the fact that he was born in Hawaii in 1961, that he married Michelle Robinson in 1992, that his mother died in 1995, that he was elected to the Illinois State Senate in 1996, and so on, as briefly outlined, for example, in Table 8.2. The full history would include the important things that happened in Barack Obama's life from the standpoint of a third-person observer—the kind of stuff that a biographer would include if he or she were preparing a full narrative account of a particular person's life.

The second way to think of the life story, however, is to take Obama's first-person perspective itself: At any given time, what does Barack Obama consider to be the story of his life? In Obama's own mind, what is the story he is working on? This second meaning, focusing as it does on the subjective perspective of the autobiographical narrator, comes much closer to what the concept of narrative identity is all about. In personality psychology, what mainly counts when it comes to the idea of a life story is the narrator's subjective understanding of how he or she came to be the person he or she is becoming—that is, the person's narrative identity. Therefore, when I use the term "life story" from here on out, I am referring to this second meaning of the term, the idea of the person's own internalized and changing story about who he or she was, is, and may become. For our purposes, then, narrative identity *is* the person's life story.

If we could see a narrative identity, what would it look like? The first thing to know is that it would *not* look like a video replay of the past. The first law of autobiographical memory and life-narrative construction is that most of what happens in the past is forgotten (no reason to remember all that stuff anyway), and what does get remembered is subjectively shaped (and sometimes distorted) by current concerns and future goals (Conway & Pleydell-Pearce, 2000). In its details, the past never was what you now remember it to be. Autobiographical memory is notoriously inaccurate for details, though it does better in conveying the emotional gist of particular events (Schacter, 1996). But the fallibility of memory is usually not a big psychological problem, at least when it comes to narrative identity. To a certain extent, memory's loose association with

**TABLE 8.2. Barack Obama's Life: A Time Line**

| | |
|---|---|
| 1961 | Born August 4, in Honolulu, Hawaii, to Barack Obama, Sr. (from Kenya) and (Stanley) Ann Dunham (from Kansas). Father abandons family. |
| 1964 | Parents divorce. |
| 1967–70 | Mother marries Lolo Soetoro; family moves to Indonesia, where Obama attends elementary school; sister (Maya Soetoro) born in 1970. |
| 1971–79 | Obama moves back to Hawaii to attend fifth grade through high school, living mostly with his maternal grandparents. His mother begins anthropological fieldwork. In 1971, Barack Obama, Sr., flies from Kenya to Honolulu for a brief visit with his son and former wife. Obama attends the elite, multicultural Punahou School in Honolulu, where he plays on the basketball team and begins to struggle with his racial identity. |
| 1979–81 | Attends Occidental College, in Los Angeles. |
| 1981–83 | Transfers to Columbia University, where he graduates with a BA, majoring in Political Science. In 1982, his father (age 46) dies in a car crash in Nairobi, Kenya. |
| 1985–87 | Community organizer in Chicago. |
| 1987 | Trip to Kenya, where he visits his father's grave and meets many members of his father's extended family. |
| 1988–91 | Attends Harvard Law School. Elected editor of the *Harvard Law Review*. |
| 1992–94 | Returns to Chicago. Marries Michelle Robinson. Begins lecturing at the University of Chicago Law School and works for a law firm. |
| 1995 | Mother dies of cancer, age 52. Publishes *Dreams from My Father*. |
| 1996 | Elected to Illinois State Senate. |
| 1999 | Daughter Malia is born. |
| 2000 | Loses Illinois Democratic primary election for U.S. House, to Bobby Rush. |
| 2001 | Daughter Sasha is born. |
| 2004 | Elected to U.S. Senate. |
| 2008 | Elected 44th President of the United States (defeats Republican John McCain). |
| 2010 | Health care reform bill is passed: The Affordable Health Care Act (aka Obamacare). |
| 2012 | Reelected U.S. President (defeats Republican Mitt Romney). |

what really happened in the past signals the creative powers of a storytelling mind. Within limits, people selectively reconstruct the past in order to make sense of it. They seek to link the past up with what they perceive to be their current situation and what they project to be their situation in years to come. Narrative identity, therefore, uses autobiographical memory to create a story that feels right to the narrator, that feels right because it captures what the narrator feels he or she has truly experienced in the past, while explaining how the narrator came to be who he or she is today, and may be tomorrow.

If we could see narrative identity, it would look like a story whose beginnings are shrouded in mystery and hearsay because human beings do not directly remember events from before the age of about 2 years. Described by Freud as "infantile amnesia," the absence of any autobiographical memories from the first 2 or 3 years of life partly reflects the human brain's delay in establishing a basic sense of selfhood, as we saw in Chapter 2. Temporally speaking, then, the life story typically starts with early childhood, as far back as the narrator can recall. What follows is typically organized into chapters, recurrent events, and specific autobiographical scenes. Cognitive scientists have shown that people routinely divide the autobiographical past into extended life periods (childhood, adolescence, my first marriage, etc.) that are punctuated by symbolic temporal markers (e.g., leaving home, turning 40) and particular episodes that stand out in memory (Conway & Pleydell-Pearce, 2000; Thomsen, 2009). The episodes may refer to repeated events of a particular type or quality, such as "arguments with my father" or "Friday night football games in high school." Whereas no particular argument or football game may be recalled in great detail, the general script of "that kind of event in my life" may be easily recalled and summarized (Abelson, 1981). In addition, however, a number of specific scenes in one's past are remembered with particular details—my wedding day, the birth of my first child, the day my father died, a great family vacation.

What are the characteristics of the specific memories that manage to "make the cut" for narrative identity? To examine this question, cognitive psychologist Dorthe Thomsen and her colleagues (Thomsen, Olesen, Schnieber, Jensen, & Tønnesvang, 2012) asked college students to keep daily diaries during an academic semester, at the end of which the students recalled three memories from the period that they considered to be "important for your life story." Compared to other memories the students recalled, those deemed important enough to be considered part of narrative identity were rated by the students as more emotionally intense, more relevant to their current goals, and more likely to have been shared with other people. Other studies have shown that when people repeatedly describe specific events in their lives to others, and when they are reinforced or affirmed for doing so, the stories of those events tend to be retained and incorporated into a person's sense of self (McLean & Pasupathi, 2011). By contrast, when narrating a personal event meets disapproval from others, or when the narration is ignored, the event fades in memory and its relevance for identity may be downgraded. Certain kinds of events are difficult to narrate, and when they are told, may incur negative reactions. Examples include stories of personal transgression and betrayal. Stories in which the narrator violates serious norms of propriety or betrays another's trust are rarely told; as a result, perhaps, they rarely assume a significant position in a person's narrative identity (Freeman, 2011b; Pasupathi, McLean, & Weeks, 2009).

Among the most revealing episodes that find their way into narrative identity are what personality and clinical psychologist Jefferson Singer (2004) has called the self-defining memory, which is "vivid, affectively charged, repetitive, linked to other similar memories, and related to an important unresolved theme or recurrent concern in an individual's life" (Singer & Salovey, 1993, p. 13). As Singer conceives it, the history of any self-defining memory begins with the person's experiencing an emotionally intense event. The event may stimulate highly positive emotions, such as joy and excitement, or negative ones, such as fear, anger, sadness, guilt, or contempt—or it may blend the positive and the negative. But strong emotion is only part of it. The event also manages to connect to important psychological issues in a person's life. The issues themselves can spell psychological conflict or fulfillment, or indeed again, both. A stinging rebuke from a romantic partner may bring to the fore past experiences of rejection in your life. An ecstatic experience on a religious retreat may connect up with other spiritual events from your past when you felt deep joy and meaning. As such, the event prompts a personal script—a predictable pattern of emotion and behavior played out over time. Eventually the script itself—the sequence of "when A happens to me, then I usually feel B and do C"—may become a central thematic line in your narrative identity. It is as if the scenes that affirm or display the script stand out in bold print. These scenes, therefore, are deemed to be "self-defining," because they reflect a central, psychologically significant pattern in the life story.

Memorable scenes in the life story may come from any period in a person's remembered life. However, certain years in life seem to have priority. In particular, many studies have shown that people tend to recall a disproportionate number of episodic memories from their emerging adulthood years—especially, say, between the ages of about 15 and 25. This well-documented phenomenon is called the *reminiscence bump*. As adults move through midlife and approach old age, they continue to give special emphasis in their reminiscences to events that occurred during that period of time when they first began to formulate a narrative identity. The finding makes sense for at least two reasons. First, the emerging adulthood years tend to contain some of the most psychologically important events in one's life—things like a person's first "date," first sexual experience, leaving home, getting a job, and so on. Second, it is in the emerging adulthood years that people first focus so much attention on figuring out who they are, how they came to be, and what their lives may mean. We may be most attuned to the narrative possibilities in life when we begin the business of composing our own life stories. As they move across the life course, therefore, autobiographical authors may hold a special place in their hearts and in their stories for those momentous events that occurred when they first became storytellers of the self (Gluck & Bluck, 2007; Thomsen & Bernsten, 2008).

Personality and developmental psychologists who study life stories typically ask research participants to narrate particular scenes in their lives, detailing for each exactly what happened in the scene, who was there, what they were thinking and feeling at the time, how the scene resolved itself, and what they think the scene may mean for their lives as a whole. In some studies, participants are asked to describe one or two key scenes in their lives; in others studies, they may describe many more, or they may consider broader temporal periods (e.g., chapters) or particular plot lines (e.g., marriage, career). In the *Life Story Interview* that my students and I typically use for research (McAdams, 2013c), participants typically begin by sketching a plot outline or overview of the main chapters in their life story, providing titles and summaries for each chapter. Then, they describe a series of key scenes, such as high points (the greatest moment of your life), low points (the worst moment), turning points, early childhood memories, and so on. Because narrative identity includes both the reconstructed past and the imagined future, participants describe what they imagine to be the next chapter in their lives, spelling out goals and plans for the future. Finally, they answer a series of questions that speak to basic beliefs and values, central challenges and struggles in life, important characters in their lives, and what they believe to be the central themes that run through the plot of their story. The interview is recorded and transcribed; then the transcripts are analyzed in different ways.

As shown in Table 8.3, researchers have developed many different coding systems for analyzing life narrative accounts. For example, some studies focus on general motivational themes that run through the story, such as the themes of *agency* and *communion* (McAdams, Hoffman, Mansfield, & Day, 1996). Stories with strong agency content feature protagonists who aim to exert mastery and control in the world; those with strong communion content feature protagonists who seek love, friendship, and community. Researchers sometimes focus on emotional shifts in life-narrative scenes, such as when a story moves suddenly from a negative situation to a positive outcome (a *redemption sequence*) or from a positive situation to a negative one (a *contamination sequence*) (McAdams, Reynolds, Lewis, Patten, & Bowman, 2001). Investigators are often interested in examining the kind of autobiographical reasoning that appears in the story—how the narrator draws conclusions about the self from specific events in life. Other approaches examine themes of personal *growth and integration*, the structural *complexity* of the story, and the story's overall *coherence*.

A significant body of research in personality psychology has examined how content themes and other features of life-story chapters and scenes relate to dispositional traits (Layer 1 in personality) and to characteristic motives, goals, and values (Layer 2). In terms of this book, these studies examine how the person as an autobiographical author (life stories) relates to the person as a social actor (traits) and motivated agent (goals and values). The research has identified many significant connections between different layers of personality, but the connections are not so strong as to suggest that one layer (e.g., narratives, Layer 3) can simply be reduced to another (e.g., goals and values, Layer 2; or traits, Layer 1). In other words, life stories are *related to but not the same thing as* a person's goals, values, and traits.

With respect to dispositional traits (the social actor), personality psychologist Amy Demorest and her colleagues at Amherst College found that students high in C tend to narrate autobiographical memories that follow a script of finding joy in accomplishment, whereas students high in A are more likely to emphasize memories about finding joy in affiliation with others (Demorest, Popovska, & Dabova, 2012). In the same study, students high in N recalled scenes of past trauma and fear. In a similar vein, other studies suggest that individuals high in N tend to construct stories about their lives that exhibit more negative emotion, less positive emotion, less growth, and less emphasis on attitudes and perspectives about the outside world (McAdams et al., 2004; Raggatt, 2006).

**TABLE 8.3. Common Dimensions of Narrative Identity, Coded in Life-Story Accounts**

*Agency.* The degree to which a protagonist is able to effect change in his or her own life or influence others in the environment, often through demonstrations of self-mastery, empowerment, achievement, or status. Highly agentic stories emphasize individual accomplishment and the ability to control one's own fate.

*Communion.* The degree to which the protagonist demonstrates or experiences interpersonal connection through love, friendship, dialogue, or connection to a broad collective. The story emphasizes intimacy, caring, and belongingness.

*Redemption.* Scenes in which a demonstrably "bad" or emotionally negative event or circumstance leads to a demonstrably "good" or positive outcome. The initial negative state is "redeemed" or salvaged by the good that follows it. Example: The narrator describes the death of her father as reinvigorating closer emotional ties to her other family members.

*Contamination.* Scenes in which a good or positive event turns dramatically bad or negative, such that the negative emotion overwhelms, destroys, or erases the effects of the preceding positivity. Example: The protagonist of the story is excited about a promotion at work but learns that it came at the expense of his friend's being fired.

*Coherence.* The extent to which a narrative demonstrates clear causal sequencing, thematic integrity, and appropriate integration of emotional responses.

*Complexity.* The level of structural differentiation and integration shown in the narrative. Complex stories evince many different, and sometimes conflicting, plots and characters, and they show how the different parts are related to each other. Simpler stories have fewer plots and characters, and they show fewer connections.

*Meaning making.* The degree to which the protagonist learns something or gleans a message from an event. The dimension ranges from no meaning, to learning a concrete lesson, to gaining a more abstract insight about life. Example of gaining insight: "It [the event] really made me go through and relook at my memories and see how there are so many things behind a situation that you never see. Things are not always as they seem."

People high in N, like individuals who report high levels of depression, are quick to identify *contamination sequences* in their life stories, wherein emotionally positive events turn suddenly negative (Adler, Kissel, & McAdams, 2006). Contamination sequences often have a fatalistic quality to them. For example, a man may describe how the perfect union he enjoyed with his first girlfriend was suddenly ruined by a mistake he made or a silly misunderstanding, or even a chance event—whatever the cause, the implication being that he will never enjoy a relationship as good as that again. Once cast out of the Garden of Eden, protagonists of contamination stories are never allowed to return to paradise. Therefore, this particular narrative form can undermine hope and suggest that the protagonist is doomed to repeat failures and mistakes again and again in the future.

High levels of O are associated with telling especially complex stories containing multiple plots and distinctions, and with higher levels of narrative coherence. In a longitudinal study of college students at the University of Illinois, the personality psychologist Jennifer Lodi-Smith found that freshmen high in O, C, and E tended, by the time they were seniors, to tell exploratory stories of change (Lodi-Smith, Geise, Robins, & Roberts, 2009). Having high O, C, and E may prepare students to experience the college years as a time of social exploration and personal transformation, much as Barack Obama did at Occidental College and Columbia. By contrast, students who are less open to experience, less focused on achievement and discipline, and relatively introverted may exhibit less soul searching in their college years and, relatedly, may shy away from personal relationships that threaten to change them in fundamental ways. Social actors who are more outgoing, open, and conscientious may, at certain times in their lives and under certain conditions, become autobiographical authors who emphasize personal exploration and change in their life stories.

A number of studies have expressly pitted dispositional traits (Layer 1 in personality) against indices of narrative identity (Layer 3) in the statistical prediction of important life outcomes. It is well established that self-report measures of E are positively associated with, and N is negatively associated with, assessments of happiness and psychological well-being. To what extent might narrative indices predict the same outcomes—happiness and well-being, for example—above and beyond the strong statistical association with traits? The personality psychologist Jack Bauer incorporated this stringent test for the utility of life-narrative measures in a study of "growth memories in the lives of mature, happy people" (Bauer, McAdams, & Sakaeda, 2005, p. 203). Bauer found that even after controlling for the variance in well-being accounted for by traits of E and N, themes of growth and intrinsic motivation in the participants' stories still accounted for sizable portions of the variance in self-reported well-being. Similarly, personality psychologist Jennifer Lilgendahl found that narrative indices of positive meaning making and self-growth, coded from extensive interview accounts provided by midlife adults, were positively associated with the adults' psychological well-being above and beyond the statistical effects of the Big Five traits and demographic factors (Lilgendahl & McAdams, 2011).

Early research on life stories shared many affinities with the practice of assessing individual differences in achievement, power, and intimacy motivation through the Picture Story Exercise (PSE; see Chapter 6 in this book). As a result, a number of studies documented linkages between motives and goals on the one hand and life narratives on the other (e.g., McAdams, 1982; Woike, 1995). The findings indicate that people with strong power motivation (Layer 2 in personality) tend to construct personal narratives that feature themes such as self-mastery, status and victory, achievement and responsibility, and empowerment; those high in intimacy motivation tend to construct more communal life narratives, emphasizing themes of love and friendship, dialogue, caring for others, and belongingness. People with strong power motivation also tend to use an analytic and differentiated narrative style when describing power-related events in their lives, perceiving more differences, separation, and opposition, compared to people low in power motivation. By contrast, people with high intimacy motivation tend to use a synthetic and integrated style when describing communal events, detecting similarities, connections, and congruences among different elements in significant life-story scenes.

Recent studies have examined the relationships between narrative and values (e.g., Frimer, Walker, Dunlop, Lee, & Riches, 2011). For example, my students and I have analyzed lengthy life-narrative interviews obtained from 128 highly religious midlife American adults, all Christian, who differ substantially on political values and beliefs (McAdams, Hanek, & Dadabo, 2013). Consistent with perspectives described in Chapter 7 of this book, we found that Christian political conservatives tended to emphasize themes of strict-father morality (Lakoff, 2002) in their life stories and to prioritize values linked to authority, loyalty, and sacredness (Haidt, 2012). By contrast, Christian political liberals tended to emphasize themes of nurturant-caregiver morality and to prioritize values linked to alleviating harm and promoting fairness.

In one of our studies, we asked devout Christians to imagine what their lives would be like if they had never adopted religious beliefs in the first place (McAdams & Albuagh, 2008). In essence, we were asking them to narrate an alternative, counterfactual life story—a story that might have happened but didn't. All of the participants imagined a negative alternative story. They described how their lives would have lacked meaning and purpose, and how they would have enjoyed much less happiness than they do today if they had never become religious. However, dramatic differences in the kind of negative stories told were also observed, and these were strongly linked to political values. Imagining a life without God, conservative Christians described scenes of personal and social chaos. They might have abused drugs, fallen into alcoholism or criminality, or engaged in any of a number of negative behaviors indicating failures in self-regulation. Without God, society would crumble, they said. Marriages would fall apart. Families would not stay together. By contrast, liberal Christians imagined an empty life and a barren world. Without God, they suggested, there would be no reason to wake up in the morning. Life would lack color, texture, and excitement. Conservatives and liberals narrated their respective counterfactual stories with very different kinds of imagery, as if to suggest that they harbor very different fears about what life would be like without a religious perspective—for conservatives, a hot and chaotic hell; for liberals, a cold and lifeless void, like the surface of the moon.

Picking up a theme I introduced in Chapter 7, the findings from our studies of politics and the life story suggest that conservatives tend to narrate life in *prevention focus* terms, telling cautionary tales about self-discipline, control, and avoiding trouble in life. By contrast, liberals tend to adopt more of a *promotion focus* perspective in life narration, privileging the discourse of growth, development, and approaching rewards. For principled American conservatives who are devoted to a Christian religious tradition, life is ideally a redemptive story of overcoming chaos, struggling to keep impulses under control in order to establish and maintain authority and social harmony. God and government function to protect the self—as agents of social control and keepers of the peace. For equally religious and principled American political liberals, by contrast, life is ideally a redemptive story of fulfillment, filling up the emptiness they sometimes sense, developing and expanding the self and encouraging others to do the same. As the Christian liberals narrate it, God and government provide nourishment for the self, filling the void with the bread of life, so that the self can grow and flourish.

## CONCLUSION

In an article titled "Becoming a Vampire without Being Bitten," the cognitive scientists Shira Gabriel and Ariana Young (2011) argue that when people experience a narrative, they become a part of the social collective described in the narrative itself. When we read stories about vampires, we become vampires, psychologically speaking, even though we never literally get bitten. Stories meet a basic human need for belongingness,

Gabriel and Young suggest. They transport us to another social world and make us temporary members of a new social group. Moreover, when we share stories of personal experiences here on earth, without the vampires and the wizards, those stories bind us to the human collectives wherein our social actions and our motivated projects find their daily meaning. Stories may be the perfect binding mechanism for the cognitively gifted, eusocial species we find ourselves to be, teaching us how to be human as they affirm our membership within human groups. In a book on the role of myth in education, John Rouse (1978) imagined our ancient ancestors' gathering around the fire at night to tell stories of the day:

> No one in the world knew what truth was until someone told a story. It was not there in the moment of lightning or the cry of the beast, but in the story of those things afterwards, making them part of human life. Our distant savage ancestor gloried as he told—or acted out or danced—the story of the great kill in the dark forest, and that story entered the life of the tribe and by it the tribe came to know itself. On such a day against the beast we fought and won, and here we live to tell the tale. A tale much embellished but truthful even so, for truth is not simply what happened but how we felt about it when it was happening, and how we feel about it now. (p. 99)

In the modern world you and I inhabit, stories are probably more important than they have ever been before. The social challenges we face are more complex and varied, no doubt, than those confronted by our ancient forebears. Under the social conditions of cultural modernity, we encounter so many different options regarding how to live and how to affiliate with fellow *Homo sapiens*. The modern world is awash in narrative. On the Internet and in face-to-face interactions, stories compete with each other for our attention. What plots do we find appealing? What characters do we want to be? Whose stories do we want to be in? What kinds of narratives will become the stories we live by?

Children begin telling stories about their own experiences shortly after they begin to speak. With repeated tellings, stories of personal events become part of children's autobiographical memory—*my* own tales of what *I* did and what happened to *me*. So begins the development of a narrative self, reinforced and articulated through conversations with parents, peers, teachers, and everybody else in the developing child's social world. By the time we hit adolescence, we are beginning to see how a broad narrative frame might apply to our individual lives as a whole. We begin to see how a life is like a novel, complete with setting, scenes, characters, plots, and themes. We begin to employ the powers of autobiographical reasoning to construe self-relevant meanings from the episodes that comprise our autobiography. In adolescence and the emerging adulthood years, many of us create narrative identities for our lives. These internalized and evolving stories reconstruct the past and imagine the future in order to describe how we have become the people we are becoming. This chapter's case of the young Barack Obama provides a vivid illustration of the development of narrative identity. Between his high school years in Hawaii and his marriage, at age 31, to Michelle Robinson in Chicago, Obama constructed an integrative story for his life to address vexing personal questions regarding race, vocation, identity, and the nature of his relationship with his mythic father.

With the emergence of narrative identity, personality adds a third perspective to the mix. The autobiographical author joins the motivated agent and the social actor. The personological trinity is now fully in place—three senses of the whole person, a single person in three related guises. In the development of personality across the human life course, stories layer over goals and values, which layer over traits. It should not come as a surprise, therefore, that corresponding features of the actor, agent, and author relate to each other in somewhat predictable ways. After all, the actor, agent, and author are all psychological features of the same human being. Research shows that people high in N (social actor) tend to tell life stories (autobiographical author) fraught with negative emotion, traumatic losses, and contamination sequences. Political conservatives (motivated agent) tend to construe their lives as narratives of self-regulation (autobiographical author).

But these kinds of linkages are not automatic in psychological reality, and many people exhibit an extraordinary degree of dissonance across the different layers of personality functioning. The *art* of personality development allows for an infinite number of variations on any general pattern. Therefore, knowing a person's standing on a dispositional profile may not tell you all that much about the kind of goals and values that same person sets forth in life. And knowing a person's traits and goals may not provide a clear window into narrative identity. We *Homo sapiens* often surprise each other in how complex and contradictory we turn out to be. Personality shows consistency and predictability for sure, but there is also mystery, and a great deal of idiosyncratic uniqueness. Our life stories manage to capture some of that uniqueness, while also showing how our lives connect to others in social and cultural communities. Our stories express how we artfully make meaning out of our unique individual lives even as they affirm our common eusocial humanity.

# chapter 9

# Generative Lives,
# Redemptive Life Stories

He was a painfully introverted adolescent. Meek and deferential in the presence of teachers, Mohandas K. Gandhi was a mediocre student in the classroom—good at English, fair in Arithmetic, poor in Geography. In accord with local custom, he was married at age 13 to a child bride, Kasturba. The couple knew nothing about marriage, beyond the fact that people dress up for weddings, eat sweets, and dance with relatives. They figured things out enough that she became pregnant a year or two later, though the baby survived less than a week. (Eventually they would have four more children.) His parents hoped Mohandas would someday succeed his father in a local political post, so they sent him off to University College London, to study Indian law and jurisprudence. Before he left, he vowed to his mother that he would abstain from meat, alcohol, and sexual relations during his time abroad. In London, he joined the Vegetarian Society and, when he was not studying law, discussed Buddhist and Hindu religious texts, including the *Bhagavad Gita*. Upon completion of his legal training, Gandhi returned to India to begin a career as a barrister. But he was beset by personal and professional misfortune. He learned that his mother had died while he was away. And his legal career was stymied because he was too shy to speak up in court. In 1893, at age 24, he accepted a modest position with an Indian legal firm in the Colony of Natal, South Africa, which was then, like India, part of the British Empire.

Gandhi's job was to represent Muslim Indian traders in the South African city of Pretoria. As a loyal subject of the British Crown, Gandhi identified at first with the white elite of South Africa. But his sentiments about race and power changed dramatically after he was thrown off a train at Pietermaritzburg because he refused, as a "colored" person, to give up his first-class seat to a white man. Gandhi came to abhor discrimination of all kinds, even as it revealed itself among the wealthy Muslim business owners in South Africa, who looked down upon their Hindu indentured servants. They were all Indians in Gandhi's mind, regardless of religion and caste. While working to expand civil rights for all Indians in South Africa, Gandhi also endeavored to bridge deeply entrenched historical divisions between Indians themselves. Over the course of his 20s and 30s, Gandhi's motivational agenda—to improve the lives of Indians living in South Africa and to bring them together as one people—seemed to trump his natural meekness and diffidence. In South Africa, he developed activist skills, and the bold political and religious philosophy that he would employ, to world-changing effect when he finally returned to India as a mature, middle-aged man.

Between his return to his homeland in 1915 and his death by an assassin's bullet in 1948, the man who would ultimately be known by the honorific "Mahatma" (meaning "high-souled" and "venerable" in Sanskrit) became the most influential leader in the drive for Indian self-rule and independence from England. Along the way, Gandhi led nationwide campaigns for erasing poverty, healing religious and ethnic strife, reforming the Indian caste system, and expanding women's rights. His effectiveness relied largely on the power of *ahisma*, or militant nonviolence. Derived from Hindu and Jainist religious traditions, *ahisma* entails passive resistance in the face of oppression. Gandhi organized nonviolent protests, political marches and demonstrations, massive boycotts, hunger strikes, and other political operations of *ahisma* in order to affect social and political change in India. These techniques have become a staple of modern political advocacy, from the American civil rights demonstrations led by Martin Luther King, Jr., to contemporary protest movements around the world. As a result of his political agitation, Gandhi endured relentless criticism from authorities, as well as imprisonment. But his status as a political and spiritual leader in India continued to increase throughout his lifetime.

Gandhi's political commitments dovetailed with his own personal quest for truth, captured in the concept of *Satyagraha* ("adherence to truth"). Borrowing ideas from Hinduism and Christianity, Gandhi conceived of his own life as a narrative of continuous development and self-realization. Going back to the vows he made to his mother before he headed off to London, Gandhi believed that in order to find truth in life, he needed to purge himself of base desires and purify his soul. His lifelong commitments to vegetarianism and nonviolence both originated in this common wellspring, as did his struggles with sexual desire. In Gandhi's mind, *Satyagraha* must entail the endurance of suffering in order to improve the self and advance society. Gandhi went so far as to conduct experiments *on himself*—"experiments with truth," he called them. Throughout his life, he put himself (and others) to the test by introducing temptations and then endeavoring to master the resultant impulses. For example, in his later years, he slept naked with his nieces, in order to test his own powers of sexual abstinence. It is not clear what his nieces thought of this; it is not clear whether Gandhi cared what they thought. He also insisted that young male relatives be put to similar tests. It should come as no surprise that such practices were resoundingly condemned, even by Gandhi's greatest admirers, and by Kasturba. Gandhi could be dictatorial and cruelly insensitive in his dealings with family members.

Despite troubling eccentricities and failings in his personal life, Mahatma Gandhi is today one of the most revered men in world history. His political activities helped to found the modern state of India, and his creative synthesis of *ahisma* and *Satyagraha* continues to serve as a model for moral heroism the world over. In 1999, Gandhi finished second behind Albert Einstein in *Time* magazine's choice for the greatest man of the 20th century.

## GENERATIVITY AND THE CHALLENGES OF MIDLIFE

In his psychological biography of Mahatma Gandhi, Erik Erikson (1969) tried to imagine Gandhi's psychological state when, at age 46, he left South Africa and returned to his beloved homeland:

> From the moment in January of 1915 when Gandhi set foot on a pier reserved for important arrivals in Bombay, he behaved like a man who knew the nature and the extent of India's calamity and that of his own fundamental mission. A mature man of middle age has not only made up his mind as to what, in the various compartments of life, he does and does not *care for*, he is also firm in his vision of what he *will* and *can* take *care of*. He takes as his baseline what he irreducibly *is* and reaches out for what only he can, and therefore, *must do*. (Erikson, 1969, p. 255, original emphasis)

By the time he returned to India, Erikson asserted, Gandhi had already developed the ideological outlook and social role commitments that would characterize his adult identity. After two decades in South

Africa, he knew who he was. As a motivated agent, he knew what he cared *for*. Moreover, he now had a vision as to what and whom he must *take care of*.

When Gandhi returned to India as a middle-aged man, he embarked upon a fundamental life mission in "generativity," which, according to Erikson, is an *adult's concern for and commitment to promoting the well-being of future generations*, as evidenced in parenting, teaching, mentoring, leadership, and other activities aimed at leaving a positive legacy for the future (McAdams & de St. Aubin, 1992). Generativity is about caring for and taking care of the next generation. In an important sense, Mohandas and Kasturba were engaged in generativity in their young-adult years as they raised their four sons. But Erikson suggested that generativity often involves life programs and projects that go well beyond parenting. The most momentous of these may, as they did in Gandhi's life, come to the psychological forefront in the middle-adult years. As such, generativity marks the central psychosocial challenge of midlife, Erikson argued. To be generative in midlife is to create, sustain, and care for the people and the valued things (and ideas) that will ultimately survive you. To fail in generativity is to experience what Erikson called "stagnation"—to feel that you are stuck or stymied, that you cannot generate anything useful, that you are unable or unwilling to be of good use to the next generation. For the middle-aged Gandhi, generativity expanded beyond the parental role to encompass his political activities in South Africa and, ultimately, his position as the symbolic *father* of an entire nation.

The normative arc of personality development culminates in the midlife adult's commitments to promoting the next generation. From the standpoint of human evolution, an individual's inclusive fitness depends on his or her ability to pass on copies of genes to the next generation. As eusocial animals, human beings meet the evolutionary challenge by not only producing offspring and caring for them but also engaging in a wide range of social behaviors that, directly or indirectly, benefit those individuals who will survive them. Obvious examples of generativity include teaching the young the skills, norms, and behaviors that make for successful group living. But other behaviors designed to bolster the group's standing in the world—from defending the group to adopting leadership roles—may serve the purposes of generativity as well. For our evolutionary ancestors, engaging in behaviors that benefited the group, then, did double duty in likewise promoting the next generation, for the survival and well-being of future generations depended critically on the survival and well-being of the group.

Social arrangements for human beings are more complex today, but generativity still bears the same moral imperative. Today the expected lifespan for humans is much longer than it was in primordial times, extending the period of "midlife" in many modern societies from, say, the late 30s through the mid-60s. In all societies, adults are expected to step up to the plate in their midlife years and take on the gamut of responsibilities that come with the psychosocial territory of being a fully functioning and mature member of a human group. Every society has its own unique demands, but the normative expectations for generativity typically increase as adults move through their 20s, 30s, and 40s (de St. Aubin, McAdams, & Kim, 2004). In modern societies, midlife adults are expected to function as stakeholders in society. Through involvement in work, family, civic life, religion, and other group affiliations, midlife adults engage in many different kinds of generative activities, from teaching Sunday school to chairing a neighborhood task force to paying taxes and voting. A teenager who shows little interest in broader society and in promoting the well-being of future generations is hardly an aberration. But a 40-year-old man or woman with the same sentiment—completely disengaged from the business of caring for society and for the well-being of those who will live on once that man or woman has died—is typically viewed to be self-centered or psychologically deficient.

As *social actors*, adults tend to show more generative *traits* and take on more generative *roles* as they move into their midlife years. The upward tick in C and A, demonstrated by many adults as they move through their 20s, 30s, and 40s (see Chapter 4 in this book), both reflects and enhances this developmental trend. Increases in C may prepare midlife adults to focus energy on serious work and on family and community commitments. Increases in A suggest a warming up of the personality and a greater emphasis on care and compassion in relationships with others. Indeed, research has demonstrated positive correlations between measures of generativity on the one hand and features of C and A on the other (Cox, Wilt, Olson, & McAdams, 2010). Generativity connects most strongly with the achievement-striving facet of C and the altruism facet of A. It is also positively associated with overall E and O, and negatively associated with N.

As *motivated agents*, midlife adults prioritize generative *goals*. As *autobiographical authors*, they begin to *narrate* their lives around hopes for their children and their efforts to make the world a better place for others. Adults invest time and resources into valued ends such as raising children and supporting their education, passing on values and skills to the younger generation at home and at work, improving their neighborhoods, volunteering for church and community groups, and accumulating resources that, they hope, will enhance the lives of those who will survive them. In one study, for example, midlife adults (around the age of 40) listed twice as many personal strivings oriented toward generativity as did younger adults in their mid-20s (McAdams, de St. Aubin, & Logan, 1993). Compared to younger adults, moreover, the midlife adults in the same study tended to place much greater emphasis on themes of care and productivity in the stories they told about important life experiences.

Of course, midlife adults list many other kinds of personal goals, too, and their life narratives cover a broad range of thematic concerns. Moreover, goals and stories that seem to have a generative quality may also serve selfish concerns. In that regard, it has almost become a cliché for corporate CEOs and sports stars in the United States to justify their obscenely high salaries by appealing to their need to "take care of my family." Research and theory suggest that there may indeed be a *selfish* component to generativity for many people (Erikson, 1969; McAdams, 2013c). Promoting the next generation often involves committing the self to the betterment of *my* children, not yours, *my* group, *my* people. Furthermore, an expansive sense of generativity may satisfy narcissistic urges for some adults, serving to bring glory to the self. Gandhi had something like that going in his life. Nonetheless, it is hard to imagine how any human society could flourish, or even survive, without the concerted commitment of adults to the pursuit of generative goals. Like many complex human sentiments, then, generativity stems from a mix of basic motivations, some selfish and some selfless.

Supporting Erikson's (1963) developmental thesis, many lines of research suggest that adults become more generative as they move from the emerging adulthood years into and through midlife (McAdams & de St. Aubin, 1998). Still, research suggests wide individual differences in generative concerns, motives, and actions among midlife adults. Like Gandhi (though less dramatically so), some adults demonstrate robust commitments to promoting the well-being of future generations. On the other end of the spectrum, some adults sink into stagnation, showing very low levels of generativity. Many find themselves positioned somewhere in the middle of the continuum. Generative inclinations, moreover, may wax and wane in any particular human life. A mother may devote her life to the care of her children, but once they grow up, she may decide, in her 40s now, to take it easy for a while and focus on her own well-being. For another person, generativity may sleep underground for decades, only to awaken with full force at midlife, when that person assumes new responsibilities at work or in the community.

Complicating things even further, people may show different levels of generativity in different domains of life (MacDermid, Franz, & de Reus, 1998). Whereas one person's generativity may flourish in the family domain, another's may express itself only through work or involvement in a religious organization. Gandhi's generativity shone brightly on the public stage. He was the father of his nation and an inspiration for millions. But as a father to his own biological children and within the context of his own extended family, Gandhi revealed a host of shortcomings. The contradictions in Gandhi's generativity were so glaring, in fact, that Erikson (1969) felt the need to step back from the biography of Gandhi in the middle of his book and write Gandhi (who had been dead for 20 years) an imaginary letter. In the letter, Erikson wondered: How could such a generative man for the world be such a bad father at home? It is a good question. Having said that, would we rather Gandhi had been a good father at home and a bad leader for India? From the standpoint of his family members, perhaps yes. From the standpoint of world history, probably no. I believe the world is better off for there having been a Mahatma Gandhi, even if he tended to ignore his own sons and sleep naked with his nieces. But I feel a little guilty when I write that. I believe that Erikson probably felt the same way about Gandhi—disturbed by Gandhi's personal failings but admiring of his awesome generativity.

Table 9.1 lists important research findings from studies of individual differences in generativity. The research suggests that people who score high on measures of generative attitudes, goals, and behaviors tend to be productively involved in a wide range of social endeavors, and tend to enjoy higher levels of psychological health and well-being, compared to adults scoring lower in generativity. Overall, generativity appears to be good for others, and good for the self, too.

Simply being a parent does not make a person more generative, but research suggests that parents who are more generative to begin with tend to be better parents. For example, parents who score high on self-report measures of generativity tend to be more involved in their children's schooling, compared to those scoring lower on generativity. They help their children with their homework, show higher levels of attendance at school functions, and evidence greater knowledge about what their children are learning and doing in school (Lewis & Nakagawa, 1995). Generative parents value trust and communication with their children, and tend to view parenting as an opportunity to pass on values and wisdom

**TABLE 9.1. The Generative Adult**

Adults who score high on measures of *generativity* tend to:

- Exhibit an authoritative parenting style with their children, insisting that children adhere to moral and instrumental standards while showing warmth and love (Peterson et al., 1997).
- Pass on wisdom and values to their children, and emphasize trust in their relationships with children (Hart et al., 2001).
- Be more involved in their children's schooling, as evidenced in setting aside time for homework, attending parent–teacher meetings, and having more knowledge about what happens at school (Lewis & Nakagawa, 1995).
- Raise children who grow up to show high levels of positive personality traits, such as conscientiousness and agreeableness (Peterson, 2006).
- Show higher levels of forgiveness and optimism in family relations (Pratt, Norris, Cressman, Lawford, & Hebblethwaite, 2008).
- Enjoy broader networks of friendships and social support (Hart et al., 2001).
- Be more engaged in providing care and support for other people in their families, at work, and in the community (Rossi, 2001).
- Attend religious services and/or be involved in a religious or spiritual tradition (Jones & McAdams, 2013).
- Show higher levels of moral development (Pratt et al., 1999).
- Be more involved in the political process, as evidenced in voting, writing letters to Congress, and political activism (Cole & Stewart, 1996).
- Exhibit strength and effectiveness as leaders, among late-midlife men (Zacher, Rosing, Henning, & Frese, 2011).
- Exhibit many signs of successful aging, including satisfaction with family roles and greater purpose in life (Peterson & Duncan, 2007).
- Enjoy higher levels of life satisfaction, subjective mental health, adaptive coping, and psychological maturity (Keyes & Ryff, 1998).
- Show low levels of neuroticism and high levels of traits related to warmth, altruism, positive emotions, assertive activity, achievement striving, dutifulness, and openness (Van Hiel, Mervielde, & Fruyt, 2006).
- Show higher levels of power motivation and intimacy motivation (Hofer, Busch, Chasiotis, Kärtner, & Campos, 2008).

to the next generation (Hart, McAdams, Hirsch, & Bauer, 2001; Pratt, Norris, Arnold, & Filyer, 1999). Mothers and fathers high in generativity tend to adopt an *authoritative* style of parenting, combining high standards and discipline with a warm, child-centered, and caring approach to raising children (Peterson, Smirles, & Wentworth, 1997; Pratt, Danso, Arnold, Norris, & Filyer, 2001).

Outside the family, generativity is commonly expressed in neighborhood, religious, and civic involvement. High scores on self-report measures of generativity consistently predict broader networks of social support, engagement with religious institutions, higher levels of voting and political participation, and more charitable giving and volunteerism, even after researchers control for educational and income factors (Cole & Stewart, 1996; Jones & McAdams, 2013). In a nationwide study of over 3,000 middle-aged American adults, researchers found that generativity was the single strongest psychological predictor of "caring and doing for others" and "social responsibility in the domains of family, work, and community" (Rossi, 2001, title page). Controlling for age and a range of demographic factors, the research team showed that individual differences in generativity (as assessed on a short questionnaire) were positively associated with a broad spectrum of prosocial behaviors, including volunteerism and contributing one's time and money to family members and to community concerns. Suggesting that the benefits of generativity also feed back to enhance the self, many studies have documented positive associations between generativity on the one hand and measures of life satisfaction, happiness, mental health, and psychological maturity on the other (e.g., Keyes & Ryff, 1998). By contrast, extremely low scores on generativity are associated with depression.

## HOW HIGHLY GENERATIVE ADULTS NARRATE THEIR LIVES

Invoking Charles Dickens's famous phrase, there is a sense in which the middle-adult years are "the best of times and the worst of times" in the human life course. By the time adults reach, say, the age of 40, the countless differences that separate them from each other—economic resources, educational opportunities, cognitive and personality differences, factors of race and class, gender norms, sheer luck—accumulate to produce dramatic disparities in life trajectories. For those adults blessed with adequate financial resources and good health, as well as meaningful involvements with work and family, midlife may indeed be the prime of life. In their 30s, 40s, and 50s, many adults feel that they are at the height of their personal and professional powers, the top of their game. For many others, however, misfortunes and disadvantages accumulate over the years. Unemployment, failed marriages, family tragedies, psychological difficulties, and a host of other debilitating factors may undermine the prospects for happiness and generativity in midlife. While many midlife adults enjoy the fruits of maturity, others fall into stagnation and despair.

Even for the winners in midlife, generativity is always a daunting challenge. More often than not, the best-laid plans for having a positive and lasting impact on the next generation go awry. Parenting may look easy—but see what happens when you try it! Among the countless sources for frustration and angst is the possibility that your children will never appreciate what you have done for them. "How sharper than a serpent's tooth it is to have a thankless child," King Lear proclaimed. Frustrations in generativity drove *him* to madness. More generally, the idea that people "do not value what I do" or "fail to appreciate the sacrifices I have made" is a recurrent refrain in midlife.

By virtue of our membership in such a peculiar eusocial species, we members of *Homo sapiens* cannot help but invest ourselves in social projects that are bound to fail, or at best meet with limited success. Nearly every effort you will ever make to be a generative adult—from parenting to teaching to professional leadership to political activism—will bring you headaches, or worse. At the same time, generativity tempts us with what many would say are the deepest rewards in human life. Parents consistently report that being a mother or father is a profoundly meaningful role for them, even if it does not reliably produce happiness. Despite failures, adults find meaning and fulfillment in many different expressions of generativity. Given the high-stakes risks and potential rewards of generativity, therefore, as well as its universal relevance to human adaptation at midlife, we might wonder: How do generative adults make sense of it all?

My thesis is this: Generativity is really hard, so *it takes a good story to be a highly generative adult.* You need a good story about your life to sustain a strong commitment to generativity for the long haul. You need a story that bucks you up when things get bad, that provides you with support for the hard work that generativity demands and the heartaches it will bring your way. As autobiographical authors, what kinds of life stories do especially generative adults construct to make sense of who they are, how they came to be, and where their lives may be going in the future? What kind of a story do you need if you are going to be a highly generative adult?

Over the past two decades, my students and I have examined closely the life stories of highly generative adults (McAdams, 2013c; McAdams, Diamond, de St. Aubin, & Mansfield, 1997). We have interviewed men and women who vary widely on self-report measures of generativity and related factors, and we have coded those interview transcripts for the narrative themes that appear to correlate with self-report generativity scores. We have also examined cultural and historical sources for generativity, such as autobiographies of especially generative men and women, memoirs, newspaper and magazine accounts, and examples from fiction and drama. Our findings dovetail with a growing literature on the life stories of moral exemplars and other midlife adults who have distinguished themselves for their positive contributions to society (Colby & Damon, 1992; Walker & Frimer, 2007).

Our studies suggest that highly generative American adults tend to narrate their lives as *stories of redemption.* In life narrative, redemption tracks a move from a demonstrably negative situation to an especially positive one. The protagonist of the story first endures suffering of one kind or another. The suffering may result from failure, loss, separation, deprivation, abuse, or any particularly difficult situation in a person's life that entails strong negative emotion. The suffering leads, however, to a positive outcome of some kind. Failure may ultimately result in victory, deprivation may give way to abundance. Importantly, the narrator describes an explicit causal link between the prior negative event and the resultant enhancement. Suffering is redeemed, and the protagonist emerges from the redemptive sequence in a position that may be better than what existed before the whole scenario began. For example, a woman is devastated by a romantic breakup, but then she finds the partner of her dreams. A student flunks out of college, then finds a great job. A boy endures extreme poverty as a child, but when he grows up, he comes to believe that early suffering has made him a better person. As in this last example, many redemption sequences involve the narrator's deriving a positive inference about a negative event *long after the event has occurred.* In the terms I introduced in Chapter 8, the narrator engages in a form of *autobiographical reasoning* whereby positive meanings come to be attributed to negative life episodes.

Personal redemption lies at the center of a constellation of six themes that together comprise a general and idealized script for the kind of life story that is often told by highly generative men and women in their midlife years, at least in the United States. Whereas nobody's narrative identity conforms to the script in every way, research consistently shows that highly generative American adults construct life stories that tend to emphasize the six themes (see Table 9.2) in the script to a greater degree than do the stories told by less generative adults. I call this script *the redemptive self.*

The redemptive self often begins with accounts of childhood wherein the protagonist felt that he or she enjoyed an *early advantage* in life (Theme 1). Perhaps, he was his mother's favorite child. Perhaps, she had a wonderful teacher in grade school who recognized her potential. Whatever the case, the protagonist feels special or blessed early on. At the same time, the protagonist of the story shows an early sensitivity to the *suffering of others* (Theme 2). The narrator recalls experiences of witnessing

**TABLE 9.2. The Six Themes That Comprise the Redemptive Self—A Common Script for the Life Narratives Constructed by Highly Generative American Adults**

How does the story begin?

1. *Early advantage.* The story's protagonist enjoys a special blessing, gift, talent, opportunity, or distinction early in life that confers a perceived advantage.

2. *Suffering of others.* The protagonist witnesses pain and suffering of others early in life, shows empathy for others, or is sensitized to social misfortune, injustice, oppression, discrimination, or the like.

3. *Moral steadfastness.* After some searching and questioning, often in adolescence, the protagonist commits the self to a personal ideology. His or her values remain strong, clear, and highly relevant in daily life for the duration of the story.

How does the plot develop?

4. *Redemption sequences.* Bad things happen, but good things follow. Negative life events are redeemed by positive outcomes, or else the narrator finds positive meanings for life in negative life experiences.

5. *Power versus Love.* The protagonist experiences strong and competing motivations for power (self-enhancement) and love (connecting to others, communion). In some stories, the competing drives lead to conflict and tension. In other stories, narrators resolve the tension and manage to integrate power and love.

How does the story end?

6. *Positive future.* As he or she looks to the future, the story's narrator projects optimism and a continued prosocial commitment to make the world a better place. The story affirms future growth and fruition.

other people's pain or describes an early realization that bad things, such as oppression or discrimination, happen to people.

The juxtaposition of the first two themes in the redemptive self sets up an implicit moral challenge in the life story: *I am blessed, but others suffer. I am the gifted protagonist who journeys forth into a dangerous world.* Because bad things happen in the world, and because I have been favored in some way, it becomes my mission to make a positive difference. Erikson (1969) identified a similar sentiment from Gandhi's childhood years. "If Gandhi selects, even from his childhood, events which could qualify as moral experiments, I will apply to them the theory that a man like him is early and painfully conscious of a special mission" (p. 100). As a young man in South Africa, Gandhi's special mission became clear: "There is every reason to believe that the central identity which here found its historical time and place was the conviction that among the Indians in South Africa he was *the only person equipped by fate* to reform a situation which under no conditions could be tolerated" (p. 166, original emphasis).

Of course, nobody is quite like Gandhi. But in a paler shade of conviction, many highly generative adults identify events in their lives that affirm an early sense of being special while sensitizing them to suffering in the world around them. Stories like these would appear to explain and reinforce an adult's generativity, couching it as an effort to give back to others (and to society) for benefits experienced long ago. Moreover, the story suggests that the world indeed *needs what the generative adult has to offer*, for the world is a dangerous place and bad things often happen. Reinforcing the generative adult's commitment to making a positive difference is the *moral steadfastness* that many protagonists in these stories tend to show (Theme 3). More than less generative adults, those high in generativity tend to describe experiences in their adolescence and emerging adult years wherein they consolidated a strong personal ideology, often linked to religion or social issues. From that point on in the life story, their values guide what they do.

Over time, the protagonist encounters one negative event after another. But negative events often lead to positive outcomes in the life stories told by highly generative adults. As such, the life story is punctuated by many *redemption sequences* (Theme 4). Redemption sequences may reinforce the generative adult's conviction that the hard work and the setbacks that go into generative pursuits may someday lead to fruition. If your life story tells you that bad things are usually redeemed by good outcomes, you may come to believe that perseverance will pay off. You have overcome adversity in the past; you will continue to persevere through the adversity that generativity brings your way.

The life stories told by highly generative adults often portray protagonists who repeatedly express strong motivations for both *power and love* (Theme 5). As I have already suggested, the very nature of generativity seems to draw on both self-oriented and other-oriented drives. Highly generative adults want to have a strong impact on the world while, at the same time, connecting to others, especially those of the next generation, in caring and compassionate ways. In some life stories, these competing motivations express a tension or conflict that the highly generative adult has often faced in life. In others, the desires for power and love are reconciled or integrated. In some of the most inspiring stories, power motives are fulfilled in the service of communion (Frimer et al., 2011). The protagonist attains recognition or even fame, as Gandhi did, but the power that comes with all of that is focused onto a life program designed to help others.

Finally, life stories told by highly generative adults tend to project an *optimistic and prosocial future* (Theme 6). Even if the world is going to hell in a handbasket, the protagonist of the story typically soldiers on, convinced that projects taken on today will grow and bear fruit in future years. The redemptive self is typically a story of growth, development, and the promise of fruition, even as the protagonist confronts setbacks and losses along the way. The optimistic belief that things will continue to improve, at least in his or her neck of the woods, reinforces an adult's generative commitments. The story keeps hope alive and affirms the redemptive potential of human life.

## TROUBLE

The redemptive stories that highly generative American adults tend to tell remind us that adversity is an inescapable feature of the human condition. The fact that human lives are inevitably marked by pain and suffering, some more so than others, is surely bad for people, but it seems to make for good stories. As Jerome Bruner (1986) observed, the best stories in literature—and in lives—result from a character's encounter with *trouble*. Had Little Red Riding Hood carried her cakes to Grandma's house without encountering the Big Bad Wolf, there would be no story to tell, or at best a very boring one. No 3-year-old is going to ask her mother to read again and again that really cool story about the little girl who walks unmolested through the forest—you know, the one where nothing happens. Indeed, when "something happens" in a story, that something is often some kind of trouble—a setback, a frustration, a loss, a challenge, an obstacle. Joseph Heller (1974) wrote a famous novel entitled *Something Happened*, in which the middle-aged main character (Bob Slocum) worries about his job, his family, his mind, and his sexual prowess for over 300 pages. But nothing happens until very near the end—when something terrible does finally occur. (I should have warned you with a spoiler alert.) The reader of *Something Happens* keeps going as the suspense builds because the reader is absolutely convinced that *something has to happen*, sooner or later. There is going to be trouble for Bob Slocum; otherwise, there would be no story to tell.

In life stories resembling the redemptive self, highly generative adults construct narratives in which trouble is often transformed into growth, insight, or enhanced well-being. When something negative occurs, a positive result often follows. But there is no law of nature that says trouble *must* lead to good things. Instead, autobiographical authors make sense of their lives in this way, some more than others. One of the great challenges in narrative identity, therefore, is figuring out how to interpret negative events in life. Experiences of failure, loss, sadness, fear, shame, and guilt seem to beg for an explanation in life stories (Pals, 2006). They challenge the storyteller to explain why the event happened and what it says about the protagonist of the story. How autobiographical authors narrate negative events, therefore, tells as much as does anything else about narrative identity, revealing recurrent themes and conflicts in the storyteller's life and expressing characteristic styles of autobiographical reasoning. To wit, personality and developmental researchers have paid special attention to the ways in which adults construct stories in response to negative life events such as divorce (King & Hicks, 2007), bereavement (Baddeley & Singer, 2008), breast cancer (Thomsen & Jensen, 2007), alcoholism (Dunlop & Tracy, 2013), child abuse (Thomas & Hall, 2008), and imprisonment (Maruna, 2001).

There are many ways to narrate negative life events. Perhaps the most common response is to discount the event in some way. The most extreme examples of discounting fall under the rubrics of repression, denial, and dissociation. Some stories are so bad that they simply cannot be told—cannot be told to others, and in some cases, cannot really be told to the self. Narrative psychologist Mark Freeman (2011b) has argued that some traumatic and especially shameful experiences in life cannot be readily incorporated into narrative identity because the narrator (and perhaps the people to whom the narrator might tell the story) lacks the world assumptions, cognitive constructs, or experiential categories to make the story make sense. Memories of these kinds of events may, therefore, be buried in what Freeman calls the *narrative unconscious*.

Less extreme are examples of what social psychologist Shelley Taylor (1983) has called *positive illusions*. Autobiographical authors may simply overlook the most negative aspects of life events and exaggerate the positive meanings: "I may be sick, but I am not nearly as sick as my good colleague at work"; "God is testing my resolve, and I will rise to the challenge." Clinical psychologist George Bonanno (2004) has shown that many people experience surprisingly little angst and turmoil when stricken with harsh misfortunes in life. People often show *resilience* in the face of adversity, Bonanno maintains. Rather than ruminate over the bad things that happen in their lives, they put it all blithely behind them and move forward.

In many cases, however, people cannot or choose not to discount negative life events. Instead, they try to make explicit narrative meaning out of the suffering they are currently experiencing, or experienced once upon a time. What is the best way to make narrative sense out of suffering? Research suggests that autobiographical authors who emerge strengthened or sustained from negative life experiences often engage in a two-step process of meaning making (Pals, 2006). In the first step, the narrator explores the negative event in depth, thinking long and hard about what the experience feels or felt like, how it came to be, what it may lead to, and what role the negative event may play in his or her overall life story. In the second step, the narrator articulates and commits the self to a positive resolution of the event, providing some temporary closure and clearing a path to the future.

Support for this two-step sequence comes from many different studies. Personality psychologist Laura King has conducted a series of investigations into how people who have faced daunting challenges in life tell stories about "what might have been" had "trouble" not occurred (King & Hicks, 2007). Among mothers of children with Down syndrome, for example, those who were able to articulate especially probing accounts of the pain and struggle they experienced as caregivers for their developmentally disabled children tended to score higher on measures of psychological maturity compared to narrators who showed less exploration, and they tended to increase in maturity over the following 2 years. Moreover, attaining a sense of positive closure in their narratives (illustrating the second step described earlier) was associated with increased life satisfaction. Similar findings were observed for (1) divorced women who imagined what their married lives might have been like had they not divorced, and (2) gays and lesbians who imagined what their experiences in love and romance might have been like had their lives followed a more conventional (i.e., heterosexual) path.

Studies examining how adults narrate life's low points, turning points, and difficult life transitions consistently show that exploring the experience in depth is associated with greater psychological maturity (Lilgendahl & McAdams, 2011). For example, personality psychologists Kate McLean and Michael Pratt (2006) found that young adults who used more elaborated and sophisticated meaning making in narrating difficult events in their lives tended also to score higher on an index of overall identity maturity. The young adults who examined their difficulties in depth and derived coherent meanings from their negative experiences appeared also to have made greater progress in developing their identities. In another study, researchers analyzed data from a famous longitudinal study of the graduates of Mills College (Lilgendahl, Helson, & John, 2013). They found that the extent to which women at age 52 explored the ramifications of negative life events predicted better clinical ratings on psychological maturity made at age 61, as well as significant increases in maturity between ages 43 and 61.

Research also shows that when autobiographical authors construct positive resolutions to difficult life experiences, they tend to enjoy higher levels of well-being and happiness. For example, the number of redemption sequences found in life-story accounts positively predicts indices of psychological well-being, above and beyond the effect of a generally optimistic narrative style (McAdams et al., 2001). A longitudinal study of emerging adults showed that those who narrated low-point events in redemptive terms, providing coherent positive resolutions to life problems, reported more positive experiences with their parents at age 17 and showed higher levels of emotional adjustment at age 26 (Dumas, Lawford, Tieu, & Pratt, 2009).

A longitudinal study of high school students revealed that those who attributed positive meanings to turning point events in their lives demonstrated significant increases in psychological health between their freshman and senior years (Tavernier & Willoughby, 2012). In a study of recovering alcoholics, the ability to create a redemptive narrative about alcohol addiction was strongly associated with maintaining sobriety (Dunlop & Tracy, 2013). Yet another study examined the theme of redemption in stories about a public trauma—the attacks on New York City and Washington, D.C., on 9/11 (Adler & Poulin, 2009). The researchers found that Americans who derived redemptive meaning from the 9/11 attacks, and who indicated greater levels of psychological closure in their accounts, had higher scores on psychological well-being than those Americans whose stories of 9/11 lacked clear positive resolutions.

## CULTURE

People face trouble in all cultures. People experience negative life events in all cultures. People cope with and often overcome adversity in all cultures. But do people tell stories about these kinds of things in the same way across all cultures? Moreover, there are highly generative midlife adults in all human societies. Generativity is a human universal. But do highly generative adults in all societies author their lives as grand narratives of redemption?

In the summer of 2000, I presented initial research findings on the life stories of highly generative adults at an academic conference in the Netherlands. The main point of my talk was that midlife adults who score high on self-report measures of generativity tend to construct narrative identities that emphasize the themes of suffering, redemption, and personal destiny. In the question-and-answer session, a woman in the front row said something like this: "Professor McAdams, this is very interesting, but these life stories you describe, they sound so, well, *American*." At the time, I took her comment as a mild criticism of the research. I responded that ideas regarding redemption in human lives—transforming negative events into positive outcomes—could likely be found in most societies in the world.

On the flight back to the United States, however, I began to think that the woman sitting in the front row was probably right, at least in part. Americans *do* seem to love stories of personal redemption. You see it in Hollywood movies and television talk shows. It seems to be reflected in stories about the nation's founding, such as the heroic tales of the 17th-century Puritan settlements, and in the very concept of *the American Dream*. It is as if the most generative adults in American society today have managed to construct narrative identities for their lives that reprise some of the most cherished, and contested, ideas in America's cultural heritage. But perhaps we should not be surprised. After all, generative adults are the norm-bearers and the destiny-shapers in any society, the adults who have taken it on themselves to pass on that society's culture to the next generation. If we are looking to find culture reflected in narrative identity, where better to look than the life stories constructed by that culture's most generative men and women?

In an interview given at the end of his presidency, George W. Bush remarked, "I have recognized I am a lowly sinner seeking redemption" (in Stout, 2008, p. A12). At a memorial service for the late Massachusetts senator Edward M. Kennedy, his son observed, "He was not perfect. But my father believed in redemption" (*New York Times*, August 30, 2009, p. A14). Upon his resignation as Attorney General of the United States, Alberto Gonzales said, "Even my worst days as Attorney General have been better than my father's best days. I have lived the American dream" (*New York Times*, August 28, 2007, p. A2). Nearly every week, somebody in the United States publishes a memoir about overcoming adversity and transforming life's suffering into enhancement. Consider this best-selling title: *Breaking Night: A Memoir of Forgiveness, Survival, and my Journey from Homeless to Harvard* (Murray, 2010). Consider that hallowed authority on American popular culture—*People* magazine. An analysis of all the article titles listed on the magazine's website for the years 2001 and 2002 revealed that 53% of them explicitly described a redemption sequence (McAdams, 2013c, pp. 5–8). Here is a lead story for September 23, 2002: "Driving ambition: Once wheelchair-bound, Kelly Sutton overcomes MS to become a hot NASCAR rookie." And September 30, 2002: "Second acts: Caught in a scandal? Here's the good news: You *can* reinvent yourself, but it takes work."

On a cultural level, the theme of redemption comes in at least four canonical varieties in American society (McAdams, 2013c). First, there is redemption via *atonement*. Reflecting America's Puritan heritage and its remarkably robust religious traditions, redemption via atonement tracks the move from sin to salvation in American lives. Especially among evangelical Christians, millions of Americans narrate religious turning points in their lives, such as conversion experiences and spiritual epiphanies whereby a depraved or unenlightened condition gave way to a more Godly, righteous, or enlightened state of being.

Captured in the idea of the American Dream, redemption via *upward social mobility* tracks the move from "rags to riches," as in immigrant success tales, Horatio Alger stories, and the like. Even though many European societies actually do a better job today of promoting upward mobility (De Parle, 2012), many people still imagine the United States as the land of boundless opportunity.

The third expression is redemption via *liberation*—a move from slavery (or oppression) to freedom. From Lincoln's Emancipation Proclamation to the current-day movement for legalization of same-sex marriage, the discourse of personal liberation features the moral cachet that accompanies the one value Americans most often endorse in public opinion polls and surveys: freedom.

Finally, there is redemption via *recovery*, which tracks the move from sickness or other related negative states (abuse, addiction, criminality) to the recovery of health, innocence, wholeness, and the like. In redemptive stories of recovery, the protagonist aims to recapture a good experience or state from long ago, a paradise lost but waiting to be found again.

For the past three decades, no American has been a more effective spokesperson for redemptive narratives of upward mobility and recovery than Oprah Winfrey. In her long-running television show, her magazine and book clubs, her movies and Internet ventures, her vast network of philanthropy, and through her powerful and ubiquitous persona, Oprah lives and sells a quintessentially American success story. Born dirt-poor in Kosciusko, Mississippi, this African American heroine survived sexual abuse as a child to become first a radio reporter, then a news anchor, talk-show host, moviemaker, publishing czar, and finally international celebrity. In an interview with *Newsweek*, she remarked, "I grew up a little Negro child who felt so unloved and so isolated—the emotion I felt most as a child was loneliness—and now the exact opposite has occurred for me in adulthood" (McAdams, 2013c, p. 124). As evidenced in her own recovery from sexual abuse, Oprah preaches that people can survive traumatic experiences and come out even stronger in the end: "Your holiest moments, most sacred moments, are often the ones that are most painful" (p. 124).

Oprah's story and her message tap into a long-running stream of American romanticism, initially identified with the writings of 19th-century intellectual Ralph Waldo Emerson (1803–1882). In essays such as *Self-Reliance* (1841/1993) and his many public lectures, Emerson taught that every adult has within him or her an inner light of goodness and vitality. Follow your light, Emerson said. Ignore the distractions of society and stay true instead to the mission that your very nature has called you to do. It is your personal *manifest destiny* to pursue that good mission, just as it was the manifest destiny, believed many Americans in the 19th century, for America itself to expand and redeem the world.

The spiritual form of rugged individualism that Emerson proclaimed has found expression in a plethora of cultural myths often associated with Americans, from the frontier romance of the Wild West (Kleinfeld, 2012) to idealistic, and sometimes imperialistic, efforts to spread American ideals—democracy and freedom—to other countries. An admirer of Emerson (she carries Emersonian aphorisms in her purse), Oprah channels cultural ideas like these into contemporary psychological and spiritual forms. She believes that her work obeys an inner calling. Like highly generative adults whose narrative identities proclaim an early advantage in life, she believes she has been chosen to make a positive difference in a troubled world, to help people take charge of their lives and change for the better. "What I teach is that if you are strong enough and bold enough to follow your dreams, then you will be led in the path that is best for you" (McAdams, 2013c, p. 124).

Oprah Winfrey is an American cultural icon, like Abraham Lincoln, John Wayne, and the Super Bowl. Her life and her story suggest a quintessentially American way to live—a coming together of American culture and the development of personality. Indeed, culture shapes human lives and personality development in a multitude of ways. Culture shapes the stories we tell about our lives, in our capacity as autobiographical authors. But culture also shapes the goals and values we develop as motivated agents. And culture impacts how we behave as social actors. In Table 9.3, I partition cultural effects into the three layers of personality development that I have described throughout this book.

At the level of the *social actor*, culture provides rules for how to perform the traits and the roles that structure social life. There are extraverts the world over, but how you perform your outgoing and gregarious nature in a rural Indian village is different from how you might perform that same dispositional profile growing up in Malibu, California. As members of a eusocial species, human beings are exquisitely attuned to the behavioral and affective standards established by groups. Groups tell us how to feel and what to do, and we perform our traits and roles accordingly.

At the level of the *motivated agent*, different cultures provide norms for the content and importance of personal goals and values. For example, the well-known distinction between cultural individualism and collectivism (Markus & Kitayama, 1991) pertains mainly to motivational and value agendas, as I argued in Chapters 6 and 7. Whereas individualist cultures like the United States may encourage the development of personal goals that privilege the expansion and fulfillment of the self, collectivist East Asian cultures may strongly encourage the development of personal goals that aim to promote social harmony and the well-being of the agent's self-defining groups.

Culture exerts its most profound influences, I believe, at the level of the *autobiographical author* (Hammack, 2008). Life stories capture and elaborate metaphors and images that are especially resonant in a given culture. Stories distinguish what culture glorifies as good characters and vilifies as bad characters, and they present the many varieties that fall between them. Culture, therefore, may provide each autobiographical author with a menu of stories about how to live, and each author chooses from the menu. In authoring a narrative identity, a person selectively appropriates and personalizes the stories provided by culture, looking for a way to convey what his or her life seems to mean within the categories of understanding that prevailing cultural narratives set forth. In contemporary American culture, then, many highly generative midlife adults appear to draw upon inspiring narrative models such as rags-to-riches stories and redemptive tales of liberation, atonement, and recovery. If those same adults grew up in a different culture, they would author their lives in different ways—both because their lives themselves would be different and because they would be exposed to different stories about how to live.

Different kinds of narrative identities make sense in different kinds of cultural contexts. In Erikson's (1958) classic study of Martin Luther's

**TABLE 9.3. Relationships between Culture and Personality**

From the standpoint of . . .

*The social actor.* Cultures provide different display rules for the expression of affect and the performance of trait-based behavior in social groups. For example, Japanese extraverts growing up in Kyoto may express their high levels of sociability and positive affectivity in ways that differ dramatically from how their equally extraverted middle-American counterparts express the same tendencies in, say, Columbus, Ohio. High neuroticism may translate into eating disorders and cutting behavior among upper-middle-class American teenage girls, whereas the same levels of emotional instability may manifest themselves as magical thinking and an extreme fear of enemies among teenage girls in Ghana (Adams, 2005). Whether different cultures promote the development of particular traits over others, however, is unclear. Some studies report cultural/geographic differences in average trait scores (e.g., Rentfrow, Gosling, & Potter, 2008), but skeptics argue that these differences are difficult to interpret because people in the same culture may implicitly compare themselves to each other when making trait judgments (Heine, Buchtel, & Norenzayan, 2008a).

*The motivated agent.* Cultures show clear influences on the content and importance of different motives and goals. For example, the well-known distinction between cultural individualism and collectivism and the corresponding emphasis on independent and interdependent self-concepts, respectively (Markus & Kitayama, 1991), appears to map much more clearly onto Layer 2 of personality (goals, motives, values) than on to dispositional traits (Layer 1). A large and growing body of research suggests that whereas individualist Western cultures may encourage the development of personal goals that privilege the expansion and articulation of the self, collectivist East Asian cultures may more strongly encourage the development of personal goals that aim to promote social harmony and the well-being of one's self-defining groups.

*The autobiographical author.* Culture may exert its most profound influences at the level of life narratives. Stories capture and elaborate metaphors and images that are especially resonant in a given culture. Stories distinguish what culture glorifies as good characters and vilifies as bad characters, as well as the many variations in between. Culture, therefore, may provide each member with a menu of stories about how to live, and each person chooses from the menu and mixes and matches different options to create a story that works. For example, highly generative American adults tend to construct their own life stories by drawing upon inspiring American narratives such as rags-to-riches stories and redemptive tales of emancipation and self-fulfillment. Identity choices are constrained and shaped by the unique circumstances of a person's social, political, and economic worlds, by his or her family background and educational experiences, and by dispositional traits and characteristic motives, values, and goals. A person authors a personal narrative identity by selectively appropriating and personalizing the stories provided by culture.

*Note.* Based on McAdams and Olson (2010).

identity formation (Chapter 8 in this book), the stories that Luther as a young man constructed to make sense of his own life—stories about physical encounters with devils and saints—made all kinds of cultural sense in 16th-century Christian Germany. But they strike the secular modern ear as somewhat odd, even delusional. A member of a rural Indian village may account for his feelings of tranquility this morning as resulting from the cool and dispassionate *food* he ate last night (Shweder & Much, 1987). His story will make sense to his peers in the village, who all believe that what you eat affects your subsequent emotional state. But it will not fit expectations for life-narrative accounts in contemporary Berlin or Los Angeles, where people do not make the same kind of narrative connections.

Within contemporary modern societies, different groups and subcultures are given different narrative opportunities and face different narrative constraints. Especially relevant here are class, gender, and race/ethnicity divisions in modern societies. For example, developmental psychologist Peggy Miller and her colleagues have shown that working-class children and adolescents learn to narrate their lives with a greater sense of humility and vigilance, compared to their middle-class peers. "The working class slant encourages children to see that they have the right and resources to narrate their own experiences in self-dramatizing ways, but that the right to be heard and to have one's point of view accepted cannot be taken for granted" (Miller, Cho, & Bracey, 2005, p. 115). In her book *Writing a Woman's Life*, late feminist author Carolyn Heilbrun (1988) remarked that many women have traditionally "been deprived of the narratives, or the texts, plots, or examples, by which they might assume power over—take control of—their own lives" (p. 17). The historical and contemporary life experiences of many African Americans do not always coalesce nicely into the kind of life-narrative forms favored by the white majority in the United States (Boyd-Franklin, 1989). Narrative identity, therefore, reflects structural and cultural boundaries in society and the patterns of economic, political, and cultural hegemony that prevail at a given point in a society's history (Rosenwald & Ochberg, 1992).

With respect to cultural effects, researchers have noted strong differences in autobiographical memory and storytelling between East Asian and North American societies. For example, North American adults typically report an earlier age of first memory and have longer and more detailed memories of childhood than do Chinese, Japanese, and Korean adults (Leichtman, Wang, & Pillemer, 2003). In addition, several studies have noted that North Americans' personal memories tend to be more self-focused than are the memories of East Asians (Chang & McCabe, 2013; Wang, 2006).

In an illuminating study of cultural differences in life narratives, developmental psychologist Qi Wang and cognitive scientist Martin Conway asked European American and Chinese midlife adults to recall 20 important autobiographical memories (Wang & Conway, 2004). Americans provided more memories of individual experiences and one-time events, and they focused their attention on their own roles and emotions in the events. In contrast, Chinese adults were more inclined to recall memories of social and historical events, and they placed a greater emphasis on social interactions and significant others in their stories. Chinese also more frequently drew on past events to convey moral messages than did Americans. The researchers suggested that personal narratives fulfill both self-expressive and self-directive functions. European Americans may prioritize self-expressive functions, viewing personal narratives as vehicles for articulating the breadth, depth, and uniqueness of the inner self. By contrast, Chinese may prioritize the self-directive function, using personal narratives as guides for social conduct.

Confucian traditions in China place a great deal of emphasis on history and respect for the past. Individuals are encouraged to learn from their own past experiences and from the experiences of others, including their ancestors. From a Confucian perspective, the highest purpose in life is *ren*—a blending of benevolence, moral vitality, and sensitive concern for others. One method for promoting *ren* is to scrutinize your autobiographical past for mistakes in social conduct. Another method is to reflect on historical events to understand your appropriate position in the social world. It should not be surprising, then, that personal narratives imbued with a Confucian ethic should draw on both individual and historical events to derive directions for life.

In all societies, a culture's stories are a powerful force in the structuring of human lives—for good and for ill. Cultural psychologist Philip Hammack (2008) describes how a culture's *master narratives* provide vital resources for the construction of narrative identity while, at the same time, severely constraining the kinds of lives that people can live. Master narratives speak to the identity of an entire group, as well as the members of the group. The group itself may be based on shared ethnicity, religion, ideology, or even its status as a nation-state. A master narrative summarizes the group's understanding of its own history and destiny. In so doing, it also suggests how members of the group should understand their place and their position in the world. As such, individuals in the group may appropriate themes from the master narrative into their personal life stories. In some cases, the effort to match the personal and the cultural is relatively easy, but in other cases, autobiographical authors struggle to line up their own unique experiences with what their culture suggests their lives should mean. Group members may sometimes *resist* the master narrative set forth by their culture (Gjerde, 2004; Polletta, Chen, Gardner, & Motes, 2011). As authors of the self, they may fight back against a master narrative that they perceive to be oppressive or inaccurate in conveying who they are.

Hammack (2009, 2011) has paid special attention to how individual stories may sometimes reproduce those features of master narratives that perpetuate conflict between different groups. His case in point is the long-running conflict between the Israelis and the Palestinians. Hammack notes that the citizens of the state of Israel and the Palestinian people who were displaced by its founding hold to dramatically different master narratives regarding the meaning of recent historical events. For the Israelis, the establishment of the state of Israel, in 1948, marked a redemptive conclusion to unparalleled suffering. Their master narrative tells how 6 million innocent Jews were exterminated in the Holocaust of World War II, and how this resilient people rallied to establish their own promised land after the war. The master narrative commemorates the horror they endured and celebrates the subsequent triumph of a democratic and enlightened nation.

By contrast, Palestinians refer to the events of 1948 as *al-Nakba*, Arabic for "the catastrophe." About 700,000 Arabs fled or were expelled from their homes during the first Arab–Israeli war. Hundreds of thousands of Palestinians were later displaced by the Arab–Israeli war of 1967, with some becoming refugees twice over. Their master narrative is about peace-loving people who were ruthlessly uprooted from their homeland. It is a *contamination story*, tracking a sudden transformation from positive to negative while holding to the desperate hope for a reversal.

Through intensive interviews of Israeli and Palestinian teenagers, Hammack has examined how individual life stories relate to master narratives. He has found a consistent tendency for the stories of Israeli youth to match the upward trajectory of their culture's master narrative, and for the stories of Palestinian youth to show the same downward spiral that is conveyed in stories of "the catastrophe." When Israeli youth in Hammack's study envisioned the time line of their own lives—from childhood past to adult future—they tended to envision an upward, redemptive arc; correspondingly, Palestinian youth imagined their own lives as downwardly mobile, declension narratives. Childhood may have been happy, but things were beginning to get worse, they suggested, and they would likely continue downhill in the future.

In the year or two following Hammack's interviews, the same Israeli and Palestinian youth came to the United States to participate in an intensive program designed to encourage friendship and understanding between the two groups. In the short term, the program seemed to be a success. Through sharing stories of their own experiences and engaging in a wide range of group activities, the young people developed close bonds across the two groups. Israeli youth reported enhanced empathy for the plight of their new Palestinian friends. Palestinian youth reported greater appreciation for the strengths and the experiences of their new Israeli friends. Members of both groups resolved to work on enhancing tolerance and mutual understanding when they returned home.

A year or two later, Hammack reinterviewed many of the youth. To his dismay, he found that the promise of the peace-making program had not been realized. Although the young people had sincere intentions when they returned to their homeland, most eventually hardened their attitudes, with some becoming even less tolerant of the other group than they were before they entered the program. Back at home, the old influences of family and friends gradually overwhelmed the more accepting attitudes they had developed in the program. Moreover, the master cultural narratives of their respective groups proved to be paramount. In Hammack's (2011) view, the discordant master narratives of Israelis and Palestinians not only produce sharply different narrative identities for individual members of their respective group but also perpetuate intergroup conflict.

As the world becomes more and more interconnected through emigration and the Internet, an increasing number of people find that they are exposed to, and may live in, multiple cultures on a daily basis. In the United States, Mexican Americans and Chinese Americans, among many other groups, often face the challenge of navigating two different cultures, each with its own prevailing language, customs, values, and social norms (Benet-Martinez & Haritatos, 2005). In crafting a bicultural narrative identity, autobiographical authors may try to blend different stories from different cultures in making sense of their own lives. Or they may aim to keep their different identities more or less separate. For many people, developing a clear and meaningful ethnic identity is an important psychological project, especially in adolescence and early adulthood (Syed & Azmitia, 2010). As different ethnic groups interact with each other and develop new modes of self-understanding, the opportunities and challenges for the construction of a meaningful narrative identity grow larger and more varied.

Indeed, for some people, becoming a *global citizen* marks a psychological and social challenge with strong moral overtones (Jensen, Arnett, & McKenzie, 2011). The construction of global citizenship suggests that people may transcend the master narratives of ethnicity and nation-states to embrace stories about being part of the human collective writ large. What kind of a life story does a good global citizen construct? How might people create stories that balance their family, ethnic, and religious affiliations with their desires to be part of a broader world community? These are relatively new questions for our eusocial species. We did not evolve to develop strong allegiances to out-groups. Yet questions like these may become increasingly important over the course of the 21st century, as people the world over aim to develop broader and more inclusive forms of eusociality.

## LIFE STORIES OVER THE LIFE COURSE

Life stories change over time. They change for two reasons. First, people's lives change. If you win the lottery or file for divorce, your life story will automatically change, for you now have an important new event to describe and to integrate. Second, people change their stories as they change their understandings of themselves. At age 30, you believed that the most important event that ever occurred in your life was your acceptance into medical school. At age 40, you see it all differently. You now believe that an *earlier* event marked the key turning point in your life—say, when your best friend died in high school. You now see that her death sensitized you to the seriousness of life, which may have awakened your desire to become a doctor in the first place. At age 50, you may end up having a very different story to tell. And on it goes.

Compared to dispositional traits such as extraversion and neuroticism, and compared to goals and values, life narratives are likely to reveal rather less continuity and more change over the course of life (McAdams & Olson, 2010). Traits may show the highest levels of stability (Layer 1 in personality), followed by values and goals (Layer 2), and then narrative identity (Layer 3). Nonetheless, people's narrative understandings of their lives have to show *some* stability over time, if we are to consider them a legitimate component of human personality. If your story changed completely from one day to the next, there would be no point in paying much attention to it.

Determining the stability and change in life stories is tricky, however. What would qualify as proof of stability over time? Would it require telling "the same story" at Time 1 and Time 2? If yes, does "same story" mean identifying the same key events in life? Showing the same kinds of narrative themes? Exhibiting the same forms of autobiographical reasoning? In a 3-year longitudinal study, my colleagues and I asked college students to recall and describe 10 key scenes in their life stories on three occasions (McAdams et al., 2006). We found that only 28% of the specific episodes described at Time 1 were repeated 3 months later (Time 2), and 22% of the original (Time 1) memories were chosen and described again 3 years after the original assessment (Time 3). Despite change in the manifest content of the stories, however, we also documented significant longitudinal consistencies in certain emotional and motivational qualities in the stories, and in the level of narrative complexity. While students did not always identify the same specific events from one session to the next, they tended to describe events in the same kinds of ways. Furthermore, over the 3-year period, students' life-narrative accounts became more complex, and they incorporated a greater number of themes suggesting personal growth and integration. In a similar study, a different research team found that the life stories of adolescents increased in thematic richness and meaning, and became more streamlined, over a 4-year period (Neegle & Habermas, 2010).

Cross-sectional studies (comparing different age groups to each other) suggest that up through late middle age, older adults tend to construct more coherent life narratives with greater insight and meaning than do younger adults and adolescents (Baddeley & Singer, 2007; McAdams & Olson, 2010). For example, researchers have found that midlife adults tend to engage in more sophisticated forms of autobiographical reasoning than do younger adults when telling stories about turning points and crises in life (Pasupathi & Mansour, 2006). Other studies have found that midlife adults tell life stories that are more thematically coherent and more illustrative of personal continuity, compared to younger adults (McLean, 2008). Whereas the stories of older adults may emphasize stability, younger adults appear to put more emphasis on change. Sampling across the age range of 20–70 years, a research team found that older respondents tended to tell more vivid and coherent earliest memories relative to younger respondents (Kingo, Bernsten, & Krogjaard, 2013). Yet another study asked adolescents (ages 15–20), younger adults (ages 30–40), and older adults (ages 60 and over) to recount personal experiences in which they demonstrated wisdom. Younger and older adults were more likely than adolescents to narrate wisdom scenes in ways that connected the experiences to larger life themes and philosophies (Bluck & Gluck, 2004).

Jefferson Singer and his colleagues asked adults to describe *self-defining memories*—emotionally vivid scenes in their lives in which they grappled with important psychological issues (Singer, Rexhaj, & Baddeley, 2007). The study showed that older adults found greater integrative meaning in their self-defining memories, compared to younger adults. Moreover, the older adults told stories that were more positive in emotional tone. Researchers have shown that older adults exhibit less conflict in their life stories compared to younger adults (Rice & Pasupathi, 2010). Findings such as these dovetail with other research, based on laboratory studies and analysis of published fiction, showing that adults use more positive and fewer negative emotion words as they age (Pennebaker & Stone, 2003). They are also consistent with research on what is sometimes called the *positivity bias* of aging—the fact that older adults tend to emphasize positive emotions in their daily lives and in their memories, compared to younger adults (Kennedy, Mather, & Carstensen, 2004). At the same time, evidence suggests that older adults tend to recall more general, as opposed to specific, event memories, tending to skip over the details and focus mainly on the memory's emotional gist (Baddeley & Singer, 2007). In our later years, narrative identity may become warmer and fuzzier.

Counselors who work with older adults sometimes employ the method of *life review* to encourage older adults to relive and reflect on past events (Butler, 1963). In life review, older adults are encouraged to mine their autobiographical memory for specific events that seem to have meaning and value. Life review therapists teach their clients how to reminisce productively about these events and to reflect upon their meaning. Some studies suggest that life review can improve life satisfaction and relieve symptoms of depression and anxiety among older adults (Serrano, Latorre, Gatz, & Montaines, 2004). Even without undergoing formal training or assistance in life review, however, autobiographical authors may draw increasingly on reminiscences as the years go by. Positive memory biases among older people may give narrative identity a softer glow. The increasing tendency with age to recall more generalized memories may also simplify life stories in our later years.

## CONCLUSION

Developmental trends in personality ideally come together in adulthood to promote generativity. Illustrated in Erik Erikson's famous case study of Mahatma Gandhi, generativity is an adult's concern for and commitment to promoting the well-being of the next generation, as evidenced in parenting, teaching, mentoring, leadership, and other behaviors aimed at leaving a positive legacy for the future. At the level of the *social actor*, developmental increases in traits related to conscientiousness and agreeableness, and decreases in neuroticism, help pave the way for the performance of generative roles in the adult years. At the level of the *motivated agent*, adults increasingly infuse generativity into their goals and values as they move into midlife. From the perspective of the *autobiographical author*, midlife adults begin to narrate their lives with an eye toward the lasting contributions they hope to make—those things, ideas, and people that will survive them after they are gone. Research reveals broad individual differences in generativity across human lives. Adults who score high on well-validated measures of generativity tend to be better parents than those who score lower, and tend to be more meaningfully involved in a range of community activities and institutions, from religious organizations to volunteer work. Generativity is also positively associated with psychological well-being and mental health.

Generativity is a universal challenge for our eusocial species. Caring for and promoting the well-being of future generations maximize the chances that an adult's genes will be passed down to posterity. Generative behaviors and commitments, moreover, typically integrate the adult more fully into the group, whether the group be a hunting and gathering tribe or the complex societal structures that prevail in the modern world. Each group context poses its own characteristic challenges for living a generative life. In contemporary American society, the most generative adults tend to narrate their lives as stories of redemption, wherein suffering gives way, again and again, to personal enhancement. Redemptive life stories help to promote generativity in the adult years. If an autobiographical author believes that bad things in life often give way to positive outcomes, he or she may be especially well prepared, psychologically speaking, to endure the difficulties that invariably accompany generativity. Whether we are talking about Gandhi or your average middle-aged mom, trying to leave a lasting positive impact for future generations is really hard work. It helps to have a good story.

The redemptive life stories told by highly generative American adults reflect quintessentially American cultural themes. In popular views of American history, in American literature, television, and movies, redemptive stories often trace how a gifted individual protagonist journeys forth into a dangerous world. Equipped with moral steadfastness and a sense of personal mission, the protagonist transforms suffering into enhancement, ultimately aiming to give back to others in light of the fortune that he or she has enjoyed. Among the most cherished American stories of redemption are those that describe religious atonement, upward social mobility (the American Dream), personal liberation from oppression, and the recovery of a paradise lost. Indeed, culture colors and contours life stories, and individual narrative identity may say as much about the culture wherein the storyteller lives as it does about the storyteller him- or herself. Research reveals strong cultural differences in the ways that adults narrate their lives. For example, European Americans often highlight key scenes that illustrate the uniqueness of their personal consciousness, whereas Asian Americans are more likely to highlight scenes in their lives in which they learned something important about how to live with others in a productive or harmonious manner. Cultures provide master narratives for identity construction. Autobiographical authors often model their own lives after these narratives, but they may also, on occasion, show strong resistance, constructing stories that defy prevailing narrative norms.

Cutting across cultures, the theme of redemption in life stories also points to a universal challenge for autobiographical authors: How do you narrate bad events? Research suggests that people make sense of negative events in their lives in many different ways. Whereas some adults blithely manage to put negative events behind them, others work hard to find explicit meaning in the disappointments, defeats, losses, and trauma they have endured. Those adults who explore the vicissitudes of negative life events tend to show relatively high levels of psychological maturity. Those who construct stories with positive resolutions to the negative events tend to enjoy relatively high levels of happiness and well-being.

Over the life course, life stories show both continuity and change. While new events may replace older ones in narrative identity, narrators may still tend to construct the new events in ways that resemble how they made sense of their predecessors. A growing body of research examines age differences in life narration. Overall, middle-aged adults tend to construct life stories that show more sophisticated forms of autobiographical reasoning compared to younger adults. Their stories may be more complex, more coherent, and more psychologically nuanced. Life stories also seem to warm up as people age. Older narrators give more emphasis to positive events and tend to downplay the conflicts and struggles they have experienced, at least through late midlife. As we get older, our stories may show a warmer glow, even as the vivid details of what we have experienced in our lives begin to fade.

# chapter 10

# The Sense of an Ending

> We live in time, it bounds us and defines us, and time is supposed to measure history, isn't it? But if we can't grasp its mysteries of pace and progress, what chance do we have with history—even our own small, personal, largely undocumented piece of it?
> —JULIAN BARNES (2011, p. 66)

In a novel titled *The Sense of an Ending*, Julian Barnes writes of a retired arts administrator named Tony Webster who confronts the fallibility of his own memory. Tony recalls a relationship he had decades ago with a mercurial young woman named Veronica. At the beginning of the novel, he remembers that Veronica and he broke things off shortly after he spent a disastrous weekend with her family at their country home. He remembers Veronica's father as a boor, her brother as an arrogant brute, and her mother as a pleasant but curious woman, who prepared breakfast for him after he slept in late Sunday morning. Veronica eventually took up with a friend of Tony's—a brilliant and eccentric student named Adrian Finn, admired by many for his brutal honesty about life and his intellectual integrity. A teacher once asked the class to define the idea of "history." Adrian gave a response that Tony still remembers and ponders: "History is that certainty produced at the point where the imperfections of memory meet with the inadequacies of documentation" (Barnes, 2011, p. 18). Tragically, Adrian killed himself a few months after meeting Veronica. He left a suicide note saying that any man has the right to examine his own life, then to decide whether or not to renounce it.

Forty years pass. Tony marries, has a daughter, divorces, has a couple of affairs, and now lives alone. He has a pleasant enough life. He keeps busy, putters around the apartment, reads books, attends regular meetings of the local historical society, gets together occasionally with a friend or two for drinks. Tony's tranquility is interrupted, however, when he receives a letter from a lawyer saying that Veronica's mother has died and left him a small sum of money. Why would she leave *him* money?

Tony met Veronica's mother only once, during that fateful weekend so long ago. He has not thought about that weekend, nor about Veronica and Adrian, for years. The letter motivates Tony to seek out Veronica and to find out what has happened over the past four decades. In a series of shocking disclosures, he comes to realize that he has completely misremembered his relationship with Veronica. She sends him a letter he once wrote to Adrian, and Tony is flabbergasted by the vicious words he once composed. He must have been a different person when he wrote this, so different that he still cannot recall ever holding the sentiments expressed in the letter.

Eventually, Tony realizes that he completely misjudged Adrian, too. Adrian's suicide, once viewed as an act of intellectual courage, appears now to have had no deep philosophical meaning. Instead, Tony comes to believe that Adrian was distraught about having gotten Veronica pregnant. But no! That turns out to be wrong, too. The baby lived on, and he is now a middle-aged man himself, developmentally disabled and living in a group home. Veronica takes Tony to meet him. But the man—Adrian's son—is not *her* son. He is instead her (half) brother, born of the affair that Adrian had with Veronica's mother. The affair, the deepest secret in the story, is revealed in the end. And Tony realizes that he may, in a sense, be culpable for the affair. In the spiteful letter that he still cannot remember writing, Tony called Veronica a "bitch" and a "cockteaser," and he claimed that she needed to see a "headshrinker." "Even her own mother warned me against her. If I were you, I'd check things out with Mum—ask her about damage a long way back. Of course, you'll have to do this behind Veronica's back . . . " (Barnes, 2011, p. 106).

Tony will never know for sure whether Adrian's first rendezvous with Veronica's mother was the direct result of his letter. But at the novel's end, he seems to be on the brink of accepting this new interpretation of time's past. History has changed, in his mind. The "certainty produced at the point where imperfections of memory meet with the inadequacies of documentation" (Barnes, 2011, p. 18) has been transformed (by new documentation from the past, which ends up changing memory). Tony now wonders what he can truly believe about his own history, about who he was, is, and may become in the future, as he approaches the end of his own life:

"How often do we tell our own life story? How often do we adjust, embellish, make sly cuts? And the longer life goes on, the fewer are those around to challenge our account, to remind us that our life is not our life, merely the story we have told about our life. Told to others, but—mainly—to ourselves." (Barnes, 2011, p. 104)

## FINAL CHAPTERS

Barnes borrowed the title for his novel from a famous treatise in literary criticism written by Frank Kermode (1967), who argued that the sense of an ending functions to shape how stories unfold and how characters' lives develop in good fiction. Similar processes may prevail in real human lives as an expression of the art of personality development. Outside the pages of literary fiction, real people imagine how their lives will end up, and those projections for the future feed back to color the way people see the present and understand the past. For everyday autobiographical authors like you and me, who I am in the present and who I was in the past are shaped in my own mind by how I believe things will end for me in the future.

We know one thing for sure: We will die in the end. Still, we may hope to leave something behind. With this in mind, the concept of adult generativity (see Chapter 9 in this book) has sometimes been seen as an artful and creative response to mortality (Kotre, 1984; McAdams, 1985). We cannot live forever, but we can live on vicariously, through our children and through other results of our efforts to provide for the next generation. For the generative adult, Erik Erikson (1968) once wrote, "I am what survives me" (p. 141). Indeed, Mahatma Gandhi's name and legacy live on, and so may yours. But this kind of immortality seems distressingly metaphorical. Autobiographical authors know that there is a literal end in store, even if they ascribe to vague notions about a religious afterlife. They organize their stories with a real ending in mind.

In his theory of the human life cycle, Erikson (1963) posited a final stage of psychosocial development. In old age, he argued, men and women address the psychological challenge of *ego integrity* versus *despair*. When "old age" occurs cannot be easily pinpointed in any particular life, Erikson acknowledged, and many people do not live long enough to experience the final stage. Nonetheless, there comes a final period in the fully extended course of human life when concerns about generativity wane somewhat in the wake of declining physical powers and the prospect of impending death. To experience ego integrity in the last stage is to accept one's life as having been a worthwhile endeavor. The sentiment has religious overtones, reminiscent of the Christian concept of *grace* (an acceptance of God's will) and St. Paul's statement at the end of his life (2 Timothy 4:7): "I have fought the good fight, I have finished my course, I have kept the faith." Ideally, the sense of an ending can be met with acceptance and gratitude. The older person is thankful for the gift of life and for a life well lived. In the opposite case of extreme despair, however, the older person rejects his or her own life as something that has not been good or worthy. The older person is filled with regrets and recriminations.

From the standpoint of narrative identity, ego integrity shifts the older person's focus somewhat from author to reader (and critic). In a sense, the person becomes the audience for his or her own life story. Rather than construct the story, the person takes it in and evaluates it. Can I *trust* my story? Is my story *good*? Does my story convey appropriately a life well lived? In the case of Tony Webster, ambivalence and doubt begin to cloud his narrative understanding of life once he receives the letter pertaining to the death of Veronica's mother. Although he is not yet what you would call an "old man," Tony begins to feel the kind of despair that Erikson suggests can occur in the later years, when the autobiographical author loses faith in his life story. Acutely aware of the aging process, Tony wonders what developing across the entire course of life really comes down to in the final analysis. In the novel's last sentences, he concludes that it all comes down to this: "There is accumulation. There is responsibility. And beyond these, there is unrest. There is great unrest" (Barnes, 2011, p. 163).

Psychological research on the development of narrative identity in the last years is sparse. Certain religious traditions and Erikson's writings on ego integrity suggest that the end of life can be a most fulfilling period. Scholars have long associated old age with the attainment of wisdom in some lives. Social gerontologists today preach the virtues of *successful aging*. The fictional case of Tony Webster, however, cautions against the rose-colored view. Beyond death itself, there are many other threats in contemporary life that cast shadows on what we might imagine to be the final stage of life for the autobiographical author. With memory loss and increasing frailty, the oldest adults may find it more and more difficult to engage in the process of life narrative construction. The autobiographical author may tell fewer and fewer stories and expend less and less energy in the construction of narrative identity.

In the cruel but common instances of Alzheimer's disease, dementia may undermine the author's fundamental reason for being, scrambling and eventually destroying the material out of which narrative identity is to be made (McColgan, Valentine, & Downs, 2000). Dementia eventually strips away the episodic memory upon which the narrative self is built. As autobiographical memory is slowly destroyed, the person may come to feel that he or she no longer has a story to live by (Freeman, 2011a). The author fades away, marking a kind of regression in the development of personality and a diminution of the self. In other lives, however, older men and women may retain control of the narrative until the very end. After a lifetime of self-authorship, people do not want their stories to slip away from them.

The final chapters in people's lives are as varied as there are people on the earth. In the same sense that every human life is a unique and artfully constructed variation on the general theme of human nature, every hero of every story ends the story in a unique way. As autobiographical authors move into old age, the stories they tell about their respective pasts tend to take on a warm and fuzzy quality, as I suggested in Chapter 9. What psychologists have identified as the positivity bias of aging is revealed in the tendency of older people to emphasize positive and deemphasize negative emotions in their autobiographical memories, and in other aspects of their lives as well. Older people may simply forget, or downplay, many of the bad things they have experienced in their lives, or else they will accept these setbacks and losses as a matter of fate. This is just how life goes, they may suggest. Erikson's concept of ego integrity depends on just such an acceptance. If you are to look back upon life and accept it as having been good and worthwhile, then you may need to be fairly selective in your remembrance of things past. Still, every autobiographical author takes on the challenges of late-life storytelling in a unique way. No two stories of life are the same, as works of art. And no two storytellers shape their artful narrations in exactly the same manner. There are comedies and tragedies to convey, romances and adventure stories. One narrator looks back upon it all with conviction and no second thoughts. Another is more like Tony Webster: "I think it happened this way, but maybe not. I thought I had one kind of life, but maybe I have been living another."

In the final chapter of life, what matters most in the story? Probably *relationships*—family, close friends, the inner circle of companionship and support. Lifespan psychologist Laura Carstensen suggests that as people get older, they winnow down their priorities to a few things in life that matter the most, such as family and friends. In her theory of *socioemotional selectivity*, Carstensen (1995) contends that when people experience a shorter time perspective for the future, they focus on keeping hold of those people and experiences that are most near and dear.

Older people, and people who believe that their lives may end soon, select the social and emotional aspects of their daily lives that provide them with the greatest degree of meaning, comfort, and satisfaction. They typically lose interest in expanding their worlds in order to gain new experiences, meet new people, or learn new things. They typically lose interest in building their lives up, or making more money, or acquiring new possessions, or doing anything that will divert their focus from those few things in life that matter most. As motivated agents, they simplify their goals. They aim to maintain their health and stay close to the people they love. It is the kind of thing you would expect of aging organisms who are members of a eusocial species like ours.

As people move into their 70s and beyond, long-term goals become less salient, for obvious reasons. At age 75, it probably does not make sense to take up a new venture in life that promises to reap benefits for you 10 or 20 years down the road, though there are surely some exceptions to the rule. An older colleague of mine jokes that he buys only the ripest bananas at the grocery store. The green ones promise to be ready to eat in 3–4 days, but by then, well, who knows?! There is also considerable research evidence to suggest that long-term planning skills erode in the later years (Kostering, Stahl, Leonhart, Weiller, & Kaller, 2014). Many studies document late-life decline in a range of cognitive abilities that are mediated by the brain's frontal lobes. Included among these is the ability to make and follow through with plans. Motivated agency must therefore adapt to our changing cognitive abilities as we age. As our abilities to make plans and pursue our valued goals in a planful manner begin to deteriorate, we need to scale back our agentic pursuits. Or we need to get help. Older adults need to obtain support from others who are better able to set up the plans that older adults want to set up, keep track of things related to the plans, and execute the actions that are required to attain valued goals.

What happens to our dispositional traits in the last years of life? Unfortunately, to date, personality researchers have not devoted considerable attention to old age, so we know relatively little about what happens to social actors in the final chapter of life. Nonetheless, a few themes can be discerned among the studies that do exist. The emerging research picture suggests that *personality stability may decline* in the later years, and people may *reverse the gains* they have made on positive personality traits.

There is evidence to suggest that the strong rank-order continuity of traits begins to break down in the last years, reversing a lifelong trend (Martin, Long, & Poon, 2002). In other words, levels of extraversion (E), conscientiousness (C), and other dispositional traits of the social actor may begin to change in unpredictable ways in the last years of life. The person's relative position in the distribution of scores for any given trait may become less easy to predict from one year to the next. An 80-year-old woman who seemed to be on the high end of the C spectrum last year may now be showing declines in self-regulation. We might have ranked her at the 95th percentile on the broad trait of C for her age group last year, but now we rank her in the middle of the distribution, or even lower.

Increases in depressiveness, fatigue, and suspiciousness in old age have been documented in a handful of studies. Over the age span of 74 to 103 years, for example, one especially thorough longitudinal study found increasingly negative emotional states with age (Smith & Baltes, 1999). Some research findings document rising levels of neuroticism (N) after age 75 (Teachman, 2006). Sharp increases in N have been shown to predict mortality (Mroczek & Spiro, 2007). Research suggests that small stresses may add up in the lives of the oldest adults to ignite debilitating negative reactions (Mroczek & Almeida, 2004). Older adults who experience a rise in N will perceive their everyday lives to be more stressful than they once did. The same high levels of N, however, render them less proficient in dealing with the stress they experience. Even for adults who do not experience increases in the trait of N, advanced aging brings with it a substantial decline in coping skills and mechanisms for defending against anxiety (Diehl et al., 2014). As frustrations mount, negative emotions increase. And as efforts to cope with negative emotions fail, feelings of anxiety and sadness increase ever more.

As social actors reach old age, they may find it increasingly difficult to sustain effective performances, especially when health fails and daily stresses mount. Nonetheless, social support from family members, peers, and paid caregivers can go a long way in dampening the negative effects of aging. Older people who are becoming higher in N by the year are difficult to be around. But being around them is what their family and friends need to be, or else arrangements need to be made whereby social support is assured.

## THE LIFE COURSE IN FULL:
## MILESTONES IN PERSONALITY DEVELOPMENT

Throughout this book, I have argued that personality follows three lines of development over the life course, each of which corresponds to a layer of psychological individuality. The first line begins with the temperament dispositions that appear shortly after birth and follows the establishment, growth, and maturation of basic dispositional *traits* in personality, such as E, N, and C. The second line follows the growth of motivated agency, which runs through the emergence of theory of mind and other important developmental landmarks in early to middle childhood. It ultimately results in the establishment and pursuit of personal *goals* and *values*. The third line has its origins in early autobiographical memory and childhood storytelling, but it does not become a salient feature of personality until the emerging adulthood years, when young people begin to formulate internalized *life stories*. The stories young people formulate reinterpret the past and imagine the future in such a way as to provide life with meaning, purpose, and temporal continuity. In personality development, stories layer over goals and values, which layer over traits.

The three lines/layers of personality development each correspond to a particular perspective on the human self. Dispositional traits are the most important features of personality from the perspective of the self as a *social actor*. Evolutionary psychologists, sociological role theorists, and Shakespeare all agree that, for *Homo sapiens*, all the world is indeed a stage, and each of us an actor upon it. From birth onward, we perform on the social stage, even before we consciously understand and appreciate our roles as social actors. As we perform, we express emotion and display characteristic behaviors, all of which is keenly observed (and evaluated) by our fellow actors on stage, who double as our audiences as well. Each actor develops his or her own unique style of performance, which ultimately confers upon that actor a corresponding reputation in the social groups within which the actor performs. The style and the reputation are essentially what the actor's dispositional traits are all about. As observers, we sort actors out (ourselves included) in terms of the broad and basic dispositional traits that personality psychologists have enumerated over the past half century, now commonly catalogued in the Big Five. In Chapters 1–4 in this book, I explored the nature, manifestation, and development of dispositional traits, following the social actor's maturation from birth through the adult years.

Human beings express rudimentary agency even in the first days of life. Babies pursue short-term goals, and they attend to and seem to appreciate goal-directed (as opposed to random) behavior in others. It is not until the age of 3 or 4 years, however, that human children understand the nature of goal-directed human action—the basic idea that human beings have desires and beliefs in their minds, and that they act upon these desires and beliefs. The emergence of theory of mind is an important step forward in the child's understanding of the self as a *motivated agent*. What developmental psychologists have named *the age 5–7 shift* tracks the emergence of a suite of psychological phenomena (e.g., cognitive development, self-esteem) and societal arrangements (e.g., elementary schooling) that work together to transform the child into a more or less rational, purposeful, and planful agent. In late childhood and adolescence, human beings articulate a motivational agenda for life, setting up long-term goals and values, and organizing their wishing, planning, and striving according to this agenda. Intrinsic needs for autonomy, competence, and relatedness shape the motivational agenda, as do values associated with morality, religion, and politics.

The self as *autobiographical author* is the last of three lines to make a distinctive appearance in personality development. In adolescence, many human beings learn how to think of their lives as ongoing narratives, complete with settings, scenes, characters, plots, and themes. These stories comprise our *narrative identity*. As authors of the self, we learn how to string together autobiographical memories in order to make a causal case about how some feature of our personality or some aspect of our lives came to be, how it developed over time and how it may continue to develop (or not) in the future. We begin to engage in what narrative psychologists today call *autobiographical reasoning*, deriving semantic meaning about our lives from the episodic evidence that we stored away in autobiographical memory. Our resultant narrative identities are strongly shaped and contoured by our own particular experiences in life; by our traits, goals, and values (the self as actor and agent); and especially by the dictates of gender, class, society, and culture. We each coauthor a story for our lives, appropriating the metaphors, images, plots, and characters that culture provides for us. Culture impacts all three lines of personality development, but its most determinative effects probably occur in the development of narrative identity. Therefore, our own life stories say as much about the social, economic, and ideological worlds in which we live as they say about us. As autobiographical authors, we continue to work on our life stories as we move through the adult years, as I suggested in Chapters 8 and 9.

The actor, agent, and author are the supreme psychological trinity for personality development over the human life course. They are the three main guises of the self in any human life, the three standpoints from which the individual human being may consider the self and its relation to the world (McAdams, 2013b). Yet the *three is always a one*. We human beings experience life as whole persons, more or less. If you and I were to get together at the local coffee shop tomorrow, neither of us needs to decide who will actually show up: Will it be the actor, the agent, or the author? The entire person—indivisible in his or her existential reality—shows up at the appointed time, drinks coffee, chats about the day, picks up the bill and pays it. The actor, agent, and author live together in one personality—not as separate selves but as three different psychological perspectives from which the self considers itself. Therefore, it should not be surprising to learn that features of the self as actor, agent, and author may overlap at times and interact, and relate to each other in meaningful ways. Our traits are likely to be related, in some way, to our goals and our values, and to the stories we live by. My central aim in this book has been to reveal the descriptive and explanatory power of distinguishing between the social actor, the motivated agent, and the autobiographical author in the art and science of personality development. But we should never forget that we are talking about one person here, not three—and one life as it unfolds over the decades of the life course.

As we reach the end of my presentation, it may be useful to consider again the whole person as he or she develops over the human life course, putting the actor, agent, and author back together. Personality develops from one moment to the next, as days become years, and years become decades. In principle, you could freeze-frame the developmental course at any moment—say, at age 7 years, 3 months, and 2 days. You could stop the clock at age 25, or 55, and examine the slice of personality that is revealed. Let us do something like that by identifying five points in the life course—five milestones on the journey of personality development. Throughout this book, I have illustrated personality development by examining the concrete lives of real people, such as Charles Darwin, Jane Fonda, and Jay-Z. But in closing, I adopt a more generic approach to review what personality development typically looks like, in general terms, at five different points in the human life course: at age 2, the transition from childhood to adolescence, emerging adulthood, midlife, and old age.

## AGE 2: I RECOGNIZE ME

The rudiments of psychological individuality—the person's unique variation on the general design of human nature—appear in the first few weeks of life. Temperament differences in characteristic mood, soothability, attention, response intensity, and inhibition provide early hints of a personality yet to come. Parents react to their infant's temperament, and these responses have impact on the development of personality over the long haul. Genotypically driven differences interact with environments in complex ways and on multiple levels as early differences gradually elaborate into more or less consistent trait-like trends in the quality of social action and emotional experience. Temperament differences, moreover, likely have effects on the development of the caregiver–infant attachment bond. Irritable babies high in negative emotionality may have an especially difficult time establishing the smooth, goal-corrected partnership that is so characteristic of securely attached infants and toddlers. Secure attachment may be easier to achieve with babies whose temperaments exude positive emotionality.

The establishment of a secure attachment bond may be seen as the first great psychosocial goal in personality development (Bowlby, 1969). But it is not a goal that the infant self-consciously sets out to achieve. In a general sense, social behavior is goal-directed from the beginning of life and, indeed, intentional, goal-directed behavior begins to capture the infant's attention by age 1. But it is not until the second and third years of life that the hints of an agentic, goal-directed self begin to show themselves, and then only haltingly. Around 18 months of age, toddlers begin to recognize themselves in mirrors and show a range of other behaviors suggesting that they now have a sense of themselves as selves—as embodied actors who move across a social landscape. The onset of self-recognition behavior roughly coincides with the emergence of social–moral emotions such as pride, embarrassment, shame, and guilt. Around the time of the child's second birthday, a sense of what William James conceived as the reflexive, duplex self—an I who observes the Me—is beginning to emerge. A social actor from day 1, the 2-year-old is now a *self-conscious* social actor who keenly observes his or her own actions (and emotions) and those of other actors in the social environment.

At the milestone marker of age 2, the toddler reveals broad and moderately consistent individual differences in temperament. The outlines of a dispositional profile can be clearly seen, even though considerable elaboration and change will surely follow. Whereas the social actor is beginning to come into profile, the motivated agent and autobiographical author are still waiting in the wings. Nonetheless, the age 2 milestone does afford a glimpse of what is to come. The emergence of the I/Me self in the second and third years of life lays the groundwork for both agency and authorship. What parents describe as "the terrible twos" refers mainly to the child's willful nature, to budding autonomy and the egocentric desire to do what it wants to do, no matter what. As a willful, intentional agent, the 2-year-old pushes hard an agenda of desire. Desire makes for immediate goals. In a few years, more stable goals will begin to crystallize, and a clearer outline of personality's second layer will become visible. Similarly, self-recognition behaviors signal the coming of autobiographical memory. The child begins to remember, own, and tell personal events after the age of 2, "my" little stories about "me" and about what "I" intended (wanted, desired) to do. The increasingly autonomous 2-year-old, therefore, takes the first steps toward becoming a goal-directed striver and autobiographical narrator, foreshadowing the expressions of both agency and authorship in personality.

## FROM LATE CHILDHOOD TO ADOLESCENCE

Whether viewed as a period of storm and stress or an uncertain limbo sandwiched between childhood and adulthood, adolescence has traditionally been identified with the teenage years. Yet marking its true beginning and end has become increasingly problematic. On the front end of things, hormonal and psychological shifts heralding a transition to come begin to occur years before the advent of puberty's most obvious signs—as early as age 8 or 9. On the back end, surveys of North Americans and Europeans show that an increasing number of individuals in their mid-20s and even older still do not consider themselves to be adults. Many have not as yet assumed those roles traditionally associated with adulthood status—stable jobs, marriage, and parenthood. Furthermore, the psychological issues facing individuals in their early teens (e.g., peer pressure, delinquency) appear to differ dramatically from those facing college freshmen and sophomores (e.g., vocation, intimacy). In that it seems to begin earlier and end later than once expected, and in that its beginning looks nothing like its ending, adolescence is not what it used to be, if it ever was. In that light, it is useful to identify two different milestones in personality development—one marking the end of childhood itself (roughly ages 8–12 years) and another marking emerging adulthood (the late teens through the 20s).

The preteen period, marking the end of childhood and the beginning of adolescence, reveals a rich and complex portrait of psychological individuality. Personality has now thickened to accommodate a second layer—goals and values layer over dispositional traits to structure psychological individuality. Factor-analytic studies of personality ratings suggest that it is around this time that a clear five-factor structure begins to appear for dispositional traits (Roberts et al., 2008). There is a sense, then, in which the structure of dispositional traits is beginning to stabilize, on the eve of adolescence. At the same time, individual differences in self-esteem have begun to emerge. As we saw in Chapter 5, self-esteem scores tend to be fairly high and not especially differentiated before the age of 7 or 8. But thereafter self-esteem drops for many children and begins to show more or less consistent individual differences. The emergence of self-esteem as an important feature of personality reflects at least two important developments: (1) rising expectations from parents and teachers regarding the child's achievements and (2) the child's newfound tendency, rooted in cognitive development and the emerging sense of the self as a motivated agent, to compare him- or herself to others in systematic ways. During the same developmental period, researchers typically note the first clear signs of depression (especially in girls) and increases in antisocial behavior (especially in boys). Scores on openness to experience also begin to rise in the preteen years.

By the time they are on the verge of adolescence, children have developed clear goals and motives that structure their consciousness and shape their daily behavior. They are now also able to evaluate the worth and progress of their own goal pursuits and projects as they play out across situations and over time. As motivated agents, they begin to see what they need to do to achieve those goals on which their self-esteem depends, be they in the realm of sports, friendship, school, or values. They also begin to withdraw investment in goals that seem fruitless—goals for which their own skills and traits, or their general life circumstances, may be poorly suited.

Older children and young adolescents may hold grandiose fantasies about accomplishment, fame, or notoriety in the future. Long ago, developmental psychologist David Elkind (1981) observed that many young teenagers secretly imagine their lives as fantastical stories of greatness and distinction, a phenomenon he called the *personal fable*. In the terms I have adopted in this book, Elkind's personal fable may be seen as a rough first draft of narrative identity. The same cognitive skills and developments that enable preteens to evaluate themselves and their goal pursuits (positively or negatively) vis-à-vis their peers may also help launch their first full autobiographical projects, as evidenced in diaries, online posts, fantasies, and conversations. It is during the transition to adolescence, moreover, that individuals begin to see in full what makes up an entire life, from birth through childhood, career, marriage, parenting, and so on, to death. They also develop facilities of autobiographical reasoning, learning how to derive personal meaning from autobiographical events. Their first efforts at imagining their own life stories may be unrealistic, grandiose, and somewhat incoherent. But autobiographical authors have to start somewhere.

## EMERGING ADULTHOOD

Many social scientists now argue that the period running from about age 17 through the middle to late 20s constitutes an integral developmental epoch in and of itself, called emerging adulthood (Arnett, 2000). This demarcation makes good sense in modern postindustrial societies wherein schooling and the preparation for adult work extend well into the 20s and even beyond. The betwixt-and-between nature of what was once called "adolescence" appears to be extending almost a decade beyond the teenage years for many young men and women today, who are putting off marriage and parenthood until their late 20s and 30s. The movement through this developmental period is strongly shaped by class and education. Less-educated, working-class men and women may find it especially difficult to sustain steady and gainful employment during this period. Some get married and/or begin families anyway, but others may drift for many years without the economic security required to become a full stakeholder in society. Those more privileged men and women headed for middle-class professions may require years of schooling and/or training and a great deal of experimentation before they feel they are able to settle down and assume the full responsibilities of adulthood. Many social and cultural factors in modern societies have come together to make emerging adulthood the prime time in the life course for the exploration and development of what Erikson (1963) described as ego identity.

Emerging adulthood marks the beginning of a gradual upward swing for dispositional traits associated with conscientiousness and agreeableness and a decline in neuroticism. As emerging adults eventually come to take on the roles of spouse, parent, citizen, and stakeholder, their traits may shift upward in the direction of greater warmth and care for others, higher levels of social responsibility, and greater dedication to being productive, hardworking, and reliable. Even as temporal stability in individual differences increases, significant mean-level changes in personality traits are to be expected, as we saw in Chapter 4. And individual differences in traits combine with many other factors, including gender and class, to shape life trajectories during this time.

For the second and third layers of personality, emerging adulthood marks the exploration of and eventual commitment to new life goals and values, and the articulation of a new and ideally integrative life story. Emerging adults begin to see life as a complex, multifaceted challenge in role performance and goal pursuit. At the same time, they seek to integrate the many different roles, goals, and values they are managing within an organized identity pattern that provides life with some semblance of unity, purpose, and meaning. Their identities should explain who they are today and how they came to be the persons they are becoming. It follows, then, that *the central developmental task of emerging adulthood in many lives is to author a suitable narrative identity.* By the time young people have "emerged" from emerging adulthood, they have ideally articulated and internalized a coherent story of who they were, are, and will be. In his first autobiography, *Dreams from my Father*, Barack Obama (1995) described how he managed to accomplish this task in his emerging adulthood years, as we saw in Chapter 8. The emerging adult's life story affirms former and ongoing explorations and newly established commitments, and it sets the emerging adult up, psychologically speaking, for the daunting challenges of generative adulthood in the modern world.

## MIDLIFE TIPPING POINTS

In many human lives, personality development reaches a crescendo in middle adulthood. Against the backdrop of ever-increasing rank-order stability in dispositional traits, conscientiousness and agreeableness rise to their apex and neuroticism bottoms out. Generativity strivings may peak as midlife adults invest heavily in their families and communities. Personal agency may be distributed across a broad spectrum of goals and responsibilities, as midlife adults negotiate the roles of parent, grandparent, child of aging parents, aunt and uncle, provider and breadwinner, colleague, neighbor, lifelong friend, citizen, leader, and so on. For the most active and generative adults, this is the prime of life, even as role demands and conflicting goals threaten to overwhelm them. Their life stories express the psychologically energizing themes of communion, growth, and redemption. For many others, however, it is a time of tremendous disappointment, mounting frustrations, and what Erikson (1963) described as *midlife stagnation.* For these people, the long-awaited maturation expected for dispositional traits never really happens; goals are repeatedly nipped in the bud; and narrative identity reveals an impoverished psychological life in which positive scenes are often contaminated by bad endings and long-term aspirations are repeatedly quashed.

Two decades of research on life stories shows that American adults in their 40s and 50s demonstrate dramatic individual differences in narrative identity. Those reporting low levels of generativity, high levels of depression, and depleted psychological resources construct life stories that fail to affirm progress and growth. Plots go round and round in vicious circles, and scenes of positive emotion are often spoiled by negative outcomes. By contrast, those who score high on measures of generativity and overall mental health construct redemptive self-narratives wherein protagonists repeatedly overcome obstacles and transform suffering into personal enhancement and prosocial engagement. As the gifted protagonist in these narratives journeys forth into a dangerous world, he or she encounters all manner of adversity, but throughout the story, bad things usually turn good, giving the plot a clearly upward trajectory.

Nonetheless, scattered research findings on personality development in adulthood show how the crescendo of midlife eventually subsides. There may be psychological tipping points in midlife when development changes directions, in a sense, or flattens out into a plateau. The complexity of thought, feeling, and desire—as expressed at all three levels of human personality—seems to peak out in the midlife years. At the same time, adults show a greater and greater positivity bias as they age. They savor positive experiences and memories and tend to downplay the negative. At some point, midlife adults may begin to scale back goal pursuits and focus their motivational energies on those areas in which they have made their strongest investments. Rather than seek out new affiliations and involvements in work and the broader social world, they may refocus their priorities around family life and their closest friends. As they begin to experience the physical and (in some cases) cognitive declines that accompany late midlife, adults may select goals and strategies for accomplishing them that optimize their best skills and compensate for their weaknesses (Freund & Riediger, 2006). Eventually, midlife adults may shift their perspective on life from one that emphasizes the expansion of the self and the bold exploration of the environment to one that emphasizes contraction, protection, and securing the gains they have already achieved. The shift is not likely to be sudden, may occur in some domains before others, and is sure to play out in different ways for different people. But however and whenever it happens, the shift marks a tipping point from a life narrative of ascent to one of maintenance and eventual decline.

## OLD AGE

In a famous article, the late Paul Baltes (1997) argued that human development reveals an "incomplete architecture" (p. 366) with increasing age. The bad news, in Baltes's view, is that evolutionary selection pressures make for decreasing flexibility and human potential once adults have matured beyond the childbearing years. It is as if natural selection gave up on designing and building the human edifice once the business of bearing children and passing one's genes down to the next generation had been assured. The good news is that culture typically tries to compensate for this loss by providing resources for middle-aged and older adults. Most societies accord older adults high levels of respect and a wide range of other goods, as members of the younger generation (assisted by the state) feel some responsibility to take care of those who have taken care of them. Nonetheless, the gain–loss ratio in life tilts toward the loss side as adults move into their later years. At the end of life, cultural resources fail to ameliorate biological constraints. Adjustment breaks down in very old age. There is no final transcendent stage of development, Baltes argued— no blissful ending, brilliant final epiphany, or surge of wisdom in the last chapter of life. Instead, the psychology of advanced aging is characterized by deterioration, entropy, and breakdown.

As I suggested earlier, research on personality traits in late life suggests a breakdown in rank-order continuity and an increase in negative traits. In their 80s and beyond, people's relative positions on Big Five trait dimensions become less and less predictable from one year to the next. Moreover, the maturational arc of dispositional traits—evident in longitudinal trends running from late adolescence through late midlife— begins to reverse itself. Neuroticism may reverse the downward slope and head upward again. Traits related to self-regulation—grouped within conscientiousness and agreeableness—may begin to decline.

As losses begin to overwhelm gains, older adults must conserve dwindling resources to invest in only the most essential goals. With advanced aging, health concerns and interpersonal losses may hijack the motivated agent's goal agenda. Fending off illness and dealing with loss may become the major goals of life. With respect to narrative identity, elderly adults may draw increasingly on reminiscences as they review the life they have lived. Positive memory biases may give life stories a softer glow in old age. However, older adults also tend to recall fewer vivid details from their past, compared to younger adults (Addis, Wong, & Schacter, 2008). As a result, narrative identity may become fuzzy and vague in the later years. In the wake of memory loss and increasing frailty, the oldest adults may feel that their stories are slipping away from them. Should serious dementia follow, autobiographical authorship itself may drop out of the picture, thinning personality out and leaving behind only two layers, where once there were three.

With further decline, motivated agency may fade away, too. As death approaches, human beings may step away from the planful, goal-directed, future-time perspective that they have regularly occupied as motivated agents, ever since the age 5–7 shift. They may return to the most basic issues of living day to day as *social actors*, conserving energy to focus on the moments left in life, surviving and holding on as well as possible, before death closes the door. And what a cruel ending it is for any member of our eusocial species. As the final insult, we must leave the *social world*—the group—wherein we first expressed our psychological individuality. *We begin life as social actors*, performing in the group. Relentlessly social until the last moment, we die *alone*.

In the art and science of personality development, the sense of an ending is ultimately about the anticipation of death. Among the very old, the prospect of dying can never be too far away from consciousness, assuming the mind is still capable of conscious, rational thought. Nonetheless, the last years of life are not invariably bleak. Many people retain significant psychological force until the very end. Consider as an example, journalist Roger Angell who, at age 93, wrote an essay entitled "This Old Man," published in *New Yorker* magazine. Angell (2014) characterizes death as "that two-ton safe swaying on a frayed rope just over my head" (p. 61). Yet Angell appears less interested in talking about death than he is in describing what *life* is like—arthritis, prosthetics, and all—in his tenth decade. He quips, "I'm not dead and not yet mindless in a reliable upstate facility . . . Decline and disaster impend, but my thoughts don't linger there" (p. 61).

Instead, his thoughts go to people. He tells touching and humorous stories about old friends and relatives, nearly all of whom are dead now. His wife (Carol) died the previous year, after nearly five decades of marriage. She always told him that he should not waste any time mourning her if she were the first to exit this world. "We didn't quite see the point of memorial fidelity," Angell (2014) recalls. "In our view, the departed spouse—we always thought it would be me—wouldn't be around anymore but knew or had known that he or she was loved forever. Please go ahead, then, sweetheart—don't miss a moment. Carol said this last: 'If you haven't found someone else by a year after I'm gone I'll come back and haunt you' " (p. 65). Angell doesn't reveal whether he has given his wife's ghost a reason to leave him alone. But like an 18-year-old guy cruising down the avenue in hopes of finding a pretty girl, Angell seems to be on the prowl, at least in his heart:

> I believe that everyone in the world wants to be with someone else tonight, together in the dark, with the sweet warmth of a hip or a foot or a bare expanse of shoulder, within reach. Those of us who

have lost that, whatever our age, never lose the longing: just look at our faces. If it returns, we seize upon it avidly, stunned and altered again. (p. 65)

Angell (2014) suffers from a couple dozen physical maladies—from macular degeneration to shingles to a herniated disc that twists and jogs his spine "like a Connecticut country road. . . . Like many men and women my age, I get around with a couple of arterial stents that keep my heart chunking. I also sport a minute plastic seashell that clamps shut a congenital hole in my heart, discovered in my eighties" (p. 61). Yet he seems remarkably more energized and vital than the much younger hero of Julian Barnes's novel, with whom I opened this chapter. Coming up on age 70, more or less, Tony Webster lives a much more phlegmatic and solitary existence, at least until he reconnects with characters in his past. By contrast, Angell seems always to have been connected. He writes:

Getting old is the second-biggest surprise of my life, but the first, by a mile, is our unceasing need for deep attachment and intimate love. We oldies yearn daily and hourly for conversation and renewed domesticity, for company at the movies or while visiting a museum, for someone close by in the car when coming home at night. (p. 65)

As he senses the end of his own life, Roger Angell exuberantly affirms the human need for connection, in a way that Tony Webster is never able to do. *Only connect*, Angell tells us—as actors, agents, and authors. Bind ourselves to other people in the social groups that give our lives meaning. Strive to connect with others in ways that advance both our own lives and theirs. Artfully render our lives into life-affirming narratives of interpersonal communion. For brainy members of a eusocial species, like us, this is the better way to live.

# References

Abelson, R. (1981). Psychological status of the script concept. *American Psychologist, 36,* 715–729.

Adams, G. (2005). The cultural grounding of personal relationship: Enemyship in North American and West African worlds. *Journal of Personality and Social Psychology, 88,* 948–968.

Addis, D. R., Wong, A. T., & Schacter, D. L. (2008). Age-related changes in the episodic simulation of future events. *Psychological Science, 19,* 33–41.

Adler, J. M. (2012). Living into the story: Agency and coherence in a longitudinal study of narrative identity development and mental health over the course of psychotherapy. *Journal of Personality and Social Psychology, 102,* 367–389.

Adler, J. M., Kissel, E., & McAdams, D. P. (2006). Emerging from the CAVE: Attributional style and the narrative study of identity in midlife adults. *Cognitive Therapy and Research, 30,* 39–51.

Adler, J. M., & Poulin, M. J. (2009). The political is personal: Narrating 9/11 and psychological well-being. *Journal of Personality, 77,* 903–932.

Adler, J. M., Skalina, L., & McAdams, D. P. (2008). The narrative reconstruction of psychotherapy and psychological health. *Psychotherapy Research, 18,* 719–734.

Alford, J. R., Funk, C. L., & Hibbing, J. R. (2005). Are political orientations genetically transmitted? *American Political Science Review, 99,* 153–167.

Allit, P. (2009). *The conservatives: Ideas and personalities throughout American history.* New Haven, CT: Yale University Press.

Allport, G. W. (1937). *Personality: A psychological interpretation.* New York: Holt, Rinehart & Winston.

Allport, G. W., & Odbert, H. S. (1936). Trait-names, a psycho-lexical study. *Psychological Monographs, 47*(1, Whole No. 211).

Andersen, C. (2002). *George and Laura: Portrait of an American marriage.* New York: Morrow.

Angell, R. (2014, February 17 and 24). This old man. *The New Yorker,* pp. 60–65.

Apperly, L. A. (2012). What is "theory of mind"?: Concepts, cognitive processes, and individual differences. *Quarterly Journal of Experimental Psychology, 65*, 825–839.

Argyle, M., & Lu, L. (1990). Happiness and social skills. *Personality and Individual Differences, 11*, 1255–1262.

Aristotle. (2004). *The Nicomachean ethics* (J. A. K. Thomson, Trans.). London: Penguin.

Arnett, J. J. (2000). Emerging adulthood: A theory of development from the late teens through the twenties. *American Psychologist, 55*, 469–480.

Arthur, W., Jr., & Graziano, W. G. (1996). The five-factor model, conscientiousness, and driving accident involvement. *Journal of Personality, 64*, 593–618.

Asendorpf, J. B., Denissen, J. J. A., & van Aken, M. A. G. (2008). Inhibited and aggressive preschool children at 23 years of age: Personality and social transitions into adulthood. *Developmental Psychology, 44*, 997–1011.

Asendorpf, J. B., & Wilpers, S. (1998). Personality effects on social relationships. *Journal of Personality and Social Psychology, 74*, 1531–1544.

Ashton, M. C., Lee, K., & Paunonen, S. V. (2002). What is the central feature of extraversion?: Social attention versus reward sensitivity. *Journal of Personality and Social Psychology, 83*, 245–252.

Astington, J. W. (2003). Sometimes necessary, never sufficient: False-belief understanding and social competence. In B. Repacholi & V. Slaughter (Eds.), *Individual differences in theory of mind: Implications for typical and atypical development* (pp. 13–38). New York: Psychology Press.

Astington, J. W., & Jenkins, J. M. (1995). Theory of mind development and social understanding. *Cognition and Emotion, 9*, 151–165.

Atkinson, J. W. (1964). *An introduction to motivation*. Princeton, NJ: Van Nostrand.

Atkinson, J. W., Heyns, R. W., & Veroff, J. (1954). The effect of experimental arousal of the affiliation motive on thematic apperception. *Journal of Abnormal and Social Psychology, 49*, 405–410.

Back, M. D., Schmukle, S. C., & Egloff, B. (2010). Why are narcissists so charming at first sight?: Decoding the narcissism–popularity link at zero acquaintance. *Journal of Personality and Social Psychology, 98*, 132–145.

Baddeley, J., & Singer, J. A. (2007). Charting the life story's path: Narrative identity across the life span. In J. Chandinin (Ed.), *Handbook of narrative research methods* (pp. 177–202). Thousand Oaks, CA: Sage.

Baddeley, J., & Singer, J. A. (2008). Telling losses: Personality correlates and functions of bereavement narratives. *Journal of Research in Personality, 42*, 421–438.

Bakan, D. (1966). *The duality of human existence*. Boston: Beacon.

Baltes, P. B. (1997). On the incomplete architecture of human ontogeny: Selection, optimization, and compensation as foundation for developmental theory. *American Psychologist, 52*, 366–380.

Bandura, A. (1989). Human agency in social-cognitive theory. *American Psychologist, 44*, 1175–1184.

Barber, B. L., Eccles, J. S., & Stone, M. R. (2001). Whatever happened to the jock, the brain, and the princess?: Young adult pathways linked to adolescent activity involvement and social identity. *Journal of Adolescent Research, 16,* 429–455.

Barnes, J. (2011). *The sense of an ending.* New York: Knopf.

Baron-Cohen, S. (1995). *Mindblindness: An essay on autism and theory of mind.* Cambridge, MA: MIT Press.

Barrick, M. R., & Mount, M. K. (1991). The Big Five personality dimensions and job performance: A meta-analysis. *Personnel Psychology, 44,* 1–26.

Bauer, J. J., & McAdams, D. P. (2010). Eudaimonic growth: Narrative growth goals predict increases in ego development and subjective well-being 3 years later. *Developmental Psychology, 46,* 761–772.

Bauer, J. J., McAdams, D. P., & Sakaeda, A. (2005). Interpeting the good life: Growth memories in the lives of mature, happy people. *Journal of Personality and Social Psychology, 88,* 203–217.

Baumeiser, R. F. (1998). The self. In D. T. Gilbert, S. T. Fiske, & G. Lindzey (Eds.), *Handbook of social psychology* (4th ed., pp. 680–740). New York: McGraw-Hill.

Baumeister, R. F., & Bushman, B. (2008). *Social psychology and human nature.* Belmont, CA: Thomson.

Baumeister, R. F., & Leary, M. R. (1995). The need to belong: Desire for interpersonal attachment as a fundamental human motivation. *Psychological Bulletin, 117,* 497–529.

Baumrind, D. (1971). Current patterns of parental authority. *Developmental Psychology Monographs, 4,* 1–103.

Behne, T., Carpenter, M., Call, J., & Tomasello, M. (2005). Unwilling versus unable: Infants' understanding of intentional action. *Developmental Psychology, 41,* 328–337.

Bekoff, M. (2004). Wild justice, cooperation, and fair play: Minding manners, being nice, and feeling good. In R. Sussman & A. Chapman (Eds.), *The origins and nature of sociality* (pp. 53–79). Chicago: Aldine.

Belsky, J., Crnic, K., & Woodworth, S. (1995). Personality and parenting: Exploring the mediating role of transient mood and daily hassles. *Journal of Personality, 63,* 905–929.

Benet-Martinez, V., & Haritatos, J. (2005). Bicultural identity integration (BII): Components and psychosocial antecedents. *Journal of Personality, 73,* 1015–1050.

Berger, P. L. (1967). *The sacred canopy: Elements of a sociological theory of religion.* New York: Random House.

Bering, J. M. (2006). The folk psychology of souls. *Behavioral and Brain Sciences, 29,* 453–462.

Bleidorn, W., Kandler, C., & Caspi, A. (2014). The behavioural genetics of personality development in adulthood: Classic, contemporary, and future trends. *European Journal of Personality, 28,* 244–255.

Bleidorn, W., Kandler, C., Hulsheger, U. R., Riemann, R., Angleitner, A., & Spinath, F. M. (2010). Nature and nurture of the interplay between personality traits and major life goals. *Journal of Personality and Social Psychology, 99,* 366–379.

Bleidorn, W., Klimstra, T. A., Denissen, J. J. A., Rentfrow, P. J., Potter, J., &

Gosling, S. D. (2013). Personality maturation around the world: A cross-cultural examination of social-investment theory. *Psychological Science, 24,* 2530–2540.

Block, J., & Block, J. H. (2006). Nursery school personality and political orientation two decades later. *Journal of Research in Personality, 40,* 734–749.

Bloom, P. (2012). Religion, morality, evolution. In S. T. Fiske, D. L. Schacter, & S. E. Taylor (Eds.), *Annual review of psychology* (Vol. 63, pp. 179–199). Palo Alto, CA: Annual Reviews.

Bluck, S., & Gluck, J. (2004). Making things better and learning a lesson: Experiencing wisdom across the life span. *Journal of Personality, 72,* 543–572.

Bogg, T., & Roberts, B. W. (2004). Conscientiousness and health-related behavior: A meta-analysis of the leading behavioral contributors to mortality. *Psychological Bulletin, 130,* 887–919.

Bohlin, G., & Hagekull, B. (2009). Socio-emotional development: From infancy to young adulthood. *Scandinavian Journal of Psychology, 50,* 592–601.

Bolger, N., & Schilling, E. A. (1991). Personality and the problems of everyday life: The role of neuroticism in exposure and reactivity to daily stressors. *Journal of Personality, 59,* 355–386.

Bonanno, G. (2004). Loss, trauma, and human resilience: Have we underestimated the human capacity to thrive after extremely aversive events? *American Psychologist, 59,* 20–28.

Bowlby, J. (1969). *Attachment.* New York: Basic Books.

Boyce, C. J., & Wood, A. M. (2011). Personality prior to disability determines adaptation: Agreeable individuals recover lost life satisfaction faster and more completely. *Psychological Science, 22,* 1397–1402.

Boyce, C. J., Wood, A. M., & Brown, G. D. A. (2010). The dark side of conscientiousness: Conscientious people experience greater drops in life satisfaction following unemployment. *Journal of Research in Personality, 44,* 535–539.

Boyd-Franklin, N. (1989). *Black families in therapy: A multisystems approach.* New York: Guilford Press.

Brosnan, S. F. (2006). Nonhuman species' reactions to inequities and their implications for fairness. *Social Justice Research, 19,* 153–185.

Brown, J. W. (2013). Beyond conflict monitoring: Cognitive control and the neural basis of thinking before you act. *Current Directions in Psychological Science, 22,* 179–185.

Brown, R. P., Budzek, K., & Tamborski, M. (2009). On the meaning and measure of narcissism. *Personality and Social Psychology Bulletin, 35,* 951–964.

Bruner, J. (1986). *Actual minds, possible worlds.* Cambridge, MA: Harvard University Press.

Buber, M. (1970). *I and thou.* New York: Scribner's.

Bush, B. (1994). *Barbara Bush: A memoir.* New York: Scribner's.

Bush, G. H. W. (1999). *All the best: My life in letters and other writings.* New York: Touchstone.

Bush, G. W. (1999). *A charge to keep: My journey to the White House.* New York: Harper.

Buss, D. M. (1995). Evolutionary psychology: A new paradigm for psychological science. *Psychological Inquiry, 6,* 1–30.

Buss, K. A., & Kiehl, E. J. (2004). Comparison of sadness, anger, and fear facial expressions when toddlers look at their mothers. *Child Development, 75,* 1761–1773.

Butler, R. N. (1963). The life review: An interpretation of reminiscence in old age. *Psychiatry, 26,* 65–76.

Byrne, R. W., & Bates, L. A. (2007). Sociality, evolution, and cognition. *Current Biology, 17,* R714–R723.

Cale, E. M. (2006). A quantitative review of the relations between the "Big 3" higher order personality dimensions and antisocial behavior. *Journal of Research in Personality, 46,* 250–284.

Campbell, W. K. (1999). Narcissism and romantic attraction. *Journal of Personality and Social Psychology, 77,* 1254–1270.

Canli, T., Zhao, Z., Desmond, J. E., Kang, E., Gross, J., & Gabriele, J. D. E. (2001). An fMRI study of personality influences on brain reactivity to emotional stimuli. *Behavioral Neuroscience, 115,* 33–42.

Carney, D. R., Jost, J. T., Gosling, S. D., & Potter, J. (2008). The secret lives of liberals and conservatives: Personality profiles, interaction styles, and the things they leave behind. *Political Psychology, 29,* 807–840.

Carstensen, L. L. (1995). Evidence for a life-span theory of socioemotional selectivity. *Current Directions in Psychological Science, 4,* 151–155.

Carstensen, L. L., Pasupathi, M., Mayr, U., & Nesselroade, J. R. (2000). Emotional experience in everyday life across the adult life span. *Journal of Personality and Social Psychology, 79,* 644–655.

Carver, C. S. (2004). Negative affects deriving from the behavioral approach system. *Emotion, 3,* 3–22.

Carver, C. S., Johnson, S. L., & Joormann, J. (2008). Serotonergic function, two-mode models of self-regulation, and vulnerability to depression: What depression has in common with impulsive aggression. *Psychological Bulletin, 134,* 912–943.

Caspi, A., Harrington, H. L., Milne, B., Amell, J. W., Theodore, R. F., & Moffitt, T. E. (2003). Children's behavioral styles at age 3 are linked to their adult personality traits at age 26. *Journal of Personality, 71,* 495–513.

Caspi, A., Houtts, R. M., Belsky, D. W., Goldman-Mellor, S. J., Harrington, H., Israel, S., et al. (2014). The p factor: One general psychopathology factor in the structure of psychiatric disorders? *Clinical Psychological Science, 2,* 119–137.

Caspi, A., Roberts, B. W., & Shiner, R. L. (2005). Personality development: Stability and change. In S. T. Fiske & D. Schacter (Eds.), *Annual review of psychology* (Vol. 56, pp. 453–484). Palo Alto, CA: Annual Reviews.

Caspi, A., Sugden, K., Moffitt, T. E., Taylor, A., Craig, I., Harrington, H., et al. (2003). Influence of life stress on depression: Moderation of a polymorphism in the 5-HTT gene. *Science, 301,* 386–389.

Champagne, F. A., & Mashoodh, R. (2009). Genes in context: Gene–environment interplay and the origins of individual differences in behavior. *Current Directions in Psychological Science, 18,* 127–131.

Chang, C., & McCabe, A. (2013). Evaluation in Mandarin Chinese children's personal narratives. In A. McCabe & C. Chang (Eds.), *Chinese language narration: Culture, cognition, and emotion* (pp. 33–56). Amsterdam: Benjamins.

Chen, X., Yang, F., & Fu, R. (2012). Culture and temperament. In M. Zentner & R. L. Shiner (Eds.), *Handbook of temperament* (pp. 462–478). New York: Guilford Press.

Clark, G. (2007). *A farewell to alms: A brief economic history of the world.* Princeton, NJ: Princeton University Press.

Clark, L. A., Watson, D., & Mineka, S. (1994). Temperament, personality, and the mood and anxiety disorders. *Journal of Abnormal Psychology, 103,* 103–116.

Clinton, H. R. (2003). *Living history.* New York: Scribner.

Clucas, J. G. (1988). *Mother Teresa.* New York: Chelsea House.

Cochran, G., & Harpending, H. (2009). *The 10,000 year explosion: How civilization accelerated human evolution.* New York: Basic Books.

Cohen, T. R., Panter, A. T., & Turan, N. (2012). Guilt proneness and moral character. *Current Directions in Psychological Science, 21,* 355–359.

Colby, A., & Damon, W. (1992). *Some do care: Contemporary lives of moral commitment.* New York: Free Press.

Cole, E. R., & Stewart, A. J. (1996). Meanings of political participation among black and white women: Political identity and social responsibility. *Journal of Personality and Social Psychology, 71,* 130–140.

Cole, S. W. (2009). Social regulation of human gene expression. *Current Directions in Psychological Science, 18,* 132–137.

Conway, M. A., & Pleydell-Pearce, C. W. (2000). The construction of autobiographical memories in the self-memory system. *Psychological Review, 107,* 261–288.

Corker, K. S., Oswald, F. L., & Donnellan, M. B. (2012). Conscientiousness in the classroom: A process explanation. *Journal of Personality, 80,* 995–1027.

Cornwell, J. F. M., & Higgins, E. T. (2013). Morality and its relation to political ideology: The role of promotion and prevention concerns. *Personality and Social Psychology Bulletin, 39,* 1164–1172.

Corry, N., Merritt, R. D., Mrug, S., & Pamp, B. (2008). The factor structure of the Narcissistic Personality Inventory. *Journal of Personality Assessment, 90,* 593–600.

Costa, P. T., Jr., Herbst, J. H., McCrae, R. R., & Siegler, I. C. (2000). Personality at midlife: Stability, intrinsic maturation, and response to life events. *Assessment, 7,* 365–378.

Costa, P. T., Jr., & McCrae, R. R. (1980). Influence of extraversion and neuroticism on subjective well-being: Happy and unhappy people. *Journal of Personality and Social Psychology, 38,* 668–678.

Costa, P. T., Jr., & McCrae, R. R. (1992). *The NEO-PI-R: Professional manual.* Odessa, FL: Psychological Assessment Resources.

Costa, P. T., Jr., & McCrae, R. R. (2006). Age changes in personality and their origins: A comment on Roberts, Walton, & Viechtbauer (2006). *Psychological Bulletin, 132,* 26–28.

Cox, K. S., Wilt, J., Olson, B., & McAdams, D. P. (2010). Generativity, the Big Five, and psychosocial adaptation in midlife adults. *Journal of Personality, 78,* 1185–1208.

Crocker, J., Canevello, A., Breines, J. G., & Flynn, H. (2010). Interpersonal goals and change in anxiety and dysphoria in first-semester college students. *Journal of Personality and Social Psychology, 98,* 1009–1024.

Crocker, J., & Park, L. E. (2004). The costly pursuit of self-esteem. *Psychological Bulletin, 130,* 392–414.

Darling, N., & Steinberg, L. (1993). Parenting style as context: An integrative model. *Psychological Bulletin, 113,* 487–496.

Darwin, C. (1903). *The descent of man and selection in relation to sex.* New York: Rand McNally. (Original work published 1871)

Darwin, C. (1965). *The expression of emotions in man and animals.* Chicago: University of Chicago Press. (Original work published 1872)

Dawkins, R. (1976). *The selfish gene.* New York: Oxford University Press.

Deater-Deckard, K., & Wang, Z. (2012). Anger and irritability. In M. Zentner & R. L. Shiner (Eds.), *Handbook of temperament* (pp. 124–144). New York: Guilford Press.

Deci, E. L., & Ryan, R. M. (1985). *Intrinsic motivation and self-determination in human behavior.* New York: Plenum Press.

Deci, E. L., & Ryan, R. M. (1991). A motivational approach to self: Integration in personality. In R. Dienstbier & R. M. Ryan (Eds.), *Nebraska Symposium on Motivation: 1990* (pp. 237–288). Lincoln: University of Nebraska Press.

Demorest, A., Popovska, A., & Dabova, M. (2012). The role of scripts in personal consistency and individual differences. *Journal of Personality, 80,* 187–218.

De Parle, J. (2012, January 4). Harder for Americans to rise from lower rungs. *New York Times,* p. A14.

Depue, R. A., & Fu, Y. (2012). Neurobiology and neurochemistry of temperament in adults. In M. Zentner & R. L. Shiner (Eds.), *Handbook of temperament* (pp. 368–399). New York: Guilford Press.

De St. Aubin, E., McAdams, D. P., & Kim, T. C. (Eds.). (2004). *The generative society.* Washington, DC: American Psychological Association Books.

De Waal, F. (1996). *Good natured: The origins of right and wrong in humans and other animals.* Cambridge, MA: Harvard University Press.

De Young, C. G. (2010). Personality neuroscience and the biology of traits. *Social and Personality Psychology Compass, 4,* 1165–1180.

De Young, C. G., Grazioplene, R. G., & Peterson, J. B. (2012). From madness to genius: The openness/intellect trait domain as a paradoxical simplex. *Journal of Research in Personality, 46,* 63–78.

De Young, C. G., Peterson, J. B., Seguin, J. R., & Tremblay, R. E. (2008). Externalizing behavior and the higher order factors of the Big Five. *Journal of Abnormal Psychology, 117,* 947–953.

Didion, J. (1979). *The white album.* New York: Simon & Schuster.

Diehl, M, Chui, H., Hay, E. L., Lumley, M. A., Gruhn, D., & Labouvie-Vief, G. (2014). Change in coping and defense mechanisms across adulthood: Longitudinal findings in a European American sample. *Developmental Psychology, 50,* 634–658.

Diener, E., Sandvik, E., Pavot, W., & Fujita, F. (1992). Extraversion and subjective well-being in a U.S. probability sample. *Journal of Research in Personality, 26,* 205–215.

Diener, M. L., Mangelsdorf, S. C., McHale, J. L., & Frosch, C. A. (2002). Infants' behavioral strategies of emotion regulation with fathers and mothers: Associations with emotional expressions and attachment quality. *Infancy, 3*, 153–174.

Dillon, M., & Wink, P. (2007). *In the course of a lifetime: Tracing religious belief, practice, and change*. Berkeley: University of California Press.

Dodge, K. A., Dishion, T. J., & Lansford, J. E. (2006). *Deviant peer influences in intervention and public policy for youth* (Social Policy Report No. 20). Ann Arbor, MI: Society for Research in Child Development.

Dodge, K. A., Pettit, G. S., & Bates, J. E. (1994). Socialization mediators of the relation between socioeconomic status and child conduct problems. *Child Development, 65*, 649–665.

Doerr, C. E., & Baumeister, R. F. (2010). Self-regulatory strength and psychological adjustment: Implications of the limited resource model of self-regulaton. In J. E. Maddux & J. P. Tangney (Eds.), *Social psychological foundations of clinical psychology* (pp. 71–83). New York: Guilford Press.

Draper, R. (2007). *Dead certain: The presidency of George W. Bush*. New York: Free Press.

Dumas, T. M., Lawford, H., Tieu, T. T., & Pratt, M. W. (2009). Positive parenting in adolescence and its relation to low point narration and identity status in emerging adulthood: A longitudinal analysis. *Developmental Psychology, 45*, 1531–1544.

Dunbar, R. (2004). Gossip in evolutionary perspective. *Review of General Psychology, 8*, 100–110.

Dunbar, R. (2010). *How many friends does one person need?: Dunbar's number and other evolutionary quirks*. Cambridge, MA: Harvard University Press.

Dunbar, R., & Sutcliffe, A. G. (2012). Social complexity and intelligence. In J. Vonk & T. K. Shackelford (Eds.), *The Oxford handbook of comparative evolutionary psychology* (pp. 102–117). New York: Oxford University Press.

Dunlop, W. L., & Tracy, J. L. (2013). Sobering stories: Narratives of self-redemption predict behavioral change and improved health among recovering alcoholics. *Journal of Personality and Social Psychology, 104*, 576–590.

Durbin, C. E., Hayden, E. P., Klein, D. N., & Olino, T. M. (2007). Stability of laboratory-assessed temperamental emotionality traits from ages 3 to 7. *Emotion, 7*, 388–399.

Durkheim, É. (1967). *The elementary forms of the religious life* (J. W. Swain, Trans.). New York: Free Press. (Original work published 1915)

Eaton, L. G., & Funder, D. C. (2003). The creation and consequences of the social world: An interactional analysis of extraversion. *European Journal of Personality, 17*, 375–395.

Eckman, P. (2003). *Emotions revealed*. New York: Times Books.

Eisenberg, N., Fabes, R. A., & Spinrad, T. L. (2006). Prosocial development. In W. Damon & R. Lerner (Series Eds.) & N. Eisenberg (Vol. Ed.), *Handbook of child psychology: Vol. 3. Social, emotional, and personality development* (6th ed., pp. 646–717). New York: Wiley.

Elder, G. H., Jr. (1995). The life course paradigm: Social change and individual development. In P. Moen, G. H. Elder, Jr., & K. Luscher (Eds.), *Examining lives in context: Perspectives on the ecology of human development* (pp. 101–139). Washington, DC: American Psychological Association Books.

Elkind, D. (1981). *Children and adolescents* (3rd ed.). New York: Oxford University Press.

Elliot, A. J., Chirkov, V. I., Kim, Y., & Sheldon, K. M. (2001). A cross-cultural analysis of avoidance (relative to approach) personal goals. *Psychological Science, 12,* 505–510.

Elliot, A. J., Conroy, D. E., Barron, K. E., & Murayama, K. (2010). Achievement motives and goals: A developmental analysis. In R. Lerner, M. E. Lamb, & A. M. Freund (Eds.), *Handbook of life-span development: Vol. 2. Social and emotional development* (pp. 474–510). London: Wiley.

Ellsworth, C. P., Muir, D. W., & Hains, S. M. J. (1993). Social competence and person-object differentiation: An analysis of the still face effect. *Developmental Psychology, 29,* 63–73.

Else-Quest, N. M., Hyde, J. S., Goldsmith, H. H., & van Hulle, C. A. (2006). Gender differences in temperament: A meta-analysis. *Psychological Bulletin, 132,* 33–72.

Emerson, R. W. (1993). *Self-reliance and other essays.* New York: Dover. (Original work published 1841)

Emmons, R. A. (1987). Narcissism: Theory and measurement. *Journal of Personality and Social Psychology, 52,* 11–17.

Emmons, R. A. (1999). *The psychology of ultimate concerns: Motivation and spirituality in personality.* New York: Guilford Press.

Emmons, R. A., & King, L. A. (1988). Conflict among personal strivings: Immediate and long-term implications for psychological and physical well-being. *Journal of Personality and Social Psychology, 54,* 1040–1048.

Erikson, E. H. (1958). *Young man Luther.* New York: Norton.

Erikson, E. H. (1963). *Childhood and society* (2nd ed.). New York: Norton.

Erikson, E. H. (1968). *Identity: Youth and crisis.* New York: Norton.

Erikson, E. H. (1969). *Gandhi's truth.* New York: Norton.

Fagles, R. (Trans.). (1990). *The Iliad.* New York: Penguin.

Fayard, J. V., Roberts, B. W., Robins, R. W., & Watson, D. (2012). Uncovering the affective core of conscientiousness: The role of self-conscious emotions. *Journal of Personality, 80,* 1–32.

Feinberg, M., Willer, R., & Schultz, M. (2014). Gossip and ostracism promote cooperation in groups. *Psychological Science, 25,* 656–664.

Feldman, R., Masalha, S., & Derdikman-Eiron, R. (2010). Conflict resolution in the parent–child, marital, and peer contexts and children's aggression in the peer group: A process-oriented cultural perspective. *Developmental Psychology, 46,* 310–325.

Fivush, R. (2011). The development of autobiographical memory. In S. T. Fiske, D. L. Schacter, & S. E. Taylor (Eds.), *Annual review of psychology* (Vol. 62, pp. 550–582). Palo Alto, CA: Annual Reviews.

Fivush, R., & Kuebli, J. (1997). Making everyday events emotional: The construal of emotion in parent–child conversations about the past. In N. L. Stein, P. A. Ornstein, B. Tversky, & C. Brainerd (Eds.), *Memory for everyday and emotional events* (pp. 239–266). Mahwah, NJ: Erlbaum.

Fogelman, E. (1994). *Conscience and courage: Rescuers of Jews during the holocaust*. New York: Anchor Books.

Fonda, J. (2006). *My life so far*. New York: Random House.

Forster, E. M. (1910). *Howard's end*. Hammondsworth, UK: Penguin.

Foucault, M. (1995). *Discipline and punish: The birth of the prison*. New York: Vintage.

Fowler, J. (1981). *Stages of faith*. New York: Harper & Row.

Fraley, R. C., Griffin, B. N., Belsky, J., & Roisman, G. I. (2012). Developmental antecedents of political ideology: A longitudinal investigation from birth to age 18 years. *Psychological Science, 23*, 1425–1431.

Fraley, R. C., & Roberts, B. W. (2005). Patterns of continuity: A dynamic model for conceptualizing the stability of individual differences in psychological constructs across the life course. *Psychological Review, 112*, 60–74.

Freeman, M. (2011a). Narrative foreclosure in later life: Possibilities and limits. In G. Kenyon, E. Bohlmeijer, & W. L. Randall (Eds.), *Storying later life: Issues, investigations, and interventions in narrative gerontology* (pp. 3–19). New York: Oxford University Press.

Freeman, M. (2011b). The space of selfhood: Culture, narrative, identity. In S. R. Kirschner & J. Martin (Eds.), *The sociocultural turn in psychology: The contextual emergence of mind and self* (pp. 137–158). New York: Columbia University Press.

Freud, S. (1961). The ego and the id. In J. Strachey (Ed.), *The standard edition of the complete psychological works of Sigmund Freud* (Vol. 19, pp. 1–66). London: Hogarth Press. (Original work published 1923)

Freud, S. (1961). Civilization and its discontents. In J. Strachey (Ed.), *The standard edition of the complete psychological works of Sigmund Freud* (Vol. 21, pp. 57–145). London: Hogarth Press. (Original work published 1930)

Freund, A. M., & Blanchard-Fields, F. (2014). Age-related differences in altruism across adulthood: Making personal financial gain versus contributing to the public good. *Developmental Psychology, 50*, 1125–1136.

Freund, A. M., & Riediger, M. (2006). Goals as building blocks of personality and development in adulthood. In D. K. Mroczek & T. D. Little (Eds.), *Handbook of personality development* (pp. 353–372). Mahwah, NJ: Erlbaum.

Friedman, H. S., Tucker, J. S., Tomlinson-Keasy, C., Schwartz, J. E., Wingard, D. L., & Criqui, M. H. (1993). Does childhood personality predict longevity? *Journal of Personality and Social Psychology, 65*, 176–185.

Frimer, J. A., Walker, L. J., Dunlop, W. L., Lee, B. H., & Riches, A. (2011). The integration of agency and communion in moral personality: Evidence of enlightened self-interest. *Journal of Personality and Social Psychology, 101*, 149–163.

Gabriel, S., & Young, A. F. (2011). Becoming a vampire without being bitten: The narrative collective-assimilation hypothesis. *Psychological Science, 22*, 990–994.

Gervais, W. M. (2013). Perceiving minds and gods: How mind perception enables, constrains, and is triggered by belief in gods. *Perspectives on Psychological Science, 8*, 380–394.

Giddens, A. (1991). *Modernity and self-identity: Self and society in the late modern age*. Stanford, CA: Stanford University Press.

Gluck, J., & Bluck, S. (2007). Looking back across the life span: A life story account of the reminiscence bump. *Memory and Cognition, 35,* 1928–1939.

Gjerde, P. (2004). Culture, power, and experience: Toward a person-centered cultural psychology. *Human Development, 47,* 138–157.

Goffman, E. (1959). *The presentation of self in everyday life.* Garden City, NY: Doubleday.

Goldberg, L. R. (1990). An alternative "description of personality": The Big Five factor structure. *Journal of Personality and Social Psychology, 59,* 1216–1229.

Graham, J., & Haidt, J. (2010). Beyond beliefs: Religions bind individuals into moral communities. *Personality and Social Psychology Review, 14,* 140–150.

Graham, J., Haidt, J., & Nosek, B. A. (2009). Liberals and conservatives rely on different sets of moral foundations. *Journal of Personality and Social Psychology, 96,* 1029–1046.

Granqvist, P., Mikulincer, M., & Shaver, P. R. (2010). Religion as attachment: Normative processes and individual differences. *Personality and Social Psychology Review, 14,* 49–59.

Gray, K., & Wegner, D. M. (2010). Blaming God for our pain: Human suffering and the divine mind. *Personality and Social Psychology Review, 14,* 7–16.

Gray, K., Young, L., & Waytz, A. (2012). Mind perception is the essence of morality. *Psychological Inquiry, 23,* 101–124.

Graziano, W. G., & Eisenberg, N. (1997). Agreeableness: A dimension of personality. In R. Hogan, J. A. Johnson, & S. Briggs (Eds.), *Handbook of personality psychology* (pp. 795–824). San Diego, CA: Academic Press.

Gregg, G. S. (1991). *Self-representation: Life narrative studies in identity and ideology.* New York: Greenwood Press.

Grolnick, W. S., Bridges, L. J., & Connell, J. P. (1996). Emotion regulation in two-year-olds: Strategies and emotional expression in four contexts. *Child Development, 67,* 928–941.

Gross, J. J. (2008). Emotion and emotion regulation: Personality processes and individual differences. In O. P. John, R. W. Robins, & L. A. Pervin (Eds.), *Handbook of personality: Theory and research* (3rd ed., pp. 701–724). New York: Guilford Press.

Gunnar, M. R., & Quevedo, K. (2007). The neurobiology of stress and development. In S. Fiske & D. Schacter (Eds.), *Annual review of psychology* (Vol. 58, pp. 145–173). Palo Alto, CA: Annual Reviews.

Gutman, L. M., & Eccles, J. S. (2007). Stage–environmental fit during adolescence: Trajectories of family relations and adolescent outcomes. *Developmental Psychology, 43,* 522–537.

Haase, C. M., Heckhausen, J., & Wrosch, C. (2013). Developmental regulation across the life span: Toward a new synthesis. *Developmental Psychology, 49,* 964–972.

Habermas, T., & Bluck, S. (2000). Getting a life: The emergence of the life story in adolescence. *Psychological Bulletin, 126,* 748–769.

Haden, C. A., Haine, R. A., & Fivush, R. (1997). Developing narrative structure in parent–child reminiscing: Across the preschool years. *Developmental Psychology, 33,* 295–307.

Haggard, P., & Tsakiris, M. (2009). The experience of agency: Feelings, judgments, and responsibility. *Current Directions in Psychological Science, 18,* 242–246.

Haidt, J. (2012). *The righteous mind: Why good people are divided by politics and religion.* New York: Vintage.

Haidt, J., & Graham, J. (2009). Planet of the Durkheimians, where community, authority, and sacredness are foundations for morality. In J. Jost, C. Kay, & H. Thorisdottir (Eds.), *Social and psychological bases of ideology and system justification* (pp. 371–401). New York: Oxford University Press.

Hamilton, W. D. (1964). The genetical evolution of social behaviour. *Journal of Theoretical Biology, 7,* 1–52.

Hammack, P. L. (2008). Narrative and the cultural psychology of identity. *Personality and Social Psychology Review, 12,* 222–247.

Hammack, P. L. (2009). Exploring the reproduction of conflict through narrative: Israeli youth motivated to participate in a coexistence program. *Peace and Conflict, 15,* 49–74.

Hammack, P. L. (2011). *Narrative and the politics of identity: The cultural psychology of Israeli and Palestinian youth.* New York: Oxford University Press.

Hampson, R. (2007, January 4). New York City cheers death-defying rescuer. *USA Today,* p. A1.

Hampson, S. E., & Goldberg, L. R. (2006). A first large cohort study of personality trait stability over the 40 years between elementary school and midlife. *Journal of Personality and Social Psychology, 91,* 763–779.

Hane, A. A., Fox, N. A., Henderson, H. A., & Marshall, P. J. (2008). Behavioral reactivity and approach–withdrawal bias in infancy. *Developmental Psychology, 44,* 1491–1496.

Harmon-Jones, E., & Allen, J. J. B. (1998). Anger and frontal brain activity: EEG asymmetry consistent with approach motivation despite negative affective valence. *Journal of Personality and Social Psychology, 74,* 1310–1316.

Hart, H. M., McAdams, D. P., Hirsch, B. J., & Bauer, J. J. (2001). Generativity and societal involvement among African-American and white adults. *Journal of Research in Personality, 35,* 208–230.

Harter, S. (2006). The self. In N. Eisenberg (Ed.) & W. Damon & R. M. Lerner (Series Eds.), *Handbook of child psychology: Vol. 3. Social, emotional, and personality development* (pp. 505–570). New York: Wiley.

Hartup, W. W., & Abecassis, M. (2002). Friends and enemies. In P. K. Smith & C. H. Hart (Eds.), *Blackwell handbook of social development* (pp. 286–306). Oxford, UK: Blackwell.

Hawks, J. Wang, E. T., Cochran, G. M., Harpending, H. C., & Moyzis, R. K. (2007). Recent acceleration in human adaptive evolution. *Proceedings of the National Academy of Sciences, 104,* 20753–20758.

Hawley, P. (2002). Social dominance and prosocial coercive strategies of resource control in preschoolers. *International Journal of Behavioral Development, 26,* 167–176.

Hay, D. F., Mundy, L., Roberts, S., Carta, R., Waters, C. S., Perra, O., et al. (2011). Known risk factors for violence predict 12-month-old infants' aggressiveness with peers. *Psychological Science, 22,* 1205–1211.

Heckhausen, J. (2011). Agency and control striving across the life span. In K. L. Fingerman, C. A. Berg, J. Smith, & T. Antonucci (Eds.), *Handbook of life-span development* (pp. 183–212). New York: Springer.

Heckman, J. J., & Masterov, D. V. (2007). The productivity argument for investing in young children. *Review of Agricultural Economics, 29,* 446–493.

Heilbrun, C. (1988). *Writing a woman's life.* New York: Norton.

Heine, S. J., Buchtel, E. E., & Norenzayan, A. (2008). What do cross-national comparisons of personality traits tell us? *Psychological Science, 19,* 309–313.

Heine, S. J., Takemoto, T., Maskalenko, S., Lasaleta, J., & Henrich, J. (2008). Mirrors in the head: Cultural variation in objective self-awareness. *Personality and Social Psychology Bulletin, 34,* 879–887.

Heller, J. (1974). *Something happened.* New York: Knopf.

Hemenover, S. H. (2003). Individual differences in rate of affect change: Studies in affective chronometry. *Journal of Personality and Social Psychology, 85,* 121–131.

Hewlett, B. S., Lamb, M. E., Shannon, D., Leyendecker, B., & Scholmerich, A. (1998).Culture and early infancy among Central African foragers and farmers. *Developmental Psychology, 34,* 653–661.

Higgins, E. T. (1997). Beyond pleasure and pain. *American Psychologist, 52,* 1280–1300.

Higgins, E. T. (2008). Culture and personality: Variability across universal motives as the missing link. *Social and Personality Psychology Compass, 2*(2), 608–634.

Hirt, E., Zillman, D., Erickson, G., & Kennedy, C. (1992). The costs and benefits of allegiance: Changes in fans' self-ascribed competencies after team victory team defeat. *Journal of Personality and Social Psychology, 63,* 724–738.

Ho, D. Y. F. (1986). Chinese patterns of socialization: A critical review. In M. H. Bond (Ed.), *The psychology of the Chinese people* (pp. 1–37). Hong Kong: Oxford University Press.

Hofer, J., Busch, H., Chasiotis, A., Kärtner, J., & Campos, D. (2008). Concern for generativity and its relation to implicit pro-social power motivation, generative goals, and satisfaction with life: A cross-cultural investigation. *Journal of Personality, 76,* 1–30.

Hogan, R. (1982). A socioanalytic theory of personality. In M. Page (Ed.), *Nebraska Symposium on Motivation* (Vol. 29, pp. 55–89). Lincoln: University of Nebraska Press.

Hogan, R., Hogan, J., & Roberts, B. W. (1996). Personality measurement and employment decisions. *American Psychologist, 51,* 469–477.

Hogan, R., Jones, W. H., & Cheek, J. M. (1985). Socioanalytic theory: An alternative to armadillo psychology. In B. R. Schlenker (Ed.), *The self and social life* (pp. 175–198). New York: McGraw-Hill.

Hogan, R., & Ones, D. S. (1997). Conscientiousness and integrity at work. In R. Hogan, J. A. Johnson, & S. Briggs (Eds.), *Handbook of personality psychology* (pp. 849–870). San Diego, CA: Academic Press.

Holtzman, N. S., & Strube, M. J. (2010). Narcissism and attractiveness. *Journal of Research in Personality, 44,* 133–136.

Hooker, C. I., Verosky, S. C., Miyakawa, A., Knight, R. T., & D'Esposito, M.

(2008). The influence of personality on neural mechanisms of observational fear and reward learning. *Neuropsychologia, 46,* 2709–2724.

Horney, K. (1980). *The adolescent diaries of Karen Horney.* New York: Basic Books.

Howe, M. L., & Courage, M. L. (1997). The emergence and early development of autobiographical memory. *Psychological Review, 104,* 499–523.

Huuskes, L., Ciarrochi, J., & Heaven, P. C. L. (2013). The longitudinal relationships between adolescent religious values and personality. *Journal of Research in Personality, 47,* 483–487.

Inzlicht, M., & Schmeichel, B. J. (2012). What is ego depletion?: Toward a mechanistic revision of the resource model of self-control. *Perspectives on Psychological Science, 7,* 450–463.

Isaacson, W. (2011). *Steve Jobs.* New York: Simon & Schuster.

Izard, C. E., Fantauzzo, C. A., Castle, J. M., Haynes, O. M., Rayias, M. F., & Putnam, P. H. (1995). The ontogeny and significance of infants' facial expressions in the first nine months of life. *Developmental Psychology, 31,* 997–1013.

Jackson, J. J., Thoemmes, F., Jonkmann, K., Ludtke, O., & Trautwein, U. (2012). Military training and personality trait development: Does the military make the man or does the man make the military? *Psychological Science, 23,* 270–277.

James, W. (1958). *The varieties of religious experience.* New York: New American Library of World Literature. (Original work published 1902)

James, W. (1963). *Psychology.* Greenwich, CT: Fawcett. (Original work published 1892)

Janoff-Bullman, R. (2009). To provide or protect: Motivational bases of political liberalism and conservatism. *Psychological Inquiry, 20,* 120-128.

Jay-Z. (2011). *Decoded.* New York: Spiegel & Grau.

Jaynes, J. (1976). *The origin of consciousness in the breakdown of the bicameral mind.* Boston: Houghton Miflin.

Jensen, L. A., Arnett, J. J., & McKenzie, J. (2011). Globalization and cultural identity. In S. J. Schwartz, K. Luyckx, & V. L. Vignoles (Eds.), *Handbook of identity theory and research* (pp. 285–301). New York: Springer.

John, O. P., & Srivastava, S. (1999). The Big Five trait taxonomy: History, measurement, and theoretical perspectives. In L. Pervin & O. P. John (Eds.), *Handbook of personality: Theory and research* (2nd ed., pp. 102–138). New York: Guilford Press.

Johnson, W. (2010). Understanding the genetics of intelligence: Can height help? Can corn oil? *Current Directions in Psychological Science, 19,* 177–182.

Johnson, W., Emde, R. N., Pannabecker, B., Sternberg, C., & Davis, M. (1982). Maternal perceptions of infant emotion from birth through 18 months. *Infant Behavior and Development, 5,* 313–322.

Jones, B. K., & McAdams, D. P. (2013). Becoming generative: Socializing influences recalled in life stories in late midlife. *Journal of Adult Development, 20,* 158–172.

Josephs, R. A., Sellers, J. G., Newman, M. L., & Mehta, P. H. (2006). The mismatch effect: When testosterone and status are at odds. *Journal of Personality and Social Psychology, 90,* 999–1013.

Jost, J. T. (2006). The end of the end of ideology. *American Psychologist, 61,* 651–670.

Jost, J. T., Federico, C. M., & Napier, J. L. (2009). Political ideology: Its structure, functions and elective affinities. In S. T. Fiske, D. L. Schacter, & R. Sternberg (Eds.), *Annual review of psychology* (Vol. 60, pp. 307–337). Palo Alto, CA: Annual Reviews.

Jost, J. T., Glaser, J., Kruglanski, A. W., & Sulloway, F. J. (2003). Political conservatism as motivated social cognition. *Psychological Bulletin, 129,* 339–375.

Joyce, J. (1964). *Portrait of the artist as a young man.* London: Penguin. (Original work published 1916)

Judge, T. A., Livingston, B. A., & Hurst, C. (2012). Do nice guys—and gals—really finish last?: The joint effects of sex and agreeableness on income. *Journal of Personality and Social Psychology, 102,* 390–407.

Kagan, J. (2012). The biography of behavioral inhibition. In M. Zentner & R. L. Shiner (Eds.), *Handbook of temperament* (pp. 69–82). New York: Guilford Press.

Kagan, J., Snidman, N., Kahn, V., & Towsley, S. (2007). The preservation of two infant temperaments through adolescence. *Monographs of the Society for Research in Child Development, 72*(Serial No. 287), 1–95.

Kandler, C., Bleidorn, W., & Riemann, R. (2012). Left or right? Sources of political orientation: The role of genetic factors, cultural transmission, assortative mating, and personality. *Journal of Personality and Social Psychology, 102,* 633–645.

Karr, M. (1995). *The liar's club: A memoir.* New York: Penguin.

Kasser, T., & Ryan, R. M. (1996). Further examining the American dream: Differential correlates of intrinsic and extrinsic goals. *Personality and Social Psychology Bulletin, 22,* 280–287.

Kay, A. C., Gaucher, D., McGregor, I., & Nash, K. (2010). Religious belief as compensatory control. *Personality and Social Psychology Review, 14,* 37–48.

Kay, A. C., Shepherd, S., Blatz, C. W., Chua, S. N., & Galinsky, A. D. (2010). For God (or) country: The hydraulic relation between government instability and belief in religious sources of control. *Journal of Personality and Social Psychology, 99,* 725–739.

Kelemen, D. (2004). Are children "intuitive theists"? *Psychological Science, 15,* 295–301.

Kennedy, Q., Mather, M., & Carstensen, L. L. (2004). The role of motivation in age-related positivity effect in autobiographical memory. *Psychological Science, 15,* 208–214.

Kermode, F. (1967). *The sense of an ending.* New York: Oxford University Press.

Kesebir, S. (2012). The superorganism account of human sociality: How and when human groups are like beehives. *Personality and Social Psychology Review, 16,* 233–261.

Keyes, C. L. M., & Ryff, C. D. (1998). Generativity in adult lives: Social structural contours and the quality of life consequences. In D. P. McAdams & E. de St. Aubin (Eds.), *Generativity and adult development* (pp. 227–263). Washington, DC: American Psychological Association Books.

King, L. A. (1995). Wishes, motives, goals, and personal memories: Relation of measures of human motivation. *Journal of Personality, 63*, 985–1007.

King, L. A., & Hicks, J. A. (2007). What ever happened to "what might have been"? *American Psychologist, 62*, 625–636.

Kingo, O. S., Bernsten, D., & Krojgaard, P. (2013). Adults' earliest memories as a function of age, gender, and education in a large stratified sample. *Psychology and Aging, 28*, 646–653.

Kirkpatrick, L. A. (2005). *Attachment, evolution, and the psychology of religion.* New York: Guilford Press.

Kleinfeld, J. (2012). *The frontier romance: Environment, culture, and Alaska identity.* Fairbanks: University of Alaska Press.

Kochanska, G., & Aksan, N. (2006). Children's conscience and self-regulation. *Journal of Personality, 74*, 1587–1617.

Koenig, L. B., McGue, M., & Iacono, W. G. (2008). Stability and change in religiousness during emerging adulthood. *Developmental Psychology, 44*, 532–543.

Kohlberg, L. (1969). Stage and sequence: The cognitive-developmental approach to socialization. In D. A. Goslin (Ed.), *Handbook of socialization theory and Research* (pp. 347–480). Skokie, IL: Rand McNally.

Kohut, H. (1977). *The restoration of the self.* New York: International Universities Press.

Kostering, L., Stahl, C., Leonhart, R., Weiller, C., & Kaller, C. P. (2014). Development of planning abilities in normal aging: Differential effects of specific cognitive demands. *Developmental Psychology, 50*, 293–303.

Kotre, J. (1984). *Outliving the self.* Baltimore: Johns Hopkins University Press.

Kroger, J., & Marcia, J. E. (2011). The identity statuses: Origins, meanings, and interpretations. In S. J. Schwartz, K. Luyckx, & V. L. Vignoles (Eds.), *Handbook of identity theory and research* (pp. 31–53). New York: Springer.

Krueger, R. F., Caspi, A., Moffitt, T. E., Silva, P. A., & McGee, R. (1996). Personality traits are differentially linked to mental disorders: A multitrait-multidiagnosis study of an adolescent birth cohort. *Journal of Abnormal Psychology, 105*, 299–312.

Lacourse, E., Nagin, D. S., Vitaro, F., Cote, S., Arseneault, L., & Tremblay, R. E. (2006). Prediction of early-onset deviant peer group affiliation: A 12-year longitudinal study. *Archives of General Psychiatry, 63*, 562–568.

Lakoff, G. (2002). *Moral politics: How liberals and conservatives think* (2nd ed.). Chicago: University of Chicago Press.

Landau, M. J., Solomon, S., Arndt, J., Greenberg, J. Pyszczynski, T., Miller, C. H., et al. (2004). Deliver us from evil: The effects of mortality salience and reminders of 9/11 on support for President George W. Bush. *Personality and Social Psychology Bulletin, 30*, 1136–1150.

Lane, J. D., Wellman, H. M., Wang, L., Olson, S. L., Miller, A. L., & Tardif, T. (2013). Relations between temperament and theory of mind development in the United States and China: Biological and behavioral correlates of preschoolers' false-belief understanding. *Developmental Psychology, 49*, 825–836.

Langbaum, R. (1982). *The mysteries of identity: A theme in modern literature.* Chicago: University of Chicago Press.

Laursen, B., Pulkkinen, L., & Adams, R. (2002). Antecedents and correlates of agreeableness in adulthood. *Developmental Psychology, 38,* 591–603.

Lee, S. J., Altschul, I., & Gershoff, E. T. (2013). Does warmth moderate longitudinal associations between maternal spanking and child aggression in early childhood? *Developmental Psychology, 49,* 2017–2028.

Lehrer, J. (2009, May 18). Don't!: The secret of self-control. *The New Yorker,* pp. 26–32.

Leichtman, M. D., Wang, Q., & Pillemer, D. B. (2003). Cultural variations in interdependence: Lessons from Korea, China, India, and the United States. In R. Fivush & C. Haden (Eds.), *Autobiographical memory and the construction of a narrative self* (pp. 73–97). Mahwah, NJ: Erlbaum.

LeVine, R. A. (1982). *Culture, behavior, and personality* (2nd ed.). New York: Aldine.

Lewis, D., & Nakagawa, K. (1995). *Race and educational reform in the American metropolis: A study of school decentralization.* Albany: State University of New York Press.

Lewis, G. J., & Bates, T. C. (2013). Common genetic influences underpin religiosity, community integration, and existential uncertainty. *Journal of Research in Personality, 47,* 398–405.

Li-Grining, C. P. (2007). Effortful control among low-income preschoolers in three cities: Stability, change, and individual differences. *Developmental Psychology, 43,* 208–221.

Lieberman, M. D., & Rosenthal, R. (2001). Why introverts can't tell who likes them: Multitasking and nonverbal decoding. *Journal of Personality and Social Psychology, 80,* 294–310.

Lilgendahl, J. P., Helson, R., & John, O. P. (2013). Does ego development increase during midlife?: The effects of openness and accommodative processing of difficult life events. *Journal of Personality, 81,* 403–416.

Lilgendahl, J. P., & McAdams, D. P. (2011). Constructing stories of self-growth: How individual differences in patterns of autobiographical reasoning relate to well-being in midlife. *Journal of Personality, 79,* 391–428.

Lischetzke, T., & Eid, M. (2006). Why extraverts are happier than introverts: The role of mood regulation. *Journal of Personality, 74,* 1127–1161.

Little, B. J. (1999). Personality and motivation: Personal action and the conative evolution. In L. A. Pervin & O. John (Eds.), *Handbook of personality: Theory and research* (2nd ed., pp. 501–524). New York: Guilford Press.

Lodi-Smith, J., Geise, A., Robins, R. W., & Roberts, B. W. (2009). Narrating personality change. *Journal of Personality and Social Psychology, 96,* 679–689.

Lodi-Smith, J., & Roberts, B. W. (2007). Social investment and personality: A meta-analysis of the relationship of personality traits to investment in work, family, religion, and volunteerism. *Personality and Social Psychology Review, 11,* 68–86.

Losh, M., & Capps, L. (2006). Understanding of emotional experiences in autism: Insights from the personal accounts of high-functioning children with autism. *Developmental Psychology, 42,* 809–818.

Lucas, R. E., & Diener, E. (2001). Understanding extraverts' enjoyment of social situations: The importance of pleasantness. *Journal of Personality and Social Psychology, 81,* 343–356.

Lucas, R. E., & Donnellan, M. B. (2011). Personality development across the life span:Longitudinal analyses with a national sample from Germany. *Journal of Personality and Social Psychology, 101,* 847–861.

Lucas, R. E., Le, K., & Dyrenforth, P. S. (2008). Explaining the extraversion/positive affect relation: Sociability cannot account for extraverts' greater happiness. *Journal of Personality and Social Psychology, 76,* 385–414.

Ludtke, O., Roberts, B. W., Trautwein, U., & Nagy, G. (2011). A random walk down university avenue: Life paths, life events, and personality trait change at the transition to university life. *Journal of Personality and Social Psychology, 101,* 620–637.

Luo, Y., & Baillargeon, R. (2010). Toward a mentalistic account of early psychological reasoning. *Current Directions in Psychological Science, 19,* 301–307.

MacDermid, S. M., Franz, C. E., & de Reus, L. A. (1998). Generativity: At the crossroads of social roles and personality. In D. P. McAdams & E. de St. Aubin (Eds.), *Generativity and adult development* (pp. 181–226). Washington, DC: American Psychological Association Books.

Mandler, J. M. (1984). *Stories, scripts, and scenes: Aspects of schema theory.* Hillsdale, NJ: Erlbaum.

Mangelsdorf, S. C., Shapiro, J. R., & Marzolf, D. (1995). Developmental and temperamental differences in emotion regulation in infancy. *Child Development, 66,* 1817–1828.

Mar, R. A., & Oatley, K. (2008). The function of fiction is the abstraction and simulation of social experience. *Perspectives on Psychological Science, 3,* 173–192.

Mar, R. A., Oatley, K., Hirsh, J., Paz, J. D., & Peterson, J. B. (2006). Bookworms versus nerds: Exposure to fiction versus non-fiction, divergent associations with social ability, and the simulation of fictional social worlds. *Journal of Research in Personality, 40,* 694–712.

Mar, R. A., Tackett, J. L., & Moore, C. (2010). Exposure to media and theory-of-mind development in preschoolers. *Cognitive Development, 25,* 69–78.

Marcia, J. E. (1966). Development and validation of ego identity status. *Journal of Personality and Social Psychology, 3,* 551–558.

Markus, H., & Kitayama, S. (1991). Culture and the self: Implications for cognition, emotion, and motivation. *Psychological Review, 98,* 224–253.

Marsh, H. W., & Hattie, J. (1996). Theoretical perspectives on the structure of self-concept. In B. A. Bracken (Ed.), *Handbook of self-concept* (pp. 38–90). New York: Wiley.

Martin, J., Sugarman, J., & Thompson, J. (2003). *Psychology and the question of agency.* Albany: State University of New York Press.

Martin, P., Long, M. V., & Poon, L. W. (2002). Age changes and differences in personality traits and states of the old and very old. *Journal of Gerontology B: Psychological Sciences and Social Sciences, 57,* 144–152.

Maruna, S. (2001). *Making good: How ex-convicts reform and rebuild their lives.* Washington, DC: American Psychological Association Books.

Mast, S. (1986). *Stages of identity: A study of actors.* London: Gower.

Matthews, G., & Gilliland, K. (1999). The personality theories of H. J. Eysenck & J. A. Gray: A comparative review. *Personality and Individual Differences, 26,* 583–626.

McAdams, D. P. (1980). A thematic coding system for the intimacy motive. *Journal of Research in Personality, 14,* 413–432.

McAdams, D. P. (1982). Experiences of intimacy and power: Relationships between social motives and autobiographical memory. *Journal of Personality and Social Psychology, 42,* 292–302.

McAdams, D. P. (1985). *Power, intimacy, and the life story: Personological inquiries into identity.* New York: Guilford Press.

McAdams, D. P. (1989). *Intimacy: The need to be close.* New York: Doubleday.

McAdams, D. P. (1994). Image, theme, and character in the life story of Karen Horney. In C. Franz & A. J. Stewart (Eds.), *Women creating lives: Identities, resilience, and resistance* (pp. 151–171). Boulder, CO: Westview Press.

McAdams, D. P. (2011). *George W. Bush and the redemptive dream: A psychological portrait.* New York: Oxford University Press.

McAdams, D. P. (2013a). Life authorship: A psychological challenge for emerging adulthood, as illustrated in two notable case studies. *Emerging Adulthood, 1,* 151–158.

McAdams, D. P. (2013b). The psychological self as actor, agent, and author. *Perspectives on Psychological Science, 8,* 272–295.

McAdams, D. P. (2013c). *The redemptive self: Stories Americans live by* (Revised, expanded ed.). New York: Oxford University Press.

McAdams, D. P., & Albaugh, M. (2008). What if there were no God?: Politically conservative and liberal Christians imagine their lives without faith. *Journal of Research in Personality, 42,* 1668–1672.

McAdams, D. P., Albaugh, M., Farber, E., Daniels, J., Logan, R. L., & Olson, B. (2008). Family metaphors and moral intuitions: How conservatives and liberals narrate their lives. *Journal of Personality and Social Psychology, 95,* 978–990.

McAdams, D. P., Anyidoho, N. A., Brown, C., Huang, Y. T., Kaplan, B., & Machado, M. A. (2004). Traits and stories: Links between dispositional and narrative features of personality. *Journal of Personality, 72,* 761–783.

McAdams, D. P., Bauer, J. J., Sakaeda, A. M., Anyidoho, N. A., Machado, M. A., Magrino, K., et al. (2006). Continuity and change in the life story: A longitudinal study of autobiographical memories in emerging adulthood. *Journal of Personality, 74,* 1371–1400.

McAdams, D. P., & Cox, K. S. (2010). Self and identity across the lifespan. In A. Freund & R. Lerner (Eds.), *Handbook of lifespan development* (Vol. 2, pp. 158–207). New York: Wiley.

McAdams, D. P., & de St. Aubin, E. (1992). A theory of generativity and its assessment through self-report, behavioral acts, and narrative themes in autobiography. *Journal of Personality and Social Psychology, 62,* 1003–1015.

McAdams, D. P., & de St. Aubin, E. (Eds.). (1998). *Generativity and adult development: How and why we care for the next generation.* Washington, DC: American Psychological Association Books.

McAdams, D. P., de St. Aubin, E., & Logan, R. L. (1993). Generativity among young, midlife, and older adults. *Psychology and Aging, 8,* 221–230.

McAdams, D. P., Diamond, A., de St. Aubin, E., & Mansfield, E. D. (1997). Stories of commitment: The psychosocial construction of generative lives. *Journal of Personality and Social Psychology, 72,* 678–694.

McAdams, D. P., Hanek, K. J., & Dadabo, J. (2013). Themes of self-regulation and self-exploration in the life stories of American conservatives and liberals. *Political Psychology, 34,* 201–219.

McAdams, D. P., Hoffman, B. J., Mansfield, E. D., & Day, R. (1996). Themes of agency and communion in significant autobiographical scenes. *Journal of Personality, 64,* 339–378.

McAdams, D. P., & McLean, K. C. (2013). Narrative identity. *Current Directions in Psychological Science, 22,* 233–238.

McAdams, D. P., & Olson, B. D. (2010). Personality development: Continuity and change over the life course. In S. Fiske, D. Schacter, & R. Sternberg (Eds.), *Annual review of psychology* (Vol. 61, pp. 517–542). Palo Alto, CA: Annual Reviews.

McAdams, D. P., & Pals, J. L. (2006). A new Big Five: Fundamental principles for an integrative science of personality. *American Psychologist, 61,* 204–217.

McAdams, D. P., Reynolds, J., Lewis, M., Patten, A., & Bowman, P. J. (2001). When bad things turn good and good things turn bad: Sequences of redemption and contamination in life narrative, and their relation to psychosocial adaptation in midlife adults and in students. *Personality and Social Psychology Bulletin, 27,* 472–483.

McClelland, D. C. (1961). *The achieving society.* New York: Van Nostrand.

McClelland, D. C. (1985). *Human motivation.* Glenview, IL: Scott, Foresman.

McClelland, D. C., Atkinson, J. W., Clark, R. A., & Lowell, E. L. (1953). *The achievement motive.* New York: Appleton-Century-Crofts.

McColgan, G., Valentine, J., & Downs, M. (2000). Concluding narratives of a career with dementia: Accounts of Iris Murdock at her death. *Ageing and Society, 20,* 97–109.

McCrae, R. R., & Costa, P. T., Jr. (1987). Validation of the five-factor model of personality across instruments and observers. *Journal of Personality and Social Psychology, 52,* 81–90.

McCrae, R. R., & Costa, P. T., Jr. (2008). The five-factor theory of personality. In O. P. John, R. W. Robins, & L. A. Pervin (Eds.), *Handbook of personality: Theory and research* (3rd ed., pp. 159–180). New York: Guilford Press.

McLean, K. C. (2008). Stories of the young and the old: Personal continuity and narrative identity. *Developmental Psychology, 44,* 254–264.

McLean, K. C., & Pasupathi, M. (2011). Old, new, borrow, blue?: The emergence and retention of personal meaning in autobiographical storytelling. *Journal of Personality, 79,* 135–163.

McLean, K. C., Pasupathi, M., & Pals, J. L. (2007). Selves creating stories creating selves: A process model of self-development. *Personality and Social Psychology Review, 11,* 262–278.

McLean, K. C., & Pratt, M. W. (2006). Life's little (and big) lessons: Identity statuses and meaning-making in the turning point narratives of emerging adults. *Developmental Psychology, 42,* 714–722.

Mead, G. H. (1934). *Mind, self, and society.* Chicago: University of Chicago Press.

Merlin, B. (2010). *Acting: The basics.* London: Routledge.

Mesoudi, A., & Jensen, K. (2012). Culture and the evolution of human sociality. In J. Vonk & T. K. Shackelford (Eds.), *The Oxford handbook of comparative evolutionary psychology* (pp. 419–433). New York: Oxford University Press.

Mikulincer, M., & Shaver, P. R. (2007). *Attachment in adulthood: Structure, dynamics, and change.* New York: Guilford Press.

Miller, P. J., Cho, G. E., & Bracey, J. R. (2005). Working-class children's experience through the prism of personal storytelling. *Human Development, 48,* 115–135.

Milyavskaya, M., Phillipe, F. L., & Koestner, R. (2013). Psychological need satisfaction across levels of experience: Their organization and contribution to general well-being. *Journal of Research in Personality, 47,* 41–51.

Mischel, W. (2004). Toward an integrative science of the person. In S. T. Fiske, D. L. Schacter, & C. Zahn-Waxler (Eds.), *Annual review of psychology* (Vol. 55, pp. 1–22). Palo Alto, CA: Annual Reviews.

Mischel, W., Shoda, Y., & Peake, P. K. (1988). The nature of adolescent competencies predicted by preschool delay of gratification. *Journal of Personality and Social Psychology, 54,* 687–696.

Moffitt, T. E., Arseneault, L., Belsky, D., Dickson, N., Hancox, R. J., Harrington, H., et al. (2011). A gradient of childhood self-control predicts health, wealth, and public safety. *Proceedings of the National Academy of Sciences, 108,* 2693–2698.

Monahan, K. C., Steinberg, L., Cauffman, E., & Mulvey, E. P. (2009). Trajectories of antisocial behavior and psychosocial maturity from adolescence to young adulthood. *Developmental Psychology, 45,* 1654–1668.

Morgan, J., & Robinson, O. (2013). Intrinsic aspirations and personal meaning across adulthood: Conceptual interrelations and age/sex differences. *Developmental Psychology, 49,* 999–1010.

Mroczek, D. K., & Almeida, D. M. (2004). The effect of daily stress, personality, and age on daily negative affect. *Journal of Personality, 72,* 355–378.

Mroczek, D. K., & Little, T. D. (Eds.). (2006). *Handbook of personality development.* Mahwah, NJ: Erlbaum.

Mroczek, D. K., & Spiro, A. (2003). Modeling intraindividual change in personality traits: Findings from the Normative Aging Study. *Journal of Gerontology B: Psychological Sciences and Social Sciences, 58,* 153–165.

Mroczek, D. K., & Spiro, A. (2007). Personality change influences mortality in older men. *Psychological Science, 18,* 371–376.

Murphy, M. L. M., Slavich, G. M., Rohleder, N., & Miller, G. E. (2013). Targeted rejection triggers differential pro- and anti-inflammatory gene expression in adolescents as a function of social status. *Clinical Psychological Science, 1,* 30–40.

Murray, H. A. (1938). *Explorations in personality.* New York: Oxford University Press. (Reissued in 2008 with a new Foreword by Dan P. McAdams.)

Murray, L. (2010). *Breaking night: A memoir of forgiveness, survival, and my journey from homeless to Harvard*. New York: Hyperion.

Neegle, A., & Habermas, T. (2010). Self-continuity across developmental change in and of repeated life narratives. In K. C. McLean & M. Pasupathi (Eds.), *Narrative development in adolescence: Creating the storied self* (pp. 1–21). New York: Springer.

Nettle, D. (2005). An evolutionary approach to the extraversion continuum. *Evolution and Human Behavior, 26,* 363–373.

Neyer, F. J., & Lehnart, J. (2007). Relationships matter in personality development: Evidence from an 8-year longitudinal study across young adulthood. *Journal of Personality, 75,* 535–568.

Noftle, E. E., & Shaver, P. R. (2006). Attachment dimensions and the Big Five personality traits: Associations and comparative ability to predict relationship quality. *Journal of Research in Personality, 40,* 179–208.

Nolen-Hoeksema, S. (2000). The role of rumination in depressive disorders and mixed anxiety/depressive symptoms. *Journal of Abnormal Psychology, 109,* 504–511.

Nusslock, R., Shackman, A. J., Harmon-Jones, E., Alloy, L. B., Coan, J. A., & Abramson, L. Y. (2011). Cognitive vulnerability and frontal brain asymmetry: Common predictors of first prospective depressive episode. *Journal of Abnormal Psychology, 120,* 497–503.

Obama, B. (1995). *Dreams from my father.* New York: Three Rivers Press.

Oberlander, T. F., Weinberg, J., Papsdorf, M., Grunau, R., Misri, S., & Devlin, A. M. (2008). Prenatal exposure to maternal depression, neonatal methylation of glucocorticoid receptor gene (NR3CI) and infant cortisol stress response. *Epigenetics, 3,* 97–106.

Oettingen, G., & Gollwitzer, P. M. (2010). Strategies of setting and implementing goals: Mental contrasting and implementation intentions. In J. E. Maddux & J. P. Tangney (Eds.), *Social psychological foundations of clinical psychology* (pp. 114–135). New York: Guilford Press.

Ogilvie, D. M., Rose, K. M., & Heppen, J. B. (2001). A comparison of personal project motives in three age groups. *Basic and Applied Social Psychology, 23,* 207–215.

Ojanen, T., Grönroos, M., & Salmivalli, C. (2005). An interpersonal circumplex of children's social goals: Links with peer-reported behavior and sociometric status. *Developmental Psychology, 41,* 699–710.

Oliner, S. P., & Oliner, P. M. (1988). *The altruistic personality: Rescuers of Jews in Nazi Europe.* New York: Free Press.

Ondaatje, M. (2011). *The cat's table.* New York: Knopf.

Oyserman, D., Coon, H. M., & Kemmelmeier, M. (2002). Rethinking individualism and collectivism: Evaluation of theoretical assumptions and meta-analysis. *Psychological Bulletin, 128,* 3–72.

Ozer, D. J., & Benet-Martinez, V. (2006). Personality and the prediction of consequential outcomes. In S. T. Fiske, A. E. Kazdin, & D. L. Schacter (Eds.), *Annual review of psychology* (Vol. 57, pp. 401–421). Palo Alto, CA: Annual Reviews.

Pals, J. (2006). Constructing the "springboard effect": Causal connections, self-making, and growth within the life story. In D. P. McAdams, R. Josselson, & A. Lieblich (Eds.), *Identity and story: Creating self in narrative* (pp. 175–199). Washington, DC: American Psychological Association Books.

Pasupathi, M., & Mansour, E. (2006). Adult age differences in autobiographical reasoning in narratives. *Developmental Psychology, 42,* 798–808.

Pasupathi, M., McLean, K. C., & Weeks, T. (2009). To tell or not to tell: Disclosure and the narrative self. *Journal of Personality, 77,* 89–123.

Pasupathi, M., & Wainryb, C. (2010). On telling the whole story: Facts and interpretations in autobiographical memory narratives from childhood through midadolescence. *Developmental Psychology, 46,* 735–746.

Paunonen, S. V. (2003). Big five factors of personality and replicated predictions of behavior. *Journal of Personality and Social Psychology, 84,* 411–422.

Pearce-McCall, D., & Newman, J. P. (1986). Expectation of success following noncontingent punishment in introverts and extraverts. *Journal of Personality and Social Psychology, 50,* 439–446.

Peck, M. S. (1978). *The road less traveled.* New York: Simon & Schuster.

Pelicano, E. (2007). Links between theory of mind and executive function in young children with autism: Clues to developmental primacy. *Developmental Psychology, 43,* 974–990.

Pennebaker, J. W., & Stone, L. D. (2003). Words of wisdom: Language use over the life span. *Journal of Personality and Social Psychology, 85,* 291–301.

Perner, J., Ruffman, T., & Leekham, S. R. (1994). Theory of mind is contagious: You catch it from your sibs. *Child Development, 65,* 1228–1238.

Petersen, I. T., Bates, J. E., Goodnight, J. A., Dodge, K. A., Lansford, J. E., Pettit, G. S., et al. (2012). Interaction between serotonin transporter polymorphism (*5-HTTLPR*) and stressful life events in adolescents' trajectories of anxious/depressed symptoms. *Developmental Psychology, 48,* 1463–1475.

Peterson, B. E. (2006). Generativity and successful parenting: An analysis of young adult outcomes. *Journal of Personality, 74,* 847–869.

Peterson, B. E., & Duncan, L. E. (2007). Midlife women's generativity and authoritarianism: Marriage, motherhood, and 10 years of aging. *Psychology and Aging, 22,* 411–419.

Peterson, B. E., Smirles, K. A., & Wentworth, P. A. (1997). Generativity and authoritarianism: Implications for personality, political involvement, and parenting. *Journal of Personality and Social Psychology, 72,* 1202–1216.

Peterson, C., Jesso, B., & McCabe, A. (1999). Encouraging narratives in preschoolers: An intervention study. *Journal of Child Language, 26,* 49–67.

Piaget, J. (1970). Piaget's theory. In P. H. Mussen (Ed.), *Carmichael's manual of child psychology* (2nd ed., Vol. 1, pp. 703–732). New York: Wiley.

Pinker, S. (2011). *The better angels of our nature: Why violence has declined.* New York: Viking.

Polletta, F., Chen, P. C. B., Gardner, B. G., & Motes, A. (2011). The sociology of storytelling. *Annual Review of Sociology, 37,* 109–130.

Povinelli, D. (2001). The self: Elevated in consciousness and extended in time. In C. Moore & K. Lemmon (Eds.), *The self in time: Developmental perspectives* (pp. 75–95). Mahwah, NJ: Erlbaum.

Pratt, M. W., Danso, H. A., Arnold, M. L., Norris, J. E., & Filyer, R. (2001). Adult generativity and the socialization of adolescents: Relations to mothers' and fathers' parenting beliefs, styles, and practices. *Journal of Personality, 69,* 89–120.

Pratt, M. W., & Hardy, S. A. (2015). Cultivating the moral personality: Socialization in the family and beyond. In J. E. Grusec & P. D. Hastings (Eds.), *Handbook of socialization theory and research* (2nd ed., 661–685). New York: Guilford Press.

Pratt, M. W., Norris, J. E., Cressman, K., Lawford, H., & Hebblethwaite, S. (2008). Parents' stories of grandparenting concerns in the three-generational family: generativity, optimism, and forgiveness. *Journal of Personality, 76,* 581–602.

Pratt, M. W., Norris, J. E., Arnold, M. L., & Filyer, R. (1999). Generativity and moral development as predictors of value-socialization narratives for young persons across the adult life course: From lessons learned to stories shared. *Psychology and Aging, 14,* 414–426.

Pulkkinen, L., Kokko, K., & Rantanen, J. (2012). Paths from socioemotional behavior in middle childhood to personality in middle adulthood. *Developmental Psychology, 48,* 1283–1291.

Quinn, S. (1988). *A mind of her own: The life of Karen Horney.* Reading, MA: Addison-Wesley.

Raggatt, P. T. F. (2006). Putting the five-factor model into context: Evidence linking Big Five traits to narrative identity. *Journal of Personality, 74,* 1321–1348.

Raskin, R. N., & Hall, C. J. (1981). The Narcissistic Personality Inventory: Alternate form reliability and further evidence of construct validity. *Journal of Personality Assessment, 45,* 159–162.

Raskin, R. N., & Novacek, J. (1991). Narcissism and the use of fantasy. *Journal of Clinical Psychology, 47,* 490–499.

Reese, E. (2002). Social factors in the development of autobiographical memory: The state of the art. *Social Development, 11,* 124–142.

Reese, E., & Newcombe, R. (2007). Training mothers in elaborative reminiscing enhances children's autobiographical memory and narrative. *Child Development, 78,* 1153–1170.

Reker, G. T., & Woo, L. C. (2011). Personal meaning orientations and psychosocial adaptation in older adults. *SAGE Open, 2011*(1), 1–10.

Remnick, D. (2011). *The bridge: The life and rise of Barack Obama.* New York: Vintage.

Rentfrow, P. J., Gosling, S. D., & Potter, J. (2008). A theory of the emergence, persistence, and expression of geographic variation in psychological characteristics. *Perspectives on Psychological Science, 3,* 339–369.

Rhodewalt, F., & Morf, C. C. (1998). On self-aggrandizement and anger: A temporal analysis of narcissism and reactions to success and failure. *Journal of Personality and Social Psychology, 74,* 672–685.

Rice, C., & Pasupathi, M. (2010). Reflecting on self-relevant experiences: Adult age differences. *Developmental Psychology, 46,* 479–490.

Ricoeur, P. (1984). *Time and narrative* (Vol. 1; K. McGlaughin & D. Pellauer, Trans.). Chicago: University of Chicago Press.

Riediger, M., & Freund, A. M. (2006). Focusing and restricting: Two aspects of motivational selectivity in adulthood. *Psychology and Aging, 21,* 173–185.

Riese, H., Sneider, H., Jeronimus, B. F., Korhonen, T., Rose, R. J., Kaprio, J., et al. (2014). Timing of stressful life events affects stability and change in neuroticism. *European Journal of Personality, 28,* 193–200.

Roberts, B. W. (2007). Contextualizing personality psychology. *Journal of Personality, 75,* 1071–1081.

Roberts, B. W., & DelVecchio, W. (2000). The rank-order consistency of personality from childhood to old age: A quantitative review of longitudinal studies. *Psychological Bulletin, 126,* 3–25.

Roberts, B. W., & Jackson, J. J. (2008). Sociogenomic personality psychology. *Journal of Personality, 76,* 1523–1544.

Roberts, B. W., Kuncel, N. R., Shiner, R. L., Caspi, A., & Goldberg, L. R. (2007). The power of personality: The comparative validity of personality traits, socioeconomic status, and cognitive ability for predicting important life outcomes. *Perspectives on Psychological Science, 2,* 313–345.

Roberts, B. W., & Mroczek, D. K. (2008). Personality trait change in adulthood. *Current Directions in Psychological Science, 17,* 31–35.

Roberts, B. W., O'Donnell, M., & Robins, R. W. (2004). Goal and personality trait development in emerging adulthood. *Journal of Personality and Social Psychology, 87,* 541–550.

Roberts, B. W., & Robins, R. W. (2000). Broad dispositions, broad aspirations: The intersection of personality traits and major life goals. *Personality and Social Psychology Bulletin, 26,* 1284–1296.

Roberts, B. W., & Robins, R. W. (2004). Person–environment fit and its implications for personality development: A longitudinal study. *Journal of Personality, 72,* 89–110.

Roberts, B. W., Walton, K. E., & Viechtbauer, W. (2006). Patterns of mean-level change in personality traits across the life course: A meta-analysis of longitudinal studies. *Psychological Bulletin, 132,* 1–25.

Roberts, B. W., Wood, D., & Caspi, A. (2008). The development of personality traits in adulthood. In O. P. John, R. W. Robins, & L. A. Pervin (Eds.), *Handbook of personality: Theory and research* (3rd ed., pp. 375–398). New York: Guilford Press.

Robins, R. W., Trzesniewski, K. H., Gosling, S. D., Tracy, J. L., & Potter, J. (2002). Global self-esteem across the life span. *Psychology and Aging, 17,* 423–434.

Rodkin, P. C., Ryan, A. M., Jamison, R., & Wilson, T. (2013). Social goals, social behavior, and social status in middle childhood. *Developmental Psychology, 49,* 1139–1150.

Rogoff, B., Sellers, M. J., Pirrotta, S., Fox, N., & White, S. H. (1975). Age of assignment of roles and responsibilities to children. *Human Development, 18,* 353–369.

Rokeach, M. (1973). *The nature of human values.* New York: Free Press.

Rosenwald, G. C., & Ochberg, R. L. (Eds.). (1992). *Storied lives: The cultural politics of self-understanding.* New Haven, CT: Yale University Press.

Rossi, A. S. (2001). *Caring and doing for others.* Chicago: University of Chicago Press.

Rothbart, M. K. (2007). Temperament, development, and personality. *Current Directions in Psychological Science, 16,* 207–212.

Rothbart, M. K., Derryberry, D., & Hershey, K. L. (2000). Stability of temperament in childhood: Laboratory infant assessment to parent report at 7 years. In V. J. Molfese & D. L. Molfese (Eds.), *Temperament and personality across the life span* (pp. 85–119). Mahwah, NJ: Erlbaum.

Rothbart, M. K., Sheese, B. E., & Posner, M. R. (2007). Executive attention and effortful control: Linking temperament, brain networks, and genes. *Child Development Perspectives, 1,* 2–7.

Rouse, J. (1978). *The completed gesture: Myth, character, and education.* New York: Skyline Books.

Rubenzer, S. J., & Faschingbauer, T. R. (2004). *Personality, character, and leadership in the White House: Psychologists assess the presidents.* Washington, DC: Brassey's, Inc.

Rueda, M. R. (2012). Effortful control. In M. Zentner & R. L. Shiner (Eds.), *Handbook of temperament* (pp. 145–167). New York: Guilford Press.

Sacks, O. (1995, January 9). Prodigies. *The New Yorker,* pp. 44–65.

Ryan, R. M., & Deci, E. L. (2006). Self-regulation and the problem of human autonomy: Does psychology need choice, self-determination, and will? *Journal of Personality, 74,* 1557–1585.

Sakharov, A. (1968). *Progress, coexistence, and intellectual freedom.* New York: Norton.

Sameroff, A. J., & Haith, M. M. (Eds.). (1996). *The five to seven year shift: The age of reason and responsibility.* Chicago: University of Chicago Press.

Saroglou, V. (2010). Religiousness as a cultural adaptation to basic traits: A five-factor model perspective. *Personality and Social Psychology Review, 14,* 108–125.

Scarlett, W. G., & Warren, A. E. A. (2010). Religious and spiritual development across the life span: A behavioral and social science perspective. In R. M. Lerner, M. E. Lamb, & A. M. Freund (Eds.), *The handbook of lifespan development: Vol. 2. Social and emotional development* (pp. 631–682). New York: Wiley.

Scarr, S., & McCartney, K. (1983). How people make their environments: A theory of genotype environment effects. *Child Development, 54,* 424–435.

Schacter, D. L. (1996). *Searching for memory: The brain, the mind, and the past.* New York: Basic Books.

Schmitt, D. P. (2004). The Big Five related to risky sexual behavior across 10 world regions: Differential personality associations of sexual promiscuity and relationships fidelity. *European Journal of Personality, 18,* 301–319.

Schneider, E. (2014, June 20). Marine Cpl. Kyle Carpenter receives Medal of Honor. *New York Times.* Retrieved from *www.nytimes.com/2014/06/20/us/ marine-cpl-william-carpenter-receives-medal-of-honor.html?_r=0.*

Schultheiss, O. C., & Pang, J. S. (2007). Measuring implicit motives. In R. W. Robins, R. C. Fraley, & R. F. Krueger (Eds.), *Handbook of research methods in personality psychology* (pp. 322–344). New York: Guilford Press.

Schultheiss, O. C., & Rohde, W. (2002). Implicit power motivation predicts men's testosterone changes and implicit learning in a contest situation. *Hormones and Behavior, 41,* 195–202.

Schwartz, S. H. (2009). Basic values: How they motivate and inhibit prosocial behavior. In M. Mikulincer & P. R. Shaver (Eds.), *Prosocial motives, emotions, and behavior* (pp. 221–241). Washington, DC: American Psychological Association Press.

Schweizer, P., & Schweizer, R. (2004). *The Bushes: Portrait of a dynasty.* New York: Doubleday.

Sedikides, C., & Gebauer, J. E. (2010). Religiosity as self-enhancement: A meta-analysis of the relation between socially desirable responding and religiosity. *Personality and Social Psychology Review, 14,* 17–36.

Seligman, M. E. P. (1975). *Helplessness: On depression, development, and death.* San Francisco: Freeman.

Selman, R. L. (1980). *The growth of interpersonal understanding.* Orlando, FL: Academic Press.

Serrano, J. P., Lattore, J. M., Gatz, M., & Montaines, J. (2004). Life review therapy using autobiographical retrieval practice for older adults with depressive symptomatology. *Psychology and Aging, 19,* 272–277.

Seybold, K. M., & Hill, P. C. (2001). The role of religion and spirituality in mental and physical health. *Current Directions in Psychological Science, 10,* 21–24.

Shaffer, D. R. (2009). *Social and personality development* (6th ed.). Belmont, CA: Wadsworth.

Sheldon, K. M. (in press). Becoming oneself: The central role of self-concordant goal selection. *Personality and Social Psychology Review.*

Sheldon, K. M., & Gunz, A. (2009). Psychological needs as basic motives, not just experiential requirements. *Journal of Personality, 77,* 1467–1492.

Sheldon, K. M., & Schuler, J. (2011). Wanting, having, and needing: Integrating motive disposition theory with self-determination theory. *Journal of Personality and Social Psychology, 101,* 1106–1123.

Shiner, R. L. (2009). The development of personality disorders: Perspectives from normal personality development in childhood and adolescence. *Development and Psychopathology, 21,* 715–734.

Shiner, R. L., & De Young, C. G. (2013). The structure of temperament and personality traits: A developmental perspective. In P. D. Zelazo (Ed.), *Handbook of developmental psychology* (pp. 113–141). New York: Oxford University Press.

Shiner, R. L., & Masten, A. S. (2012). Childhood personality as a harbinger of competence and resilience in adulthood. *Development and Psychopathology, 24,* 507–528.

Shweder, R. A., & Much, N. C. (1987). Determinants of meaning: Discourse and moral socialization. In W. M. Kurtines & J. L. Gewirtz (Eds.), *Moral development through social interaction* (pp. 197–244). New York: Wiley.

Silvia, P. J., & Duval, T. S. (2001). Objective self-awareness theory: Recent progress and enduring problems. *Personality and Social Psychology Review, 5,* 230–241.

Singer, J. A., Rexhaj, B., & Baddeley, J. (2007). Older, wiser, and happier?: Comparing older adults' and college students' self-defining memories. *Memory, 15,* 886–898.

Singer, J. A., & Salovey, P. (1993). *The remembered self.* New York: The Free Press.

Sloane, S., Baillargeon, R., & Premack, D. (2012). Do infants have a sense of fairness? *Psychological Science, 23,* 196–204.

Smillie, L. D., Cooper, A. J., Wilt, J., & Revelle, W. (2012). Do extraverts get more bang for the buck?: Refining the affective-reactivity hypothesis of extraversion. *Journal of Personality and Social Psychology, 103,* 306–326.

Smillie, L. D., Pickering, A. D., & Jackson, C. J. (2006). The new reinforcement sensitivity theory: Implications for personality measurement. *Personality and Social Psychology Review, 10,* 320–335.

Smith, C., & Denton, M. (2005). *Soul searching: The religious and spiritual lives of American teenagers.* New York: Oxford University Press.

Smith, J., & Baltes, P. B. (1999). Trends and profiles of psychological functioning in very old age. In P. B. Baltes & K. U. Mayer (Eds.), *The Berlin aging study* (pp. 197–226). Cambridge, UK: Cambridge University Press.

Smith, T. W. (2006). Personality as risk and resilience in physical health. *Current Directions in Psychological Science, 15,* 227–231.

Specht, J., Bleidorn, W., Dennissen, J. J. A., Hennecke, M., Hutteman, R., Kandler, C., et al. (2014). What drives adult personality development?: A comparison of theoretical perspectives and empirical evidence. *European Journal of Personality, 28,* 216–230.

Speer, N. K., Reynolds, J. R., Swallow, K. M., & Zacks, J. M. (2009). Reading stories activates neural representations of visual and motor experiences. *Psychological Science, 20,* 989–999.

Spera, C. (2005). A review of the relationship among parenting practices, parenting styles, and adolescent school achievement. *Educational Psychology Review, 17,* 125–146.

Spink, K. (1997). *Mother Teresa: A complete authorized biography.* New York: HarperCollins.

Srivastava, S., Angelo, K. M., & Vallereux, S. R. (2008). Extraversion and positive affect: A day reconstruction study of person–environment transactions. *Journal of Research in Personality, 42,* 1613–1618.

Stanislavski, C. (1936). *An actor prepares* (E. R. Hapgood, Trans.). New York: Theatre Arts Books.

Stern, D. N. (1985). *The interpersonal world of the human infant.* New York: Basic Books.

Stewart, A. J., & Vandewater, E. A. (1999). "If I had it to do over again . . . ": Midlife review, midcourse corrections, and women's well-being in midlife. *Journal of Personality and Social Psychology, 76,* 270–283.

Stout, D. (2008, November 29). Bush shows a reflective side to an unusual interviewer. *New York Times,* p. A12.

Streib, H., Hood, R. W., Jr., Keller, B., Csoff, R. M., & Silver, C. F. (2009). *Deconversion: Qualitative and quantitative results from cross-cultural research in Germany and the United States of America.* Gottingen, Germany: Vandenhoek & Ruprecht.

Sullivan, H. S. (1953). *The interpersonal theory of psychiatry.* New York: Norton.

Suls, J., & Martin, R. (2005). The daily life of the garden-variety neurotic: Reactivity, stressor exposure, mood spillover, and maladaptive coping. *Journal of Personality, 73,* 1485–1509.

Suskind, R. (2004). *The price of loyalty: George W. Bush, the White House, and the education of Paul O'Neill.* New York: Simon & Schuster.

Sutin, A. R., Ferrucci, L., Zonderman, A. B., & Terracciano, A. (2011). Personality and obesity across the adult life span. *Journal of Personality and Social Psychology, 101,* 579–592.

Syed, M., & Azmitia, M. (2010). Narrative and ethnic identity exploration: A longitudinal account of emerging adults' ethnicity-related experiences. *Developmental Psychology, 46,* 208–219.

Tajfel, H., & Turner, J. C. (1979). An integrative theory of intergroup conflict. In W. G. Austin & S. Worchtel (Eds.), *The social psychology of intergroup relations* (pp. 33–47). Monterey, CA: Brooks/Cole.

Tamir, M. (2009). Differential preferences for happiness: Extraversion and trait-consistent emotion regulation. *Journal of Personality, 77,* 447–470.

Tangney, J. P., Stuewig, J., & Mashek, D. J. (2007). Moral emotions and moral behavior. In S. T. Fiske & D. Schacter (Eds.), *Annual review of psychology* (Vol. 58, pp. 345–372). Palo Alto, CA: Annual Reviews.

Tavernier, R., & Willoughby, T. (2012). Adolescent turning points: The association between meaning-making and psychological well-being. *Developmental Psychology, 48,* 1058–1068.

Taylor, C. (1989). *Sources of the self: The making of the modern identity.* Cambridge, MA: Harvard University Press.

Taylor, S. E. (1983). Adjustment to threatening events: A theory of cognitive adaptation. *American Psychologist, 38,* 624–630.

Teachman, B. A. (2006). Aging and negative affect: The rise and fall and rise of anxiety and depressive symptoms. *Psychology and Aging, 21,* 201–207.

Tellegen, A., Lykken, D. J., Bouchard, T. J., Jr., Wilcox, K. J., Segal, N. L., & Rich, S. (1988). Personality similarity in twins reared apart and together. *Journal of Personality and Social Psychology, 54,* 1031–1039.

Thomas, S. P., & Hall, J. M. (2008). Life trajectories of female child abuse survivors thriving in adulthood. *Qualitative Health Research, 18,* 149–166.

Thompson, R. A. (1998). Early socio-personality development. In W. Damon & N. Eisenberg (Eds.), *Handbook of child psychology: Vol. 3. Social, emotional, and personality development* (5th ed., pp. 25–104). New York: Wiley.

Thomsen, D. K. (2009). There is more to life stories than memories. *Memory, 17,* 445–457.

Thomsen, D. K., & Bernsten, D. (2008). The cultural life script and life story chapters contribute to the reminiscence bump. *Memory, 16,* 420–435.

Thomsen, D. K., & Jensen, A. B. (2007). Memories and narratives about breast cancer: Exploring associations between turning points, distress and meaning. *Narrative Inquiry, 17,* 349–370.

Thomsen, D. K., Olesen, M. H., Schnieber, A., Jensen, T., & Tønnesvang, J. (2012). What characterizes life story memories?: A diary study of freshmen's first term. *Consciousness and Cognition, 21*(1), 366–382.

Tomasello, M. (2000). Culture and cognitive development. *Current Directions in Psychological Science, 2,* 37–40.

Tomasello, M., & Vaish, A. (2013). Origins of human cooperation and morality. In S. T. Fiske, D. L. Schacter, & S. E. Taylor (Eds.), *Annual review of psychology* (Vol. 64, pp. 231–255). Palo Alto, CA: Annual Reviews.

Tomkins, S. S. (1987). Script theory. In J. Aronoff, A. I. Rabin, & R. A. Zucker (Eds.), *The emergence of personality* (pp. 147–216). New York: Springer.

Trautwein, U., Ludtke, O., Kastens, C., & Koller, O. (2006). Effort on homework in grades 5–9: Development, motivational antecedents, and the association with effort on classwork. *Child Development, 77,* 1094–1111.

Triandis, H. C. (1997). Cross-cultural perspectives on personality. In R. Hogan, J. Johnson, & S. Briggs (Eds.), *Handbook of personality psychology* (pp. 439–464). San Diego, CA: Academic Press.

Trivers, R. L. (1971). The evolution of reciprocal altruism. *Quarterly Review of Biology, 46,* 35–57.

Trobst, K. K., Herbst, J. H., Masters, H. L., & Costa, P. T., Jr. (2002). Personality pathways to unsafe sex: Personality, condom use, and HIV risk behaviors. *Journal of Research in Personality, 36,* 117–133.

Trull, T. J., & Sher, K. J. (1994). Relationship between the five-factor model of personality and Axis I disorders in a nonclinical sample. *Journal of Abnormal Psychology, 103,* 350–360.

Tsai, J. L., Knutson, B., & Fung, H. H. (2006). Cultural variation in affect valuation. *Journal of Personality and Social Psychology, 90,* 288–307.

Turiano, N. A., Hill, P. L., Roberts, B. W., Spiro, A., III, & Mroczek, D. K. (2012). Smoking mediates the effect of conscientiousness on mortality: The Veterans Affairs Normative Aging Study. *Journal of Research in Personality, 46,* 719–724.

Turkheimer, E., Pettersson, E., & Horn, E. E. (2014). A phenotypic null hypothesis for the genetics of personality. In S. T. Fiske, D. Schacter, & S. E. Taylor (Eds.), *Annual review of psychology* (Vol. 65, pp. 515–540). Palo Alto, CA: Annual Reviews.

Twenge, J. M., & Crocker, J. (2002). Race and self-esteem: Meta-analysis comparing whites, blacks, Asians, and American Indians and comment on Gray-Little and Hafdahl (2000). *Psychological Bulletin, 128,* 371–408.

Vail, K. E., III, Rothschild, Z. K., Weise, D. R., Solomon, S., Pyszcynski, T., & Greenberg, J. (2010). A terror management analysis of the psychological functions of religion. *Personality and Social Psychology Review, 14,* 84–94.

Van Egeren, L. A., Barratt, M. S., & Roach, M. A. (2001). Mother–infant responsiveness: Timing, mutual regulation, and interactional context. *Developmental Psychology, 37,* 684–697.

Van Hiele, A., Mervielde, I., & de Fruyt, F. (2006). Stagnation and generativity: Structure, validity, and differential relationships with adaptive and maladaptive personality. *Journal of Personality, 74,* 543–573.

Vazire, S., & Funder, D. C. (2006). Impulsivity and self-defeating behavior of narcissists. *Personality and Social Psychology Review, 10,* 154–165.

Vazire, S., Naumann, L. P., Rentfrow, P. J., & Gosling, S. D. (2008). Portrait of a narcissist: Manifestations of narcissism in physical appearance. *Journal of Research in Personality, 42,* 1439–1447.

Veroff, J. (1982). Assertive motivations: Achievement versus power. In A. J. Stewart (Ed.), *Motivation and society* (pp. 99–132). San Francisco: Jossey-Bass.

Walker, L. J., & Frimer, J. A. (2007). Moral personality of brave and caring exemplars. *Journal of Personality and Social Psychology, 93,* 845–860.

Walton, K. E., Huyen, B. T. T., Thorpe, K., Doherty, E. R., Juarez, B., D'Accordo, C., et al. (2013). Cross-sectional personality differences from age 16–90 in a Vietnamese sample. *Journal of Research in Personality, 47,* 36–40.

Wang, Q. (2006). Earliest recollections of self and others in European American and Taiwanese young adults. *Psychological Science, 17,* 708–714.

Wang, Q., & Conway, M. A. (2004). The stories we keep: Autobiographical memory in American and Chinese middle-aged adults. *Journal of Personality, 72,* 911–938.

Warren, R. (2002). *The purpose driven life.* Grand Rapids, MI: Zondervan.

Weaver, K. C. G., Cervoni, N., Champagne, F. A., D'Alessio, A. C., Sharma, S., Secki, J. R., et al. (2004). Epigenetic programming by maternal behavior. *Nature Neuroscience, 7,* 847–854.

Weisberg, J. (2008). *The Bush tragedy.* New York: Random House.

Wellman, H. M. (1993). Early understanding of mind: The normal case. In S. Baron-Cohen, H. Tager-Flusberg, & D. J. Cohen (Eds.), *Understanding other minds: Perspectives from autism* (pp. 10–39). New York: Oxford University Press.

Wellman, H. M., Cross, D., & Watson, J. (2001). Meta-analysis of theory of mind development: The truth about false-belief. *Child Development, 72,* 655–684.

Westenberg, P. M., Blasi, A., & Cohn, L. D. (Eds.). (1998). *Personality development: Theoretical, empirical, and clinical investigations of Loevinger's conception of ego development.* Mahwah, NJ: Erlbaum.

White, R. W. (1959). Motivation reconsidered: The concept of competence. *Psychological Review, 66,* 297–333.

White, S. H. (1965). Evidence for a hierarchical arrangement of learning processes. In J. P. Lipsett & C. C. Spiker (Eds.), *Advances in child development and behavior* (pp. 187–220). New York: Academic Press.

Widiger, T. A. (2005). Five factor model of personality disorder: Integrating science and practice. *Journal of Research in Personality, 39,* 67–83.

Widiger, T. A., & Costa, P. T., Jr. (2012). Integrating normal and abnormal personality structure: The five-factor model. *Journal of Personality, 80,* 1471–1506.

Williams, P. (2002). *Mother Teresa.* Indianapolis, IN: Alpha Books.

Wilson, D. S. (2002). *Darwin's cathedral: Evolution, religion, and the nature of society.* Chicago: University of Chicago Press.

Wilson, D. S., van Vugt, M., & O'Gorman, R. (2008). Multilevel selection and major evolutionary transitions: Implications for psychological science. *Current Directions in Psychological Science, 17,* 6–9.

Wilson, E. O. (2012). *The social conquest of earth.* New York: Liveright.

Wilt, J., & Revelle, W. (2009). Extraversion. In M. R. Leary & R. H. Hoyle (Eds.), *Handbook of individual differences in social behavior* (pp. 27–45). New York: Guilford Press.

Wink, P. (1992). Three types of narcissism in women from college to midlife. *Journal of Personality, 60,* 7–30.

Winter, D. G. (1973). *The power motive.* New York: Free Press.

Winter, D. G. (1987). Leader appeal, leader performance, and the motive profiles of leaders and followers: A study of American Presidents and elections. *Journal of Personality and Social Psychology, 52,* 196–202.

Woike, B. (1995). Most-memorable experiences: Evidence for a link between implicit and explicit motives and social cognitive processes in everyday life. *Journal of Personality and Social Psychology, 68,* 1081–1091.

Wolfe, A. (2003). *The transformation of American religion: How we actually live our faith.* New York: Free Press.

Woodward, A. L. (2009). Infants' grasp of others' intentions. *Current Directions in Psychological Science, 18,* 53–57.

Wright, R. (1994). *The moral animal.* New York: Pantheon.

Wuthnow, R. (1998). *After heaven: Spirituality in America since the 1950s.* Berkeley: University of California Press.

Zacher, H., Rosing, K., Henning, T., & Frese, M. (2011). Establishing the next generation at work: Leader generativity as a moderator of the relationship between leader age, leader–member exchange, and leadership success. *Psychology and Aging, 26,* 241–252.

Zurbriggen, E. L. (2000). Social motives and cognitive power–sex associations: Predictors of aggressive and sexual behavior. *Journal of Personality and Social Psychology, 78,* 559–581.

# Index

Page numbers followed by *f* indicate figure, *t* indicate table

353